San Diego Christian College
2100 Greenfield Drive
El Cajon, CA 92019

THE GEORGE GUND FOUNDATION
IMPRINT IN AFRICAN AMERICAN STUDIES

The George Gund Foundation has endowed this
imprint to advance understanding of the history,
culture, and current issues of African Americans.

The publisher gratefully acknowledges the generous
contributions to this book provided by the
Center for Black Music Research and the
African American Studies Endowment Fund
of the University of California Press Foundation,
which is supported by a major gift from the
George Gund Foundation.

Lining Out the Word

MUSIC OF THE AFRICAN DIASPORA

Edited by Samuel A. Floyd, Jr., and Rae Linda Brown

Lining Out the Word

Dr. Watts Hymn Singing in the Music of Black Americans

William T. Dargan

UNIVERSITY OF CALIFORNIA PRESS

Berkeley   Los Angeles   London

CENTER FOR BLACK MUSIC RESEARCH

Columbia College Chicago

University of California Press, one of the most distinguished
university presses in the United States, enriches lives around the
world by advancing scholarship in the humanities, social sciences,
and natural sciences. Its activities are supported by the UC Press
Foundation and by philanthropic contributions from individuals and
institutions. For more information, visit www.ucpress.edu.

University of California Press
Berkeley and Los Angeles, California

University of California Press, Ltd.
London, England

Center for Black Music Research
Columbia College Chicago

Library of Congress Cataloging-in-Publication Data

Dargan, William T.
   Lining out the word : Dr. Watts hymn singing in the music
of Black Americans / William T. Dargan.
      p.   cm.—(Music of the African diaspora ; 8)
   Includes bibliographical references (p.), discography (p.), and
index.
   ISBN 0-520-23448-0 (cloth : alk. paper)
   1. Hymns, English—Southern States—History and criticism.
2. Church music—Southern States.   3. African Americans—
Music—History and criticism.   I. Watts, Isaac, 1674–1748.
II. Title.   III. Series.
ML3111.D24   2006
782.27'089'96073075—dc22   2004019700

Manufactured in the United States of America

15   14   13   12   11   10   09   08   07   06
10   9   8   7   6   5   4   3   2   1

This book is printed on Natures Book, which contains 50% post-
consumer waste and meets the minimum requirements of ANSI/NISO
z39.48–1992 (R 1997) (Permanence of Paper). ∞

To the memory of the elders who fired this interest:
James Dargan (1866–1943), grandfather
William Dargan (1912–1992), father
Vashti Brewer Dargan (1912–2002), mother
Rev. C. J. Johnson (1913–1990), mentor

CONTENTS

ILLUSTRATIONS

TABLES

PREFACE

My fullest sound images of "Dr. Watts"–style hymns are accompanied by other sensate memories, all hearkening back to the Piedmont sandhills of South Carolina. Gum Springs Missionary Baptist Church is situated there in Chesterfield County, halfway between Pageland and Mount Croghan, two blink-your-eyes-and-you'll-miss-them towns. My late father was the adult Sunday school teacher from about 1954 until 1984 and also served as a deacon from the early 1970s till his death in 1992.

After a hearty Sunday-morning breakfast, we would leave for Sunday school promptly at 9:45. Riding for about five minutes over sandy side roads, we turned off onto a narrow path where wild plum bushes would scrape the truck, as if to remind us that we were not yet out of the woods. The white frame church there in the clearing faced a dirt road. My mother, Vashti Brewer Dargan, tells me that when she was a child in the 1910s and 1920s, an older church building faced in the opposite direction, toward the cemetery that is behind the present edifice. The church was then at the center of a country community called Guess, where the daily train stopped and there was a country store. Her parents, Thomas and Nannie Brewer, were the free undertakers who kept a stock of inexpensive caskets and "laid out" the deceased. They were beloved by and, shall we say, indispensable to the community.

During my own childhood, all Gum Springs church activities took place in a one-room frame building. The same group of early arrivals would always greet us: Mrs. Rene Sinclair, the matriarch of her family; Mrs. Julia Gregory; and her husband, Deacon Gregory, the church janitor. The Sunday school superintendent, Deacon Ed Jackson, was responsible for starting and ending the classes on time, and a succession of adolescent female secretaries read the minutes after classes and before the recess (my favorite part of the church day). Because public education for Negroes in the state's rural areas was underfunded in the 1930s and 1940s, most of the adult class members I occasionally sat next to in the 1950s could not read. So the adult Sunday school was a literal search for the holy grail of the scripture lesson.

There was a big round stove in the center of the sanctuary, homemade rough-hewn pews, an outdoor baptismal pool, and an outhouse at the edge of the woods. But somehow the big breakfast, the Sunday-go-to-meeting garb, and the excitement of seeing the folk muted the indignities. That pot-bellied stove became the source of winter comfort, and wafting breezes, aided by funeral-parlor fans, ventilated the space in summer. The wooden floors, ceiling, and makeshift pews afforded a lively resonance for mingled voices, clapping hands, and patting feet.

In this early 1950s ambience, powerful lining-out hymn performances called me to attention from churchyard play between the close of Sunday school and the devotionals that preceded the twice-a-month preaching services. A committed core of worshipers whose names and faces still hover in memory—Deacon Jackson and his wife, Mrs. Lillie Mae; Mrs. Roxie Rivers and her son-in-law, Brother Alec Edgeworth; Mrs. Rene and her children; Sister Sue Nicholson and Deacon Hardin Sinclair—sang the Dr. Watts hymns, which still begin the ten- to fifteen-minute devotions before preaching service in old-time black Missionary Baptist churches. Following the old tradition of lining out, the hymns were performed in a call-and-response pattern, first intoned, line by line or verse by verse, by the pastor or song leader, then echoed by the congregation.

Though I was by no means religious as a child, these hymns instilled in me a peculiar awe of the sacred that forcefully set apart the worship and singing from any mundane associations. Paradoxically, even then I could hear in these hymns the gestures and intonations that would mark my developing sense of rhythm and blues and black gospel. The slow pace of the renditions, coupled with what seemed a paltry few interchangeable melodies that were sung with the hymn texts, gave the sound an ever-present sameness, but also a gorgeous familiarity and rock-solid stability. In hindsight, this kind of fixed sound idea invoked not so much quaking fear as reflective awe. Such a sound affects the ear much the way images of movement in scenes like Michelangelo's Sistine Chapel ceiling are absorbed by the eye. One is supremely aware of grandeur, space, and unhurried yet gracious movement. So upon hearing the first hymn begin, I knew it was time to go inside the church—and right away! The sounds were profoundly human—slow and deliberate, yet quickly building in an aural ascent toward the divine. This sense of a most stern and solemn yet soulful call to worship has become indelible in memory. Although I could seldom decipher a word of the chanted calls and droned-out responses in the slowly undulating hymns, they charmed me nonetheless, and as childhood mysteries have grown into adult questions the attraction has only become more compelling.

The edifice of Gum Springs Baptist Church, where my sound image was fixed, now has a modern exterior complete with a handicapped ramp, stained-glass windows, and a brick façade. The interior is equipped with central heat and air conditioning, plush red carpeting, Sunday school rooms, indoor toilets, and an adjacent kitchen-fellowship hall.

The sounds within the church have also changed with time. As late as the 1960s, unaccompanied hymns and songs comprised the major repertory for worship in small, rural Baptist churches such as the one at Gum Springs, few of which had anyone trained or hired to provide keyboard accompaniment. Like gospel hymnody and shape-note singing schools during the late nineteenth century, jubilee and quartet singing have affected twentieth-century style and performance practice in the hymns and songs. But in many places the old-time repertory has remained central even as newer genres have been integrated into the order of worship. Such changes occurred in the 1970s when small rural churches formed "gospel choirs" that rehearsed and sang recorded selections (most often in unaccompanied quartet style), and larger churches hired part-time musicians who could improvise accompaniments to the gospel selections as well as the old-time songs and hymns. Today in Gum Springs Baptist, the Dr. Watts sound of my youth has been silenced with the passing of the elders. But as we shall see, Dr. Watts hymn singing continues in many other quarters.

The physical modernization of Gum Springs Baptist Church is reflected, to some extent, in the socioeconomic conditions of its present-day congregation as people's aspirations for bettering their status have led to improved housing, job opportunities, and financial security, and with these changes has come participation in the consumer-oriented world of media marketing and technology. Nevertheless, the subculture of the working poor persists, their daily subsistence sustained through barter arrangements with family and neighbors for goods and services. And while the level of education and literacy at Gum Springs has also risen, the shadow of illiteracy that for three hundred years has hovered over slaves, then sharecroppers, and now their descendants, has yet to disappear. Two wide and unfettered entrances now open onto the church ground at Gum Springs church. But the wagon path between the wild plum bushes is still there. And the practice of lining out the word using Dr. Watts hymns, though now only a memory at Gum Springs, continues to resonate in African American musical traditions—both sacred and secular—up to the present day.

ACKNOWLEDGMENTS

Early inspiration to write this book came during conversations with Bernice Johnson Reagon, the renowned singer, activist, and founder of Sweet Honey in the Rock. When I was a predoctoral scholar at the Smithsonian in 1981–82, my talks with her—which I remember as understated yet strident debates—seeded and incubated the ideas developed here.

A Pew Evangelical Scholars Fellowship as well as supplementary assistance from Saint Augustine's College enabled me to complete the first draft in 1997. These sources supported my leave from teaching and administrative duties for an uninterrupted year of research and writing, an odyssey for which all my previous writing in shorter forms could not prepare me.

My heartfelt thanks go to Samuel Floyd, the editor of the series in which this volume appears and a longtime mentor, who has provided encouragement and advice at so many turns. My lifelong mentor and friend T. J. Anderson also read early drafts and encouraged this project throughout. C. Eric Lincoln offered sage and caring advice. I regret his demise before the project's completion. I also mourn the more recent death of our mutual friend William Brown, who read an early version of this manuscript and did much else to keep me, as he put it, "on the case."

Through their faculties and resources, Duke University and the University of North Carolina at Chapel Hill have provided invaluable assistance over the last two decades. Music librarian John Druesedow of Duke University read the manuscript and offered helpful advice, and he, along with Duke Divinity reference librarian Rebecca Schaafsma, guided me at turns in the study. I am also indebted to Roger Lloyd, librarian at Duke Divinity School, who made a graduate student carrel space available to me for two years. The team of administrators and librarians at the Library of Congress's American Folklife Center—Alan Jabbour, Peter Bartis, Judith Gray, Jennifer

Cutting, and especially Joe Hickerson—made "ways out of no ways" for me whenever searching seemed destined to become a career enterprise.

My son James, now twenty-one, studiously read the first draft as a twelve-year-old and is fondly thanked for his helpful criticisms and encouragement. Those who gave me "somewhere to lay my head" while I conducted research on a shoestring include my cousins Margaret Washnitzer, Nannie Brewer Young, and Josh and Mae Wright, and especially my late friend Marie Grant Leatherman (1908–2002).

Based on their extensive knowledge of shape-note hymnody, Daniel and Beverly Patterson responded in detail to my query about possible melodic sources for hymns. Their insights opened areas of understanding about ethnic transfers that might have remained inaccessible to me. Marsha Vick gave this manuscript a thoughtful and caring perusal and made helpful comments. From the beginning, Pamela Grundy and Jerma Jackson, my writers' group colleagues, have read and discussed the parts and the whole with care and insight. Without the force of their convictions, my writing process might have flagged for lack of energy. They made it plain that certain of my questions were important enough to merit answers. Fred Mohammed of Saint Augustine's College read and offered helpful responses to chapter 7; Alisea McLeod and Frederick C. Jones of Saint Augustine's College and Houston Baker of Duke University read various chapters and offered helpful comments. John King directed the Reformation Seminar at Ohio State in which I participated, read two chapters, and offered invaluable guidance; Georgiary McElveen provided insight and attention to detail in critiquing the introduction and chapter 1; Cleveland Flowe, Scott Tilley, and Craig Denunzio copied the musical examples; Louise Meintjes discussed important ethnomusicological issues with me; Eddie Meadows read an early draft of chapter 3 and offered helpful insights; Jacquelyn DjeDje pointed me to Willie Collins's work on moaning and to J. H. Kwabena Nketia's book on the Akan dirge tradition; Michael Taft and Terry Miller read drafts of the introduction; Jon Michael Spencer offered advice and hospitality; and William Cole and his colleagues at Ohio State opened and recovered a computer file of chapter 3 that might have been lost without their timely help. Rev. Edward Davis loaned me several books on black preaching.

None of these people bears any responsibility for what may be lacking in this effort. Now, at the close of this project, it is time to move on and hope for another opportunity to treat at length some aspect of this gracious body of African American music.

Introduction

The tradition of African American hymn singing known as "Dr. Watts" derives from the collection of hymn texts written in the eighteenth century by the Dissenting English theologian Isaac Watts and others, including Charles Wesley, brother of the founder of Methodism. These hymns, sung to a limited selection of familiar tunes, were most commonly "lined out"— intoned a line at a time—by someone who could read the text, and were then taken up by the congregation, most of whom could not read.[1] Such a method was ideally suited to the worship practices of Christianized slaves in the American South in the early nineteenth century, who were mostly illiterate, a condition generally enforced by law. This hymnody, infused with enduring vestiges of African musical forms, created the complex heterophony, subtle rhythms, and unhurried intricacies of the musical corpus that became known simply as Dr. Watts.

DR. WATTS HYMNS AND THE "LONG BLACK SONG"

The title of this book refers, in the first instance, to the practice described above in which a leader and a congregation would sing, one line at a time, the texts from those hymns that had contributed to the worship liturgies of various Christian traditions since the eighteenth century. Implicit within this reference, though, is the idea that these Dr. Watts hymns have been "blackened" by African American worshipers who take part in the lining-out tradition. Often such "blackened" performances result in exquisitely extended renditions of the hymns, for which the title of Richard Wright's short story "Long Black Song" provides an apt description.[2] Not only is Wright's title appropriate for describing the literal length of many such lining-out performances, but it also stands, metaphorically, for the length and breadth of contested spaces between descendants of Africa and Europe living out a common American destiny.

Wright's "Long Black Song," set in the post–World War I era, teems with ironies of "the blues life." The story's protagonist, Silas, is a hard-working farmer who owns a small piece of land and is determined to throw off his stifling poverty by the sweat of his brow. While he is away selling his cotton, his wife is seduced by a white phonograph salesman who plays her a hot blues record and plies her with fantasies of big-city life. Silas discovers the betrayal, kills the salesman, and, surrounded by vigilantes, dies in the charred ruins of his own house. Just before the final conflict, Silas complains out of his broken heart, "Lawd, yuh die ef yuh fight! Yuh die ef yuh don fight! Either way yuh die n it don mean nothin" (Wright and Fabre 1997: 283).

African American worship traditions have developed within similarly contested spaces between white control and black self-determination. During the antebellum period, black slaves worshiped both with white owners (seated separately along the walls or in a rear gallery) and in their own secret meetings. During Reconstruction and the period of Jim Crow segregation, despite the proliferation of new black congregations led by black clergy, the pattern of plantation churches (still controlled indirectly by whites) continued. Bruce Hilton relates a story told to him by a black pastor in Denver: "When I graduated from seminary, I went back to Mississippi, and they gave me a plantation church out near Leland. The second day I was there, the boss-man called me in. He handed me a ten-dollar bill and said, 'Your job is to keep my niggers happy. Do that, and I'll keep you happy.' I packed up . . . and left Mississippi the next day" (1969: 183–84).

But despite the pangs caused by genteel duplicity, or outright intimidation and violence, black worship has continually nurtured self-esteem and group solidarity. In turn, the spirituals and especially the blues have come to signify black identity. Bluesman Son House pointed to field hollers as a source for blues, and noted that hollers came from the practice of long-meter hymn singing (House 1965). This kind of approach to spoken song can also be heard, for example, in the work of early bluesman Charlie Patton.[3] Such singing, which stems from elaborate speech rhythms, is freely articulated through formulaic melismas, alternately pulling against and flowing with the regular pulse of the bluesman's guitar.

The archaic linkage running from the field hollers through long-meter hymns to the blues provided a foundation of shared memory. With the popular emergence of the blues, the ramifications of long meter were felt more broadly, beyond the secret and sacred places of worship in the rural South. This concept of vocal style later became the basis upon which Thomas Dorsey's blues-laden gospel songs found acceptance in black urban communities during the 1930s. Black gospel music sought a social prestige and economic base commensurate with the developing class aspirations of blacks in the urban North. These composed gospel songs, popularized through sales of sheet music, both affirmed the old-time tradition and offered something new. The musical discourse ranged more freely between Standard English and dialect, and the whole was clothed in the urbane context of rehearsed performances, physical separation of performers and audiences, and elaborate keyboard accompaniments.

In such a way did Dr. Watts hymn singing play a seminal role in the transition from spirituals—through the secular course of blues—to classic gospel. The music that became popular was often rooted in less visible, more amorphous forms such as (secular) cries, calls, and hollers, or (sacred) moans (Collins 1992) and hymn singing. These discursive and open-ended yet generative moments that commingled black singing and black speech were the crucibles where black vocal styles developed before meeting with wider popular acceptance. Although certain vocal inflections and bends are routinely called *blue* notes, for example, descriptions of black singing from the eighteenth and nineteenth centuries make it clear that such vocal pyrotechnics long predated both the spirituals and the blues (Allen 1867: v–vi).

Thus, musical identities—sound imprints that become referents for association—are formed from the circuitous interaction of varied social forces. Three points made by Kwame Anthony Appiah (1992: 178) about the nature of identities are relevant here: first, that they are multiple and complex responses to change that oppose other identities; second, that they flourish despite their "roots in myths and lies"; and third, that although reason can study and manage identities, their construction is well beyond such rational forces (1992: 178). I engage Appiah's perspective more fully in the conclusion. For the moment, what is significant is the implication of paradox and multiplicity in his analysis. Paradoxically, lining out was an English form, and Dr. Watts himself was a Dissenting English minister with roots in the Anglican Protestant tradition. These developments have more to do with the formation of an African American musical identity than might be expected. The practice of lining out, despite its European origins (or perhaps because of the cultural sanction those origins afforded) became an early but seminal phase in the development of a modern identity for black music. The ritual legacy of Dr. Watts as an early-modern form was inherited from the archaic tradition of sixteenth- and seventeenth-century psalm singing.

The proliferation of hymn books and Bibles in the eighteenth century coincided with the rise of a semiliterate middle class, the growth of cities, and the Industrial Revolution in England; these conditions also marked the early stirrings of print media as popular culture. Through its relationship to mass production, popular culture fashions icons that compress the multiple and complex facets of a given tradition into a single local or personal embodiment of that essence. The moniker "Dr. Watts," which stands not only for hymns by Watts but for the corpus of *all* hymns in the repertory of black lining out, is such a reduction. Representing the inherent oppositions between the African oral heritage of slaves and the hegemony of writing that was set against them, "Dr. Watts" came to stand for what was inaccessible in outward form and meaning, but ownable, knowable, and unassailable in its essence. Thus, Dr. Watts represents a seminal dimension in the evolution of a black musical identity.

It is this rich tradition that forms the focus of this book. The practice of lining out Dr. Watts hymns was foundational to a variety of worship traditions in antebellum slave communities; it was encouraged by white missionaries in the early 1800s as the most appropriate form of black singing (see Jones 1842), and it can be seen in retrospect as the most fitting pre-Emancipation repository for unresolved contradictions between slaves as children of God and the dehumanization of slavery. Found today chiefly among concentrations of black Baptists throughout the United States, and having particular signification only in such worship settings, the practice holds general significance for the development of African American music since 1800.

While no singer of Dr. Watts hymns has ever referred to these hymns as "long" or "black" or "songs," Richard Wright's titular metaphor still holds currency for this book, for the concepts of resiliency, tradition, and "blackening" found in the title are also implicit in the tradition of lining out Dr. Watts hymns. These concepts gesture toward the primacy of the Dr. Watts tradition as seminal to a lineage of specifically African American vocal genres and style epochs, extending from spirituals to blues to rap. Therefore, this consideration of Dr. Watts hymn singing reexamines a turning point in the transition from African musical identities to those that are distinctively and diversely African American.

FIVE KEY THEMES

Building on my childhood experiences with Dr. Watts, four research experiences have furthered my thinking about this tradition. First, the Pageland Religious Folksong Documentation project (1982) revealed a correlation between the overall vitality of congregational singing in a given church and the particular strength of Dr. Watts hymn singing in that same location.[4] The pattern emerged in an inventory of over two hundred song and hymn performances from revival services in thirty churches in the Piedmont region of South Carolina. Second, the 1989 Smithsonian Institution Workshop on Black Congregational Singing brought together five groups of singers from diverse regions: Washington-Baltimore, Piedmont and coastal South Carolina, and Piedmont and southwest Georgia (recordings of these five groups are included in *Wade in the Water*, vol. 2; see pages 46 and 47).

Third, Project Senior Culture (1990–95), a regional survey of congregational singing in South Carolina, substantiated the correlation between hymns and congregational singing in general. For the first time, it became apparent to me that several regional styles continue within that state's boundaries (see Dargan 1995). Most recently, my survey of the recorded hymn-singing performances that are archived at the American Folklife Center of the Library of Congress confirmed both the diversity and dispersion of the tradition among clusters of black worshipers throughout the Southeast and its urban extensions in the East, Midwest, and Far West.

In the course of these researches, five themes have surfaced that point to the most general significance of Dr. Watts for black music: (1) the tensions between regional and local style traditions, constant social change, and fundamental cultural patterns, which I have labeled "unified diversities"; (2) cultural adaptation (as opposed to assimilation); (3) musical change and consistency; (4) language contact; and (5) black music as ritual. Of this constellation, the issue of change and nonchange in African American music is the central theme of this book. Attention to lining out elucidates the ways in which inward continuities are balanced by outward change in the expressive character of African American music. Even as the outward changes reflect movements from one geographical place and social station to another, the inward consistencies suggest more pervasive cultural patterns.

The most important, yet largely unexamined, nonchanging feature of black music between about 1800 and 1970 was the generative structural relationship in vocal music between intoned words as timbral gestures, on one hand, and percussive rhythms and bodily movement, on the other. The creative tensions between these structuring features have forged a ritual style that has come to determine what happens not only in black worship but in disparate secular performances as well. The specialized nature of the present comparative study, seeing one genre across regions and through time, limits the treatment of such a complex and general relationship between elements of musical style, and especially between speech and song. These must be more fully investigated in a subsequent work.

Unified Diversities

While the hymn "Blest Be the Tie That Binds" is not a core text in African American religious circles, it remains popular among black and white Baptist congregations alike as a musical benediction at the close of worship. Quoted in the titles of chapters 1 and 2, it symbolizes the links of race, faith, language, and music that have created a distinctive religious culture among African Americans. The ground of this bond is an African-derived social framework that looks at all of life as sacred and deemphasizes Euro-American Christianity's well-defined boundaries between the church and the world.

Stemming from the old origins controversy—the debate as to whether the spirituals originated from black or white sources—the tendency of positivist scholarship has been to search for one or two "authoritative" black vocal styles, and certainly there are abiding points of continuity or unity between the regional congregational singing traditions that remain. But a significant yet neglected area of commonality among various regional styles and across genres is the range of ways in which singers treat the generative relationship between words and vocal gestures (interjections such as "yes," "yeah," "well," and "oh," as well as an endless catalogue of hums, wails, calls, cries, yells, and the like), on one hand, and pitches and rhythms, on the other. This network of ways with words seems to have been an ever-present basis of continuity among the host of black genres that developed in the two centuries between the American Revolution and the early 1970s.

This network of oral traditions that links some black churches more than others to the religion of slave culture—its language, beliefs, and ritual style—remains most vital in churches that continue the old-time devotional practice of singing songs and lining out hymns. Because the white Baptist version of the gospel—tainted with the motive that slaves should obey their masters—was the first successful effort at mass evangelization of slaves, it is no accident that most of the churches that continue these practices are Missionary Baptist. Although early on and well into the twentieth century many moaning and shouting congregations were also Methodist, the community-based links with slave worship traditions have continued longer and with more vitality under the Baptist pattern of autonomous congregational polity. The absence of a top-down governance structure has encouraged a diversity of regional style traditions among Baptists, a diversity embracing a unified range of style elements, about which Portia Maultsby (1985, 1991), Olly Wilson (1992), Samuel Floyd (1991, 1995), and others have forged a broad scholarly consensus.

Building from these sources, one can see with increasing clarity how styles have changed as they have moved through time and across the map of cultures in the United States and throughout the world. Perhaps it is no coincidence that the music of oral transmission, which developed as a by-product of the illiteracy attending colonial-era slave culture, has become the world medium of commercial entertainment in the postcolonial era. Where deacons and congregations continue the practice of lining out hymns, the form has weathered the inexorable rhythms of change. Where the old-time hymns have lost their voice, other ways of moaning and shouting, as well as new tunes and styles for rendering the old texts, have come into vogue. Beyond the church as a generative ritual locus for African Americans, the ever-growing, multivalent possibilities for change—whether more or less urban or rural, sacred or secular, Euro-American or African—have pushed the musical and cultural latitudes and longitudes in widely varying directions.

The hymns of Watts and Wesley have served a variety of useful functions in black congregations since they were introduced to North Americans by George Whitefield, the Wesley brothers, and others in the mid-1700s. They have provided a popularly accessible approach to the master's language, they have sustained and empowered voices of hope and aspiration, they have offered a language in which to peal out the thunder of pain and anguish, they have silenced souls in meditation, they have produced an irreducible common stock of phrases utilized in ritual performances, and they have served as "etudes" for the interactive elements of music making that are peculiar to African American worship.

Cultural Adaptation

In cultural terms, the European worship tradition of hymn singing provided a new and perhaps unlikely site for African American self-definition. As I shall argue, the ancient African circle dance tradition of the ring shout[5] may have signified *adaptation* among slave worshipers in the North American colonies, while lining out of psalms and hymns, an English-originated tradition, signified *assimilation*. This thesis presupposes (1) that, because slave owners and clergy who likely discouraged or forbade the ring shout also sanctioned lining out, the two forms played complementary roles in language contact and musical syncretism; (2) that the ring shout became the earliest African American ritual context for song, dance, and story; (3) that slaves later adapted English oral performance to African cultural tendencies through the practice of lining out; and, (4) that vocal gestures built upon the dialectic between the ring shout and lining out animate spirituals, blues, and rap, as well as the performative tropes of modern jazz.

In the Second Great Awakening (1800–1820), the Baptist missions to the slaves, in which lining out was a key element, were envisioned as a means of saving souls while reinforcing the control of masters over slaves. Perhaps because more obviously African forms were more easily discovered and discouraged by overseers, missionaries, or both, hymns—together with the preaching of those portions of Paul's Epistles that were used to justify slavery—came to be the part of black worship that was most acceptable to white overseers. Hymn singing may well have been the one aspect of these worship services that was the least susceptible to the taint of a perverted gospel. To the extent that blacks shaped these texts into autonomous singing styles, they successfully mediated the tensions between white and black expectations. Therefore, where old-time hymn singing continues, there is an implicit reverence for the practices that brought the ancestors through the wildernesses of slavery and segregation.

As a primary stage of change and adaptation, the English hymns and the African ring shout became complementary elements in a core African

American worship tradition. Building upon these developments, hymns have not abided in stasis but have come under the influence of shape-note singing and white gospel hymnody in the late nineteenth century, and black gospel in the twentieth. There has been a tendency to view the old-time traditions as either closed or endangered. However, they continue in balance with the perpetual forces of change.

Prior to Walter Pitts's book *Old Ship of Zion: The Afro-Baptist Ritual in the African Diaspora* (1993), the most frequent explanation for the apparent readiness of slaves to embrace Dr. Watts had been the similar call-and-response structure in both the African musical heritage and in the English form of lining out.[6] It had also been observed that slaves warmed to the immediacy of Watts's language, which was conceived to reach the sensibilities of commoners via the King's English. However, Pitts cogently argues that "retentions of antiquated prayer speech and hymn singing that appear to be African American imitations of early Euro-American Protestant practices can only be explained sufficiently as religious custom inherited from Africa" (91). Pitts's identification of an African basis for lining out follows from George Pullen Jackson's observation about the origin of "surge songs," as he called the hymns: that "no scholar . . . has to my knowledge tried to trace [lining out hymns] or merely their movement back to Africa. But why not? Nothing could seem at first hearing more exotic, weird, or 'African.' . . . And the negro [*sic*] sang surge songs half a century before there was such a thing as a revival Spiritual. Why should not the earlier custom be more 'African' than the latter?" (1943: 257).[7]

Despite Jackson's unwarranted conclusion that the slaves sang hymns before they sang spirituals, Pitts took seriously his mention of possible African sources and found that two distinct ritual paradigms are common to eight New World rituals that are traceable to African origins. These two complementary paradigms comprise an opening devotional in which subdued hymns with texts by European authors are interspersed with intoned prayers, and a closing African-derived service that emphasizes non–Standard English speech, percussive rhythms, and bodily celebration.

In the way that enslaved Africans, and later, freedpersons, stretched out toward the God of Baptist missions there was an earnest seeking for freedom that has not passed from the souls of black folk, especially community elders who see themselves as bearers of the spiritual or social standard. This resolute spirit of questing after the things that matter—the "move on up a little higher" mentality, whether to heaven or to the East Side—is expressed in the text of "Father, I Stretch My Hands to Thee," a Charles Wesley hymn that, despite its conspicuous absence from the *New National Baptist Hymnal*, remains ready on the lips of oral culture in black Baptist, Methodist, and Pentecostal churches stressing either the archaic congregational singing or modern gospel traditions.

Musical Change and Continuity

In reaching out toward God, slaves received a voice of their own, a sound of crying and laughing, a musical language that codified the developing blend of Standard English and the black vernacular termed "Spoken Soul" by Rickford and Rickford (2000). Therefore, in the Watts paraphrase of Psalm 116, "I Love the Lord, He Heard My Cries," we can hear the believer's gratitude not only that the Lord heard the cries but that there was an effective means of crying out. Through Dr. Watts, the ambient cries, calls, and hollers, which reflect the most direct of African musical transfers to American soil, were fashioned into a new form as the slaves and later freedpersons learned the verses of Watts and Wesley. During the nineteenth century, this new voice of weeping and wailing, the "moaning" sound, became a fixed pattern and a reference for still other African American musical styles.

The concept of nonchange being as important to this book as the notion of change, I hold that hymn singing enriched an existing body of African American ritual practices and became a new entry point into English-language performance for individuals and worshiping communities. My premises are (1) that Dr. Watts hymns occupied a ritual function somewhere between singing and speech, yet encompassed both; (2) that the hymns played changing roles in three aspects of social development which have been pivotal for African Americans: language and culture contact, black urban migrations following the industrial revolution in the South, and the cultural politics of race and class; and (3) that the most interesting and characteristically human features of the Dr. Watts tradition have not been "stylistic change and individual variation in performance, but nonchange and the repetition of carefully rehearsed passages of music" (Blacking 1995: 154).[8] The vocal techniques concentrated in Dr. Watts hymn singing have been replicated in every major genre of black music produced from 1800 to 1970.

While slaves mastered English-based dialects in their first century of contact with North American colonists, the introduction of Watts hymns into eighteenth-century slave communities marked an early watershed in the parallel development of Standard English performativity and black vocal styles and genres. Eighteenth-century sources indicate that slaves aggressively sought both access to the written word and the opportunity to express their newfound Christian faith through hymn singing. Hymns offered the promise but could not deliver the impossible reality of literacy to the masses of enslaved Africans who were evangelized only in the nineteenth century. Therefore, Dr. Watts came to symbolize the power of the word in both spiritual and cultural terms, without threatening to alter the power relationship between slaves and masters. The hymns of Watts, along with the King James

Version of the Bible, provided a vehicle through which ever-greater numbers of enslaved Africans internalized the rhythmic lilt of English prosody.

Language Contact

Given the apparent expressive correlation between pitch and vocal gestures
or speech in black vocal sound, I have assumed an inherent connection
between them. This connection has led me to ponder how West African
associations between phonemic elements and their musical surrogates were
perhaps transformed through the process of North American language contact into English phonemic elements that carry expressive rather than lexical signification. The question presupposes (1) that both continuities and
distinctions exist between West African musical speech surrogates and
African American performative styles; (2) that the presence of hymns characterized by iambic prosody, prevalent during the time of the First Great
Awakening and the coincidental growth in the slave population of the
1740s–1750s, established iambic prosody as an aural referent not only for
African American oral culture but also for a larger stream of white American
literary traditions; and (3) that the case for such a larger stream of aesthetic
influence can be substantiated by reference to contemporary black poets
such as Jupiter Hammond and to white poets such as Emily Dickinson.

Dr. Watts hymns and African American spirituals embody a dialectical
tension among speech, timbre, and pitch, on one hand, and, on the other,
percussive rhythm and bodily celebration. Speech is to song as rhythm is to
movement. While pitch-inflected speech and song concretize and channel
the dramatic tension between indeterminacy and predictability, the combination of rhythm and movement creates and sustains intensity and pushes
toward the altered states of consciousness that can lead to personal and
social transformation in black worship. One or the other of these tendencies is emphasized in the various regional styles of Dr. Watts singing. One
moves in rhythms that approximate speech by their interaction with subtly
varying pitch and timbral inflections. The other builds from a multilayered
texture of rhythmic interest, increases in tempo and intensity, and culminates in varied types of shouting and spirit possession. The former, especially, is related to the creative way with spoken words that Zora Neale
Hurston called black poesy. She was describing the power and lyricism captured in the rhetorical style of black extemporaneous preaching, which is
closely intertwined with the old-time songs and hymns. This is the preaching tradition that culminated in the often extemporaneous sermons of the
Rev. Dr. Martin Luther King Jr. (see Lischer 1995). The visceral effectiveness of black preaching is ruthlessly caricatured in a number of jokes and
stories about the proverbial woman who heard the preaching and got carried

away by the spirit but didn't remember the subject of the sermon. As a cultural practice, this way of speaking or preaching formulates a sense of voice and a way of performing that utilizes rhythm, tone, and timbre to manipulate gestures and words, whereby an individual celebrant leads a worship community toward concurrence around a particular theme or issue and thence to active celebration. These ways of preaching (and singing) the gospel came of age by producing subtly varying sound templates, each uniquely adapted to a particular community's self-vision. As a marker of identity, the sounds of Dr. Watts hymn singing, in their various regional guises, have become cultural sites of self-definition.[9]

The notion of speech as generative to music is more explicit in John Storm Roberts's observation that "In both Haiti and Africa the specific drumbeats replicate tones and rhythm of spoken language; thus the drums 'talk' to the loa" (1974: 2). Although African words or semantic links between words and tones are absent from regional singing traditions in the United States, no study has analyzed the music stemming from the North American confluence of African linguistic patterns and English worship forms.

African drum languages have been studied as musical speech surrogates, but neither this nor any other generative relationship between speech and music in African American culture has been firmly established. *Lining Out the Word* interprets Dr. Watts as a distant analogy to the musical speech surrogates associated with West African tonal languages (Agawu 1996, Chernoff 1979, Locke 1990, Nzewi 1974), and hypothesizes that slaves embedded remnants of African speech intonation patterns into various regional styles of Dr. Watts hymn singing.[10] Despite the growing base of excellent studies of modern styles (jazz, juju, rhythm and blues) and their relation to West African traditions (Monson 1995, Waterman 1990, Wilson 1974), structural analogies *between* language and music in West Africa and in the Diaspora remain to be sufficiently integrated into a theory of black music performance in the United States.

It is toward such an end that my hypothesis is directed:[11] that, building upon the English hymn form and African worship forms, lining out first defined quasi-linguistic and musical terms by which a sequence of Anglo-American forms (religious, popular, and classical) would be imbued with African elements, structures, and tendencies. Serving as musical speech surrogates, residual but nonsemantic associations between music and speech guided the reinterpretations of the English verse forms found in Dr. Watts hymnody. Although language (and cultural) contact between the two traditions began with the earliest continuing African presence in North America, my claim is that during the First Great Awakening, Dr. Watts performances became an artistic watershed for language contact between slave dialects and English verse. Intensified and expanded during the Baptist missions to slaves, which occurred during the Second Great Awakening, this shift in speaking and singing styles employed in worship occurred as a linguistic response and sociocultural reaction to the growing English-language dominance.

Therefore, I will argue the paradox that, in adapting these English forms to residual intonation patterns, slaves discovered what became a seminal range of expressive but nonsemantic associations between nonstandard *and* Standard English speech, on the one hand, and African patterns of pitch inflection, on the other. It seems a paradox because, being denied access to literacy, the more they sought to sound "English," the more they sounded "African." Delving beneath the iambic "jog trot" of the hymns, the slaves forged an African American oral aesthetic in which the sing-song character of ballad verse provided the basis for many of the musical patterns—the licks and riffs—which generate from words in black music.

Throughout the eighteenth century such approaches to performance proliferated into as many regional styles as there were black speech communities in the slave states. By the early nineteenth century, black speech communities had formed from the linguistic interference between English and African languages, and the spirituals—an older tradition that was revitalized by its interaction with the hymn texts—surfaced during the Second Great Awakening as an expression of persisting African-language loyalties.[12] Throughout, English-language dominance vied with loyalties to regional dialects. But despite the leveling influences of time and media technologies, such speech communities still coincide with an array of parallel Dr. Watts traditions. These couplings of interference phenomena with language loyalties have fostered both myriad regional traditions and a sequence of popular forms synthesizing African "mood and feeling."[13]

Black Music as Ritual

The hymn "Come Ye That Love the Lord" sounds a call to worship that welcomes the faithful and marks a difference between them and others. Wherever events within a community perplex and confound the notion of neat categories like "the church" and "the world," preachers and laypersons may muse upon how "God moves in a mysterious way / His wonders to perform." While the phenomenon of movement across sacred/secular boundaries is not at all mysterious to social scientists, the particular stratagems of this movement are more elusive, especially when we consider the changing dynamics of this process in the present day. Black sacred traditions have ritualized musical structures and forms that, through the continuum linking hymns to blues to gospel to rhythm and blues to rock 'n' roll, have gained currency throughout the world. Invariably, such styles emphasize the interrelations between the performance event and both its immediate and its larger contexts.

For over two centuries, Dr. Watts hymn singing has provided worshipers with regular occasions to perform a fixed repertory of hymn texts with a limited, interchangeable set of melodies. The studied but impassioned repetition of this act may be seen as the sacred equivalent of the games practiced by black children and women that Kyra Gaunt has termed "cultural etudes" (1997: 26–99). By attention to a particular style and form of expressing oneself within the group context, Dr. Watts has taught worshipers how to be "religious" within the culture. This perhaps ungenerous assessment points to a deeper and not specifically religious level of musical and cultural transfer that crosses boundaries of religion and class.

The musical impact of lining-out performances can be analyzed not only in terms of the form itself but also for its relationship with proximate events as well as the entire ritual. Such references to larger contexts underscore the functional nature of black performance, wherein singing is judged good or not-so-good based upon what it *does* (its effect) more than how it *sounds* (its affect). The affect of the sound potentially effects a collective mind to carry the worship in the direction that the song leader has charted. Perhaps it is obvious that *effect* can also trigger *affect*. When either course has met or exceeded its implicit goals, the felicitous moment is said to confirm that the singer, and by extension, the whole group, was moving by divine guidance. The sound coalesces the loose aggregation into a oneness that can facilitate personal and collective wholeness. Therefore an "excellent" Dr. Watts performance, which may not, of itself, *sound* so pleasing to the ear, nonetheless leads the service of worship onward to the proverbial "higher heights and deeper depths."

While the ways with words considered above in the discussion of language contact may be regarded as structuring conventions of black vocal style, they are not ends in themselves but means of guiding a musical performance toward certain ends. During the period of the Great Awakenings, Baptist and Methodist clergy adapted the Anglican heritage to the less formal and more flexible styles of worship that were common in outdoor revivals and camp meetings. From such fervor emerged the devotional, the informal gathering and hymn singing that still prefaces the call to worship in black Baptist churches. While blacks and whites practiced these more informal modes of worship separately and together in the fervent religious Awakenings of the eighteenth and nineteenth centuries, the sense of immediacy and communal participation was particularly well suited to both the African background and the exigency of clandestine slave worship. Therefore, to the extent that they have been continued and standardized among black Baptists, devotions, as the first element of a two-part ritual form, represent a possible African American innovation in Protestant worship tradition.

THE FOREST AND THE TREES

Lining Out the Word issues from the premise that until the musical "forest" of black performance—the cultural context—is more clearly mapped, the debate over the nature of its various musical "trees" will continue unabated. To this extent, this book does not lead to semantic certainty about the tradition itself or the theory it explicates, but it does seek to discuss without pretense both what is known and what remains for further investigation. I would hope, for instance, that as a result of this writing, it will be easier to think more clearly about musical interrelationships between sacred and secular forms in African American culture. For example, although they don't sound at all alike in their outward gestures, Mahalia Jackson's performance of "What a Friend We Have in Jesus" and the bebop masterpiece "Parker's Mood" are linked in ways that carry to the foundations of style in black music.

To continue the arboreal metaphor, the "myths and lies" that veil our understanding of music, movement, and dance as core elements in black religious experience can be understood as the choking vines and covering underbrush that conceal the true meaning and importance of the common cultural history. These overgrown pathways of music, movement, and dance mark the trek of African slave communities to an African American consciousness: from slaves to freedpersons, from country folk to urbanites, and from Negroes to African Americans—one among many hyphenated ethnicities, all being American citizens.[14] Much has been done in black music scholarship, especially in the past three decades, but much more remains. For example, the broad outlines of the black church's covert origins are visible and well known, but too much of that history remains hidden or obscured.

Lining Out the Word looks at lining out as one of the "invisible" (or autonomous) forms of music in contemporary black churches and considers it in relation to language and ritual. The rubric "Dr. Watts," which is heard chiefly among African Americans, coincides with the prophetic implications of Isaac Watts's "system of praise" for the evolution of black musical identity. As an adaptation of orthodox Christian belief to the particularities of one's own culture, that system of worship, which combined received tradition with accessible innovations, has replicated itself time and again in the spread of evangelical Christianity as a populist movement in the United States. Of course, neither belief nor culture is fixed; rather, the one is ever pulling and being pulled by the other. Conforming to the template of the worship practices imposed upon them, but also acting in opposition to it, slave worshipers cultivated a particularity that has been transformed by bluesmen and blueswomen into the dominant language, the template for commercial music genres that have swept the world.[15]

Given that African precedents for black hymn singing have been well substantiated (see Pitts 1993), questions remain as to how, when, and where slaves embraced what must have seemed to them a strange and unfamiliar language of worship. To those thought to be subhuman, praising God in the master's tongue must have been deemed a high—almost revolutionary—privilege.[16] Moreover, the burgeoning population in slave quarters during the first half of the nineteenth century included non-English speakers and those speaking various dialects, as well as others speaking Standard English. Coming to slave communities long after the African circle dances that became the ring shout, the English tradition of lining out was one of few means by which shared praise could link these diverse groups of slaves. Reaching beyond the slave consciousness, the hymn texts, which offered spiritual succor even as they met the expectations of white overseers and ministers, made it possible for blacks to sing, without fear of rebuke, Standard English words with which they could personally identify. Laid upon the profoundly African basis for worship that was the core of slave culture, Anglo-American hymns signified for slaves, and later, freedpersons, a catholic Christian identity that paralleled the larger quest for freedom and full citizenship.

The key point of this book is that the tradition of lining out has served as a powerful "gatekeeper," sustaining both continuity *and* transformations, through which new forms have emerged from the recombination of existing elements. When musicians practice the same things over and over, the sameness of repetition can, of course, lead to boredom. But the routine can also provide a framework out of which one arrives at new plateaus of either virtuosity or insight, or both. In this last sense, where Dr. Watts still thrives, it gives witness to a form out of which slaves sang the blues before there was a blues; where it has ceased, other forms have encased the functions formerly served by lining out. Its strength has been demonstrated in unceasing adaptation; its weakness lies in its resistance to its own adaptive potentials. This dynamic historical process has placed lining out and the ring shout in a geosocial relationship of thesis-antithesis out of which the spirituals, blues, and rap have emerged.

With the advent of the hymns, the spirituals were renewed and enlarged—as ways with words—through the verse forms of Dr. Watts. So did the blues reinterpret that same tradition of *singing* and *saying* to found a new cult of performativity,[17] corresponding to the historical moment and social ethos of modernism. Adapted from the lining-out tradition (as well as from cries, calls, hollers, and worksongs), the sound of blues intonation mediated between the church and street in black parlance, as well as between the sacred community of the elders and the modernism of the Harlem Renaissance and beyond.[18] In like manner, rap has reformulated the means of *singing* and *saying* in still more radical terms, such that song is completely sublimated to speech. Thus what may appear in the pejorative controversies of popular culture as regressive and illogical is guided by an inward sense of logic that betrays structural and functional origins in the interstice between speech and song.

The writing of this book arose from the felt need for a theory of music *as an extension of language* in African American culture. Of course, since speech and song are traceable to the same impulses within the central nervous system, all human cultures share in some degree this pairing of sensible phenomena. However, the majority of enslaved Africans spoke tonal languages prior to their forced migration, and these linguistic backgrounds were transferred in varying degrees to the English ways of speaking and singing they developed in North America. It is one thing for a linguist like Geneva Smitherman to hear the "music" that abounds in black speech (1977); but the prescience and relevance of her linguistic analysis—along with the more recent discussion of the "speakerly" character of black literature and music by Henry Louis Gates, Jr. (1988)—begs for a corresponding explanation of the "speech" that is implicit in black music.

Three sources have provided resonance to my interpretation of rhythmic styles in lining out and other black music genres from the period between 1800 and 1970. Willis Laurence James posited in "The Romance of the Negro Folk Cry" three vocal textures found in cries, calls, and hollers: plain, florid, and coloratura (1955). My purpose is to offer more comprehensive definitions of such categories by a fuller contextualization of their origins and implications. Such a notion is reinforced from an African perspective by Gerhard Kubik's study of Yoruba chantefables from Nigeria (1989), which identifies at least three ways of structuring songs: the rhythms of underlying time lines; a short text line covering an uneven number of pulse units so that entire phrases are sung out of phase with the prevailing pattern; and "constructive use of timbre sequences in rhythmic structure [that] can also lead to offbeat rhythmic accentuation" (148–49). Finally, I reiterate the overall resonance of Kofi Agawu's *African Rhythm: A Northern Ewe Perspective* (1995) with the character of African American music making. Coming to his work only after this book was substantively complete, I was emboldened by his conceptual model of rhythms among the Northern Ewe, one that coheres with the more modest range of concepts outlined here. Moreover, his arguments and conclusions suggest the need for a comparable study of speech and singing within a single African American community.

Lining Out the Word seeks to further the integrative approach to arts criticism developed in African American literary criticism by Houston Baker (1984), Henry Louis Gates (1987), and Eric Sundquist (1995) and applied to certain aspects of black music by Sterling Stuckey (1987) and Samuel Floyd (1995). While Floyd, in *The Power of Black Music,* applies an integrative approach to the gamut of black music in the United States, my project is to explicate an important performative genre omitted from his landmark study, and to sustain attention to that genre as the focal point for queries about the changing role and status of black musical performance. Although the most innovative aspect of Walter Pitts's *Old Ship of Zion* is its identification of African structural roots for Baptist worship ritual, the core of his field observation is a linguistic analysis of praying and preaching in a central Texas association of black Baptist churches. *Lining Out the Word* proposes a broader focus of study that includes a survey of black hymn-singing styles, as well as analysis of other black genres that embody the same concepts. Its interpretation of the history of African American performance style is limited only by its focus upon Dr. Watts.

The Dr. Watts tradition, embracing intoned sermons, prayers, testimonies, moans, shouts, and songs, as well as hymns, stems from the fervent evangelical Christianity of the North American frontier and from an African lineage more ancient and multifarious. One source links it with a common American culture, and the other renders it a unique and distinctive mix of sound and feeling. While the precise mechanisms of the tradition's development can only be guessed at, its broad outlines are clear: English hymns, stemming indirectly from plainchant in the mingled line of European praise forms, underwent reinvention in the mouths of the enslaved Africans who were "babes and sucklings" in the faith. It is commonplace to say that the slaves "deconstructed" the hymns. More precisely, though, they stripped away the European preoccupation with melody as the primary musical impulse and emboldened the hymns with an African rhythmic character that, in its variance and constancy, stems from both speech and dance.

Part I of this book, "The Proverbial Trees," considers the branching network of influences that created the Dr. Watts singing style, which, in turn, influenced the development of later styles in black music, from the blues to jazz to rap. Chapter 1 describes Dr. Watts hymn singing in general musicological and historical terms, as a unity forged from its disparate origins. This African American religiomusical identity harbors a diversity of regional styles that challenge the unity without overthrowing it, and chapter 2 considers this diversity. Chapters 3 and 4 focus more closely on the English and African historical contexts, respectively, in order to comprehend more fully the hyphenated character of the tradition. Chapter 5 ponders the process of musical transformation from English forms to African American hymns and songs to the blues, for a close relation is apparent between blues ways of speaking and the "long meter" hymns upon which they followed. Chapter 6 traces a parallel path, considering the role of *words* in the Dr. Watts style and the rise of its modern progeny.

Black hymn singing is one of many Christian worship traditions, and it also encompasses its own wide range of regional styles. Although the range of substyles has diminished before the onslaught of popular culture in the digital age, vital remnants can offer instruction not just about worship traditions within church walls but also about a musical culture that, through the agency of commercial recording technology, dominated the twentieth century. As the various regional styles partook of the larger tradition, secure and well-trodden pathways connected modern jazz and the concert music of certain American composers with the substance, feeling, and tone of congregational singing.

Part II, "The Proverbial Forest," represents an effort to resituate the discrete topics discussed in part I within broadly social, theoretical, and critical terms. Chapter 7 explores the trajectory of African American socioeconomic aspirations, offering as a case study the life of a minister, the Rev. C. J. Johnson (1913–1990), as a testament to a search for something better in which songs and hymns were key sustaining elements. Chapter 8 sets forth a theoretical framework for appreciating the gradations of style and expression that are distinctively African American, positing a continuum of ritual and musical styles connecting the ring shout and lining out. Using this framework, chapter 9 critiques selected blues and jazz performances, including the signature pieces of Billie Holiday and Charlie Parker, in terms of their connections to the lining out and ring shout traditions. The conclusion returns to the question of cultural identity I raised above and finds its root in linguistic usage, that bubbling cauldron that has fed both continuity and change in African American music.

Each chapter in the book takes its title from, and provides an epigraph of, one of the hymns in the Dr. Watts tradition whose text evokes or reflects a particular aspect of my theme.[19] Heading chapters 1 and 2, "Blest Be the Tie That Binds" stands for the unified diversities that draw from a common wellspring of African American style traditions yet render each worshiping community distinct. "Our God, Our Help in Ages Past," the Watts hymn most universally accepted in England during the author's lifetime, leads the chapter that focuses on the origins of the hymns with Dr. Watts himself. Two hymns that carry special currency among African Americans, "Father, I Stretch My Hands to Thee" and "I Love the Lord, He Heard My Cries," are invoked upon those chapters that deal with the African-derived elements in the historical and musical development of black lining out.[20] The theme of chapter 6, which examines the treatment of the texts in Dr. Watts singing, is suggested by the hymn "Go Preach My Gospel, Saith the Lord." The hymn "I Heard the Voice of Jesus Say" evokes the calling answered by Rev. C. J. Johnson, whose story provides the framework of chapter 7. In the black experience, "Come Ye That Love the Lord" calls the faithful to worship but also invites the unsaved to "come and take of the water of life freely," a gesture of inclusivity that reflects the continuum running through and linking lining out and the ring shout, which is the subject of chapter 8. The oft-repeated notion that "God moves in a mysterious way" is manifest when we see how what began as a musical form among the lowly came to provide an aesthetic basis for the acceptance of jazz as a form of "high culture," as described in chapter 9. The phrase is by now a facile cliché invoked by African Americans in a host of difficult, painful, or perplexing situations, often associated with racial conflicts; but as an attempt to understand what is ultimately unknowable, it also reflects the open-ended and inconclusive nature of this book, which raises questions about black music and ritual that have yet to be fully answered.

The Proverbial Trees

Patterns of Change in African American Music Making

For you shall go out in joy
And be led back in peace;
The mountains and the hills before you
Shall burst into song,
And all the trees of the field
Shall clap their hands.

ISAIAH 55:12 *(New Revised Standard Version)*

Chapter 1

"Blest Be the Tie That Binds"

Part I: Congregational Singing as a Worship Ethos for Dr. Watts Hymns

The service will not be completed until we can hear from Dr. Watts.
Deacon's exhortation before lining out the hymn "A Charge to Keep I Have"
(Wade in the Water, *vol.* 2)

A distinctive form of congregational singing originated among enslaved Africans who were converted to Christianity before Emancipation, and it reached its apogee in late-nineteenth- and early-twentieth-century black Baptist and Methodist churches. Slaves hid themselves in the woods to worship or went to plantation praise houses, and after Emancipation the sound of the leader-group, call-response singing, accompanied by only hand and foot rhythms, resonated across the plains from the uplifted windows of the spacious frame buildings that dominated African American communities (see Rankin 1993). Known as devotions or the devotional, the cycle contains an opening song or hymn, a scripture reading, a second song or hymn, and a prayer. Although they can be interrupted at any point by the shout that signifies the divine presence, devotions are freely extended through repetitions of the song-saying (i.e., prayer, exhortation, or testimony) sequence.[1] Led by lay office-holders of the church, congregational singing seeks to transform the separate frames of mind that individuals have brought to a service into a corporate urgency and readiness to worship. In its insistence upon active call-response participation in the multilayered ritual pattern of talking back, the devotional prepares the congregation for the high worship of preaching, or for a special anniversary service that may follow. With the exception of funerals, which begin more formally, such devotionals introduce most services in the Missionary Baptist tradition. Interspersed with interludes of exhortation, testimony, or shouting, the repeated song-saying sequences typically occupy from fifteen to forty-five minutes and conclude when the clergy take their seats in the pulpit.

Skilled and gifted lead singers can foster the palpable and exquisite rapport and intimacy that has produced not only a distinctively African American character but particular style features identified with various congregations, church associations, locales, and regions. While the remnants of such regionalism remain discernable, rapid urbanization since the 1950s has led to the replacement of the older repertoire with the songs from sanctified or charismatic churches and gospel recordings, and with a performance style that features accompaniments improvised on keyboards, bass guitars, drums, and tambourines.

Richard Foster's definition of worship as "an ordered way of acting and living that sets us before God so he can transform us" (1998: 166) embraces many Christian traditions. But it plumbs the essentials of African American congregational singing. This animating idea of placing the human self before his or her god applies both to the tradition's African origins, stressing communication between the seen and unseen worlds, and to the Christian doctrine of God's immanence throughout the domain of created beings and things. The movement-centered and reflexive character of African American worship blends the African experience of ancestral and divine spirits as a felt presence in the worship event with the American revivalist stress upon the indwelling presence of the Holy Spirit (who is also the third person of the Christian Godhead) in believers.

In this network of actions and belief—famously dubbed by W. E. B. Du Bois "the music, the preaching, and the frenzy"—words embody and communicate beliefs, both literally and figuratively. The more immediately and viscerally the words impact the community of participants in black worship, the more power is ascribed to the utterance as truly significant and to the speaker as a divinely gifted messenger. While our central concern in this book is the music (i.e., the singing), the preaching and the frenzy (i.e., the words and body movement) are no less germane to congregational singing. Their relevance stems from the interaction among particular (danced) rhythms, specific (spoken or "moaned") texts, and definite (sung) pitches in the worship of black folk. The three mold and shape each other from one moment to the next, working in harmony to invoke the divine presence in worship as the Agency of communion between humans, who are often broken and hurting, and the Christian God of forgiveness and redemption.

Four general statements describe the character of worship in Baptist and Methodist bodies that continue the congregational singing tradition.[2] (1) These bodies emphasize charisma, or gifts of the spirit, and believe that dancing in the spirit or speaking out, along with other signs, can give evidence of God's presence in the midst of worshipers. In a more general sense, (2) there is an openness to subjective or intuitive perceptions, and a corresponding lack of insistence upon deductive reasoning or objective conclusions.[3] Nevertheless, (3) such inductive learning must prove itself beneficial in the practical world of personal and social experience. And (4) because the direction of communication in such worship settings is circular rather than linear, and its meaning process-oriented rather than static, clock time is deemphasized as long as participants believe that God is working or manifesting himself in the worship service. This flexible perspective has produced a worship tradition that, especially in the decentralized Baptist congregational polity, accommodates a wide range of both continuity and change in worship styles. The absence of episcopacies or supremely governed districts allows neighboring Missionary Baptist churches, associations, or regions the freedom to differ radically, some retaining old-time congregational worship, some resembling the sanctified church, and others practicing nondenominational or charismatic worship styles and doctrines.[4]

James Cone (1978) cites six elements of black Christian worship: preaching, conversion, shouting, singing, prayer, and testimony. All are means toward the common end of making the presence of God felt in the worship process. While not all black preaching, strictly speaking, is allied with the congregational singing tradition, intoned preaching (also known as "whooping" or "tuning") proceeds directly from the continuum linking speech, song, and movement that encompasses prayer, testimony, singing, and shouting. Intoned preaching differs from these four in that it serves to culminate rather than begin the worship service, and it is performed by preachers, who, after showing evidence of a divine calling, have been set apart through licensure and ordination. Conversion is the central mode of experiencing religious experience (e.g., "I once was lost, but now I'm found"). Shouting, despite the term's aural connotation, denotes an individual's bodily response to stimuli (visual, aural, or tactile) that signify the divine presence. Infinitely personalized, shouting can be dancelike, or more irregular and agitated. Singing, no less pliable, is an elemental form of heightened speech that gathers unto itself preaching, prayer, and testimony. The full expressive character of these six forms, ranging freely among speech, recitation, chant, and song, stems from and culminates in the act of singing, which the church practices to achieve the spiritual state of "one accord" that sets the stage for a visitation of the Holy Spirit.[5] This verbal and physical gathering process, whereby a distinctive ethnic community of Christian worshipers offers diverse yet proximate expressions toward God, is both an in-the-moment creative interaction and a received tradition with African and European sources.

DR. WATTS HYMN SINGING

The name "Dr. Watts" connotes the oral tradition of hymn singing among black Missionary and Primitive Baptists in the United States. In such places Dr. Watts underscores the unimpeachable authority of history and tradition. As in the English Reformation, the metrical psalms were but "one slight remove" from the Bible; in a less rigid sense, hymns have anchored black Baptist worship for as long as 250 years. Synonyms for Dr. Watts include the lexical term "lining out" and the poetic term "meter hymns." The practice is also known among adherents as "long meter," "reading out," "wording out," "deaconing," and "the old one-hundreds." While this range of terms has been used by both black and white Americans to describe their folk traditions, common use of the Dr. Watts sobriquet has been noted only among African Americans.[6] An instance of this usage can be heard on volume 2 of *Wade in the Water,* when, before lining out the hymn "A Charge to Keep I Have," the deacon says, "The service will not be completed until we can hear from Dr. Watts." Like preachers who put their words in the mouth of the source by saying, for instance, "I heard John say," the deacon is voicing the hymn out of the mouth of its putative author. Because the name of Watts with his honorific title designates the entire corpus of hymns carried in the tradition, it does not matter that the author of "A Charge to Keep I Have" was actually Charles Wesley. The Dr. Watts designation is not somehow more "correct" than others, but its use raises the question of why the rhetorical homage is paid to Watts by African Americans.

The moniker "Dr. Watts" connotes the particular call-and-response form and style wherein a hymn text is read or chanted by a worship leader and then sung by the congregation. Call-and-response songs in general consist of formulas, such as the statement "Oh, set down, servant," followed by the repeated exclamation "Set down," or the narrative declaration "When Israel was in Egypt land," followed by the recurring request "Let my people go." However, in Dr. Watts, or lining out, the preacher or singer sings or intones a line, couplet, or verse that is repeated in its entirety by the congregation. Though the Reverend Isaac Watts (1674–1748) was not the first to compose or publish hymns, as opposed to the psalm paraphrases of the Calvinist tradition that followed the English Reformation, his published collections achieved unprecedented popularity in England and the American colonies, and this currency continued throughout the eighteenth and early nineteenth centuries. Therefore, slaves who learned hymns by various authors through the lining-out form apparently came to associate the entire tradition with the name and honorific title "Dr. Watts." Hence, this cryptic sobriquet, which has been heard especially among blacks, symbolizes the more general acknowledgment of Watts as the father of English-language hymnody.

The form became a setting wherein African concepts of musical structure coincided with the worship practices of English Dissenters. In the eighteenth and nineteenth centuries, new black ways of singing developed when African musical tendencies blended with styles that colonials called the "old" and the "regular" ways of singing. This acculturative process emphasized the reinterpretation of African musical and linguistic concepts within Anglo-American forms and contexts. Unaccompanied congregations performed

texts by Anglo-American hymnists after a rote call-and-response pattern
that was designed to facilitate participation despite the scarcity of hymn
books and widespread illiteracy. Lining out hymns are (1) unaccompanied;
(2) slow throughout or moving from slow to fast; (3) sung in unison, "folk
organum," or heterophony;[7] (4) styled along a vocal continuum from
moaning to speaking to chanting to singing; (5) iambic texts composed by
English and Anglo-American hymnists; (6) the oldest vocal forms commonly practiced in black Baptist churches; (7) situated in authoritarian,
male-dominated settings; and (8) a conservative yet dynamic core of hymn
texts that continue alongside other, more rapidly changing and less stable
styles and genres.

One who "lines out" reads, intones, or chants the lines or couplets of a
hymn stanza in the manner of a "call," to which the congregation "responds"
by singing the same words. To get the singing started, a member then
"raises" the hymn by offering a "suitable tune"—one that is known within
that particular community and coincides with the poetic meter of the hymn
stanza. Following the lead, the congregation swells the throng of sounds.
The iambic texts most often sung in this manner are set in either common
meter (8–6–8–6), short meter (6–6–8–6), or long meter (8–8–8–8).[8] The
Missionary Baptist hymn repertory in most regional traditions contains
fewer than ten texts, which might include "Amazing Grace," "I Heard the
Voice of Jesus Say," "Come Ye That Love the Lord," "I Love the Lord, He
Heard My Cries," "Father, I Stretch My Hands to Thee," "A Charge to Keep
I Have," and "Must Jesus Bear the Cross Alone." Similarly restricted are the
range of tunes to which the texts are sung. Larger repertories of hymn
texts are common only among black Primitive Baptists, whose unaccompanied hymns and songs are not limited to devotional services but occur
throughout the worship ritual. The need for a larger repertory of hymn
texts arises because whereas Missionary Baptists often include in their
services gospel music and standard hymns with accompaniment, most
Primitive Baptists hold a doctrinal objection to the use of instruments in
worship. Whereas the former may perform a hymn only once or twice per
month, the latter do so on a weekly basis (see discussion of repertory in
chapter 4).

Dr. Watts hymn singing cannot be understood or appreciated apart from
the worship traditions that govern its performance. Hymn texts are still
lined out and sung without accompaniment among Old Regular, Primitive,
and Missionary Baptists in the United States. With few exceptions (see
Smith 1987), the Old Regular congregations are white. Because orders of
worship among black and white Primitive Baptists adhere to a consistent
form and manner of expression, these remain ideal sites for observing
subtle distinctions between ethnic traditions within certain regions. Such
comparative studies of hymns in black and white Primitive Baptist worship

include Jackson (1943), Sutton (1982), and Cauthen (1999).[9] However, as a direct link between secret slave gatherings and the modern era, Missionary Baptist worship reveals a wider range of apparently more radical distinctions between black and white traditions in the United States. While black lining out is also practiced among other groups, its widest geographic and social dispersion is among Missionary Baptists, the largest black church body. By contrast, there is no indication that the practice continues among white Missionary Baptists. The practice was universal among both black Baptists and black Methodists in the late nineteenth and early twentieth centuries. But while hymn singing remains current among a few Methodists (within three organizations: the African Methodist Episcopal [AME], the African Methodist Episcopal Zion [AMEZ], and the Christian Methodist Episcopal [CME]), the number of Methodists congregations who continue the hymns is miniscule compared to the larger minority of Baptist churches where Dr. Watts is still heard. The hymns are the primary vocal form among conservative Primitive Baptists, but a significant minority of Missionary Baptists, who are far more widespread throughout regions and social status groups, continue the hymns alongside other genres and styles.

DEVOTIONS

Devotions, the first period of the worship ritual, is typically called to order by two male leaders, seated on either side of a table at the front facing the congregation. One of these leaders offers a song to quiet the people, and the other follows with a scripture reading. Then the chosen verses of the opening hymn are read aloud and the formal request is made for a "suitable tune." The hymn text is read from a hymn book that includes the texts without music. The most common of these in the Eastern Seaboard states is the *Baptist Hymnal for Use in the Church and Home* (1883). In the Deep South and the Southwest, the *National Baptist Hymn Book* (1906) is popular. The person who offers the suitable tune in effect "raises" the hymn by intoning the first line or couplet of the hymn and following with the first line of the melody. He or she is quickly joined in this initiative, first by other key singers, then by the swelling whole as individuals recognize and join the first lines of winding and deliberate melody. The teeming vocal intensity often raises the key center one or two semitones during a hymn performance. Even where the stability of a strong lead singer anchors the pitch itself, rising intensity remains a concomitant of good hymn singing. Certain traditions feature unison singing, but even in these, there is a "looseness" that disallows any effort to mingle all the voices in a unified melodic whole. But whether the ensemble texture of lining out is unison, organum, or triadic harmonies, each individual finds his or her place of vocal comfort in a variegated heterophony. A special favorite in many black congregations is the hymn text written in 1846 by the Scotsman Horatius Bonar:

> I heard the voice of Jesus say
> Come unto me and rest
> Lay down, thy weary one, lay down
> Thy head upon my breast.

This became the signature hymn of the Rev. C. J. Johnson, who was billed during the 1960s and 1970s as "the world's greatest hymn singer." His most successful recorded performance begins with an ornate opening phrase, which is answered by the congregation (see the recording *Dr. Watts Hymn Singing among African Americans*—hereafter *Dr. Watts*—no. 10). Before the second quatrain, Johnson intimates that this is his favorite verse in the hymn and, without detailed explanation, gives some indication of what the hymn text means to him:

> You know this verse is the one that I love so well:
> I came to Jesus—
> I wonder are y'all holding me?—
> I, I, I came, I came to Jesus—
> I didn't wait till I got a new pair of shoes
> I came to Jesus
> I didn't wait for my little sisters and brothers
> Every now and then my burden get heavy, my trials give misery
> And I like to get away and say
> I came to Jesus as I was
> Weary, worn, and sad
> I found in him a resting place
> And he has made me glad.

Once chosen verses of the hymn have been sung, the melody may be "moaned" or hummed softly as a deacon kneels and begins to pray in a measured, formulaic style. An oral genre in themselves, these formulaic prayers are invoked by leaders on behalf of the congregations, who yea-say throughout their course. The focus of such a ritual moment is upon invoking the presence of the Holy Spirit among the worshipers (see Jones-Jackson 1994). Such prayers open in a measured speaking voice that allows ample space between phrases for freely placed verbal responses of "yes" or "amen." Then the tone of voice shifts from speaking to rhythmic intonation. Formulaic prayers begin by acknowledging God's omnipotence and the believer's dependence (lines 1–3 below), then thanks is offered for earthly blessings (4–9), the Father's mercy and grace are sought and God's faithfulness is declared (10–20), the preacher or speaker is remembered (21–25), and a petition for eternal life after death (26–36) most often closes the form. The following example, transcribed by Andrew Polk Watson, illustrates such a form:

Almighty! and all wise God our heavenly Father!
Tis once more and again that a few of your beloved children are gathered to
    call upon
your holy name.
We bow at your foot-stool, Master, to thank you for our spared lives.
We thank you that we were able to get up this morning clothed in our right
    mind.
For Master, since we met here, many have been snatched out of the land of
    the living
and hurled into eternity.
But through your goodness and mercy we have been spared to assemble
    ourselves
here once more to call on a Captain who has never lost a battle.
Oh, throw round us your strong arms of protection.
Bind us together in love and union.
Build us up where we are torn down and strengthen us where we are weak.
Oh Lord! Oh Lord!
Take the lead of our minds, place them on heaven and heavenly divine things.
Oh God, our Captain and King!
Search our hearts and if you find anything there contrary to your divine will
just move it from us, Master, as far as the east is from the west.
Now Lord, you know our hearts, you know our up-rising. Lord you know all
    about us
because you made us.
Lord! Lord!
One more kind favor I ask of you.
Remember the man that is to stand in the gateway and proclaim your Holy
    Word.
Oh, stand by him.
Strengthen him where he is weak and build him up where he is torn down.
Oh, let him down into the deep treasures of your word.
And now, oh Lord;
when this your humble servant is done down here in this low land of sorrow:
done sitting down and getting up;
done being called everything but a child of God;
Oh, when I am done, done, done, and this old world can afford me a home
    no longer,
Right soon in the morning, Lord, right soon in the morning,
Meet me down at the River of Jordan, bid the waters to be still,
Tuck my little soul away in that snow-white chariot,
and bear it away over yonder in the third heaven where every day will be Sunday
and my sorrows of this old world will have an end,
is my prayer for Christ my Redeemer's sake and amen and thank God.
    (Watson 1932, quoted in Washington 1986)

This particular prayer is exemplary for its pith and concision. Building upon both slave creoles and dialects, the Jacobean influences of biblical prose and English evangelical hymns, and the poignant fervor of personalized state-ment, the prayers are formulaic phrase structures comprised of alliterations, contrasts, and metaphors. During the prayer's course, some local traditions will interject the moaned hymn verse while other communities interject free-standing moans.[10] Just prior to or upon the prayer's conclusion, a con-gregational song such as "Set Down, Servant" might begin:

[Leader] Oh, set down servant
[Congregation] Set down
[Leader] Oh, set down servant
[Congregation] Set down
[Leader] Oh, set down servant
[Congregation] Set down and rest a little while.

The song might continue with verses such as

2. I know you tired
3. Well, you come from a long way
4. Been runnin' a long time
5. I know you tired
6. Goin' home with Jesus.[11]

Then comes a scripture reading, and perhaps a second song-and-saying sequence. During devotions, anyone so moved can lead a spiritual from the pews. By contrast, hymns usually begin with the intonation of hymn lines chanted by a leader or deacon and given out from the front. Devotions are formally closed when the clergy have entered the sanctuary and are seated in the pulpit, or when the leaders relinquish their roles before a formal call to worship or a choir processional.

Dr. Watts hymns still begin devotionals only in Baptist churches sustain-ing what is called the old-time way. This is the "black folk church" that Walter Pitts describes as Afro-Baptist. Such churches generally adhere to a fundamentalist belief in the Bible, encourage vocalized call-and-response interactions throughout the ritual, and celebrate the occurrence of various levels of spirit possession as central to the efficacy of worship (1995: 28). While indications are that this stratification is loosening, the socioeconomic status of a local church's membership has largely determined the extent to which a black Baptist church will either pursue this course or one more the-ologically liberal, less participatory, and less rooted in the song-dance-story heritage of African rituals. Though music is often performed from written scores and speakers more often use Standard English in middle-class Baptist worship, such worship also includes varying degrees of black performativity as the central component of a diverse range of worship styles. Whether lining out occurs in such settings depends upon the balance between the congregation's customs and the influence of clergy and musicians. Congregations that are in status, age-group, or style transitions may continue deacon-led devotionals yet freely insert other songs instead of, or in addition to, the old-time hymns and spirituals.

The shifts in ministry focus, ideas about music in worship, or both that come with changes in leadership or demography have often signaled the demise of Dr. Watts in a given congregation, locale, or region. For example, a church included in the study of lining out by William Crowder (1978), New Silver Mount Baptist (in Charlotte, North Carolina), has not continued the tradition under its new pastor. Where the tradition has remained, comparably conservative views about doctrine and musical style have often persisted as well.[12] While core participants in lining out may listen to or enjoy other sacred genres, the style elements of congregational singing—with lining out at its core—stand apart from the smoother harmonic textures and heavier rhythms of gospel style.

DR. WATTS HYMNS AS A CORE ELEMENT OF THE BLACK CONGREGATIONAL SINGING TRADITION

In our time, what is slow is seldom thought to be good. Nevertheless, the dirgelike Dr. Watts hymns can wax eloquent as they launch the unspeakable burdens of worshipers upon the wings of their own speech rhythms. Hymns being songs of praise to God, Dr. Watts hymns are texts in the evangelical style originated by the Rev. Isaac Watts. They were taught to colonial slaves and poor whites in Virginia and the Carolinas during the 1740s and 1750s, in the religious fervor of the First Great Awakening. The antiphonal form of lining out had been sanctioned by the Westminster Assembly in 1644 as what was to be a temporary means of congregational psalm singing in English parish churches.[13] But even prior to this formal authorization, English settlers of North America brought the practice with them to the New World. Though Puritan congregations abandoned lining out early in the eighteenth century, it has achieved permanence among three groups within the United States: chiefly white Old Regular Baptists in Eastern Kentucky; black and white Primitive Baptists scattered more widely in states east of the Mississippi River; and black Missionary Baptists throughout the United States. In all cases, the practice has become an expression of the cultural conservatism attending a range of Baptist positions from strict to moderate Calvinism.

Whereas the congregational singing tradition encompasses surviving examples of the ring shout, moans, and spirituals as well as Dr. Watts hymns, the other forms have received greater notice than Dr. Watts. The controversy that raged among early-twentieth-century scholars over black and white origins tended to reify the spiritual as a more "folk" expression and to marginalize black hymn-singing traditions as less "original." More recently, spirituals, and the "freedom songs" modeled after them, inspired solidarity in Civil Rights meetings and marches during the 1950s and 1960s, while the intricate melodic detail of regional hymn-singing styles proved less useful in solidifying protesters from diverse regions and ethnic backgrounds. The particular character of a regional singing tradition is often founded upon the melodic and rhythmic intricacies of Dr. Watts, and, to that extent, the hymns form the core of regional traditions that parallel linguistic speech communities. In this sense, the Standard English of the hymns (and of the King James Version of the Bible) balances the African-American English of the songs and sayings, which issue from the hearts of worshipers. Black Baptist worship styles blend the hymns as symbols of formality and literacy with a core of improvised and orally transmitted ritual elements.

Although distinctively black singing styles were well-developed prior to Emancipation, they were no doubt further stabilized in the late nineteenth century as black congregations became independent of white Baptist supervision. The congregational singing tradition flourished in rural churches, and it spread to cities through the massive urban migrations that occurred between 1880 and 1950. The great majority of black Baptist churches were founded around the turn of the twentieth century—before and after the 1897 founding of the largest black denomination, the National Baptist Convention, U.S.A., Inc. Although Baptist polity resides with each local congregation, most belong to regional associations of fifteen to twenty-five churches. This autonomy within loosely confederate regional associations (who joined together for hymn choir anniversaries or periodic singing unions) accounts for the prolific diversity of Dr. Watts hymn-singing styles that blossomed in the nineteenth century.

Although the musicality of hymn singing is inextricable from its worship function, many hymns have nevertheless been commercially recorded. During the 1920s and 1930s era of race records (recordings produced for distribution among Negro audiences), the Rev. J. M. Gates of Atlanta, Georgia, recorded several Dr. Watts hymns with his sermons. From the 1940s through the 1960s, Rev. C. L. Franklin (father of Aretha Franklin) followed the same practice. The 1960s and 1970s recordings of the Rev. C. J. Johnson, also of Atlanta, constitute the largest body of hymns and songs commercially recorded by any one song leader. The vocal ensemble Sweet Honey in the Rock, founded by Bernice Johnson Reagon, a veteran of the Freedom Singers who were active in the Civil Rights movement, has recorded and performed songs and hymns to international acclaim. Dr. Reagon's achievements bring full circle the legacy of the Fisk Jubilee Singers, who drew international plaudits for their formalized renditions of spirituals. Whereas that group represented movement toward assimilation, she and Sweet Honey have garnered critical acclaim for their professional and sophisticated yet unmediated synthesis of congregational songs and hymns as well as other African Diaspora vocal traditions.

A progressive blend of aesthetic sensitivity, cultural awareness, and social accountability is also apparent in the worship and outreach of large urban churches like Hartford Avenue Baptist of Detroit and Canaan Baptist in New York City. These are complex ministries led by high-profile pastors who bring to their work both academic training and fluency in the worship practices of oral tradition. For his blend of theological erudition with moaning intonations, the Rev. Charles Adams of Hartford Avenue has become known by the honorific "Harvard Hooper," and the Rev. Wyatt T. Walker of Canaan is an accomplished song and hymn leader and the author of *"Somebody's Calling My Name": Black Sacred Music and Social Change*. While Dr. Watts remains vital in these places, such churches seem to be exceptions to the apparent association of hymn singing with autonomous but nonactivist status-quo thinking among black Christians.

MOANING, SHOUTING, AND LINING OUT

Where Dr. Watts has continued, it has appreciated in value as a symbol of black culture's resilience. But the form inherited this role from the ring-shout tradition which preceded it (see Rosenbaum 1998). In the low country, comprising the coastal counties south of Charleston, and on the Sea Islands of South Carolina where there were few sanctions against African worship traditions, the ring shout, the Gullah language, and an entire complex of Creole culture has dominated.[14] By contrast, lining out, as an African adaptation of an English form, has anchored congregational singing in upland areas throughout the Southeast, particularly those areas in North and South Carolina and around the Blue Ridge Mountains. In these areas, white and black clergy's sanctions against the African-derived ring shout were compensated by at least tacit approval of European-derived lining out. Lining out provided a sufficiently European "mask" behind which the African feeling for expressive poignancy and rhythmic eloquence might continue, restrained yet unabated.[15]

Given the cycle of economic and social upheavals such as the American Revolution, the Civil War, and Emancipation, the field-to-factory migrations, and the Civil Rights movement, it is impossible to know how much and precisely what kind of change black lining out has undergone since 1758, when English missionary Samuel Davies wrote about the slaves who lodged in his quarters and sang "a torrent of sacred harmony that carried [his] mind away to heaven" (Southern 1983: 29). Repeated references indicate that slaves were developing a distinctive style of hymn singing by the mid-eighteenth century. Prefaced by indications of psalm singing among blacks and whites fifty years earlier, these sources document a developing pattern whereby slaves must have adapted English evangelical hymns to suit inherently African musical tendencies.[16]

The earliest record—from the 1750s—of a distinctive style of hymn singing among slaves coincides with the first organized black Baptist congregations. It was not until after the establishment of independent Methodist denominations and the camp-meeting revivals of the Second Great Awakening (1800 to 1820), though, that congregational songs in arranged and rehearsed forms known as "spirituals" emerged. Although excellent scholars of theology and literature have documented the story of "how the spiritual was hammered out," no thorough-going musicological study of the spirituals (also called congregational songs, or simply songs)[17] could ignore its chief precursors, the African ring shout and the English practice of lining out.[18]

Hymns and songs constantly mediate the timbral and expressive space between the extremes of talking and singing. Songs are begun out of the unction to speak a certain thing, and they unfold in patterned structures that develop those ideas and feelings through repetition and contrasts. Where speech utterance is vivified through song, the rising intensity can provoke a periphery of spoken interjections. In extreme cases, these terse exclamations can overtake the singing and become an interlude of celebration. Individual leaders of hymns and songs play a key role in moving words and phrases back and forth between the poles of speech and movement. Where a song is not coming together as it should, a leader will occasionally explain to the congregation why she or he is singing the song and urge their participation. In the back and forth of such a process, the singing congregation of individuals is ideally gathered into fuller communion with the divine and with each other. This movement from many different agendas to the unanimity that facilitates worship is understood by Christians as a central mystery of the faith. But it is the work of individual worship leaders to summon the divine presence that creates and sustains such communion.

Black congregations perform Dr. Watts hymns along a style continuum that ranges from moaning to shouting. While the softer, closed-lip, melismatic pitch inflections or the "dirty" sounds of glottal groans characterize the wordless moan or humming sound, the strident cries of the upper vocal range implicate shout-style hymn singing. Although no comprehensive inventory of regional hymn-singing styles is available, those styles that have been documented on sound recordings correspond either with the vocal colors and implicit rhythms of moaning or with the body movements and explicit rhythms of shouting. These apparently opposed yet complementary gestures—one brooding and inward, the other celebratory and percussive—have become engrained as structural components of African American worship. Moaning and shouting exist at the two ends of the continuum between relative reflection and relative intensity, respectively, as

TABLE 1   Patterns of Interaction in Congregational Singing

Focus of Action	Relative Reflection		Relative Intensity	
Singing and movement	Moans	Hymns	Songs	Shouts
Speech, intonation, and exclamation	Scripture	Prayer	Exhortation	Testimony

shown in table 1. Both of these traditions are dialogical and revolve around a leader's ability to communicate with and motivate the group in terms afforded by the ritual style.

The following descriptions of moaning (commonly associated with lining out) and shouting (which has been traced to the ring shout) survey the most general relationship among these elemental forms, Dr. Watts, and the entire tradition of congregational singing.

Moan Styles

The term "moaning" refers either to the humming chorus of a hymn performance or to more variegated and ambient sounds that can be heard during intoned prayers, moans, and hymns. Performed with the mouth open or closed, these sounds nuance the entire continuum of vocal colors between speech and song, including melismas, ghosted notes, slides, and blue-note inflections. Moaning is not synonymous with a moan, which is a text-based form that uses some or all of the above-mentioned variants of moaning for expression and coloration. Willie Collins defines the moan as a genre distinct from moaning and also explains the interrelation between the two:

> [The moan is] a sacred chant of one sentence repeated two or three times of approximately thirty seconds duration whose text is generally based on personal experience and is of individual creation but may occasionally be based on a hymn title or psalm and is disseminated by oral tradition. Moans are initiated and expressed a cappella during prayer in prayer service, devotion, and occasionally during the preacher's sermon. A number of these moans may be led successively by one of several individuals during the course of a prayer. The moan is generally uttered in the following manner: a leader moans most of the sentence and near the end the congregation joins in, in degrees sometimes initially humming then uttering the words with the leader. Moans are of relatively low amplitude as compared with song, are melodically embellished with melismas, having a unison and heterophonic texture usually done in a slow manner. (1992: 246)[19]

Collins describes a long-standing tradition of moans as an improvised devotional genre that builds from the repetition of a phrase given out by a

2. **Sinners are dying,**
   Sinners are dying,
   Sinners are dying,
   Save me Lord.

Music example 1. Transcription of moan no. 1 heard during prayer, by the Blue Spring Baptist Association, Tennessee. Transcription by Dr. Bernice Johnson Reagon; by permission of Dr. Reagon and Smithsonian Folkways.

leader. A moving example can be heard in the performance of "A Charge to Keep I Have" by the Blue Spring Missionary Baptist Association (*Wade in the Water*, vol. 2). In such traditions, once the chosen hymn text has been sung, it is moaned softly under the introductory phrases of the prayer that follows. The moaning-praying counterpoint continues against the background of yea-sayers who "bear up" the prayer (see music example 1). The praying continues over the chant, perhaps audible to at least some of those bearing him up with the moan, but the prayer is unintelligible on the recording cited here. As the solemn prayer builds in intensity, a second chant is heard, this time in three lines (see music example 2).

Once a sense of pulse is established in a moaning-style Dr. Watts performance, that flexible yet audible ictus remains constant throughout. The apparent exception to this pattern is the break in rhythm where the leader chants the following line(s) in speech rhythm, devoid of pulse. However, especially in moaning-style hymns, the pulse recedes but does not abate completely, for the underlying pulse often remains powerfully implicit while the hymn lines are being chanted. The chant is given out in a two- or three-note formula—most often, a segment of the pentatonic scale—which begins and ends on the home note of the key or mode (for instance, the

2. We are in yo' name,
   We are in yo' name,
   We are in yo' name.

3. Come by here,
   Come by here,
   Come by here.

Music example 2. Transcription of moan no. 2, by the Blue Spring Baptist Association, Tennessee. Transcription by Dr. Bernice Johnson Reagon; by permission of Dr. Reagon and Smithsonian Folkways.

lined-out phrases that begin "A Charge to Keep I Have" on *Wade in the Water*, vol. 2). Bret Sutton (1982) found that while black Primitive Baptists in the Blue Ridge Mountains commonly lined out hymns in such a manner, whites in the same region more often began by reading out the words and then singing continuously thereafter. Black Primitive Baptists more consistently alternate between intoned chant in speech rhythms and hymns sung in a variety of free or measured rhythms. This penchant for radical and immediate changes in vocal texture and rhythmic context—ones that are apparent more than real—are subtle reinterpretations of the African tradition that encourage polyrhythmic layered sounds (see Keyes 1996: 231–38).

   While a moaning chorus may follow a hymn in any tempo, moaning sounds ordinarily occur in and around slow tempos. In the slowest of moaning-style hymns, not a couplet but a single hymn line of six or eight syllables can occupy a twenty-five- to thirty-second time frame. Since such a tempo can make the words difficult to follow and cause one to lose track of where the melody is at any given point, the form itself offers no general welcome to the uninitiated. However, despite the slowness, such performances are not unmeasured, but rather are rhythmic and melodic expressions that move along in tension with implicit speech rhythms. This extreme slowness and rhythmic license is also an inheritance from the "old way" of lining out psalmody (see Temperley 1981), a slow and unmeasured style of lining out that held currency in North America throughout the seventeenth and early eighteenth centuries. Whereas the slowness of such singing became a wearisome bore to many colonials in New England, the practice may have enabled slaves (and, in a different sense, ethnic Europeans in the South) to freight their cries with the weight of feeling, torn between belonging and alienation.

Although the moaning gesture can be insinuated at any tempo, its speechlike character is most compatible with slow to moderate tempos. While an elastic yet audible sense of measure reigns in even the slowest hymns, other factors such as speech rhythms, melodic contours, and subtly varying vocal colors undermine the sense of regularity. Therefore, I agree with John Work's notion that such moaning-style melodies are not purely "derived out of measure and beat." Work describes the hymns he heard among black Primitive Baptists in Nashville, but his description applies to the best of all moaning-style hymn singing:

> There is something epic, something elemental, something overwhelmingly religious about the rendition of these old songs. Starting softly and informally, as one of them does after the half-intoned wordphrase by the leader, a melody is spun-out melismatically with no rhythm derived out of measure and beat, only punctuated by the wordphrase of the leader. The crescendo is gradual but relentless, and at a high point in the song the membership rises and engages in a very dignified formal clasping of hands between members right and left. Sometimes the singers, particularly the deacons, circulate among the membership. There is nothing trite, banal, or sensational in this performance. (Work 1949, quoted in Southern 1983: 284)

If, according to Work, "no rhythm [is] derived out of measure and beat," from where is it derived? An answer to this question is offered in chapters 5 and 6, which address the how and why of rhythm in Dr. Watts hymns at the rhetorical, one-note-to-the-next level in which Work's observation is grounded. What is important for the present is Work's description as a general statement about the character of ritual and the quality of sound that is projected in moaning-style hymn performances.

Shout Styles

The moaning utterances of first-frame hymns, prayers, and songs are preparatory to second-frame choir selections and preaching that more often establish or build upon motor rhythms and culminate in ecstatic forms of worship. Such expressions include exuberant vocal responses from the congregation, the religious dance known as the shout, and accompanying musical vamps or hand-clapping patterns. While worshipers speak of getting happy, letting the Spirit have His way, and shouting, studies of black music and ritual link these practices with African traditions of spirit possession, especially the circle-dance tradition known as the ring shout (see Stuckey 1987).

The ring shout was covertly practiced by slaves as a way of merging African worship patterns, which embraced sacred dance, with Calvinist doctrine, which saw dancing as antithetical to faith. Though waning, the practice has persisted in a few island and coastal locations up to the present. While a group of "shouters" shuffle forward counterclockwise in a circular formation, they do not lift the feet; therefore they do not "dance." This movement is always accompanied by a congregational song with text variations that sustain a deceptively simple call-and-response phrase pattern over the steadily growing intensity of cross rhythms, which are produced by feet, hands, and a stick on the floor (see Rosenbaum 1998: 17–52). Sterling Stuckey argues that the counterclockwise ring shout has continued among enslaved and free Africans in North America from the 1600s till the present. He also parallels the form to numerous West and East African circle-dance traditions, all directed to the ancestors and deities and increasing in tempo as the movement around the circle progresses. The circular movement symbolizes "the four moments of the sun" as the earth rotates counterclockwise, both on its axis and in its orbit (1987: 79, 96, 256). The singing that accompanies the ring shout begins in a stately tempo with little or no body movement. After the first stanza or chorus, the tempo of the opening pulse is doubled to reveal a fully articulate, layered texture of hand, foot, and stick-on-the-floor beat patterns that achieve a balance between predictable yet conflicting rhythms. While the sound of singing in the offbeat shout style may be breathy and richly varied as in moaning styles, singing in the cross-rhythmic shout style of Gullah-speaking areas is—as in West African traditions—nasal, straight-toned, and placed high within the vocal range (for an example of offbeat shout, see *Dr. Watts*, no. 7; for cross-rhythmic shout, see no. 1).

Whereas there is a rock-steadiness about moaning hymns, shout-style hymn singing does accelerate—either dramatically in one or several places, gradually throughout the performance, or in a composite of both ways. Shout-style hymn singing begins much like the moaning style, then moves in either of two directions, depending upon local tradition. During the slave era, the occurrence of various forms of sacred dancing, which African slaves and white observers alike referred to as shouting, was documented in most of the slave-holding states. Of these, two very different shout styles of hymn singing have continued in the Carolinas and Georgia: an offbeat syncopated style in the Central Piedmont region that surrounds Charlotte, North Carolina, and a cross-rhythmic style in the Sea Island communities off the coast of South Carolina and Georgia. While the former embodies accelerating tempos, offbeat syncopated hand clapping, attendant body movement, and occasional spirit possession, the latter is more apparently descended from the African tradition of circle dances.

The question arises as to why a shout style with various cross-rhythmic clapping patterns should be found only in Gullah-speaking coastal areas. In sum, the singing is no less unique than the language. The fixity of the coastal traditions can be understood at least in part as a function of the geographical and labor needs of the rice plantations common on the coast compared with those of the tobacco, corn, or cotton plantations that were prominent in the upland and Piedmont regions. The particular geographical demands of rice-growing meant that rice plantations could not easily be relocated, while tobacco and corn plantations could be located in many more places and thus moved, particularly after large amounts of land were made available through the Louisiana Purchase. Likewise, the specific labor needs of rice growing called for a greater consistency of laborers than on the tobacco or corn plantations. Whereas almost anyone could learn how to farm tobacco or corn, farming rice required more specialized skills. The dearth of influences from other regions, along with the consistency of the laborers, mitigated any tendency of the musical traditions of the coastal regions to evolve or assimilate other musical styles over time. Hence, it comes as no great surprise to learn that a specific shout style and specific rhythmic tendencies developed among the Gullah-speaking peoples of the coastal areas.

Shout-style hymn singing continued in the low country at least through the 1960s. For example, a shout-style performance of "What a Friend We Have in Jesus" was recorded by Guy and Candie Carawan in a New Year's watch night service in January 1964 (*Dr. Watts*, no. 1). This and several other Dr. Watts hymns were performed in the earlier, more formalized portions of that service, and as the spirit of celebration intensified, congregational songs like "Ain't You Got a Right to the Tree of Life" (see *Wade in the Water*, vol. 2, for a performance of this song) replaced the hymns and the length of the performances increased. The singing itself is in a nasal, high-pitched, intensely felt style that is also common to West Africa and the Caribbean. While pitch inflections are somewhat liquid, the singing implicates the insistence of a holler or cry more than the introspection of a moan. This kind of gesture seems to follow from the nature of calls by leaders that are expected to elicit visceral group responses. In sum, while a poignant moan moves or implores others to response, a shouting call demands a vocal response in a certain rhythmic place. In the terms of African culture, the absence of either kind of affirmative response can be an embarrassing rebuke to an inept leader (see Smitherman 1977: 109).

Although the congregational singing tradition as a whole is persisting—despite frequent eulogies—the cross-rhythmic shout style is, by all accounts, endangered. Such singing ceased long ago in larger black churches in and around Charleston and Savannah, and it can still be heard in only a few rural "praise houses," where elders gather to pray, testify, and sing. Such praise houses were constructed in slave quarters by masters and missionaries to facilitate worship during the Baptist mission to slaves that continued from the 1830s throughout the antebellum period.

Marked by an accelerating offbeat syncopation, perhaps adapted from the unaccented-to-accented pattern of iambic hymn meters (see chapter 3), the upland and Piedmont Carolinas shout style exerts a prevalent influence throughout the worship ritual. The vigor of this offbeat syncopated style occurs within a church culture that includes both large urban and small rural churches in Charlotte and continues southward between interstate highways 85 and 77 to Gastonia, North Carolina, and to Rock Hill and Chester, South Carolina. As one moves north from Charlotte toward the Virginia border and the Blue Ridge Mountains, there seems to be a softening of the shout impetus and more moderate tempos and tune-based melodies.[20]

At its beginning, the sound is moaning, organumlike, and disembodied or distant-sounding compared with the more extraverted spirituals. But as the couplets are lined out, foot patting becomes more insistent, intoned "talking back" as a signifying gesture thickens the texture, and miscellaneous hand claps begin. After the first verse of the hymn, the choir stands. By the last verse, a faster tempo has been stabilized over a consistent clapping pattern. From this point, the closing couplet of the hymn's final verse is repeated over a steady and urgent rhythmic pulse. This may carry for only two or three "choruses" or may, at length, deconstruct into shouting, walking, testifying, continuation of the clapping and patting without the singing, moaning (humming) of the hymn tune over the clap, or an extended reprise of the couplet. Completely subject to the tenor of the moment, the byword for this portion of the worship ritual is "let the Spirit have His way." There is no ring or communal pattern for shouting (i.e., dancing), and shouters are watched or shielded—so as not to injure themselves or others—but not restrained by ushers or friends.

THE BLACK BAPTIST WORSHIP ETHOS

Whether large-scale or small-scale, formalized or informal, impoverished or upwardly mobile, old-time, eclectic, or charismatic, in and through all the fluidness between moaning and shouting is a discernable constancy about black Baptist worship. It moves from songs, testimonies, hymns, and prayers entreating and invoking God's presence to climactic events such as preaching and shouting that celebrate the experience of Christian conversion and

TABLE 2   Order of Worship and Approximate Time Frames
for Each Ritual Segment

Devotions: 15–20 minutes	Exhortation
	Opening hymn
	Prayer
	Song
Service—part 1: 10–15 minutes	Call to worship
	Procession of choir or choir and clergy
	Responsive reading
	Prayer of consecration
	Choral response or selection, hymn, or song
Service—part 2: 10–15 minutes	Announcements
	Introduction of visitors
	Welcome to visitors
	Pastoral remarks
	Choral selection, hymn, or song
Service—part 3: 15–20 minutes	Offertory prayer
	Missionary offering (optional)
	Ministry of tithes and offering
	Offertory response
	Choral selection
Service—part 4: 60–80 minutes	Scripture
	Choral selection
	Sermon
	Altar call
	Benediction

God's presence in the midst of worshipers. Although the binary form observed
by Pitts (1993)—the opening devotions frame and the culminating service
frame—is insightful, no fixed pattern can apply to the highly reflexive and
interdependent nature of the ritual style that Baptist churches have inherited from slave worship and adapted to the changing needs of each generation. However, a typical order of service in a local Baptist church follows this
general outline (see table 2).

The service frame of black Baptist worship, though apparently more
fixed than devotionals in form, is no less fluid and malleable in structure.
This notion of structure accrues from the sequence of relative emphasis
and deemphasis, or prolongation and abbreviation, that changes with each
ritual performance. The prayer of consecration that was a peak experience
in the service on one Sunday is noticeable as a useful but passing moment
of the next service. The habitude of announcements in one service
becomes a time of interactive, even jovial fellowship in the next. The choir

selection that evokes no congregational response on one occasion brings active participation and causes members to bear witness through verbal responses and shouting on another. In place of the celebratory sermon of the previous Sunday, the pastor talks in almost conversational tones to the congregation. The altar call that draws no response on one Sunday lasts for thirty minutes on another and new converts are taken into the church. The contingent nature of the entire ritual emphasizes the belief that the individual and collective needs of the congregation are more important than any established pattern of worship forms.

Wherever oral tradition prevails, the order of service is flexibly performed, and songs are chosen based upon a leader's inspiration. Only in the most literate churches is there strict adherence to a printed order of worship. What the words appearing on the printed program actually mean can be determined only by each local setting and its regional context. In highly literate congregations, few deviations from the printed program are tolerated. In mixed settings, the program is only a guide. Where oral tradition rules, the same printed program is circulated from week to week. But everyone knows that the inspiration of the moment will choose certain hymns and songs, and will often modify the entire order of worship as well.

True to the congregational polity of Baptist tradition, each church embodies a distinctive worship character that expresses the tensions between discrete and, at times, opposing cultural perspectives. James Washington has identified four historical currents that create, in his terms, a fractious pattern of unity among black Baptists. They are (1) black Baptist folk culture, (2) a sense of the church as "a haven in a heartless world," (3) a middle-class ethos, and (4) a prophetically progressive political current.[21] Since the post-Emancipation era, divisions have occurred and tensions have persisted between clergy steeped in folk culture, for example, and the formally educated clergy who serve in middle-class settings. In perhaps the most apparent of these rifts, many prominent ministers and leaders in the National Baptist Convention, U.S.A., Inc. never assumed a public role in the Civil Rights movement, which was led by Dr. Martin Luther King Jr., a Baptist minister and doctoral graduate of Boston University. Yet the latter's sermons and oratory were as replete with the gestures and spirit of black folk preaching as they were erudite and rational (Lincoln and Mamiya 1990).

Along with sermons, prayers, moaning, shouting, and songs, hymn singing is a core element of Washington's "black Baptist folk culture," which finds its African basis in the dynamic relationship among speech, body movement, and ritual celebration. Although Baptist congregational polity has hindered the consolidation of the denomination's organizational and political potentials, the pattern of local autonomy has sustained the old-time traditions associated with Dr. Watts hymn singing. While there are black Baptist churches that do not continue the practice (and they are often proximate to those that do), no other network of black church associations has sustained the lining-out tradition throughout the twentieth century in every major region of the United States. The very emergence of the black Baptists as a national organization grew from confederations between networks of small, regional associations that began to take on national significance. On one hand, certain associations have become networks for the retention of folk culture in worship. On the other, the forces of "progress"—whether toward social and political initiatives or toward rehearsed choirs and gospel music performance in worship—have tended to be national in scope and vision. Nevertheless, whether altered to reflect urban influences or performed in the old-time way, opening devotions seed the ground of black Baptist worship for the desired outcomes of praise, proclamation, and power.

Chapter 2

"Blest Be the Tie That Binds"

Part II: Regional Style Traditions
of Dr. Watts Hymn Singing

Blest be the tie that binds
Our hearts in Christian love;
The fellowship of kindred minds
Is like to that above.

JOHN FAWCETT, *1782*

In the universe of Dr. Watts hymn singing, the particular qualities of regional styles and their unifying similarities are of equal importance. This chapter focuses on regional traditions of hymn singing, building upon both the local ethnography by Pitts (1993) and the regional styles described by Reagon and Brevard (1994). The quiltwork of musical dialects stretches itself across the southeastern United States, with more random urban intersections in the North and West. The precise number of these styles is unknown, and the process of discovering or recovering them from obscurity might continue for years to come. But it is not too early to posit a regional typology of rhythmic styles and ensemble textures in black hymn singing.

Because they are among the most widely distributed and currently available examples of black hymn singing, thirty-three recorded performances have been selected for analysis in this and subsequent chapters. These performances, listed in table 3, part A, can be heard on three recordings: *Wade in the Water*, volume 2: *African American Congregational Singing: Nineteenth-Century Roots* (1994; hereafter *Wade in the Water*, vol. 2); *Benjamin Lloyd's Hymn Book: A Primitive Baptist Song Tradition* (1999; hereafter *Benjamin Lloyd*); and *Dr. Watts Hymn Singing among African Americans* (2002; referred to throughout this book as *Dr. Watts*).[1] Save numbers 8 and 19, which are songs and will be discussed in other chapters, all of the selections on *Dr. Watts* may be categorized as hymns and so come under the discussion in this chapter. These thirty-three performances chronicle various regional styles of black hymn singing. Tunes that have been traced to printed sources are indicated by name. Where a source is unidentified but the tune sounds as if

TABLE 3   Lining-Out Hymn Performances and Their Locations

A. Hymn Performances Analyzed in This Book

Wade in the Water, volume 2

Location	Selection	Texture/Tune/Rhythm
Baltimore, MD	8. I Heard the Voice of Jesus Say	Offbeat-shout/s
Philadelphia, PA	11. Am I a Soldier of the Cross	Moaning harmony/*Arlington*/f
	12. Early, My God, without Delay	Moaning harmony/unknown/s
Southwest Georgia	15. A Charge to Keep I Have	Moaning organum/*Idumea*/f

Benjamin Lloyd's Hymn Book

Location	Selection	Texture/Tune/Rhythm
Alabama	5. The Day Is Past and Gone	Moaning unison/*Idumea*/f
North Carolina	8. Dark and Thorny Is the Desert	Offbeat-shout/s
	9. O May I Worthy Prove	Moaning unison/unknown/s
Livingston, AL	12. Amazing Grace	Moaning unison/*Pisgah*/f
	13. That Doleful Night before His Death	Moaning unison/f
Loachapoka, AL	15. What Wondrous Love Is This	Moaning unison/*Wondrous Love*/s
Notasulga, AL	16. While Sorrows Encompass . . .	Moaning organum/unknown/s
Eutaw, AL	20. Father, I Stretch My Hands to Thee	Moaning organum/f

Dr. Watts Hymn Singing among African Americans

Location	Selection	Texture/Tune/Rhythm
South Carolina: Sea Islands	1. What a Friend We Have in Jesus	Cross-shout/*Restoration*/s
Low country	2. Come Ye That Love the Lord	Off-shout/*Idumea*/s
Sandhills	3. Go Preach My Gospel, Saith the Lord	Moaning organum/f
Sandhills	4. Father, I Stretch My Hands to Thee	Moaning organum/f
Sandhills	5. A Charge to Keep I Have	Moaning organum/*Idumea*/f

(continued)

TABLE 3 (continued)

Dr. Watts Hymn Singing among African Americans

Location	Selection	Texture/Tune/Rhythm
Piedmont—north central	6. Father, I Stretch My Hands to Thee	Offbeat-shout/s
Piedmont—north central	7. Amazing Grace	Offbeat-shout/s
Piedmont—north central	8. You May Bury Me in the East	Offbeat-shout/s
Piedmont—southwest	9. Jesus Invites His Saints	Moaning triadic harmony/unknown/s
Georgia—Piedmont	10. I Heard the Voice of Jesus Say	Moaning organum/f
Florida—north central	11. A Charge to Keep I Have	Moaning organum/*Idumea*/f
Mississippi—delta (near Memphis)	12. A Charge to Keep I Have	Moaning unison/*Idumea*/f
Louisiana—south central	13. Amazing Grace	Off-shout triadic harmony/*Willow*^{a}/s
Central Texas	14. Must Jesus Bear the Cross Alone	Moaning unison/f
	15. I'm Not Too Mean to Serve the Lord	Moaning unison/f
Detroit, MI	16. Before This Time Another Year	Moaning unison/f
Kentucky/North Carolina/Virginia	17. What a Friend We Have in Jesus	Moaning unison/*Restoration*/s
	18. My Work on Earth Will Soon Be Done	Moaning unison/f
Central Texas	19. A City Called Heaven	Moaning unison/f
	20. A Few More Years Shall Roll	Moaning unison/f
Detroit, MI	21. Remember Me	Moaning triadic harmony/unknown/s

B. Other Locations Where Black Lining Out Was Observed or Reported in the Late Twentieth Century

Location	Number of Item	Source or Site of Observation
Hartford, CT	22	Horace Boyer, professor emeritus of music, University of Massachusetts
New York, NY	23	Dr. Wyatt Tee Walker, Canaan Baptist Church
Philadelphia, PA	24	Rev. Charles Walker, pastor, Nineteenth Street Baptist Church

TABLE 3   (continued)

*B. Other Locations Where Black Lining Out Was Observed or Reported
in the Late Twentieth Century*

Location	Number of Item	Source or Site of Observation
Washington, DC	25	United Southern Prayer Band
Chicago, IL	26	Rev. Clay Evans, pastor, Fellowship Baptist Church
Kansas City, MO	27	Dale Taylor, professor of music therapy, University of Wisconsin, Eau Claire
Nashville, TN	28	Various Primitive Baptist churches
Memphis, TN	29	Rev. Kenneth Whalum, pastor, Mt. Olivet Baptist Church
New Orleans, LA	30	Bishop Paul Morton, pastor, Greater St. Stephen Full Gospel Baptist Church
Los Angeles, CA	31	Rev. Allen Iverson, Paradise Baptist Church

NOTE: These performances correspond to those mapped in figure 1 (page 57).
a The full name of the tune is *The Weeping Willow* or *Go Bury Me beneath the Willow*. It is paired with a secular lyric folksong that can be found in Frank C. Brown, *The Frank C. Brown Collection of North Carolina Folklore* (Durham: Duke University Press, 1952–64), vol. 5, 189–90.

it might be from a written source (bearing in mind that the very process of notating a tune imposes a certain regularity), it has been marked "unknown." Where no such sense of tunefulness is evident, I have assumed an oral origin. Thus, questions of origin and originality do not turn solely upon whether a written source can be identified, but focus upon the singing style as well.

Among these thirty-three performances, twenty-three were recorded among Missionary Baptists and ten among Primitive Baptists (all eight *Benjamin Lloyd* selections as well as *Dr. Watts*, nos. 17 and 18), and the regional styles are shared between both traditions. Whereas the Primitive Baptist performances are evenly balanced between the strictly measured moaning style (s) and the freely measured moaning style (f)—five strict and five free—the freely measured rhythms are both dominant and more widespread across regions among Missionary Baptists—ten strict and thirteen free. Altogether, eighteen performances are in free rhythm, and fifteen incorporate moaning gestures in singing that has a stricter rhythm.

While freely measured rhythms implicate the gestures of either moaning or speaking, the motor rhythms of the shout are intimated in strictly measured singing. The rhythmic character of freely measured moaning derives from dynamic interactions among the iambic hymn texts, the rhythmic and melodic tendencies of pitch combinations sung on each syllable, and the

sense of rapport and timing between leader and group in each performance. Flowing along a continuum that marks the expressive range
between the moan and shout, this speech-centered form of expression can
also utilize pitch inflection, diverse vocal timbres, and accentuation to intimate strictly measured rhythms. This range of rhythmic nuances is
grounded in ritualized patterns of speech intonation, the genesis and substance of which are considered further in chapters 5 and 6.

Ensemble textures are a more constant and neutral element than the
subtle approaches to timbre and rhythm that underlie moaning and shouting. Moaning hymns are heard in textures that are either unison, organum,
or triadic harmony. Unison moaning (uni-moan) is a linear composite of
melodic sounds, including formulaic melismas, variegated timbres, and
bent-note intonations. These timbres and gestures produce a distinctive
thickness or density of sound, which Olly Wilson has described as "the heterogeneous sound ideal" in African American music (1992). Moaning
organum has the same character of "liquid" and languid heterophony, but
with consistent two-part harmonies moving in the parallel fourths, fifths,
and thirds that William Tallmadge (1984) describes as folk organum. The
liquid pitch inflections of moaning also occur in hymn tunes that incorporate triadic harmonies (i.e., moaning harmonies). All three moaning textures incorporate the range of sounds—grunts, groans, humming,
melismas, ghosted notes, slides, and pitch inflections up or down—that
have been subsumed under the concept of "blue notes." Although both
moaning and the blues can connote sadness, exigency, or pain, each suggests a domain of human experience that is less particular and more ineffable within its own context. Thus moaning is the religious counterpart of
the third- and seventh-degree blue-note complexes described and illustrated by Jeff Todd Titon in *Early Downhome Blues* (1977: 154–65).

Heard in inland regions of South Carolina, Georgia, and Florida, moaning organum (see *Dr. Watts*, nos. 4, 5, 10, and 11) features the sound of two
principal vocal parts as well as occasional heterophony. Whereas moaning
organum in slow-to-moderate tempos is common in upland and Piedmont
areas of the Eastern Seaboard states, moaning unison performances from
the Deep South (e.g., *Dr. Watts*, nos. 13 and 15–20, save no. 16, which was
recorded in Detroit by singers who practice a hymn-singing tradition with
roots in the Deep South) demonstrate a remarkable consensus of both
melodic outline and melismatic nuances. The pockets of organum heard
among Primitive Baptists in the north-central Tennessee area around
Nashville and in Eutaw, Alabama (see *Benjamin Lloyd*, no. 20), may be heard
as a combination of the density of moaning organum with the florid quality
of unison moaning. This slower and rhythmically freer, echolike organum
creates a grandly spacious yet full sound in which one can hear certain
notes spreading out, or "liquefying," beyond their normal duration.

Though only two lines are sounded in organum, strategic delays and antic-ipations create a peculiar echo effect of swirling sound that flows and ebbs around a discernable pulse reference.

All three types of moaning-style hymn performances approximate the texture and tempo of what Nicholas Temperley has described as "the old way of singing" (1981), a style that passed out of currency among whites even as blacks adapted its slow and lugubrious terms to African ritual forms. Rejecting the old way in the popular quest for musical literacy, Southern whites embraced shape-note hymnody in the early nineteenth century. However, similar shape-note singing schools did not achieve wide currency among blacks until long after Emancipation (Dyen 1977).[2]

Given the prevalence of slides, melismas, and variegated tone colors in moaning-style performances, such melodies can be difficult to pair with published hymn tunes from sources such as the *Original Sacred Harp (OSH)*.[3] And to think of the gestures as mere ornaments, in the conventional sense, is to misunderstand their generative significance to the character of each regional style. For although there is much freely conceived call-and-response heterophony on certain selections (e.g., *Wade in the Water*, vol. 2, nos. 11 and 15; *Dr. Watts*, no. 18), many freely measured moaning hymns also demon-strate remarkable similarities in the intricate details of their formulaic melodies (e.g., *Benjamin Lloyd*, no. 5; *Dr. Watts*, nos. 12, 14, 15, 16, and 21).

The intricate transformations that written tunes have undergone in oral tradition call into question the hegemony of written sources, even as they invite comparisons with them. For, as Lawrence Levine has observed, the toughness and resilience of a culture is not determined by [its] ability to withstand change . . . but by its ability to react creatively and responsively to the realities of a new situation" (1978: 5). George Pullen Jackson (1943) acknowledges or explains only white-to-black transfers, but the 1844 publi-cation of the *OSH* was the culmination of a period of tunebook publication when *two-way* transfers occurred between black and white worshipers who attended the same camp meetings. Had black-to-white transfers not been common, there would have been no need for the Rev. John Watson's stern 1819 warning against the infusion of black worship practices into white worship (see Southern 1983: 62–64).

Despite apparent similarities between recorded oral performances and written tunes, the historical remove of centuries and the lack of documen-tation for oral performances before the era of recorded sound render absurd the very idea of certifying racial influences in either direction. An example of such historical complexity, which is especially widespread among black worshipers throughout the United States, is the slow, moaned-out hymn tune *Idumea* (*OSH* 47). The phrase contours of the written melody closely parallel the tunes of *Wade in the Water*, vol. 2, no. 15; *Benjamin Lloyd*, no. 5; and *Dr. Watts*, nos. 2, 5, 11, and 12. Save *Dr. Watts*, no. 2, all feature a moaning-style melody, and, other than *Benjamin Lloyd,* no. 5, all are paired with Charles Wesley's short-meter hymn text "A Charge to Keep I Have." The regional styles are situated in two South Carolina locations, as well as in Georgia, Florida, Alabama, and Mississippi.

The textures of these moaning-style performances vary from moaning organum in *Wade in the Water,* vol. 2, no. 15, and *Dr. Watts,* nos. 5 and 11, to moaning unison in *Benjamin Lloyd,* no. 5, and *Dr. Watts,* no. 12.[4] Yet there is notable consistency among them. First, all are sung in an extremely slow duple meter rather than the triple meter of the printed source. If this oral version were directly and simply based upon the written version, one would expect some groups of black worshipers to still be singing something more akin to the written melody. Second, all five versions adhere to a certain melodic outline, sharing consistent detail in the melismatic shape and context of each syllable. This suggests that a remarkable rhythmic-melodic consensus has overspread virtually the entire Southeast, not just about each melodic phrase, but also about each syllable, which constitutes a kind of subphrase within the larger shape. The resemblance between *Idumea* and these five performances is distant, yet it is discernable in the contour of the larger phrases. However, more apparent is the resemblance between *Idumea* and the tune heard in *Dr. Watts,* no. 2, "Come Ye That Love the Lord." This tune is set in a strictly measured rhythm that insinuates moaning and bent notes but accelerates to a rhythmic bounce, with backbeat claps on two and four. By contrast with the five moaning performances, this "near-shout" hovers much closer to the melodic outline of *Idumea.*

The similarities and distinctions among these six recordings and the tune *Idumea* correspond with the more general range of rhythmic-melodic transformations in both jazz standards and classic gospel songs. In such cases, the resulting melodies resemble their melodic sources in macrostructures or form, but the microstructures or subphrases constitute entirely different terms of expression. Michael Harris explains, for example, the close similarities and the distinctions among the melody *Maitland,* the associated text, "Must Jesus Bear the Cross Alone," and Thomas Dorsey's signature gospel song "Take My Hand, Precious Lord" (1992). Of course, in Dorsey's song, the structural impetus overtook and transformed the broader outlines to accommodate something that was different from the hymn, the moaning tradition itself, or his blues background, yet synthesized all three.

In shout-style singing, the formulaic melismas that embellish the moaning style are often incorporated into the fabric of given melodies. Where melodies are traceable to written sources, the tunes have evidently been simplified or "flattened out" to approximate the pentatonic modality of intoned chant. In performance, the rhythms inherent in such recontoured melodies are "drummed out" interactively by voices, so as to approximate, in much less intricate detail, the layered effect of time lines in, say, Ghanaian drumming from West Africa (Nketia 1974). As prime examples of this layering, the cross-rhythmic shouts (cross-shout) from the Sea Islands of South Carolina and Georgia reflect the most direct African influence. Although only one hymn having this texture has been included for discussion here (*Dr. Watts*, no. 1), similarly textured songs can be heard on *Wade in the Water*, vol. 2.

Hymns are heard least frequently in this cross-rhythmic shout style, which is also the least widely dispersed. By contrast, offbeat syncopated shouts occur more frequently in the collections cited, mirroring their wider geographic distribution throughout various regions of the Southeast. This more ubiquitous presence may also derive from the prominence of iambic prosody in oral speech patterns, which will be examined in chapter 5.

In the body of recordings in table 3, part A, strictly measured moaning-style hymns are about equal to shout-style hymns. Of the styles and textures described, these most nearly resemble the structure and character of written hymn tunes, such as those from the *OSH*. Where a written source has not yet been identified, the connection with written sources is inferred from the regular rhythms and the melodic faithfulness to standard Western intonation. Of the seven strictly measured moaning performances, most faithful to this ideal are *Dr. Watts*, nos. 9 and 21, which utilize triadic harmonies more than the open intervals of organum. Although a written source for the tune of no. 9 has not yet been identified, it is apparently a tune-based melody. The Phinizy Chorus, which performs this hymn, represents a regional tradition of designating hymn tunes by names consistent with those used in *OSH* and similar sources.

Well defined as it is, the tune-based tradition to which the Phinizy Chorus belongs is the exception to the rule. More common and widespread across regions and locales is the oral patterning that has followed from tune-and-text pairings in printed sources. Among the most frequently heard are "Amazing Grace" in the tune of *New Britain* and "Must Jesus Bear the Cross Alone" in the tune of *Maitland*. The former match appeared first in William Walker's *Southern Harmony* of 1835, and the latter pairing issued from George Allen's *Oberlin Social and Sabbath School Hymn Book* of 1844 (*Handbook to the Baptist Hymnal* 1992: 190–91). These more common tune-based performances build upon the moaning concept a richly textured foreground of liquid melismatic interpolations to "put the song over." Because such melodies are grounded in triadic harmonies, this kind of hymn tune has been more generally adaptable to gospel accompaniments.[5] Among commercially recorded, tune-based, moaning-style performances, few have rivaled the broad popularity of *Aretha Franklin: Amazing Grace, with James Cleveland and the Southern California Community Choir* ([1972] 1987).

A much earlier sense of triadic singing embellished by melismas and bent notes is heard in the *Pisgah* hymn tune (*OSH* 58), here paired with "Amazing

Grace" (*Benjamin Lloyd*, no. 12). Though the tune is but thinly veiled, Doc Reed and Vera Hall (two performers who sang together frequently in field recordings made by Alan Lomax) mesh their voices in a startling array of unison melismas. This congruity suggests an intimate musical rapport between the singers, perhaps based upon a strong consensus about the rightness of their chosen pitches and rhythms. (This matter of melodic detail or microstructure will be examined at greater length in chapter 6.) Since the performers adhere closely to melodies and rhythms outlined in the written tune, and therefore utilize vocal gestures as embellishments in the conventional sense, this local style is situated very much halfway between adherence to the hymn-tune and unison moaning gestures.[6] *Dr. Watts,* no. 21, projects the same melodic directness and simplicity, but its languid articulation places it further afield from the tune-based sound of strictly measured moaning. Of the seven strictly measured moaning performances, *Dr. Watts,* no. 21, is most apparently oral in conception.

As vocal gestures, both moaning and shouting are matters of degree as well as kind. Either can be performed within a range of emphasis that may vary from subtle intimation to bold insistence. In the freely measured moaning of "Must Jesus Bear the Cross Alone" (*Dr. Watts,* no. 14), for example, pitches are pulled and twisted on almost every syllable to achieve a delicate poignancy. By contrast, the flattened-out, chant-like hymn tune of "What Wondrous Love Is This" (*Benjamin Lloyd*, no. 15) uses the moaning impetus in a strictly measured rhythm to convey the divine awe alluded to in the text. This vast expressive range is filled in by the seemingly infinite number of variations adopted by different speech communities and individual speech patterns, which are continually modified from one generation to the next.

MAPPING REGIONAL STYLE TRADITIONS

Regional hymn-singing styles have developed through a complex web of interactions between Baptist and Methodist congregations. Regional organizations of choirs and congregations, allied with local Baptist associations, have established the musical equivalent of linguistic speech communities— groups of people who use the same language varieties. Just as a dialect (in the nonpejorative linguistic sense) is distinguished by such features as accent, grammar, vocabulary, lexical meaning, semantics, and orthography, its associated regional singing tradition might be distinguishable by the nature of its ensemble textures (unison, organum, or triadic harmony), its use of call-and-response structures, and its emphasis upon either moaning or shouting as the predominant vocal gesture. For example, there is a self-evident point of distinction between the Gullah language of the Sea Islands and coastal regions and the less distinct speech patterns of Piedmont South

Carolina, and certain distinctions between those speech patterns are intimated in the rhythmic character and intonation patterns of congregational
singing in these neighboring regions (see Dargan 1995). More detailed
study of parallels between speech communities and congregational singing
within neighboring regions is needed, and the relationship between speech
and singing in local Baptist associations remains to be tested. But, for now,
a useful hypothesis can be proposed between the ways people talk and their
ways of singing.

Several neighboring Baptist associations may, over time, interact in such
a way that common patterns of worship reinforce a certain range of predominant style elements that hold currency over a large area. Such patterns
of dissemination suggest the dynamism and fluidity of regional style
"boundaries." Any geographical notion of such boundaries is, of course,
indefinite and ever-changing, depending as it does upon the personal incli-
nations of prominent song leaders, which are reinforced by group consensus about what is good singing.

A way of singing shared among congregations throughout a certain
region marks what is unique about that people and signifies a religious and
social identity (see Lincoln 1996). In this sense, not all regions are created
equal. While some enjoy a vital and distinctive tradition of congregational
singing, forces for change such as media and migration have destabilized
the social equilibrium in other regions. For example, the twentieth-century
pattern of rapid change in the Sea Islands sharply contrasts with the continuities in the Carolina Piedmont and suggests that those African American
traditions reflecting the smallest degrees of European influence, such as
the ring shout and the Gullah language, are also the most difficult to sustain in the face of modernity.[7]

Within distinctive regional traditions, each Baptist congregation main-
tains its own worship style to some degree. It is reasonable to assume that
churches emphasizing the priestly function—often termed the "haven in a
heartless world"—would privilege continuity over innovation and be more
disposed to retain the singing of Dr. Watts hymns and songs. By contrast,
the progressive tendencies of churches exerting a prophetic political
impact upon black social welfare would lead them to more readily embrace
gospel and other musical expressions at the expense of the archaic traditions. Although this assumption presumes that most congregations are not
prone to embrace both directions, both old and new forms continue in a
visible minority of large and prominent churches within the black Baptist
connection.

Because each regional singing tradition is, in some measure, a law unto
itself, interregional worship—at events such as Baptist state conventions—
relies upon gospel songs or other forms sourced from the media and thus
known to all. What is shared across genres and regions in black sacred music

has most often held the attention of collectors and scholars. This bias is implicit, for example, in the convention of categorical references to *the* spiritual. However, given the premise of regional styles, there is evidently no one right way to perform a certain spiritual, nor is one region's tradition necessarily more authoritative than its neighbor's. The present need is to explicate the vast (but declining) range of style traditions that coexist within African American music and culture.

Just as African vocal traditions adhere to common principles of rhythm, color, and modality yet exhibit extreme diversity, a similar pattern obtains in regional styles of Dr. Watts hymn singing in the former slave states. The parallel can be explained at least four ways: (1) continuity in patterning among myriad African traditions led to similarly diverse "dialects" of African American music; (2) slaveocracy imposed legal and social partitions between slaves on neighboring plantations as a means of minimizing insurrections; (3) prior to the development of the modern transportation infrastructures, rivers and other natural boundaries limited local travel and, with it, style transfers (Dargan 1995); and (4) three migratory patterns have disrupted or at least altered regional traditions: the early colonial course of migration and agribusiness from North to South, the expansion to the West in the early 1800s, and the field-to-factory migrations of the late nineteenth and early twentieth centuries. Although styles are generally consistent within each region, hymns or songs are frequently heard that do not conform to the regional style. Black Americans have seldom been wedded to *any* notion of style for its own sake, but rather have adapted styles to more pragmatic social and ritual functions. This lack of self-conscious restrictions to any certain style may be explained by the fact that the regional backgrounds of shared memory form a cultural map of archaic regional styles that predated the rise of popular culture in the late nineteenth century. Therefore, any congregation may, at a point in the service, leave the melodic-harmonic style associated with its own area to offer a tune-based melody such as "Amazing Grace" in the tune of *New Britain,* which has been widely disseminated through recorded and written sources. This capacity for mediating change relies upon a layered coexistence of multiple vocal traditions, as evidenced by the choirs maintained in many large Missionary Baptist churches.

Part B of table 3 is a general supplement to part A and shows that the area where Dr. Watts hymn singing extends beyond the predominantly southeastern locations listed in part A. Figure 1 maps the locations of the performances included in table 3, parts A and B. Specific locations are identified because, while the tradition is widely disseminated across regions of the United States, its continuance in each location is limited to the few congregations where strong hymn singers are still alive and influential as worship leaders.[8]

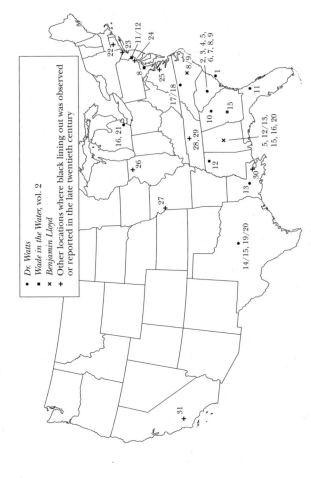

Figure 1. Map of locations where lining-out hymn performances discussed in this book were recorded. The numbers on the map correspond to the number of each performance in its respective collection. Each collection has its own symbol, as shown in the key. See also table 3, part A (page 47). The "other locations" represent performances not discussed in this book, as listed in table 3, part B.

The fine points of texture, rhythm, and manner of expression and the differences among varying styles within the same regions were discussed earlier in this chapter. A more comprehensive picture is rendered in figure 1 and table 3, taken together. Viewed in tandem, they illustrate the essential patterns that seem to pertain to larger regions and thus stress similarities across regions. Four musical textures emerge from this consideration: cross rhythms, organum, unison moans, and triadic harmonies. Either with or without a ring formation, cross-rhythmic clapping supports the singing in both the Sea Islands proper and the neighboring coastal plains. Moving north and west from the coasts of South Carolina and Georgia, the organum sound can be heard in the midlands and sandhills of the Piedmont region of South Carolina and, by extension, inland regions of Georgia, Florida, Alabama and Tennessee, as well as the Mid-Atlantic (including New York) and New England states in which migrants from the Eastern Seaboard have settled. Organum textures encompass perhaps the widest range of varying tempos and moods, from spacious echolike effects in central Tennessee and Alabama to slow stately movement in parts of Georgia and the Carolinas to the impassioned shout style of the Piedmont Carolinas that the prayer bands have carried with them to the Washington-Baltimore area (see Reagon 2001: 42–67). However, one should not assume that it is necessary to travel great distances to hear these distinctions. For example, *Dr. Watts* nos. 4, 5, and 6 are organum textures. But the rhythmic styles of *Dr. Watts* nos. 4 and 5, both of which are moaned, and of *Dr. Watts* no. 6, a slow bouncelike shout, are separated by only a thirty-minute drive through the South Carolina sandhills. Further westward and well beyond the Appalachian and Great Smoky Mountains, the plaintive sound of unison moaning pervades parts of Louisiana, Mississippi, western Tennessee, and Texas (and perhaps Oklahoma and Arkansas as well, although no recorded examples have been located from these states). As figure 1 shows, these bluesy plaints also mark the sound of Dr. Watts in places further afield, like Los Angeles, Chicago, and Detroit, where migrants from the Deep South have clustered.

Eighteenth-century writings confirm that en route to and in the New World, enslaved Africans sang in the mix of styles they brought with them (see Epstein 1977, Stuckey 1987). When the hymns were later introduced in such areas, the texts were simply adapted to those prior forms and styles, which have become known as the ring shout. From such roots did the low country–Sea Island shout style of South Carolina and Georgia develop. This cultural distinction, along with the agricultural pattern of rice farming in coastal areas, set Sea Island slave communities apart from those less apparently African and further inland. Stuckey's (1987) argument that the ring shout was practiced by African slaves in North America as early as the late 1600s is corroborated by the primacy of songs as opposed to hymns in

Gullah-speaking communities. For if something akin to the songs that accompany the ring shout was practiced before the American advent of Watts and Wesley hymns in the mid-1700s, then the hymn singing in Gullah-speaking areas has apparently conformed to the shout style of the songs. The context for the earliest song performances would have been the secret places and occasions for slave worship, which existed among slaves in coastal areas during the early colonial era (see Creel 1988).

In the course of the eighteenth century, inland slave communities with less prevalent African worship patterns were more deeply influenced by Anglo-American practices. These influences were first felt in Virginia—which had the largest eighteenth-century slave population and became the early center of development for black Baptist churches. Following the Second Great Awakening and during the subsequent Baptist mission to the slaves, this growth spread southward to the Carolinas, Georgia, and Florida, and later westward to the Mid- and Deep South, including West Virginia, Kentucky, Tennessee, Alabama, Mississippi, Louisiana, and Texas. Direct beneficiaries of the expanding tradition also included states immediately west of the Mississippi River, such as Missouri, Arkansas, and Oklahoma. Both moaning and shouting styles were likely performed in Virginia and the Carolinas in the late eighteenth century. Noncoastal styles multiplied as whites and their slaves migrated southward into Georgia and Florida, and westward into the mountain, delta, and Gulf coast regions.

Slave communities had been introduced to the slower and more hetero-phonic "old way" of singing in the eighteenth century, and as the popular-ity of formal singing schools moved south from New England in the early nineteenth century the faster, harmonic, and formalized "regular way" was popularized as shape-note singing. However, the latter movement had little direct impact among black worshipers until the late nineteenth century. The heterophony of the old-way influence continues in the vast range of interlocking, improvised rhythms, and in the melismatic or deeply textured moans that still permeate Dr. Watts hymns.

One indication that shape-note singing did influence the Dr. Watts tra-dition is the presence of two-part organum harmonies. These archaic-sounding open intervals preceded the tertian pattern of thirds and triads that came with the gospel hymns and their keyboard accompaniments in the latter part of the nineteenth century (Tallmadge 1984). In various regional adaptations of either moaning or shout styles the open harmonic sound of organum was disseminated throughout the colonial South and as far west as central Tennessee and western Alabama.

The quasi-organum sound can efficiently seed the ground for the high celebration that occurs in black Baptist worship. Bernice Johnson Reagon locates the foundation of her prodigious vocal and creative gifts in the congre-gational singing tradition of southwest Georgia, a powerful quasi-organum style of hymn and song singing. A less heterophonic version of the same organum texture is heard in the hymns performed on certain recordings by the Rev. J.M. Gates of Atlanta, who achieved popularity during the race-records era of the 1920s. The same ensemble sound supports the histrionics of the Rev. C.J. Johnson, also of Atlanta, who was influenced by Gates and who recorded on the Savoy gospel label during the 1960s and 1970s. In general, these organum fourth and fifth harmonies mark the moaning sound in noncoastal areas of the Eastern Seaboard states from Virginia to Florida.

As the westward migration continued to west Tennessee, Mississippi, Louisiana, and Texas, a new synthesis of Dr. Watts was codified. The unison moaning of this starkly melodic style developed with no harmonies other than the resonance of different individuals singing similar versions of the same line at different times. This sound of unison moaning has achieved a certain signature as emblematic of all black "soul" expression, and this perception follows from the popularizing influence of legendary performers like Blind Willie Johnson (see "Dark Was the Night and Cold the Ground" on *The Blues: A Smithsonian Collection of Classic Blues,* vol. 2), the Rev. C.L. Franklin, and his daughter Aretha.

Unison moaning is heard in still slower tempos here and there throughout the south-central and Deep South in places such as Memphis, the Mississippi delta, Louisiana, and Texas. Perhaps as slaves migrated to these areas of westward expansion during the antebellum period the dislocation and disruption of existing cultural norms, as well as new environmental and social stimuli, led to a redefinition of what was essential to Dr. Watts. Between 1875 and 1950, as blacks migrated to the North, Midwest, and Far West, various Dr. Watts styles moved with them. Although Rev. Franklin and his daughter Aretha have emerged as the most visible urban bearers of this rural tradition, it should be remembered that the elder Franklin's childhood and early ministry took place in the Mississippi delta, Arkansas, and Memphis.

DR. WATTS HYMNS:
A NOTE ON THE TRANSCRIPTIONS

The songs and hymns transcribed beginning on page 62 and included on my recording *Dr. Watts Hymn Singing among African Americans* were chosen to reflect the widest possible diversity of black hymn-singing styles and to document the role of Dr. Watts within a larger tradition. Missionary and Primitive Baptists spanning a range of regional styles are represented. These include the cross-rhythmic shouts associated with coastal and Sea Island areas; the off-beat clapping rhythms of upland shouts from the Carolinas and Louisiana; the tune-based moaning from Aiken County, South Carolina, that is traceable to blacks' worshiping with whites during the slave era and to tunes that are still known by name in some circles; the moaning organum sound of fourth and fifth harmonies from portions of South Carolina and Georgia; and the unison heterophony of moaned melodies from Texas, the Mississippi delta, and their migratory extensions in cities like Detroit and Chicago.

Most of the transcriptions *prescribe* the linear course of performances by indicating in simple form (but with care to avoid reduction) basic constituent elements of melody and harmony that comprise the singing. Detailed *descriptive* musical representations of sound appear only where a lead singer is utilizing vocal gestures to guide or inspire the whole. These melismatic "flowers and feathers" illustrate passages that integrate subtleties of vocal color, rapid-fire pitch inflections that follow from them, and a certain sense of "rhythmic poetry" that constantly mediates between the *feelings,* or expressive moment, and rhythm as a more direct implication of body movement. Transcriptions of such intricacies are therefore stylized to emphasize the essence without obfuscating the whole. The long-term goal of such a dual approach to transcription—simplicity without reduction—is to build upon appropriate notational conventions and idioms commonly applied in various forms of African American music.[9]

Music example 3. Transcription of *Dr. Watts,* no. 1, "What a Friend We Have in Jesus," Sea Islands, South Carolina. Transcription by the author; a lining-out hymn cataloged as no. 3538 in the N.C. Archives, recorded by Guy Carawan in a Johns Island watchnight meeting in January 1964 in which hymns and songs were led by Mr. Macky, Mrs. Bligen, and others; by permission of Guy and Candie Carawan.

Music example 4. Transcription of *Dr. Watts,* no. 2, "Come Ye That Love the Lord," low country, South Carolina. Transcription by the author; a lining-out hymn performed and recorded at Oak Grove Baptist Church in Salters, South Carolina, on November 7, 1994, by a mass choir that performed at the Annual Session of the Jerusalem Missionary and Educational Baptist Association; by permission of Maudest Rhue-Scott.

Music example 5. Transcription of *Dr. Watts,* no. 3, "Go Preach My Gospel, Saith the Lord," sandhills, South Carolina. Transcription by the author; a lining-out hymn performed and recorded in a meeting of the Kingston Lake Baptist Association at Flag Patch Baptist Church on October 14, 1994; by permission of Adolph Lewis.

Music example 6. Transcription of *Dr. Watts,* no. 4, "Father, I Stretch My Hands to Thee," sandhills, South Carolina. Transcription by Judith Gray. Subsequent couplets repeat the musical form of B, mm. 10–16.

Charles Wesley

Music example 7. Transcription of *Dr. Watts,* no. 5, "A Charge to Keep I Have,"
sandhills, South Carolina. Transcription by the author; sung by Deacon Mack Bittle
and congregation and recorded at the August 30, 1981, meeting of the 5th Sunday
Singing Union of the St. Paul Baptist Association at Gum Springs Baptist Church
near Mt. Croghan, South Carolina; by permission of Deacon Mack Bittle.

Music example 8. Transcription of *Dr. Watts,* no. 6, "Father, I Stretch My Hands to Thee," north-central Piedmont, South Carolina. Transcription by the author; performed and recorded on July 20, 1981, at Gethsemane Baptist Church, Kershaw, South Carolina; by permission of Waldo Robinson.

John Newton, 1779

Music example 9. Transcription of *Dr. Watts,* no. 7, "Amazing Grace," north-central Piedmont, South Carolina. Transcription by the author; performed by the Hymn Choir at Boyd Hill Baptist Church in February 1992; by permission of John H. Walton.

(continued)

Music example 10. Transcription of *Dr. Watts*, no. 8, "You May Bury Me in the
East," north-central Piedmont, South Carolina. Transcription by the author; performed by the Hymn Choir at Boyd Hill Baptist Church in February 1992; by permission of John H. Walton. (In this performance, the verb is changed from "may
bury" to "can bury.")

Music example 10 (continued)

Music example 11. Transcription of *Dr. Watts,* no. 9, "Jesus Invites His Saints,"
southwest Piedmont, South Carolina. Transcription by the author; performed in a
rehearsal of the Phinizy Chorus of New Ellenton, South Carolina, held at the home
of Isiah Phinizy in Augusta, Georgia, on September 3, 1994; by permission of
Joseph H. Wilborne.

Music example 12. Transcription of *Dr. Watts,* no. 10, "I Heard the Voice of Jesus Say," Piedmont, Georgia. Transcription by the author; by permission of Tommy Couch, Malaco Co.

(continued)

Music example 12 (continued)

Music example 13. Transcription of *Dr. Watts,* no. 11, "A Charge to Keep I Have,"
north-central Florida. Performed by Rev. Cross in an informant interview and
recorded in the early 1970s by interviewer A. A. Pinkston (a doctoral candidate in
music at the University of Miami); transcription by Judith Gray.

(continued)

Music example 14. Transcription of *Dr. Watts,* no. 12, "A Charge to Keep I Have," Mississippi delta (near Memphis). Performed by Rev. Ribbins and congregation; recorded by Alan and Elizabeth Lomax and Lewis Jones; transcription by Judith Gray.

Music example 14 (continued)

Music example 15. Transcription of *Dr. Watts*, no. 13, "Amazing Grace" (modified), south-central Louisiana. Performed by Huddie Ledbetter of Shreveport, Louisiana, in a 1940 interview by Alan Lomax. Transcription by Judith Gray.

Music example 16. Transcription of *Dr. Watts*, no. 14, "Must Jesus Bear the Cross Alone," central Texas. Performed in August 1941 at St. Stevens Baptist Church in Austin; recorded by John Faulk; transcription by Judith Gray.

Music example 17. Transcription of *Dr. Watts,* no. 15, "I'm Not Too Mean to Serve the Lord," central Texas. Performed in August 1941 at St. Stevens Baptist Church in Austin; recorded by John Faulk; transcription by Judith Gray.

Music example 18. Transcription of *Dr. Watts,* no. 16, "Before This Time Another Year," Detroit. Recorded and transcribed by Jeff Todd Titon; performance led by Deacon Milton Hall, with the congregation of the New Bethel Baptist Church, Detroit, November 27, 1977.

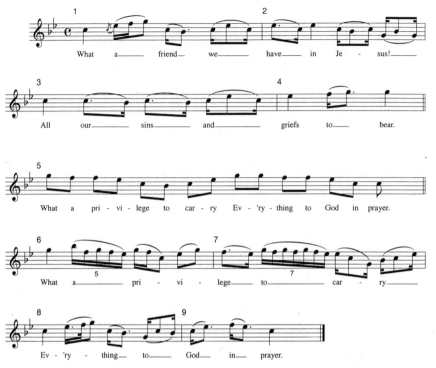

Music example 19. Transcription of *Dr. Watts,* no. 17, "What a Friend We Have in Jesus," Kentucky/North Carolina/Virginia. 1997. Transcription by the author; performed at a meeting of the Shiloh Primitive Association at the Shiloh Primitive Baptist Church, North Carolina, and recorded by Joyce Cauthen; by permission of Elder Ronald Houser.

Music example 20. Transcription of *Dr. Watts*, no. 18, "My Work on Earth Will Soon Be Done," Kentucky/North Carolina/Virginia. Transcription by the author; performed by Elder Thomas Givens and Sister Tamara Givens at a meeting (date unknown) of the Primitive Baptist Associations from Kentucky, North Carolina, and Virginia and recorded by Drew Armstrong; by permission of Elder Thomas Givens.

Music example 21. Transcription of *Dr. Watts,* no. 19, "A City Called Heaven," central Texas. Performed in 1941 at Barton Creek Baptist Church, Austin; recorded by John Faulk; transcription by Judith Gray.

(continued)

Music example 22. Transcription of *Dr. Watts,* no. 20, "A Few More Years Shall Roll," central Texas. Performed in 1941 at Barton Creek Baptist Church, Austin; recorded by John Faulk; transcription by Judith Gray.

Music example 22 (continued)

Music example 23. Transcription of *Dr. Watts*, no. 21, "Remember Me," Detroit. Recorded and transcribed by Jeff Todd Titon; performance by deacons of the New Bethel Baptist Church and the Mt. Zion Baptist Church at New Bethel Baptist Church, Detroit, June 4, 1978.

Chapter 3

"Our God, Our Help in Ages Past"

*The Tradition of Dr. Watts
in English Historical Perspective*

*Our God, our help in ages past
Our hope for years to come
Our shelter from the stormy blast
And our eternal home.*
ISAAC WATTS, The Psalms of David Imitated, *1719*

While Isaac Watts (1674–1748) is called the father of English hymnody, the form he brought to prominence, with its innate orality and biblical symbolism, has proved itself the foundation for a complex of sacred and secular African American genres. Although the hymn texts belong to the larger tradition of English-language hymnody, for black Baptists both the sound and the verse forms of Dr. Watts hymn singing have become style repositories out of which a larger range of congregational singing traditions continues. Almost without exception, wherever the old-time hymns are still heard, the vitality of the larger congregational singing tradition continues.

It was written texts of evangelical hymns that black Baptists appropriated into oral tradition. Ironically, these verse forms themselves were inherited by Watts from the English oral tradition of ballad meters that had thrived for more than two centuries before his day. Psalmody and hymnody had long been popular traditions of bardlike verse, aurally conceived and then transmitted both orally and in writing. Protestant writers wrote in the "plain voice" of the English folk and from the new-found religious (and nationalist) authority of the Bible in its various translations into the English vernacular. The movement toward vernacular language in worship that marked the English Reformation under Henry VIII and Edward VI had been gradual. It was leavened by the worship practices initiated by John Calvin, who influenced the English churchmen who had sought exile in Switzerland in the 1550s, fleeing from the terror that Queen Mary exerted upon non-Catholics. Upon Mary's death and the accession of Elizabeth I to the throne, the tradition of performing metrical translations of the biblical psalms began to flourish again on English soil. In parish churches where there was neither an instrument nor anyone trained to accompany the singing, the lining-out practice developed, in which a leader read or recited the psalm text and the congregation sang it back without instrumental accompaniment and in a tune agreeable to the text's poetic meter. Existing tunes were called into service for worship, and others were composed in conformity with the verse structures of ballad or "common" meter (four lines with 8–6–8–6 syllables per line) and its variants, long meter (8–8–8–8) and short meter (6–6–8–6).

Even prior to these developments, English courtier-poets had met the double challenge of faithfully translating the psalms into English, which meant not only translating the words but also rendering Hebrew poetry into metrical English verse. These poets, known as gospellers, eschewed imported forms such as the sonnet, ottava rima, and terza rima for the staples of popular culture such as ballad measure, fourteener couplets (two lines of fourteen syllables each, or common meter), and poulter's measure (two lines of twelve and fourteen syllables, or the equivalent of short meter). Their "popular ballads and plain style appealed to the king at the same time that they were read by a broad popular audience" (King 1982: 210).[1] This poetic impetus foreshadowed Elizabethan Puritanism and was inspired, in part, by the call of Erasmus, who sojourned in England, "for creation of a body of popular scriptural poetry in the vernacular so that even the lowliest peasant could sing Bible songs" (211). The contributions of gospeller poets such as Christopher Tye, William Samuel, and Robert Crowley were noteworthy, but none have ramified throughout the lifeblood of Protestant heritage like the work of Thomas Sternhold. "Appearing in more than five hundred editions during the next century, the 'old version' of the Psalms by Sternhold and [John] Hopkins became the most familiar collection of English verse during the sixteenth and seventeenth centuries" (218).

The first complete edition of what later became known as the Old Version was published as the *Whole Booke of Psalmes* by John Daye in 1562. Two-thirds of these texts were in common meter and set to a limited range of tunes. They achieved wide popularity among all strata of the population as social and devotional songs. Yet over time the artless predictability and clumsiness of the old-version texts in this edition caused such dissatisfaction among the most literate that it was gradually supplanted by *A New Version of the Psalms of David* . . . , collected and edited by Nahum Tate and Nicholas Brady and published in 1696. Although countless English translations of the biblical psalms were published during the period (see Rogal 1991: 38–44 for a detailed list), these two psalters held sway until the era of Isaac Watts. The work of the gospellers in general, including the psalters that achieved wide currency, was part of a developing Protestant, even Calvinist, aesthetic that flourished among sixteenth- and seventeenth-century poets.

In her study of the major devotional poets of the seventeenth century, Barbara Lewalski contends that the primary influences upon John Donne,

George Herbert, Henry Vaughan, Thomas Traherne, and Edward Taylor were "contemporary, English, and Protestant, and that the energy and power we respond to in much of this poetry has its basis in the resources of biblical genre, language, and symbolism, the analysis of spiritual states, and the tensions over the relation of art and truth which were brought into new prominence by the Reformation" (1979: 5). Lewalski also underscores "an overwhelming emphasis on the written word as the embodiment of divine truth. In this milieu, the Christian poet is led to relate his work not to ineffable and intuited divine revelation, but rather to its written formulation in scripture" (6).

This emphasis upon the written word and a concomitant deemphasis of other artistic expressions, including music, marked the long-term development of English Puritan worship from its roots in Calvinist practice.[2] Fewer tunes than texts were recycled, and though a handful of tunes, such as *Old Hundred,* have remained in use, they were distinctive not of themselves but for the endlessly varying texts that congregations sang upon them. Thus the sense of English congregational singing as distinctly unmusical is owing to both practical necessity and the restrained musical expression of Calvinist tradition. Whether by necessity or choice, this lack of emphasis upon the music pertained only outside the major cathedrals, where choirs and musicians were supported (directly or indirectly) by royal patronage. Therefore, in contrast with the Anglican High Church tradition of trained choirs, full-time musicians, and prominent composers—from Christopher Tye to Thomas Tallis to Henry Purcell—the essence of "music" in parish churches and among Puritan sects was spoken and intoned words. Although the Anglicans embraced anthem settings of the biblical psalms and, in some measure, congregational psalm singing, the Puritan practice developed in tension with the centrist Anglican Church and the radical orthodoxy of Roman Catholic influence. While neither lining out nor psalmody in general were restricted to the Puritans, both are associated with that heritage, which has been a nebulous and long-standing dimension of English spirituality.

THE LIFE AND CONTRIBUTIONS OF ISAAC WATTS

The paraphrase of Psalm 90 quoted in the epigraph to this chapter, which became Watts's signature hymn text, celebrates God's past and future providence. It is also a possessive exclamation, not to the divine as a general case but to *our* God. The balance between the abandon of this opening cry and the divinely ordered yet vast expanse of time etched in "ages past" and "years to come" is exemplary of how texts by Watts and others mediated between the English Puritan heritage of heartfelt religion and the rationalism espoused by the established Church of England.

Though his mature life was spent in the eighteenth century, Watts was a child of the seventeenth, having been born in the year of John Milton's death. The English Puritan aesthetic of that century was captured in George Herbert's rhetorical question "Is there in truth no beautie?" (Lewalski 1979, Collinson 1988). Watts provided an affirmative answer in his "system of praise," which embraced both the old psalmody and the new hymnody.[3]

In the seventeenth century, Milton's *Paradise Lost* and John Bunyan's *Pilgrim's Progress* were the standards in English literature. Both poets were Nonconformists, and Milton's work in particular influenced Watts, whose hymns and psalms are a more utilitarian, if less original, expression of a kindred poetic and spiritual vision. It was Milton's poetic sensibilities, more than those of poets of Watts's own age, such as Pope (see Escott 1962: 261), that provided the literary ideal that informed Watts's verse style. This ideal was lucid yet teeming with powerful metaphors, plainly articulate yet deeply personal in its description of religious experience, politically subversive but shrouded in religious symbolism and mythology, and deeply invested in the mastery of language as a godly yet practical form of social empowerment for a dispossessed religious minority. Although Watts's poetic stature was certainly not comparable to Milton's, critics have taken his work seriously.

Numbered among those who might be called the latter-day gospellers of the late seventeenth and early eighteenth centuries, Watts signaled the culmination of the old practice of psalmody and the emergence of the new hymnody. While his "system of praise" broadened the "Bible only" basis for texts to include contemporary readings—as opposed to only metaphrases, or literal translations of ancient texts—his hymns epitomized the plain speech enriched by metaphors that became a literary hallmark of English Nonconformity. In his first publication—a collection of poems with selected hymns and metrical psalms, titled *Horae Lyricae* (1706)—Watts expressed the Puritan inclination toward both plain speech and practicality, placing in the collection only hymns with "bolder figures of speech." Similarly, the readers of *Hymns and Spiritual Songs,* which followed in 1707, were assured in the preface that its metaphors had been "generally sunk to the level of vulgar capacities" and that he had "endeavored to make the sense plain and obvious." Watts's plainspokenness could acquit itself notably; witness his classic paraphrase of Psalm 72:

> Jesus shall reign wher'er the sun
> Does his successive journeys run;
> His kingdom stretch from shore to shore,
> Till moons shall wax and wane no more.

The same plainspokenness, however, could also wax awkward and trite:

> Furnish me, Lord, with heavenly arms
> From grace's magazine,

And I'll proclaim eternal war
With ev'ry darling sin. (Watts 1707, bk. 2, no. 81)

Evangelical hymnody did not originate with Isaac Watts. Others, such as the Particular Baptist Benjamin Keach (*Singing of Psalms, Hymns, and Spirituals Songs*, 1691), the Presbyterian Richard Baxter (*A Paraphrase on the Psalms, with Other Hymns*, 1692), the Anglican John Mason (*Songs of Praise to Almighty God upon Several Occasions*, 1683), and fellow Congregationalist John Patrick (*A Century of Select Psalms*, 1679), had each originated various components of the "system of praise" articulated by Watts. But he surpassed them all in combining a pious freedom of expression with disciplined (and learned) poetic forms (Rogal 1991: 84). When Watts died in 1748, his *Hymns and Spiritual Songs* had appeared in eighteen editions, thousands of copies had been sold, he had become renowned in England and abroad, and his paraphrase of Psalm 90, "Our God, Our Help in Ages Past" had become a signal moment in the English Puritan epoch. A recent study of *Hymns and Spiritual Songs* identifies more than six hundred editions over the last 250 years (Bishop 1974).

The Rev. Dr. Isaac Watts, hymnist, educator, and theologian, was born in the period following the restoration of the monarchy, when "Dissenters" from the Church of England—General and Particular Baptists, Congregationalists, and Presbyterians—were caught between the pretenses of Charles II toward toleration and a Parliament that employed all legal and economic means to suppress and punish Dissenters (see M. Watts 1978: 239–62). Watts's father, a cloth-maker and teacher living in the port city of Southampton, was, like many Nonconformists, a prosperous and influential man, and his mother had descended from Huguenots exiled in England. An Independent meeting-house deacon, the elder Watts was imprisoned for Nonconformity twice during his son's infancy and boyhood. Therefore, Watts spent his formative years encircled by the maelstrom of persecution for religious convictions. His most constant vantage point was the rigorous yet innovative education he received in one of the Dissenting academies to which the children of those outside Anglicanism were limited. There he studied Latin, Greek, Hebrew, mathematics, geography, philosophy, and theology. Excelling in languages and showing some poetic gift even at seven years of age, he read with zeal "Homer, Sophocles, Plato, Virgil, Horace, and the neo-Latin poets George Buchanan and Casimire Sarbiewski." Watts made note that he was "falling under considerable conviction of sin" in 1688, and, the following year, expressed hope of being "taught to trust in Christ" (Escott 1962: 15–16). Although the Dissenters' political standing improved considerably following the 1689 Act of Toleration and remained stable throughout Watts's lifetime, the personal religious experience and piety out of which he lived and wrote—for example, his way of speaking on behalf of God's embattled people—was fashioned in the crucible of Nonconformist persecutions. His decorous speaking and writing expressed deeply personal accounts of religious experience. "Nonconformist literature bore an invaluably sympathetic witness to the apprehensions and aspirations of individuals in an age of increasingly complacent dismissal of any manifestation of individuality as a reprehensible aberration" (Keeble 1987: 24). This sense of spiritual extroversion can be seen in the way that Watts rewrote, intentionally or not, the old-version translation of the opening lines of Psalm 51. Whereas the version by Sternhold and Hopkins reads, "O Lord, consider my distresse, / And now with speed some pity take," Watts reworked and accentuated the word "pity" into a more fervent plea: "Show pity, Lord, O Lord, forgive, / Let a repenting rebel live."

Paradoxically, the more vividly that personal experiences are recounted, the more likely they are to transcend their particularity and speak as universal expressions. Watts's insistence upon Christianizing and modernizing the psalmist David through such I-we transformations made an important connection between the psalmody that preceded him and the Romantic-era and gospel hymnody of the mid-nineteenth century that followed. Through his critical reading of the psalms, Watts also freed biblical texts from the strictures of the letter and, despite his moderate approach to change, opened to the Protestant aesthetic a freedom of expression that would have been unthinkable a century before.

Though Watts was ordained and served as pastor of Mark Lane Congregational Church in London for several years, serious infirmities and weakness cut short his active ministry. Soon thereafter, he went for what was to be a week or so of recuperation to the country home of then Lord Mayor of London, Sir Thomas Hartopp, who was a member of Mark Lane Church. He remained there for the rest of his lifetime, living a devout but apparently not ascetic life. While his chief vocations became teaching (as a private tutor to wealthy families) and writing, he also enjoyed an active social life among London's elite, both Dissenting and Anglican, maintained regular correspondence with prominent friends on both sides of the Atlantic, and accumulated considerable means through the success of his publications. He corresponded with New Englanders such as Cotton Mather and Jonathan Edwards and was well acquainted with the cofounder of Methodism George Whitefield and with the Presbyterian Samuel Davies, an early president of Nassau Hall, later Princeton University.

Watts wrote most of his psalm paraphrases and hymns before he was forty years old (writings from the balance of his life include essays, correspondence, and books on logic and theology). Producing so much writing within a fairly limited period of time greatly increased the likelihood of repetition, and one finds an abundance of repeated ideas, words, and phrases in his work. Certain turns of phrase appear repeatedly in his corpus of more than six hundred psalms and hymns. In reading his work, my eye and ear seized immediately upon recurring phrases from those hymns that have been most popular among black Baptists, such as "I Love the Lord, He Heard My Cries," "Our God, Our Help in Ages Past," and perhaps the most universally popular of all his works, "Joy to the World."[4] Some examples:

Phrases from familiar hymns by Watts	*Phrases from lesser-known hymns by Watts*
And pitied every groan (Ps. 116)	He pities all our groans (Ps. 6)
When I survey the wondrous cross (Watts 1707, bk. 3, no. 7)	When I survey the stars (Ps. 8)
And chased my griefs away (Ps. 116)	That chase my fears away (Ps. 13)
Long as I live, when troubles rise (Ps. 116)	When troubles rise and storms appear (Ps. 26)
I love the Lord, he bowed his ear (Ps. 116)	He'll bend his ear to your complaints (Ps. 31)
Under the shadow of thy wings (Ps. 90)	Fly to the shadow of thy wings (Ps. 36)
. . . heard my cry; . . . bowed his ear (Ps. 116)	He bow'd to hear my cry (Ps. 40)
Under the shadow of thy wings (Ps. 90)	The shadow of thy wings (Ps. 63)
Under the shadow of thy wings (Ps. 90)	Beneath the shadow of thy wings (Watts 1707, bk. 1, no. 80)
While fields and floods, rocks, hills, and plains	Hosannah! Let the earth and skies Repeat the joyful sound;
Repeat the sounding joy (Ps. 98)	Rocks, hills, and vales, reflect his voice In one eternal round. (Watts 1707, bk. 2, no. 35)
Am I a soldier of the cross A follower of the Lamb.[5]	Amongst the chosen of his love The followers of the Lamb! (Watts 1707, bk. 2, no. 99)
I love the Lord, he bowed his ear (Ps. 116)	I love the Lord that stoops so low (Watts 1707, bk. 2, no. 141)

Beyond the character and forms of the language they use, the hymns and psalms of Watts display a balanced, almost exhaustive coverage of biblical topics. While those hymns that express praise, adoration, or exultation, such as "When I Survey the Wondrous Cross," have remained most beloved, his texts either literally or freely translate passages from almost every book of both the Old and New Testaments. Watts's intention to Christianize the language and symbolism of the Old Testament is exemplified in his version of Psalm 63:

> Thou great and good, thou just and wise,
> Thou are my Father and my God;
> And I am thine by sacred ties;
> Thy son, thy servant, bought with blood.

Coupled with Watts's Christianizing project was his sense of the psalmist as well as the Lord Jesus Christ as figures of particular relevance to the English as a people. Perhaps as a heritage from the military stridency of Puritans during the period of Oliver Cromwell, many of Watts's psalms and hymns are marked by this zealous nationalism:

> Shine, mighty God, on Britain, shine
> Reveal thy power through all our coasts,
> And show thy smiling face.
> Amidst our isle, exalted high,
> Do thou our glory stand,
> And, like a wall of guardian fire,
> Surround the fav'rite land. (Ps. 67)[6]

Not only a hymnist, Watts was also a published logician whose works were in use as textbooks at major English universities for some time after his demise. This sense of order and balance is expressed in verses 9–12 of Psalm 148. By reordering the panoramic flash of inspiration suggested by the biblical text into a verse-by-verse catalog of each being's particular means of rendering praise, Watts fashioned a childlike yet ordered vision of nature and animal life. These crescendo to "the earth-born race" as the pinnacle of God's creation and to Christian believers who might see themselves as best qualified to praise their Lord:

> Ye lions of the wood,
> And tamer beasts that graze,
> Ye live upon his daily food,
> And he expects your praise.
>
> Ye birds of lofty wing,
> On high his praises bear;
> Or sit on flowery boughs, and sing
> Your maker's glory there.
>
> Ye creeping ants and worms,
> His various wisdom show,
> And flies, in all your shining swarms,
> Praise him that dress'd you so.

By all the earth-born race
His honours be express'd;
But saints, that know his heav'nly grace
Should learn to praise him best.

Perhaps the most striking element of Watts's verse, as Bernard Manning (1942) has noted, is its concisely telescopic vision of the whole universe of sacred time and space expressed in the fleeting interval of a single line or stanza. This sense of sweeping movement in his verse is balanced by a complementary depth of perspective, which now and then transfixes itself upon the divine subject and sustains this concentration on the divine with a child-like and guileless sense of awe or fascination. No more shining example of this gift can be found than the following:

When I survey the wondrous cross
On which the prince of glory died
My richest gain I count but loss
And pour contempt on all my pride. (Watts 1707)

A less well-known example of the same awestruck sense of God's grandeur is

Bright King of glory, dreadful God!
Our spirits bow before thy seat,
To thee we lift an humble thought,
And worship at thine awful feet. (Watts 1707, bk. 2, no. 51)

N.H. Keeble argues persuasively that "nonconformity created a committed Christian literature of distinctive character." He demonstrates— through the writings of Bunyan and Milton, as well as those of a host of lesser-known writers and divines—that "this literary dissent was misrepresented by contemporary conformists as incontrovertibly sectarian, retrogressive," as well as obscurantic. Keeble avers, however, that "it was rather creative, positive, and salutary in its demotic realism, its subjective authenticity, its metaphorical richness, and its sensitivity to the numinous" (1987: 282). The literary complexities of Nonconformity are reflected in the psalms and hymns of Isaac Watts, whose life spanned the height of Dissenter persecutions, the forty years of relative calm that followed, and the dawning of the age of Methodist revivalism. Coupling decorous reserve with thoughtful reflections on personal religious experience, the simple lyricism of Watts stands astride the relative calm of his own time and the revivalist zeal of the age following. Indeed, as Keeble argues, an affinity is apparent between the Romanticism that surfaced later in the works of Blake, Wordsworth, and Coleridge and the place of personal experience in Nonconformist literature.

A parallel affinity is evident among subsequent hymn writers in the extent to which they built vivid verse upon rhetorical ideas faintly yet clearly outlined in Watts. A most obvious example may be seen in the third verse of the ever-popular gospel hymn "Beneath the Cross of Jesus," written by Elizabeth Clephane in 1868, and the second verse of the little-known Watts hymn "Not with Our Mortal Eyes" (Watts 1707, bk. 1, no. 108):

Watts	Clephane
Now, for the love I bear his name,	I take, o cross, thy shadow for my abiding place
What was my gain I count my loss;	The very dying form of One Who suffered there for me
My former pride I call my shame,	Content to let the world go by, to know no gain nor loss
And nail my glory to his cross.	My sinful self my only shame, my glory all the cross.

Watts developed not only an English Protestant system of praise embracing hymns as well as psalms but also a classical hymnodic style. In his hymns, congregational texts echo human experience through a personal voice by evoking a scene and a situation at the outset, sustaining coherence as the main thought is developed, limiting figurative language to biblical sources, and summoning vocabulary that is neither obscure nor inane but widely accessible (Parker 1985: 400–402; 415–16). These attributes are still more abundant in the larger corpus of hymns authored by Charles Wesley. One might see Watts and Wesley in the way that music historians look upon the steady reliable creativity of Haydn and the genius of Mozart. Wesley's first collection of hymns appeared in the year of Watts's demise; the brilliance of the later and more advanced figure was facilitated by the established terms of a received style that had been most fully developed by Watts.

In his freely metrical translations of the psalms, Isaac Watts sought without apology to make the psalmist David not only speak like a Christian but address issues and ideas pertinent to contemporary England. Only after his *Hymns and Spiritual Songs* of 1707 had been through six editions did Watts publish *The Psalms of David Imitated* (1719). Following the model of Calvin's Geneva Psalter, most Dissenting bodies held that the psalms of David, translated literally into English verse, were the only approved forms of singing in worship. Watts appended to the first edition of his *Hymns and Spiritual Songs* his case for change, which he called "An Essay Towards the Improvement of Christian Psalmody, by the Use of Evangelical Hymns in Worship as well as the Psalms of David," in which he argued that congregational singing should not merely replicate the word of God; rather, "songs are . . . expressions of our own experiences or of His glories; [in them] we breath[e] out our souls toward him" (Watts 1707: 243). Without denying the efficacy of scripture for Christian instruction and edification, he called for free translations of the psalms that would speak as David might have done had he been a Christian. Watts believed that the Hebrew psalms were useful primarily as patterns for what praise should be. Beyond this, he posited, if metrical psalms are to a degree "human inventions," then we should we go further to create "human composures." This view of worship was built upon Paul's concept, from the Galatian epistle, of Christian freedom from slavery to Jewish forms. The project of translating all 150 psalms had, by Watts's time, become a genre unto itself. But Watts argued for selectivity, affording that neither all the psalms nor all parts of certain psalms convey moments or ideas appropriate for Christian worship. Applying that principle, he translated only 137 psalms into metrical verse, and only certain portions of some of these.

Watts gave impetus and prestige to the practice of hymn and psalm singing by freeing both genres from the letter of static deference to tradition and focusing them upon the enlivened human spirit of those gathered into redeemed communities. Asking what the nature of those souls' response to God and his Providence should be, Watts supposed that "Every beam of new light that broke into the World gave occasion of fresh Joy to the Saints, and they were taught to sing of Salvation in all the Degrees of its advancing Glory" (1707: 254). He saw his own efforts at praising God, and those of the universal church, as man's progressive apprehension of God's will. Harry Escott argues that Watts sought to "set in motion a reform of Christian praise that should continue through all ages of the Church's mission upon earth—a reform to be renewed as fresh circumstances in the work and worship of the Christian Fellowship arose" (1962: 131).

While being faithful to the Bible that Herbert called "truth," Watts quietly abandoned what St. Paul had described as the deadness imposed by adherence to the letter of the word. Instead, through the means of "human composures," Watts made it possible for succeeding generations to perpetuate the Davidic practice of singing a new song to the Lord. While "beautie" cannot follow as a guarantee from this or any other formula, what is experienced as eternal truth can be readily apprehended when it is clothed in the language of one's own time and place. All of these dimensions—the old plain speech, the biblical symbolism, and the pithy utterances, as well as the new personal voice of experiential religion—were bequeathed, through Watts, to the black Baptist worship tradition.

Watts offered not only the hymns and psalms (which can scarcely be distinguished at sight from his hymns) but also a rationale—or, in the tone of Peter's epistle, "a reason of the hope" (I Peter 3:15)—for why a more open-ended panoply of praise forms should exist. That reason, which was inimitably of its age, sought rectitude in the very tradition of psalm singing that Watts challenged. It established a theological foundation not only for Dr. Watts among black Baptists but also for the continuing development of a modern hymnody that, out of the mouths of slaves in the New World, has embraced the trilogy invoked by Paul in Colossians 3:16—"singing with grace in your hearts to the Lord" not only psalms and hymns but "spiritual songs" as well.

WATTS'S NEW WORLD LEGACY

By virtue of their exile from the British crown and the established church, religious minorities from England became the majority voice throughout New England and other North American colonies. Indeed, the contradiction between the search for religious freedom and the enslavement of Africans was creating an increasing tension in America (Morgan 1975). Although neither hymns nor other writings of Isaac Watts that address directly the issue of slavery have been located, it is well documented that he maintained regular correspondence with a number of prominent religious figures in New England. Therefore, he would have been aware of the growing North American white audience for his hymns and psalms, even if he remained largely unaware of the popularity of his songs among African Americans.

The invocation of an English cleric's name by enslaved Africans in North America to describe an oral tradition of folk hymnody dramatizes the historical connection between the pressures put upon English Nonconformity in the seventeenth century and the outbreak of American religious awakenings in the eighteenth and nineteenth. However, while both the English Reformation and the American Great Awakenings impacted the oral cultures of illiterate "common" folk, the rush toward literacy among English Puritans and the powerful oral tradition that developed within the constraints of enforced illiteracy among African slave converts in North America brought about commensurate yet differing patterns of change. In the former case, a vital sixteenth-century oral tradition built upon secular ballad meters and tunes gave rise to austere and pious psalm singing without musical accompaniment. In contrast, the slaves came to the American continent neither to sing, dance, pray, nor preach. But not being easily alienated from their traditions and linguistic patterns, they did not leave their religious beliefs and ritual practices behind. Works since Lawrence Levine's 1978 groundbreaking study *Black Culture and Black Consciousness* have substantiated his hypothesis concerning slave acculturation, which argued that "Africans were so imperfectly acculturated into the secular American society into which they were thrust . . . that they were forced to" rely upon African cultural frames of reference (1977: 53). Due to the widespread fear of owners that the Christian conversion and baptism of slaves would lead to their freedom, from 1619 till 1820 or so, no sustained effort at mass evangelization had been successful.

There has been an enigma concerning the place of hymn singing in the life of slave communities. On one hand, Jackson (1943) pondered it wistfully as the most purely African of vocal singing styles, and, on the other, Higginson reported that "they sang reluctantly, even on Sunday, the long and short meters of the hymn-books, always gladly yielding to the more potent excitement of their own spirituals" (Higginson [1870] 1960: 172–73). Yet there is truth on both sides of this seeming contradiction. Jackson heard the slow moaning-style hymn singing of upland Piedmont regions, and Higginson observed the practice in the low country region of South Carolina. And, while Higginson was reporting primarily on encamped soldiers' practice of singing songs, Jackson was primarily describing the use of hymns in a worship service in a church edifice. Given these qualifications, a general correlation between hymns and songs still pertains. For although a people's own songs may function as a crowning musical celebration, hymn texts not written by black authors have also endured as an entry point into devotional worship. And wherever the older songs of celebration have been discontinued as the entry point, they have been superseded by standard hymns with accompaniment, praise songs, or gospel choirs. The issue of originality is less important. As Levine observed: "It is not necessary for a people to originate or invent all or even most of the elements of their culture. It is necessary only that these components become their own, embedded in their traditions, expressive of their world view and life style" (1977: 24).

Therefore, when Baptist missionaries brought the gospel to the masses of slaves, more than two centuries after the slave trade had begun, the latter grafted texts by Watts onto living oral traditions, which were by default grounded in an admixture of African orientations toward the universe, human existence, and family relations, as well as the ritual celebrations embracing these perspectives. It is no wonder that the continuing song- and hymn-singing traditions still emphasize florid and stylized forms of speech intonation that, through repetition and variation, initiate collective and individual responses, beginning with speech-song, progressing toward dance movements, and culminating in shouting as an embodiment of divine inspiration.

Chapter 4

"Father, I Stretch My Hands to Thee"

The Tradition of Dr. Watts in African Historical Perspective

> *Father, I stretch my hands to thee*
> *No other help I know;*
> *If thou withdraw thyself from me,*
> *Ah, whither shall I go?*
>
> CHARLES WESLEY, *1741*

The first illustration in *Black Art and Culture in the Twentieth Century*, by Richard Powell, is of a late-seventeenth-century slave drum (Powell 1997: 6–7; see also Epstein 1977: 48). Now housed in the British Museum, the drum was acquired in Virginia by the physician and naturalist Sir Hans Sloane in the early eighteenth century, "at the height of mass importation of enslaved Africans." Such tangible evidence—"African-in-design, American-in-origin, and transatlantic in praxis" (Powell 1997: 7)—indicates the conscious practice of African cultural expressions within North American slave communities and denies that colonial slavery was a total separation from the artifacts of African culture. African or African American adaptations of such drums remained in Virginia fifty years after Sir Hans's acquisition, when the first colonial congregation of black Baptists was chartered there in 1758 (Sobel 1979: 250, 296). Such a coincidence between the visible artifact and the unrecoverable sounds of ritual suggests the persistence of African performance contexts and concepts in the singing of slave communities and inspires the reconstruction of those sounds.

The drum's unchanging appearance is significant because African rituals and music making were legally suppressed after the Stono Rebellion of 1739 in South Carolina, and a century later, ministers taught slaves to turn from their own "heathenish" songs to the hymns of Isaac Watts. Because only a small minority of slaves were converted to Christianity or allowed to read the Bible before the 1830s, various Pidgin English or creole languages had been the lingua franca between slaves and masters since the colonial era. The First and Second Great Awakenings hastened the process of cultural change through geographical migrations and especially language contact.

Another layer of rapid change followed when, after Emancipation, industrialization in the South and less outward racial oppression in the North
drew the children of former slaves to the cities. Throughout these transitions—from African to slave to American—Dr. Watts hymn singing was pivotal in the shaping of black people's identity.

This chapter is an account of that transformation. My quest here is not
for definitive origins—which in any case are impossible to trace—but for a
generative concept that can make "something appear which [has] remained
invisible [and] . . . unintelligible in the natural object" (Barthes 1972:
214–15). The continuity of unaccompanied congregational singing in congregations where Dr. Watts remains vital (Dargan 1995) suggests the importance of lining out to subsequent genres and forms. Lining out became the
primary slave model for Standard English–language singing in Christian
worship. Beneath the surface was the historical contrast and seeming disjunction between a short-term need in seventeenth-century English parish
churches for engaging illiterate worshipers in congregational singing and
the longer-term illiteracy enforced by North American slavery. In retrospect, we can see that the politics of literacy in a developing print culture
both aligned and distinguished these disparate social settings. As an aesthetic moment, black lining out became the point of origin or *genotype*[1] for
myriad regional and local singing styles that have become analogous to
speech communities and were defined by plantation property lines as well
as rivers and other natural boundaries.

The history of Dr. Watts hymn singing balances between persistent
African continuities and the perpetual change factors—such as migration
and especially language contact—that have shaped the practice of Christianity in African American communities. Because Dr. Watts hymns have
persisted longer in more diverse black communities than in comparable
white ones, socioeconomic isolation alone cannot account for their centrality to African American culture. So we may assume that these performance styles developed on colonial slave plantations of North America,
where enslaved Africans were alienated from the linguistic "letter" of their
cultural origins, but not from its generative "spirit." These approaches to
performance conceived in African terms what New World vocal expression
should be and could be. In a word, "New ideas were recycled through age-
old concepts to produce new music styles" (Maultsby 1990: 205).

In nineteenth-century congregational singing, that generative force
became the speechlike song, which stemmed from both African ritual and
linguistic practices and the performance pattern of lining-out hymns. In
the following century, this song-talk approach to singing emerged as "the
strongest marker of in-group identity among African-Americans" (Brothers
1997: 179). To explain the relevance of this claim to black music, Thomas
Brothers identifies (180) the blues style of Charley Patton, who studied

field hollers, as a poignantly expressive blending of speechlike song and polyrhythmic textures within a unified form. Building upon the blues form and style, and upon the popularity of blues recordings in the 1920s, in the following two decades the same merging of gestures occurred in swing and bebop. However, before the blues emerged as a modern synthesis of those archaic sound complexes, moaning (the locus of the "speechlike song" identified by Brothers)[2] and shouting (a key application of his polyrhythmic paradigm) developed in some regions separately and in others in tandem through the convergence of the African ring shout, on one hand, and, on the other, the English heritage of Dr. Watts.

Although the consistent importance of speech rhythms to black music is clear at least as far back as nineteenth-century congregational singing, the specifics of the African and Anglo-American origins of speech rhythms are not as clear. Though we can generally identify the patterning of African tonal languages as foundational for "songified speech," we have only begun to investigate the specific ramifications of such vocal styles in the United States.

The slaves received the hymns from missionaries as an entirely new body of speechlike song which they superimposed upon an African-derived repertory that was substantial. From this commingling, patterns of cross-influence occurred between the Standard English of the hymns and the various regional and local dialects. Dr. Watts bequeathed to song leaders a core of formulaic and rhythmic English prosody, all set in easy-to-remember metrical patterns and rhyme schemes. The hymn texts serve as verses in songs passed on through oral tradition, into which other formulaic "wandering verses" (texts that are freely applied to any number of melodies)—some in the familiar ballad meters and others in less symmetrical yet generally conforming rhyme schemes—are freely inserted. Gilbert Chase, Charles Hamm, Wiley Hitchcock, Eileen Southern, and Wilfrid Mellers, for example, note the adaptability of lining out, as an English pattern of rote response, to patterns of call and response embedded in African practice.[3] But no less important to the acculturation process in the hymns was the interaction of speech or chant with singing, as well as with moans and exclamations, all contributing to a ritual context that expressed the African preference for speechlike singing and variegated timbres.

In African American rituals, speechlike song also connotes the attribute of being plainspoken. Watts hymns and black spirituals share this emphasis upon direct and genuine accounts of experiential religion. It is not enough, in the rhetoric of black Baptist tradition, to merely report that one has been converted. One is obliged to offer such details as "I looked at my hands and they looked new; I looked at my feet and they did too." The cultural significance of plainspoken details that also rhyme, alliterate, or otherwise reinforce the movement of speech to song is that they integrate the rhetorical act with the kinetics of body movement, a union that is at the heart of

African and African American ritual. The dynamics of this rhetorical style are distinct from those of both Nonconformists and Anglicans, who differed in the English seventeenth century over what it meant to be plain-spoken (see Keeble 1987: 240–62). Plain speech in black worship enables respondents to "get on one accord" in their responses to the song leader's calls and to quickly reinforce the rhythmic implication of his or her words. Such basic and redundant forms provide performers with mnemonic and rhythmic markers that outline a certain sonic shape and thus identify the song. This practice explains why so many texts can share the same melody and be considered different songs: the particulars of each song are carried in the rhythms of the text, which lend emphasis to the words.

AFRICAN PARALLELS WITH AFRICAN AMERICAN FORMS

Rhythm and pitch inflection are central to the tonal languages of many of the various Bantu-speaking peoples who were sold into North American slavery. Slaves were imported from a wide range of Bantu areas along the western coast of Africa, and linguists such as Winifred Vass and Joseph Holloway have argued that perhaps the greatest element of unity existed among Bantu-speaking slaves from diverse areas in Africa. In turn, this linguistic character has persisted in African American dialects and vocabulary:

> Bantu speech has a proven ability to move into a culture, to absorb it, and to change its language. It has adopted and adapted each new culture group as it has spread from its original Nucleus area, probably in the Nok region of Nigeria, down over almost the entire African subcontinent south of the Sahara. The outstanding linguistic homogeneity of this tremendous geographic region is due to this central body of inherited Proto-Bantu vocabulary that still ties all Bantu languages together and proves their once common source. Bantu-speaking slaves from Central Africa enjoyed a linguistic unity and ability to communicate with their fellow-captives that slaves of West Africa did not share. (Vass 1979: 3)

Holloway (1990) has documented the Bantu language influence throughout the southeastern United States, and Dillard (1972) certifies that the slaves in certain areas continued the equivalent of a lingua franca. But because the Bantu influence upon neither African nor African American rhythms or patterns of intonation has been examined, we can only speculate about the extent to which such language transfers carried with them intonations that derived from Bantu.

Two dirge-singing traditions, one from Central Africa and the other from West Africa, offer graphic precedents for the kind of slow speechlike intonation that predominates in African American lining out. A musical corollary to the Bantu language dominance that Holloway and Vass have identified is suggested by style similarities between a recorded example of dirge singing among the Ngeende, a subgroup of the Kuba in northwestern Zaire, and the moaning style of black lining out common in the Mississippi delta and East Texas.[4] Both offer plaints in slow-to-moderate tempos with intricate melodies that are sung in meticulous unison, and variant pitch and moaning sounds are prevalent. While few reliable conclusions can follow from one pair of examples, this similarity does suggest that African linguistic and musical influences have interacted with European ones to produce a striking patchwork of black lining-out styles. Although the Ghanaian dirges recorded and transcribed by Kofi Agawu sound much less "African American" than the Ngeende, both forms are identical to that of lining out: a leader speak-sings a call in free rhythms and the group responds in a more metrical rhythm upon definite pitches (Agawu 1995: 76–83).[5] Taken together, these examples from West and Central Africa suggest how widespread the practice of dirge singing may have been in the areas from which slaves were imported to North America.

The speechlike inflection of dirge singing resembles the speech-song inflection in lining out, which, coupled with the circle dance known as the ring shout, creates the binary "mood frames" that Walter Pitts (1993) identifies in Afro-Baptist worship as well as in eight Africa-derived rituals in the Western Hemisphere.[6] These rituals illustrate "the durability of an African perspective that continues . . . although deities and cosmologies have changed." Pitts has presented answers to broad questions as to what ritual forms moved from Africa to the New World and how they function in black Baptist worship—answers that posit linkages between the African past and the Christianized slave communities of the late-eighteenth and nineteenth centuries.[7]

While slave social hierarchies directed certain groups of slave converts to embrace and develop the lining-out practice, local and regional speech communities shaped by African origins, as well as by geographic separation on the American continent, produced an intricate network of performance styles. Speech patterns outlined a sociolinguistic hierarchy at three levels: house slaves speaking more or less Standard English, field slaves fluent in plantation creoles, and new arrivals who spoke little or no pidgin or creole. Slave oral traditions retained African patterns even as the number of slave converts to Christianity multiplied throughout the antebellum period, and Dillard also shows that, despite the superimposition of new social structures, African hierarchies were not destroyed (1972: 73–96). By contrast, the most literate blacks, many of whom had been house servants and artisans, would continue neither lining out nor other oral practices after Emancipation. Nevertheless, the decision to follow either black oral or white written aids to worship was probably due less to group preferences than to the skills and preferences of individual leaders in various communities (Blacking 1995: 160).

Although speakers of various African languages were deliberately mixed, some owners also preferred slaves from certain language areas either for their presumed competence as house servants, rice farmers, and craftsmen or for their durability as field laborers. Owners in South Carolina, for example, expressed preferences at various time periods for house servants and craftsmen from Senegambia or field slaves from Bantu-speaking areas of Central Africa. While it is impossible to claim any direct correspondence between an African language area and a particular African American singing style, because of the high volume of Bantu speakers among field slaves, a Bantu influence was likely pivotal in the majority of regional lining-out styles that have been, with few exceptions, orally transmitted.[8] Following Emancipation, fluent speakers of Standard English and plantation creoles were intermingled in the same segregated communities and schools. While "creolization had occurred largely independent of the white man's language influence, . . . [what was to be a long-term] decreolization . . . would almost by definition be traceable to the influence of the white man's English" (Dillard 1972: 83).

THE DEVELOPMENT OF DR. WATTS HYMN SINGING, 1750–1900

Before the mid-eighteenth century, Standard English had no lasting influence upon the way slaves worshiped (away from the eye of the masters) because, until that time, no mass evangelism had been attempted among slaves held on large Southern plantations. Only in New England and New York did blacks and whites commonly worship together (see Southern 1997: 28–33). In that period, lining out was practiced primarily among the Puritans of the Massachusetts Bay Colony and the Dutch Reformed in New York—locations with limited slave populations. The first book published in North America, *The Whole Booke of Psalms Faithfully Translated into English Metre* (1640), was used extensively by churches in Massachusetts and surrounding areas. Because Puritan divines such as John Cotton had become wholly dissatisfied with the accuracy of the Old Version and the Ainsworth Psalter (1612), the stated emphasis of the new publication, which became known as the *Bay Psalm Book,* was upon faithful translation. This emphasis implied a lack of concern for prosody and rhyme, which severely limited the psalter's potential for influencing a nascent oral culture. This fact, plus the small number of slaves in New England, may be the reasons why no distinctive style of hymn singing developed among early colonial blacks.

From the mid-1700s forward, three general periods stand out in the development of Dr. Watts hymn singing. In the first period, from 1750 to 1800—excepting the years of the American Revolution—the lining-out practice grew among enslaved blacks as an "aural primer," a means of facilitating individual literacy and corporate worship. Of eleven black Baptist congregations organized before 1800, six were in Virginia and the remainder were in the Carolinas and Georgia (see Sobel 1979, 1987). For such groups, lining out must have been a symbolic subversion of the enforced illiteracy among slaves. However, mere symbolism would not suffice for the house slaves and for certain other rebels against the status quo who were determined to read and write the English language.

In the second period, from 1800 to 1865, slaves' continuing practice of lining out was first minimized by the enthusiastic furor of camp-meeting revivals, then reemphasized as a strategic component of organized Baptist missions to the slaves. The waning of large camp meetings combined with the rising tide of abolitionist rhetoric to provide an ideal environment in which widespread white missions directed to slave plantations in the antebellum period could flourish. In such efforts, the orthodoxy of Dr. Watts hymn singing mediated the cultural tensions between black aspirations toward freedom and the stated expectations of white ministers and owners.

The third period, comprising the post-Emancipation years of 1865–1900, saw the consolidation of the Missionary Baptists as the largest independent black denomination and the ready inclusion of the old-time hymn singing in the worship repertoire of black folk. As the Pentecostal movement of the 1900s and the waves of black urban migration that reached a climax between the world wars brought massive changes, black Baptists either brought the lining-out practice from rural to urban churches with them, or they transformed the sound textures and modalities of lining out (and also blues) to forge the classic gospel style. Or else they found ways to continue the old and include the new by retaining lining-out hymns in devotions and incorporating gospel performances in the service frame of the worship. We will consider accounts of lining out from each of these periods.

The first detailed description of black lining out, and the one most often cited, is from the First Awakening of the mid-1700s. The Presbyterian Samuel Davies marveled at the singing of hymns by slaves in Virginia and begged his sponsors for the psalms and hymns of Watts (as well as more Bibles). Although only a small minority of the slaves were evangelized during that period, the letters of Davies and other ministers report an intense desire among the slaves to read and sing Watts's hymns. Davies wrote in March 1755 that "Negroes above all the human species I ever knew, have an ear for music, and a kind of ecstatic delight in Psalmody." About a year later, he was struck by the force of what was apparently an emergent singing style he heard among the slaves: "The books were all very acceptable; but none more so than the 'Psalms and Hymns,' which enabled them to gratify their peculiar taste for Psalmody. Sundry of them have lodged all night in my kitchen; and, sometimes, when I have awaked about two or three o-clock in the morning, a torrent of sacred harmony poured into my chamber, and carried my mind away to Heaven. In this seraphic exercise, some of them spend the whole night."[9]

Davies was apparently not alone among those in the 1750s who noted in journals and letters the receptivity of enslaved converts to Bibles and to the psalms and hymns of Watts. From Hanover, Virginia, the Rev. Mr. Todd wrote in 1758 that "multitudes of Negroes and white people flock to my house to get books. . . . The poor slaves are now engaged in learning to read; some of them can read the Bible, others can only spell; and some are just learning their letters—But there is general alteration for the better. The sacred hours of the Sabbath, that used to be spent in frolicking, dancing, and other profane courses, are now employed in attending upon public ordinances, in learning to read at home, or in praying together, and singing the praises of God and the Lamb." Working in Cumberland County, Virginia, the Rev. Mr. Wright wrote in 1761 that "they heard the Slaves at worship in their lodge, singing Psalms and Hymns in the evening, and again in the morning, long before the break of day. They are excellent Singers." From South Carolina, the Rev. Mr. Hutson noted that the vital part of religion was among Negroes and that they gladly received Bibles and Watts psalms and hymns (Southern 1983: 27–30).[10]

Despite the legal prohibition against teaching slaves to read, the conversion of slaves and owners during these revivals generated both zeal among slaves for reading, hearing, and memorizing hymns and Bible verses and corresponding liberty among certain masters and overseers to permit these activities. Pitts recontextualizes these eighteenth-century cultural exchanges by reading Samuel Davies' comment—that "Negroes above all the human species I ever knew, have an ear for music, and a kind of ecstatic delight in Psalmody"—from the slave viewpoint:

> Just as the Reverend Samuel Davies was perplexed as to why colonial slaves were so enthralled with the . . . hymn, these newly arrived Africans in North America were probably elated, or religiously moved beyond the Europeans' comprehension, to find a musical song style so close to their own that they had heretofore been forced to sing in secret. . . . While the arcane knowledge of Africa was waning, the fervent Protestant revivals were gaining popularity and spreading to slave quarters. . . . Black people in North America had to borrow the doctrines and ritual practices, including speech and song forms, of a new, somewhat strange religion, namely, Protestant Christianity, to create the content of their reinterpreted esoteric frame. What could have been more esoteric to Africans, disembarking in North America with only the knowledge of . . . their own indigenous language[s], than to hear seventeenth-century English spoken when addressing God, taught them by a slave-holding clergy? (Pitts 1993: 124–25)

"A musical song style so close to their own" must refer to dirge singing and other African precedents for freely measured, speechlike singing. Early on, these signs of continuity between African and African American practice prevailed in black churches founded by both Methodist and Baptist denominations. The first hymnal for use by an all-black congregation was published at Philadelphia in 1801 by the founding bishop of the African Methodist Episcopal (AME) Church, Richard Allen. The second edition of *A Collection of Hymns and Spiritual Songs from Various Authors,* published the same year, contained sixty-four hymn texts without music, of which thirteen were by Watts. Though not formally educated, Allen was an intelligent and highly articulate pastor, and his flock apparently lined out the hymns and sang songs of their own composing (Southern 1997: 73–80). An Englishman, William Faux, wrote, "After the sermon they began to sing merrily, and continued, without stopping, one hour, till they became exhausted and breathless. . . . While all the time they were clapping hands, shouting and jumping, and exclaiming, 'Ah Lord! Good Lord! Give me Jasus! Amen'" (quoted in Southern 1997: 78). Although under Bishop Daniel Payne, who followed Allen, many AME churches dispensed with the oral tradition of hymns and songs for trained choirs, Mother Bethel, the founding AME congregation, was apparently a moaning and shouting church in the early 1800s.

Until the 1830s, the Methodist body led by Richard Allen had been unrivaled in its appeal to the masses of free blacks in the mid-Atlantic region. However, the masses of blacks on Southern plantations—far removed from the Rev. Allen's congregation in Philadelphia—were not evangelized until after the camp meetings of the Second Great Awakening in the early 1800s. As late as 1837, Charles Ball, a former slave, noted: "There is, in general, very little sense of religious obligation, or duty, amongst the slaves on the cotton plantation; and Christianity cannot be, with propriety, called the religion of these people" (quoted in Epstein 1977: 192–93). The majority of enslaved Africans—most of whom were perforce unable to travel to extended camp meetings in faraway places—embraced Christianity during the Baptist mission to the slaves between 1820 and 1850.

In what has become a signature statement of the Baptist mission to slaves, Charles Colcock Jones, a missionary serving in Liberty County, Georgia, wrote in 1842: "One good advantage in teaching them good psalms and hymns is that they are thereby induced to lay aside the extravagant and nonsensical chants, and catches and hallelujah songs of their own composing; and when they sing, which is very often while about their business or of an evening in their houses, they will have something profitable to sing" (201). In fifty years, the number of Baptist slave converts increased sixfold, from 25,000 in 1800 to 150,000 in 1850. Following slavery's end, the number swelled to one half million by 1870. The oldest and largest black Baptist body, the National Baptist Convention, was founded in 1895 (Lincoln and Mamiya 1990: 23–30).

Baptist missionaries taught slaves to line out hymns in the hope that they might abandon supposed "nonsensical chants, and catches and hallelujah songs of their own composing." Instead, the slaves "blackened the hymns" (Whalum 1973) and retained the practice long after folk hymn singing had ceased in comparable white bodies. Baptist missionaries prescribed the singing of lining-out hymns as part of a larger ritual form for slave worship that was to include:

1. an opening hymn and prayer,
2. scripture,
3. singing,
4. the sermon or lesson, and
5. the close. (Jones 1842: 69)

Pitts hypothesizes that slave worshipers embedded African initiation rites into this five-part ritual form:

> By alternating lined hymn and chanted prayer until the initiation had run its course . . . the obligation of ritual purification could continue before congregants entered trance with the Holy Spirit (126). Segments 2 through 4 [then] became the Service, or second ritual frame, with the sermon as the focal point of trance, as it was during the camp meeting revival. The singing of hymns, that is, segment 3, allowed slaves to create their own rhythmic song—especially in the secrecy of their bush meetings—using various music sources, which they accompanied with percussive hand clapping and foot stomping. . . . The closing segment, 5, containing a hymn and benedictory prayer, remained the same in the slave ritual. By means of imbedding, the African initiation . . . found a place in what was to become the Afro-Baptist ritual structure. . . . Slave worshippers utilized this format, not only in meetings with whites, but in secret slave arbors as well. (Pitts 1993: 126–27)

A still more specific sense of how the Baptist mission to the slaves influenced the pattern of slave worship can be gleaned from a letter of November 15, 1863, written by William Francis Allen, the principal author of *Slave Songs in the United States* (1867), the first substantive book published on African American music. Allen and his colleagues had been sent to the Sea Islands near Charleston to teach slaves who had been freed at the outset of the Civil War. What Allen described was a merging of the African ritual style and the sequence of worship events that slaves appropriated from Baptist missionaries. A Harvard-trained historian with some background in music, he reported to a large circle of friends that

> Molly, Katy, Winsor and I went to the Praise House in the Quarters. . . . They were just beginning a hymn, which the preacher (a stranger) deaconed out, two lines at a time. The tune was evidently Old Hundred, which was maintained throughout by one voice or another, but curiously varied at every note so as to form an intricate intertwining of harmonious sounds. It was something

very different from anything I ever heard, and no description I have read conveys any notion of it. There were no *parts* properly speaking, only now and
then a hint of a base or tenor, and the modulation seemed to be just the inspiration of the moment—no effort at regularity, only that one or two voices kept
up the air—but their ears are so good, and the time is so perfectly kept
(marked often by stamping and clapping the hands) that there was very
seldom a discordant note. It might be compared to the notes of an organ or
orchestra, where all harmony is poured out in accompaniment of the air;
except that here there was no base [*sic*]. Exhortation, prayer, another hymn,
benediction, and then a "shouting song" I believe they call them, beginning
"Good Morning," at which all began to shake hands and move about the room
in measure. The chorus was "Hallelujah," but the words were very hard to
catch. (Quoted in Epstein 1977: 308)

This remains the most complete and detailed description of black
lining out written prior to the twentieth century. First, Allen informs us
that the meeting was held in the "praise house." In keeping with common
practice, he refers to the speech or chant that began the performance as
"deaconing." Consistent with the wider pattern (see chapter 1), Allen
notes that the service began with a hymn sung in the tune of *Old Hundred*
and closed with a shouting spiritual (which he does not describe in
detail). As hymns opened slave worship, so the ring shout consummated
the experience at or after the close of the service. The slow pace of lining
out, or at least its slow beginning, likely moved the congregation imper-
ceptibly from nonmetrical speech patterns to the order and rhythm of
singing as a context for movement, dance, and spirit possession. Although
Allen cites the long-meter *Old Hundred* tune (most commonly associated
with the doxology text, "Praise God from Whom All Blessings Flow"), he
is silent about the text.

He then describes what he finds deeply affecting. The tune is "curiously
varied at every note," which results in an "intricate intertwining of harmo-
nious sounds" wherein there is "seldom a discordant note."[11] These "varied"
notes were likely melismas and ornaments, or perhaps well-placed rhythmic
interjections, freely interpolated to add expressive emphasis to the melody.
As much rhythmic as melodic, such gestures in effect shape or place
"English"—much the way a calculated spin is placed on a billiard ball—
upon the expressive meaning of a given melody. The "intertwining of har-
monious sounds"—as they create the effect of but differ from harmony—is
assuredly a heterophony resulting from several or many worshipers freely
interpolating the melody at the same time, but not in concert.[12] Because he
compares the effect of the whole to an "organ or orchestra," either of which
can produce an overpowering fullness, Allen must have heard something akin
to what Olly Wilson has described as the tendency in black music making to
fill up all the temporal space with sound (Wilson 1992). This fullness also

implies the tendency of black speech and speech-song to evoke "demonstrations of the spirit and power" as the ritual unfolds.

Such demonstrations imply physical body movement, and, as with the melodic dimension, all the participants do not move in concert, but all are coordinated with and governed, first, by an inwardly intuitive pulse and, as the performance develops, by "stamping and clapping of hands." This must have been the cross-rhythmic Sea Island tradition; while many regional styles of black lining out do not include clapping or patting, such rhythmic accompaniments can still be heard in the Sea Islands, where Allen worked. By his inclusion of the subsequent order of service—"exhortation, prayer, another hymn, benediction, and then a shouting song"—we understand that at least two hymns were performed before the shouting song closed the service.

The historical moment of Emancipation forced all black churches into a larger, more encompassing role of responsibility for not only for the souls of their members but also their emergent social and economic welfare. Freedpersons sought to affirm their humanity as both children of God independent of white control and as participants in a capitalist democracy. Thus, social class and economic agency took on greater significance. The invisible institution of secret slave worship continued in the local churches and regional associations of black Baptists, who, with the quest for literacy, aspired to more formal orders of service. Yet even as it became outwardly more formal, black Baptist worship retained the inward flexibility and openness to divine inspiration that slaves had found in the "hush arbors" of backwoods hideaways. Reflecting this creative tension between the heritage of oral forms and aspirations toward literacy, black Baptist worship has demonstrated a special genius and uncanny ability to be malleable and fluid without appearing formless or disorganized. Of course, the corresponding weakness is that when these fluid structures disintegrate on occasion into uninspired formlessness, the given order of worship provides few guidelines back to clarity.

The renowned minister and hymn singer Wyatt Tee Walker argues that meter music—as he calls the hymns—reached its ascendancy around 1875. He posits that blacks learned the hymns and continued them following Emancipation because they were easy to memorize and were conducive to the more formalized worship patterns befitting actual church buildings (as opposed to brush arbors); they also affirmed the membership of blacks as free agents in a larger Christian community (1979: 90).[13] The hymn texts were of the dominant white culture, but slaves were then free, and the impulse to embrace the hymns as a symbol of power was strong (84).

Word-only hymn books, and before them psalters, had long been used by black and white deacons or ministers to line out hymns. But as the nascent black Baptist organization grew in solidarity at the turn of the twentieth century, the demand for a denominational hymnal (with words and music) increased. Modeled after the Southern Baptist Convention's *Baptist Hymnal* of 1883, *The National Baptist Hymnal* of 1903 met this demand and became the first hymnal published by a black Baptist body.

However, soon after publication of the hymnal, "there arose a petition for a pocket-size hymn book," and, in response, *The National Baptist Hymn Book* was published by the National Baptist Publishing Board. The book's subtitle—*A Collection of Old Meter Songs*—refers to the "long meter" handle for lining out that is common among black folk. Having nothing to do with long meter as a poetic form, this subtitle refers to the slower, moaning style of *singing* the hymns. As the publication embraced an existing tradition, the preface declared that its contents "were selected from among the many thousand hymns that have been sung in churches by our parents and grandparents for centuries back. In the arrangement of this collection of hymns the editor has endeavored to answer the calls of a long felt want. . . . Thousands of earnest inquirers have continued to ask us for the old style pocket edition of the Baptist Hymn Book" (1906: 3).[14] The book's continuing publication for the past century indicates the strength of Dr. Watts in black Missionary Baptist churches. Its greatest popularity is concentrated in the Gulf states of the Deep South between Texas and Florida. In 1998, for example, almost three thousand copies of the *National Baptist Hymn Book* were sold, and seven states—Georgia, Florida, Alabama, Mississippi, Louisiana, Texas, and Tennessee—accounted for more than 80 percent of these sales. (At least one order for this hymn book was filled that year from thirty-two of the forty-five states listed in the company's database.)[15] The data confirms that while many black Baptists have ceased the practice, a certain cadre of churches continues to sing Dr. Watts.

In the Carolinas and Georgia, *The Baptist Hymnal for Use in the Church and Home* has become the common printed source for lining out among black Baptists. A word-only adaptation of the *Baptist Hymnal* of 1883 for lining out or private devotions, it was published in the same year by the same editorial board. Whereas the *Baptist Hymnal,* in 5½-by-7½-inch format, contains 704 hymns and 60 chants, its slightly more portable 4-by-6-inch black Baptist counterpart fits easily into a coat pocket and contains 632 hymns and no chants. The *Baptist Hymnal for Use in the Church and Home* includes a more diverse compilation of the evangelical hymnody of Isaac Watts, John Wesley, John Newton, Augustus Toplady, Philip Doddridge, and Horatius Bonar, plus Romantic contributions primarily from James Montgomery, and the gospel hymnody of Philip Bliss and Fanny Crosby. The long-standing popular bias of blacks and whites toward Watts hymns is vividly indicated by inclusion of 115 of his texts in the *Baptist Hymnal for . . . Church and Home.* However, the greater emphasis by blacks on both his hymns and his name as a rubric is underscored by the inclusion of 127 Watts texts in the *National Baptist Hymn Book.* Hymns commonly lined out by blacks but not included in the *Baptist Hymnal for Use in the Church and Home* are "I Love the Lord, He

Heard My Cries" and "Dark Was the Night and Cold the Ground." Popular hymns omitted from the *National Baptist Hymn Book* include "God Moves in a Mysterious Way" and "My Soul Be on Thy Guard." The hymns shown in table 4 are performed with some frequency in various regional traditions.[16]

Although a tune is listed above each text in the *National Baptist Hymn Book,* few of those melodies are utilized in the performances discussed in this chapter or in others known to me. Exceptions include *Maitland* ("Must Jesus Bear the Cross Alone"), the tune upon which Thomas Dorsey structured the melody of "Take My Hand, Precious Lord," and *Arlington,* to which the common-meter hymn "Amazing Sight! The Savior Stands" has been sung in my hearing. It is also heard in the re-creation of "Am I a Soldier of the Cross" as sung from the Richard Allen hymnal of 1801 (see *Wade in the Water,* vol. 2).

Two early-twentieth-century descriptions of lining out—by W.C. Handy and by George Pullen Jackson—may be read as indications of what lining out had become by 1900. Handy emphasized that the individual voices he heard in a Mississippi church during the late 1800s were both independent and interdependent. After the preacher lined out verses of the hymn with blues intonation, "from every note each singer would start on a vocal journey of his own, wandering in strange pentatonic figures, but returning together at the proper moment to the next note of the melody. . . . To an unaccustomed listener close at hand, the result would be chaos, but at the distance the sounds merged into a strange and moving harmony" (quoted in Sundquist 1992: 50).

Writing about black Primitive Baptist hymn singing in Alabama, Jackson (1943: 248–49) begins with a measured and clear description of the "long meter" hymns that he describes as "surge song." Then he frankly confesses puzzlement: "It seems perfectly simple and easy for the singers. But the listening white person is utterly confused. His concepts of melody, rhythm, music, fail to help him through the maze. He cannot even check the trend by the words he has heard lined out; for the singing surges on with so many graces and strings of graces . . . that all words, syllables even, lose their identity and evade recognition. It becomes vaguely evident . . . that each complicated tone surge or tone constellation accompanies a single syllable of text."[17] Handy as an insider and Jackson as an outsider to African American culture both call attention to the heterophonous, ambient, and complex range of harmonies heard in Dr. Watts.

Inasmuch as Isaac Watts affirmed and wrote about religion as inward personal experience, the outward and bodily character of black worship would no doubt have been antithetical to his polite and moderate view of religious service (see description in M. Watts 1978: 312–13). Nevertheless, much as Watts himself caused a revolution by extending to hymns the status previously reserved for biblical psalms, the expressive rhythms of slave

TABLE 4   Frequently Performed Hymns

Hymn	Meter[a]	Judson Number[b]	National Baptist Hymn Book Number[c]	Composer	Tune
"A Charge to Keep I Have"	S.M.	454	89	Charles Wesley	Boylston
"A Few More Years Shall Roll"	S.M.	631	620	Horatius Bonar	Laban
"Alas! And Did My Savior Bleed"	C.M.	125	153	Isaac Watts	Salzburg
"Amazing Grace How Sweet the Sound"	C.M.	492	364	John Newton	Warwick
"Amazing Sight! The Savior Stands"	C.M.	248	275	Unknown	Arlington
"Am I a Soldier of the Cross"	C.M.	417	416	Isaac Watts	York
"Blest Be the Tie That Binds"	S.M.	463	340	John Fawcett	Dennis
"Come Ye That Love the Lord"	S.M.	350	348	Isaac Watts	St. Thomas
"The Day Is Past and Gone"	C.M.	65	50	John Leland	Dennis
"Did Christ o'er Sinners Weep"	S.M.	260	277	Benjamin Beddome	Boylston
"Father, I Stretch My Hands to Thee"	C.M.	293	304	Charles Wesley	St. Ann's
"God Moves in a Mysterious Way"	C.M.	81	—	William Cowper	From Scottish Psalter, 1615
"Go Preach My Gospel, Saith the Lord"	L.M.	559	259	Isaac Watts	Grostette
"Guide Me, O Thou Great Jehovah"	—	99	112	William Williams	Zion
"I Heard the Voice of Jesus Say"	C.M.	487	472	Horatius Bonar	Haven
"I Love the Lord, He Heard My Cry"	—	—	399	Isaac Watts	Retreat
"Jesus, Thou Art the Sinner's Friend"	C.M.	391	588	Richard Burnham	Peterborough
"Must Jesus Bear the Cross Alone"	C.M.	449	437	George Nelson Allen	Maitland
"My Hope Is Built on Nothing Less"	L.M.	309	333	Edward Mote	Solid Rock

(continued)

TABLE 4   (continued)

Hymn	Meter[a]	Judson Number[b]	National Baptist Hymn Book Number[c]	Composer	Tune
"My Soul Be on Thy Guard"	S.M.	422	—	George Heath	?
"Our God, Our Help in Ages Past"	S.M.	66	94	Isaac Watts	*Selbourne*
"Prayer Is the Soul's Sincere Desire"	C.M.	396	391	James Montgomery	*Dundee*
"Savior, Visit Thy Plantation"	—	565	533	John Newton	*Oliphant*
"There Is a Fountain Filled with Blood"	C.M.	231	—	William Cowper	?
"There Is a Land of Pure Delight"	C.M.	684	621	Isaac Watts	*Varina*
"What a Friend We Have in Jesus"	—	406	404	Joseph Scriven	*What a Friend*

[a] Abbreviations in this column: S.M. = short meter; L.M. = long meter; C.M. = common meter.
[b] Hymn numbers in this column are for the *Baptist Hymnal for Use in the Church and Home*, published by the white-owned Judson Press.
[c] Hymn numbers in this column are for the *National Baptist Hymn Book*, published by the black-owned National Baptist Publishing Board.

singing combined with the language of realism in Watts hymns to institutionalize a new style of worship. The slaves and their progeny composed folk hymns in ballad form, inserted hymn texts whole cloth as verse lines into their congregational songs, and developed a free pattern of formulaic wandering verses for their songs—all still reflecting the iambic gait of the hymns (see chapter 5 for examples).

One interpretation of this phenomenon might link the backbeat feeling of the most colloquial African American rhythms to the unaccented-to-accented iambic stress pattern prevalent in African American singing. That is, the conventional emphasis in white hymn singing upon beats one and three in 4/4 meter has shifted in black music to beats two and four. Even if this speculation cannot be proved, the question of why African descendants in North America have turned the musical beat around, so to speak, begs for answers. For this dominant emphasis upon two and four is replicated in neither African nor other Diasporan cultures that have not been so subject to the impact of Dr. Watts hymnody.

It may be that, in the absence of a musically *developed* liturgical tradition such as Lutheranism or high Anglicanism—and having been denied access to intact African continuities such as those in the Caribbean and Brazil— black Americans were, paradoxically, more at liberty to develop a range of forms and a rhythmic style associated directly with neither Africa nor England but with the plight of how to sing what became their Lord's song in a strange land with its own tongue.

The drum was to some degree silenced on the North American frontier. However, the ritual function of the percussive and expressive beat came to be performed by an aggregate of not only patting hands and feet, along with available idiophones and drums, but also pulsating voices that commingled African gestures and English texts. And the whole has differed profoundly from the sum of its parts.

Chapter 5

"I Love the Lord, He Heard My Cries"

The Role of Dr. Watts Hymns in the Musical Acculturation of African Americans

I love the Lord, he heard my cries
And pitied every groan
Long as I live, while troubles rise
I'll hasten to his throne.
ISAAC WATTS, *1719*

Not only in Dr. Watts hymns, but also in spirituals, blues, gospel, rhythm and blues, and jazz, African-European encounters have shaped a persisting core of relationships between language and music. From about 1800 to 1970, this sequence of genres emerged out of the cauldron of wars and disenfranchisement that marked the African American trek from autonomous existence to crossover with or assimilation into the American cultural mainstream. These observable continuities include a field of nonsemantic, psychoemotional expression in African American music that is analogous to language surrogates (or drum languages), speechlike song, and other synergies between speech and song in African ritual expression. The African affinity between speech and song has been noted many times in this book but has not yet been considered at length. While chapter 6 considers African and English factors in the language of the hymns and related genres, this chapter examines the interrelationship between speech and song in the sound of Dr. Watts, while positing a conceptual model that places musical performances on a continuum of rhythmic styles.

In chapter 4, I identified a network of style concepts in recorded performances of Dr. Watts and compared them with contemporary accounts of pre-twentieth-century performances. The performances hold in common certain ways of treating pitch and stress that are guided by particular ways of apprehending and organizing time. Although these rhythmic styles transcend genre and pertain to African American performance in general, my conceptual model emerges solely from Dr. Watts. My concentration upon the hymns alone, spanning three continents and three centuries of development, seeks to achieve the depth of historical perspective. But as a broadly comparative study, it is grounded in localized ethnographies of African and African American music, for such intricate relationships between systems cannot be substantiated without resort to a coherent range of particular cases. What I am seeking to reconstruct is not a history but a musical and cultural process. My quest is to interpret an inherently archaic form that was born of exigency at the early dawning of modernity, when all New World cultural authority proceeded from at least the semblance of Old World identifications. In this regard, no study of African music is more relevant than *African Rhythm: A Northern Ewe Perspective* by Kofi Agawu (1995). The detail and clarity of this work lend credence to the speech-song parallels between African and African American cultures, which have been hypothesized by the anthropologist Melville Herskovits and the linguist Geneva Smitherman.

Rooted in the notion that "without African languages, African music would not exist" (Bebey 1975: 115), Agawu's premise is: "If song lies at the heart of African musical expression . . . then a productive approach to the analysis of song will include primary emphasis on the rhythms of language" (1995: 2). Agawu finds that "singing is by far the most prevalent mode of musical expression among the Northern Ewe" and that many different types of song follow from this prevalence (61). Following the received scholarship on African music, he describes song rhythms as either free or strict. Free rhythm lacks "a specific meter and clear sense of periodicity. . . . A comparison with recitative in opera, oratorio, or cantata is not entirely inappropriate. Strict rhythm by contrast refers to the presence of a tactus, a palpable metric structure, and a resultant periodicity" (73).

Like many of its African counterparts, Ewe is a tone language, and Agawu looks in detail at the interrelationship between what we consider music and the language with which it is interwoven. He finds that despite the effect of pitch on the lexical meaning of Ewe words, the melodic contour of songs often conflicts with the contours of speech. As with other African languages, no Ewe word exists for either music or rhythm. In the case of rhythm, Agawu concludes that this absence suggests "a binding together of different dimensional processes, a joining rather than a separating, an across-the-dimensions instead of within-the-dimension phenomenon" (7). Seeking to apprehend the unity among these dimensions, he "begins with a 'soundscape' of Northern Ewe society, a fictional ethnography which allows us to listen to manifestations of 'rhythm' in the spectrum of physical activities that take place during a single twenty-four period" (3).

Postulated as the primordial expressive event, gesture is "the physical manifestation of a more fundamental communicative urge." Dance, then, is "stylized gesture." The gesture and the spoken word are reflexive: "Gesture is both generated by, and in turn generates, the spoken word." Agawu's model moves in a circular direction, from gesture to spoken word to vocal music to instrumental music to dance and back to gesture again. However, he notes exceptions that either move counter to the given sequence or interrupt it by, for example, linking the spoken word to instrumental music rather than to the stages that precede or follow it (1995: 28). This model seems to explain the deep structure by which the Northern Ewe rhythmic style draws unto itself many ambient elements of a culture and, through the semantic propensities of sound, symbolizes a whole and unified sense of human experience.

As gesture generates speech in Agawu's view of Ewe culture, so hymn singing is the primordial form of speechlike song in African American culture. There is little if any conscious effort to sing in cleanly articulated harmonies or to render melodies that apparently correspond to the conventions of written notation: it is an aurally conceived sound concept. Therefore, Dr. Watts is a repository for "sound gestures"—moaning, shouting, or both. Heightened speech or singing in this context often achieves the level of metacommunication that maximizes the effectiveness of a performance.

Within a unified range of African American worship traditions, each region and locality expresses its own character. The unifying formal features include devotions and preaching services (as dual and complementary worship frames) and the antiphonal dynamics of speech-song that produce heterophony, polyrhythmic textures, and the tendency toward cyclically developed songs, hymns, prayers, and sermons, as opposed to fixed "pieces" of music or rhetorical forms. In tandem with the other elements of this expressive complex, the speech-oriented musical patterns discussed in this chapter point to what is most distinctive about each regional style tradition. Ingrid Monson (1996) and Thomas Brothers (1997) have noted this speechlike quality in gospel, blues, and jazz. But as an antecedent form, Dr. Watts affords a means of examining closer to its sources the transformation of an English form to suit African linguistic and ritual patterns.

As Jack Berry notes, "Almost every one of the languages spoken south of the Sahara [uses] pitch distinctions to differentiate words" (1970: 87). J.L. Dillard (1972) and Molefi Asante (1991) have investigated grammar as a semantic dimension and pitch as an expressive element of black English in North America and compared these patterns with African linguistic models. But neither phonology in black English nor its possible analogies with African tonal languages seems to have become a serious topic of linguistic study. We know, however, that African tonal languages were paralleled by musical surrogates of language that conveyed explicit semantic references through instrumental music.[1] The question that follows is how, if at all, these African ways of speaking, singing, and playing were adapted or reinterpreted in a radically different linguistic context.

Noting that the "same 'musical' quality is prominent in Negro-English and Negro-French everywhere," Melville Herskovits affirms the possibility "that the peculiarly 'musical' quality of Negro-English as spoken in the United States and the same trait found in the speech of white Southerners represent a nonfunctioning survival of [the tonal character of] African languages" (Herskovits 1941: 291, quoted in Smitherman 1977: 136). Following the study of African American speech by Arthur L. Smith (1970), Asante notes that "African American language behavior is characterized by a significant control over vocal inflection and modulation. . . . Vocal color [also] plays a vital role for the black public speaker, particularly the preacher, who utilizes various intonations and inflections to modify or amplify specific ideas, concepts, or emotions" (Asante 1991: 25).

In an empirical analysis of style in black speech, Smitherman isolates four modes of black expression: call-response, signification, tonal semantics, and narrative sequencing (1977: 103). Signification (indirect expression through analogy or metaphor) and narrative sequencing (the conventions that define black storytelling) are critical dynamics of praying, preaching, and other speech events in black worship, while call-response and tonal semantics are more germane to the rhythmic character of musical performances. Each of these modes has at least some bearing upon my discussion of style in lining out. Both the African-derived ring shout and the European-derived lining out are archaic call-response forms underlying African American performance styles. Acknowledging this past-present relationship, Smitherman (1977) illustrates the point with reference to a Dr. Watts performançe. Call and response comprise

> spontaneous verbal and non-verbal interactions between speaker and listener in which all of the speaker's statements ("calls") are punctuated by expressions ("responses") from the listener. . . . (104)
>
> Not only has the call-response pattern been employed consistently by twentieth century gospel and rock groups, it has an older history than that, as it is used in the long-metered, hymnal singing style in the traditional black church. This is a style of singing dating way back to slavery times when "church" was anywhere black people were: in the fields, back in the woods. . . . The leader-caller begins by a kind of talk-singing of the opening line for the hymn: "I love the Lord, he heard my cry." The congregation of responders then sing-chant each word, in a long, slow, drawn-out fashion, with the leader joining in with them, becoming part of the group-response. Then the leader calls out the next line: "And pitied every groan." The congregation sing-chants this line, and the song continues in this fashion to the end. (112)[2]

Smitherman also posits connections between tonal semantics and African speech patterns. "Whereas English is quite limited in its use of the features of tone to signal meaning, African languages have a very complex, highly sophisticated system of tone. Caught between a tone language (i.e., their native African tongue[s]) and a 'toneless' language (i.e., the English they were forced to adopt), Africanized English speakers seem to have

mediated this linguistic dilemma by retaining in their cultural consciousness the abstract African concept of tone while applying it to English in
obviously different ways" (135). Slaves retained this concept of tonal semantics, which is

> the use of voice rhythm and vocal inflection to convey meaning in black com-
> munication. In using the semantics of tone, the voice is employed like a musi-
> cal instrument with improvisation, riffs, and all kinds of playing between the
> notes. This rhythmic pattern becomes a kind of acoustical phonetic alphabet
> and gives black speech its songified or musical quality. . . . The speech rhythms
> and tonal inflections of Black English are, of course, impossible to capture in
> print. But you have heard these rhythms in the speech-music of James Brown
> and Aretha Franklin, in the preaching-lecturing of Martin Luther King, Jr.
> and Jesse Jackson, in the political raps of Stokely Carmichael and Malcolm X,
> in the comedy routines of Flip Wilson and Richard Pryor. (134–35)

It is interesting to note how her four pairs of exemplars move along a song-
talk continuum from singing by way of preaching to oratory and stand-up
comedy. The pairing of James Brown and Aretha Franklin implies, perhaps
coincidentally, the complementary style relation between Brown's driving
speech rhythms and Franklin's ability to moan and groan her way into and
out of grooves.

Smitherman also makes the oft-cited point that these "improvisations,
riffs, [and] all kinds of playing between the notes . . . [are] impossible to
capture in print." This—from the European perspective—"uncivilized"
dimension of the slave songs is what troubled William Allen, Charles Ware,
and Lucy Garrison in their landmark 1867 publication *Slave Songs of the
United States* and provoked their famous qualification that "The best that we
can do . . . with paper and types, or even with [our own] voices, will convey
but a faint shadow of the original. . . . The odd turns made in the throat,
and the curious rhythmic effect produced by single voices chiming in at different irregular intervals, seem almost as impossible to place on the score
as the singing of birds or the tones of an Aeolian Harp" (iv, vi). Although
lining out heightened the spirituals' propensity for habitual transgression
of the boundaries between speech and song, Dr. Watts has attracted far less
scholarly attention than the spirituals due to its relative obscurity. Smitherman
continues the discussion by grouping tonal semantics within the categories
of "talk-singing, repetition and alliterative word play, intonational contouring, [and] rhyme" (137). She explains: "Talk-singing . . . achieves its meaning from the listener's association of the tone with the feeling of being
'happy' and gittin the [spirit]. In repetition and alliteration, key words and
sounds are repeated in succession, both for emphasis and effect. . . . Intonational contouring is the specific use of stress and pitch in pronouncing
words in the black style" (142, 145).

TABLE 5   The Speech-Movement Continuum

Freely Measured Speech Rhythms	*Strictly Measured Speech Rhythms*
Portraiture sound—Poetic rhythms————Speech rhythms—Percussive rhythms	

THE SPEECH-MOVEMENT CONTINUUM

Although call-response and tonal semantics are the interactive modes pertinent to the lining-out practice, a general comment from Smitherman's introduction more nearly anticipates my view of tonal semantics as an explicitly musical dimension of black performativity. She mentions that "the real distinctiveness—and beauty—in the black sound system lies in those features which do not so readily lend themselves to concrete documentation— its *speech rhythms, voice inflections,* and *tonal patterns*" (Smitherman 1977: 3; italics mine). In the discussion that follows, I have subsumed these three categories within my own set of conceptual approaches to understanding the styles of lining-out performances. This will continue the approach begun in chapter 2, where I noted that in Dr. Watts singing, speechlike rhythms occur in either "freely measured" or "strictly measured" styles, which in turn lie across a *speech-movement continuum* of rhythmic approaches.[3] Ranging from subtlety of rhythm to extreme emphasis, the continuum moves from *portraiture sound* through three increasingly rhythmic categories: *poetic rhythms, speech rhythms,* and finally *percussive rhythms* (see table 5).

Freely Measured Rhythms

The word *measured* underscores that virtually all black lining out issues from inherent tensions between a metronomic pulse and patterns of speech inflection. Compared with strictly measured rhythms, freely measured rhythms are slower in tempo, more heterophonic in texture, and tend to fill up all the temporal space created by the roughly equal prolongation of every syllable of the hymn text, save the last of each line. Two kinds of freely measured rhythms are common in Dr. Watts: portraiture sound builds or sustains intensity through moaning (or liquid pitch inflection), timbral variations such as growling or falsetto, and interpolated exclamations or narrative; poetic rhythms encourage certain gestures, attitudes, or moods through episodic and formulaic patterns of discrete pitches.

Portraiture Sound.   Portraiture sound derives from the blend of spoken word and rendered gesture that William Turner describes as a "kratophony" (Spencer 1987: x). The fullness of such power enlivens intoned preaching and prayers. Whether portraiture sound occurs in such sacred sites of origin or in a secular style like rhythm and blues, it intimates something to be said transcending what mere words—or mere pitches—can symbolize. Such changes in vocal color result from shifts in the size, shape, and direction of the air column projected through the windpipe and directed upon the nasal cavities. In the improvised moment, this way of performing a text (or by extension, a melody) depends upon the leader's skill and emotional engagement to structure timbres in such a way that affective force is accumulated as a continuing and coherent gravity upon the hearer's sensibilities.

While the other three categories on the speech-movement continuum are called rhythms, this is not to say that portraiture sound is utterly arhythmic. The static connotation of portraiture sound suggests the degree to which periodicity can be "immobilized" or fully sublimated to speech rhythms that are both verbal and nonverbal. This is the kind of melodic indirection one hears in the trumpet solo on Duke Ellington's *Concerto for Cootie* (see *Smithsonian Collection of Classic Jazz,* vol. 3). Our conventional ways of thinking about rhythm must be redrawn to see Cootie Williams's trumpet solo as a *rhythmic* masterpiece. Most discussions of this solo center on timbre. However, rhythm as a calculated yet dramatic sense of where to place each event in time enables the moaning, groaning, hollering, and laughing sounds of this virtuoso performance to cohere as a "story" form, complete in itself.

Especially effective as portraiture sound, in differing ways, are *Dr. Watts* nos. 14 and 18, "Must Jesus Bear the Cross Alone" and "My Work on Earth Will Soon Be Done." The former is sung with a quality of simple and unadorned pathos that seems to probe the marrow of human vulnerability. Literally every note of this plaint is pulled and stretched in the gentlest way, so as to evoke comparisons between the human voice and a string instrument. The twanging yet rounded nasality of the female lead voice invites comparison not just with string instruments in general but with the softness and agility of a sitar or perhaps a drone instrument from the Hindustani tradition. The poignancy of each note melding into the next makes it easy to see the bridge between Dr. Watts in church, the "thinking out loud" kind of Dr. Watts lines that plowmen sang in the field hollers, and the guitar accompaniments that fashioned these plaints into early blues.

A much more disparate and interactive sort of portraiture is effected in "My Work on Earth Will Soon Be Done." The text seems to belong to a genre of African American folk verse modeled upon common meter (8–6–8–6) hymns. The vocal gestures of the lead singer include both the liquid intonation of slides and sweeps and improvised patterns of discrete pitches. However, the sense of community generated by his lead produces no concerted vocal effect but rather a powerfully charged aggregate of inspired cooperation. In most familiar hymn-singing styles, the leaders, who must carry the singing, intersperse moans and vocables between the syllables only at critical points in the performance.[4] However, as an obvious and integral part of this melody, moans are thoroughly interwoven with the syllables of this text. In addition, the unimaginably slow pace of the singing creates a peculiar yet moving sense of parts hanging together in suspension, as it were. Although portraiture sound is the least outwardly rhythmic style in the lexicon of Dr. Watts, the degree of fluidness heard in this performance is, in my experience, without precedent. George Pullen Jackson notes that whereas certain white congregations sang a chorus or four-line stanza in fifteen to twenty-two seconds, black Primitive Baptists spread the same passage over sixty-six seconds (1944: 250–51). This one four-line verse of "My Work on Earth" as recorded in *Dr. Watts* no. 18 requires more than three minutes![5]

Poetic Rhythms.   While portraiture sound paints a graphic picture of what the singer has to "say," poetic rhythms consist of formulaic pitch clusters, sequentially ascending or descending. Neither portraiture sound nor poetic rhythms may be heard as rhythms in the literal or metronomic sense, but such intonational gestures shape the rhythmic contours of song to implicate speech and, in so doing, articulate rhythm in what might be thought of as qualitative more than quantitative terms.

While poetic rhythms occur in a variety of tempos, they predominate in slower, freely measured hymns. These licks of repetitive melisma add a conversational, metacommunicative quality to the religious and musical characteristics of the performance. The adjective "poetic" denotes the formalized and formulaic character of the style, which is organized into patterns not as means for achieving motor regularity but as recognizable formulas connoting images and moods of black vocal expression. Repeated and varied like instrumental riffs, poetic rhythms are interpolated in the "cracks" between melodic phrases.[6] While they often insinuate the blue and liquid sound of moaning intonation, they consist of discrete pitches and articulate rhythms. The role of a forceful lead singer is central in this approach, for once such melismatic figures are stated, they are likely to be in some degree replicated by group members. But the whole is reliant upon the inward fullness and vocal skills of a talented "instigator" who can initiate and sustain a certain musical and emotional assertiveness. Given the virtuosity they imply, poetic rhythms have gained wide currency not only in Dr. Watts but also in the gospel "feathers and flowers" of Mahalia Jackson and the "bird feathers" of Charlie Parker.

Poetic rhythms abound in *Wade in the Water,* vol. 2, no. 15. After a faster opening song, members of the Blue Spring Missionary Baptist Association continue their devotional service with "A Charge to Keep I Have." The leader announces the hymn and lines out the first verse in a voice that hovers between recitation and chant.[7] He then raises the hymn upon a melody akin to the shape-note tune *Idumea* (see chapter 2). The group sings the hymn in an organum texture of fourths and fifths with occasional thirds and sixths.

The vocal texture is thickened further by another male singer who bears up the leader with impromptu responses strategically placed to fill the breath gaps in the lead voice. The poetic rhythms of the leader as well as those of the singer bearing him up are built upon three notes: a flat third, a tonic, and the flat seventh below, the last two pitches being repeated at will. (A similarly structured poetic rhythm is uttered in *Dr. Watts* no. 16, "Before This Time Another Year.") As the singing gains intensity, individuals clap their hands out of rhythm several times in rapid succession. Perhaps related to the claps, the gradual rise in pitch by a whole step suggests a corresponding intensity in the singing itself. After the second verse has been lined out in couplets and sung, as the leader tells them to "moan it, children," a traditional prayer begins over the moaning. Further along in the prayer, after the general moaning has ceased, discreet moans are sung in the background. In this excellent hymn performance, the poetic rhythms of both leaders somehow coalesce with the group sound to form a diverse but coherent heterophony. The astounding density of the sound belies the small number of singers—fewer than a dozen—who are carrying the hymn.

A similar level of intensity is achieved by poetic rhythms in *Dr. Watts* nos. 10 and 12, "I Heard the Voice of Jesus Say" and "A Charge to Keep I Have." The poetic rhythms and a singular vocal quality—the kind that must have inspired James Weldon Johnson's vision of *God's Trombones*—make the Rev. C. J. Johnson's signature hymn "I Heard the Voice of Jesus Say" unforgettable. Both his opening flourishes and the intoned testimony between verses are expansive strokes of virtuosity. Yet, given his rare combination of sincere passion and vocal agility, there is no hint of ostentation or sensationalism. "A Charge to Keep I Have" is similarly effective for its blending of effective speech with commanding poetic rhythms.

Strictly Measured Rhythms

Strictly measured singing—as *rhythmic strings of words*—stems from the creoles and dialects traced by Victor Turner, Joseph Holloway, and Winifred Vass to African languages. Within this context, they proceed from either the motor regularity of cross-rhythmic clapping patterns (percussive), or the standard sense of melodic organization owing chiefly to written sources (speech). Strictly measured rhythms are often interrupted by the freer rhythms of speech, but the "hook" of such melodies is a dominant rhythmic pattern that recurs throughout. While speech rhythms embellish a line within the given melodic contours, percussive rhythms exert a generative influence that transforms a melody. As the former nuances a given melody through a pattern of discrete speech inflections, so the latter isolates a rhythmic motive, even a single-note pattern such as that patented in jazz singing by Louis Armstrong, as a variation theme. While lyricism can "flatten out" melodic contours to effect the chantlike insistence of a reciting tone with upper and lower neighboring tones, percussive rhythms assert as "melody" the percussive impulse itself (sometimes coupled with the impetus of speech). Both kinds of strictly measured rhythms occasionally pair formulas of one to several pitches with each syllable. Whereas such melismas may nuance speech rhythms, the percussive approach utilizes them to accelerate tempo and heighten intensity (note the latter approach in *Dr. Watts* nos. 1 and 7, "What a Friend We Have in Jesus" and "Amazing Grace").

This heightened percussive intensity is often accompanied by vigorous body movement and episodes of shouting. This is, of course, in keeping with the African tradition of rhythmic dancing and drumming as means of invoking a divine presence. Speech rhythms may implicate some percussive character, but, maintaining the contour and spirit of the given melody, they more clearly observe the restraint of Anglo-American ritual traditions.

Whether in hymns or congregational songs or other genres, speech rhythms are well-suited to periodic melodies with a half cadence following the second line, or to arrangements or singing styles that feature parallel harmonic movement. Speech rhythm performances bend the melodic lines to accommodate gentle speech inflections, and to elicit the mood and feeling of African ritual without utterly transforming the given melodic form. However, when the rhythmic momentum of a performance effects a complete melodic transformation, the percussive impulse is doing its work. Both styles commonly occur in Dr. Watts and other sacred genres, as well as the speechlike jazz singing styles that began with Louis Armstrong and Bessie Smith and culminated in the performances of Billie Holiday.

Speech Rhythms.   Benjamin Lloyd no. 15, "What Wondrous Love Is This," exemplifies the character of speech rhythms. The melody (no. 159 in the *Original Sacred Harp*) typifies the kind of traceable adaptation that tunes published in written sources have undergone within black congregations. The contour of the "Wondrous Love" tune is retained but flattened out, as it were, and elaborated through repetition. What remains is more spare and iterative and lends emphasis to the rhythm. To the uninitiated, this might seem to take away what cannot be replaced. The majority of the pitches in the duet by Amanda Smith and Ella Pearl White hover around two notes, the home pitch of the key and the third above it. But this narrowed melodic range causes the ear to hearken to any note rising above or falling below these poles as being of special importance. This is the contoured economy of up-and-down idiomatic expressions, the question-and-answer musical phrases that drive the chantlike intonation of African American spirituals, as well as sermons and prayers.[8] A contrasting example of speech rhythms is "Remember Me" (*Dr. Watts*, no. 21), an African American chant that does not lean heavily upon either the moaning inflection or the flattening out

process just described. The entire idea of the song stems from a single rhythmic motive. The repeated invocation opens on the root of the triad, moves
to the third, and then closes on the fifth as the melody approaches the half
cadence. The interjection "O Lord" marks the expressive peak of the
singing, and the thought comes to rest again on the tonic. This pithy chant
contains the whole of what is a common formula in the congregational
songs. The a-a-b-a textual germ begins with an opening phrase centered
upon the tonic, a second moving from the third of the tonic triad to a half
cadence, and a third contrasting phrase, which is also the melodic climax,
followed by a reiteration of the opening thought. While various kinds of
decoration may be added to this plaint, its power is its simplicity. Although
moaning intonations are not explicit in the fabric of this melody, because of
its emphasis upon the third degree of the scale it is easily whined out in portraiture sound or adorned with poetic rhythms.

Percussive Rhythms.   An outstanding example of percussive rhythms is *Benjamin Lloyd* no. 8, "Dark and Thorny Is the Desert." In the way that mass concentrations of meaning (or "mascons") like "Jesus is a rock in a weary land,"
"Go down, Moses," or "I got a home in that rock" can mark points of reference in sermons and sayings, so can a percussive melodic line encapsulate a
certain gravity of momentum. Melodically reminiscent of the famous congregational song "Wade in the Water," this shouting performance of "Dark
and Thorny Is the Desert" accelerates throughout its course. Despite the
strophic text, the percussive repetition of the melody implicates chant, and
the tension between strictly measured singing and freely measured lining out
lends intensity to this extended performance. Not only is the chantlike
melody itself sung by the full congregation, but as the performance develops,
the congregation joins the leader in lining out each verse. Chanted out of
measure, these spoken passages float over the prevailing pulse but do not
stem its flow. This seeming redundancy underscores the primacy of lining out
as a rhetorical gesture in black music and ritual. Over the stress of the prevailing beat pattern, the lined-out passages frame a tension-producing
moment or inhalation, as it were, wherein a speechlike diction proceeds in
unmeasured rhythm. Then, in the percussive measured rhythms that quickly
follow, that same energy finds release in the rhythmic flow of exhalation.[9]
Whereas this uplands shout style is founded upon offbeat syncopated
rhythms, the more African ring shout of the low country and Sea Island areas
builds upon cross-rhythmic clapping and stomping patterns. (An example of
the latter tradition is *Dr. Watts* no. 1, "What a Friend We Have in Jesus.")

These four approaches to music making are, in practice, interrelated
and overlapping. However, for the sake of illustrating them as organizing
principles of structure and form, the hymns that form the basis of the present study have been so identified in table 6, based upon which of the four

TABLE 6   Hymns Categorized by Rhythmic Styles

Wade in the Water, volume 2

Rhythmic Style	Selection	Texture/Tune
Percussive rhythms	8. I Heard the Voice of Jesus Say	Offbeat-shout
Portraiture sound	11. Am I a Soldier of the Cross	Moaning-harmony/*Arlington*
Speech rhythms	12. Early, My God, without Delay	Moaning-harmony
Poetic rhythms	15. A Charge to Keep I Have	Moaning-organum/*Idumea*
Poetic rhythms	16. (Traditional prayer with moans)	Unison-moaning

Benjamin Lloyd's Hymn Book

Rhythmic Style	Selection	Texture/Tune
Poetic rhythms	5. The Day Is Past and Done	Moaning-unison/*Idumea*
Percussive rhythms	8. Dark and Thorny Is the Desert	Offbeat-shout
Speech rhythms	9. O May I Worthy Prove	Unison-moaning
Poetic rhythms	12. Amazing Grace	Unison-moaning/*Pisgah*
Poetic rhythms	13. That Doleful Night before His Death	Unison-moaning
Speech rhythms	15. What Wondrous Love Is This	Unison-moaning/*Wondrous Love*
Speech rhythms	16. While Sorrows Encompass	Unison-moaning
Portraiture sound	20. Father, I Stretch My Hands to Thee	Moaning-organum

Dr. Watts Hymn Singing among African Americans

Rhythmic Style	Selection	Texture/Tune
Percussive rhythms	1. What a Friend We Have in Jesus	Cross-shout/*Restoration*
Percussive rhythms	2. Come Ye That Love the Lord	Off-shout/*Idumea*
Percussive rhythms	3. Go Preach My Gospel, Saith the Lord	Moaning-organum
Percussive rhythms	4. Father, I Stretch My Hands to Thee	Moaning-organum
Portraiture sound	5. A Charge to Keep I Have	Moaning-organum/*Idumea*
Percussive rhythms	6. Father, I Stretch My Hands to Thee	Offbeat-shout

(continued)

TABLE 6   (continued)

Dr. Watts Hymn Singing among African Americans

Rhythmic Style	Selection	Texture/Tune
Percussive rhythms	7. Amazing Grace	Offbeat-shout
Percussive rhythms	8. You May Bury Me in the East	Offbeat-shout
Speech rhythms	9. Jesus Invites His Saints	Moaning-harmony
Poetic rhythms	10. I Heard the Voice of Jesus Say	Moaning-organum
Poetic rhythms	11. A Charge to Keep I Have	Moaning-organum/*Idumea*
Percussive rhythms	12. A Charge to Keep I Have	Unison-moaning/*Idumea*
Percussive rhythms	13. Amazing Grace	Off-shout/*Willow*[a]
Portraiture sound	14. Must Jesus Bear the Cross Alone	Unison-moaning
Portraiture sound	15. I'm Not Too Mean to Serve the Lord	Unison-moaning
Poetic rhythms	16. Before This Time Another Year	Unison-moaning
Percussive rhythms	17. What a Friend We Have in Jesus	Unison-moaning/ *Restoration*
Portraiture sound	18. My Work on Earth Will Soon Be Done	Unison-moaning
Percussive rhythms	19. A City Called Heaven	Unison-moaning
Poetic rhythms	20. A Few More Years Shall Roll	Unison-moaning
Speech rhythms	21. Remember Me	Moaning-harmony

[a] The full name of the tune is *The Weeping Willow* or *Go Bury Me beneath the Willow*. It is paired with a secular lyric folksong that can be found in *The Frank C. Brown Collection of North Carolina Folksong* (Durham: Duke University Press, 1952–64), vol. 5, 189–90.

approaches exerts the dominant influence upon the style of the performance.[10] The texture of the performance is also indicated, together with an identification where possible, of the tune.

IMPLICATIONS OF THE SPEECH-MOVEMENT CONTINUUM

Pondering the elements of the speech-movement continuum has led me to three further areas of consideration: empirical speculations about possible African sources for these rhythmic concepts, a return to the question of their genesis on American soil, and observations about their wider significance within African American music. Regarding the first, from the observation of parallels between Dr. Watts as an African American tradition and various African music and ritual practices, three correspondences may be hypothesized: (1) that the strictly measured speech rhythms of Dr. Watts reinterpret the time-line concept by which African drumming traditions accompany and interact with ritual and social dancing; (2) that the portraiture sound of Dr. Watts reinterprets the West and Central African traditions of dirge singing; and (3) that the poetic rhythms of Dr. Watts reinterpret the musical speech surrogates that link semantic references to relative pitch sequences in African languages.

1. Fundamental to many West African drumming traditions, the ostinato, or rhythmic time line, is an externalization of "subjective metronomic time," a pattern that may accompany dance by sustaining rhythmic motion (Nketia 1974: 131–32). New World reinterpretations apply this concept in at least two ways: ostinato clapping patterns accompany the Sea Island shout songs heard in the Gullah language areas of South Carolina and Georgia (*Dr. Watts* no. 1, for example), and words themselves outline repeating patterns in songs from the South Carolina Piedmont region like *Dr. Watts* no. 8, "You May Bury Me in the East." Where words either conform to the singing or become its primary rhythmic reference they parallel the bell rhythm that anchors many African drumming styles. This use of words as a propulsive force in themselves mediates between the ritual power of words as generative ideas, or *nommo,* and rhythmic movement as embodied celebration.

2. The impassioned moods and multiple facets of portraiture sound may be traceable to African dirge-singing traditions, such as those from Central and West Africa discussed in chapter 4. Although the sound of dirge singing from Central Africa is especially similar to black lining out, the overall style and the ritual form and placement (within the dual ritual frame posited by Pitts) of the Ghanaian practice from West Africa described by Nketia also parallels the context of Afro-Baptist moaning. Nketia describes dirge singing among the Akan-speaking peoples of Ghana as a "wailing" tradition, performed only by women, because wailing does not become a man (1955: 8).

> The dirge *frequently begins the funeral ceremony* and remains its mainstay for a long time until it is reinforced and *eventually overshadowed by music and dancing.* . . . [In this sense,] the dirge is . . . the culminating point of the preparation for the funeral as well as the beginning of public mourning. . . . (8) One of the requirements of a performer is that *she should really feel the pathos of the occasion* and the sentiments embodied in the dirge. Pretense is condemned and mock-sadness is discouraged. A tear should fall, lest you are branded a witch and a callous person. . . . (9)
>
> There are *two* [*vocal qualities* employed in singing the dirge]: a wailing voice, and the normal singing voice or something near to it. In the first case the musical intonation commonly used in songs is not followed. *Notes are*

indeterminate in pitch and less sonorous; the quantitative differences between successive notes are reduced, though perceptible [pitch] differences are still maintained. In the second type of wailing a musical intonation much nearer that of the song is used, though the voice quality may have a tinge of the wail in it. . . . (113)

The dirge piece is usually made up of musical phrases and sentences corresponding to verbal linear units. . . . (113) The *frame of the melody carried by the verbal linear units is guided by the frame of the speech tones of the words.* . . . (114) The rhythm of dirge tunes follows the rhythm of the verbal linear units. The relative duration of syllables in speech is reflected in the duration of the notes of the dirge. . . . (116)

The usual way of performing dirges at funerals is *for each individual mourner to perform on her own,* singing dirges of her choice when and where she likes, without regard to what others may be singing at the same time or how they may be singing them. . . . (116) Traditional tunes may be associated with many fragments of the dirge and a mourner may find many of them useful. But for the most part a singer must make her own tunes as she goes along whether it is for the wail-dirge or the song-dirge. (117; italics mine)

Correlations abound between the prayer-moan context of black hymn singing and that of dirge singing at Akan funerals. Just as lining out begins Afro-Baptist devotions, so does dirge singing set an opening tone of gravity and solemnity. Both convey pathos ("she should really feel the pathos of the occasion and the sentiments embodied in the dirge") through a diverse range of vocal qualities, from speech to song to wailing (the two vocal qualities among dirge singers use notes of indeterminate pitch and song, respectively). Both styles utilize speech as a formal determinant for singing ("the frame of melody . . . is guided by the frame of the speech tones"); both melodic contexts are flexible enough to allow for each individual performer to express his or her own sense of the song(s). ("Each individual mourner perform[s] on her own, singing dirges of her choice when and where she likes, without regard to what others may be singing at the same time.") Finally, dirges, like lining out, are followed by a ritual frame in which they are "eventually overshadowed by music and dancing." So is there full correspondence between the ritual grammars linking the two musical forms.

3. Both African language surrogates and African American poetic rhythms impose an apparent tension between free and strict rhythms. That is, while the question of whether they derive from the same linguistic-musical sources cannot be settled here, both musical phenomena do effect a "rhythmic suspension," as it were, which enables the soloists in the one tradition or the master drummer in the other to "say" what he or she has to say somehow within yet outside the frame of a metronomic pulse. Whether that tension proves as brief as a momentary syncopation, as emphatic as a two-against-three polyrhythm, or as prolonged as two

opposing rhythmic meters is only a matter of degree. In subjective terms, such rhythmic placements lend a conversational character to the musical rhetoric, which, in combination with call-and-response interactions as well as the range of more obviously vocally derived timbres and inflections (here described as portraiture sound), reinforces the dialogical and communal signification of a musical performance. While poetic rhythms are certainly prominent in sacred and secular vocal styles, they have become no less common as part of the complex of instrumental sounds that lend to jazz improvisation much of its speechlike character.

The line of reasoning outlined in this chapter—seeing rhythmic styles as the basis for melodic ordering and expressive context—brings us again to the question of how these ways of singing and conceiving hymns and songs came into being. The songs that likely accompanied the ring shouts (e.g., *Wade in the Water,* vol. 2, nos. 1–4) entered the black sacred tradition long before the First Awakening revivals of the mid-eighteenth century (Fisher 1963, Stuckey 1987, Pitts 1993). The initial encounters between slaves and evangelists featured the "old way" of singing, wherein all words were sustained for roughly equal durations and the extreme slow pace of singing obfuscated a regular pulse. Then, in the "regular way" of singing that followed, the length of each note was predetermined by a livelier written melody.[11]

While it is impossible to estimate precisely where or when free and strict rhythms came to bear upon North America cultures, observers from the fifteenth through the eighteenth centuries wrote that slaves sang "dirges," "pines," and "melancholy lamentations" (see Epstein 1977: 3, 4, 8, 9). What technical means were employed to convey such effects? Could these have been moaning sounds produced by the variant pitch of wails, hollers, or vocables? In describing an 1835 slave hymn performance, visitors from England and Wales noted that "they have no books, for they could not read; but it was printed on their memory and they sang it off with freedom and feeling. There is much melody in their voices; and when they enjoy a hymn, there is a raised expression of the face, and an undulating motion of the body, keeping time with the music, which is very touching" (Reed and Matheson 1835: vol. 1: 217–22). What was the fullness of "melody" or the freedom heard in their voices? Could it have been rhythmic interpolation or moaning? The comments of Reed and Matheson indicate that, while perhaps not as incessantly rhythmic as the ring shout, this way of singing was notable and deeply affecting.

Four general conclusions, applying to a wide range of genres and styles of African American music, may be drawn from these comparisons and parallels:

First, *African and African American singing styles link tone (timbre and pitch) and rhythm in linear patterns of narrative discourse that subordinate other musical elements such as melody and harmony.*

There has been a reductionist tendency to overstate the primacy of rhythm in African and African American music. Although the formulation of a melody around pitches, rhythms, or both will affect its lyric or recitative quality, it does not as a direct consequence become either more or less melodic. Even the invocation of the categories "lyric" and "recitative" sends us in the wrong direction, for the maps we have developed about these complementary vocal expressions are different. More pertinent to the forms and structures of both African and African American vocal music are the tension and complementarity *between* tones and rhythms that performances bring into play, with tones being emphasized in the early stages of ritual celebration and percussive rhythmic patterns growing in importance as the ritual unfolds. However, whether at home in Africa or in Diaspora, rhythm has been only the head of a highly adaptive musical body that, without fear for losing itself, is ever in pursuit of wholeness.

Most distinctive have been the stylistic implications of this linking of tone and rhythm for various popular forms over the last two centuries. Slave performances of work songs and ring shouts predated the Dr. Watts hymns in African American culture. Following upon lining out and emerging in the 1800s, the "Christianized" spirituals exerted a certain creative mastery over the rhetoric of the English language that exploded into a range of formal permutations. Many of these spirituals were rhythmic chants with melodic formulas that were latent in the chanted calls of leaders who intoned the remembered lines of a favorite hymn. But unlike the droned-out hymns, spirituals and ring shouts took the shape of speechlike, thematic rhythms that followed more closely the dialects of local speech communities. Later, blues singers with guitar accompaniment broke up words into still more irregular and unpredictably long or short phrases. The work of the early bluesman Charley Patton is quintessential of such "talking blues" rhythms.[12] Gospel and, later, rhythm and blues reflected homogenization of the same complex of styles. Rap, in turn, has intensified both the speech rhythms of spirituals and the variable phrase lengths of blues to attain, in its best instances, an unprecedented spoken virtuosity.[13]

Speech rhythms can supply the underlying structure for a song, a sermon, or, metaphorically, an instrumental work. The metaphor of speech rhythms also surfaces in the practice of scat singing—for example, Louis Armstrong's inimitable display of an entire chorus of three-against-two rhythms in "Hotter Than That." The same kind of irrepressible energy of word rhythms resurfaces in songs by Stevie Wonder, such as "Living for the City." Such talking rhythms capture the momentum of word patterns as a counterpoint to the ostinato rhythms that underlie rhythm and blues songs.

As an extension of this same impetus, no rhythm and blues singer has done more with powerfully repetitive (percussive) speech rhythms that rivet the listener's attentions than has James Brown in songs like "Papa's Got a

Brand New Bag" and "The Funky Drummer."[14] By contrast, and also during the 1960s and early 1970s, Aretha Franklin demonstrated an unequalled mastery of portraiture sound and poetic rhythms. Like Sam Cooke before her, she brought these concepts to the marketplace from the sanctum of the black church, where they had been stirring hearts for more than a century.[15] However, direct transfer is not the sole means by which these ways of making music have become public domain. The modern style of jazz improvisation that Lester Young pioneered and Charlie Parker perfected is rife with profoundly elaborated poetic rhythms. Poignantly poetic rhythms are heard in the formulaic three- and four-note rhythmic motives that adorn hymns raised by preachers like C. J. Johnson and C. L. Franklin.[16] In turn, rhythm and blues masters such as Sam, Aretha, and Stevie personalized these approaches as they developed soulful styles around bases of experience gained in church performances. Despite the cultural partitions among the church life, the world of rhythm and blues, and the jazz life, the concepts of portraiture sound and poetic rhythm point up striking similarities among the sound structures of the old-time church, gospel, rhythms and blues, and jazz. Across these genres there is an ascending scale of abstraction, but the ways that instrumental soloists develop ideas and the interrelations between vocal soloists and groups share this common body of generative principles.

In such ways have the heterogeneous textures of portraiture sound and the expressive gesturing of poetic rhythms enriched instrumental as well as vocal styles.[17] Portraiture sound utilizes subtly varying vocal inflections to implicate rhythms without embracing them. Such gestures underscore structural and formal attributes of sound or tone by setting into relief paired contrasts, such as rise/fall, loud/soft, pitched/indeterminate, accented/ghosted, to magnify the cumulative and sequenced impact of word signifiers. As a similar strategy, poetic rhythms signify upon expressive functions more commonly associated with melody and timbre on at least two levels: structurally by segmenting a song, sermon, or improvisation into an irregular sequence of lines punctuated by natural phrase endings, "amen"-like interjections, aspirate breath accents, or group entries; and functionally by creating a synergy of rhythmic counterpoint between a soloist and the group.

Second, *just as slave converts reinterpreted African relationships between language and music, supplanting the semantic content of African language surrogates with the emotional content of spirituals, so singing in the black church seeks to transcend mere words through the evocation of emotional content.*

Although Leonard Meyer's primary research base is European music, the fundamental logic of his hermeneutic on the emotions and music facilitates an understanding of African to African American transformations. In reference to the conjunctive effect of music and other stimuli (including words) upon the emotions, Meyer suggests a system of relations among images, connotations, and the moods they elicit. He argues that referential and absolute meanings are not mutually exclusive (1956: 1). "Whereas there is a concrete relation between a musical stimulus, perhaps another [medium such as poetry], and an image evoked thereby, aside from any such particularity, music may . . . be experienced as mood or sentiment" (266). While images may be conscious or unconscious, private or shared among a group of individuals within a culture (257), "connotations are shared in common by a group of individuals within a culture. A complex of related connotative associations are [*sic*] most often used in combination so that each reinforces the other. . . . A particular epoch may develop quite an elaborate system of connotations in which certain melodic, rhythmic, or harmonic practices become signs of certain states of mind or are used to designate specific emotional states" (260). These connotative relationships between certain sounds and relatively habitual or automatic responses spell out the dynamic function of conventions in African American music.

For example, prior to lining out a hymn, many leaders will evoke the spirit of the "elders" by painting a picture of the potential for transformation that the elders found in the experience. Before a sermon preached in 1942 by a guest minister, the host pastor of a Mississippi church prepared the congregation to sing "A Charge to Keep I Have" (see *Dr. Watts*, no. 12) with this exhortation:

> I want to ask you to join in and sing two verses of a hymn. You know, we just can't get away from those good ol' hymns. They will stir you when nothing else will. You can get up some morning feeling bad and feeling tired and feeling worn out. And just go to humming one of those ol' hymns that you used to hear Mother hum and walk around the floor and hum them until the Spirit of God would come and get in her soul and cause a great shout. Let us sing this hymn.

In his singing of "A Charge to Keep I Have" that follows, his deftly poetic rhythms are conventional and formulaic, and the volume and intensity of the performance mount rapidly as individuals join the singing during the first few syllables of the first line. This mixture of poignant words, gently undulating rhythms, a recognizable melody, and the story about the mother's singing becomes a connotative complex of powerfully evocative images that interact to effect a certain mood. Through such means, the elders receive homage within acceptably Christian terms, and the legacy of black suffering and degradation is ritually adorned by reference to "those good ol' hymns." Far from being an easy nostalgia, this is a mythical episode wherein the culture and moment of the elders is visited upon the present gathering, so as to center the past, present, and implicitly the future in the circle of present-tense reality. Through this mechanism, the semantic content that could not be carried by Standard English has been filled in by images and moods that are evoked in the singing itself through portraiture sound and poetic rhythms.

Third, *through such processes, black vocal styles project an economy of means that is analogous to the limited vocabulary and stock phrases that are structured by conventions and elaborated for the sake of clarity in African language surrogates.*

Both systems also utilize emphatic signification (semantic references in African language surrogates and evocative images in African American performative style) that is frequently innovative but seldom pursues originality for its own sake. There is a rigor in this kind of approach to music making, as principles of composition and improvisation that depend upon and reflect patterns of social interaction are scrupulously observed. This correspondence between singing and speaking goes to the core of African American cultural identity. It is the means by which the webs of sound the slaves spun around them "blackened" the Standard English hymn texts. In this way does the *sound* of the hymns reveal, in its starkest, most abstract forms, what is African-sounding about African American music. Much of this Africanness is the liminality between speech and song that one hears in "speech on its way to becoming song" (Agawu 1995: 180–82).

Finally, *lining-out hymns serve a ritual function both radically different from and complementary to intoned sermons, ring shouts, and holy dances, and the style distinctions, as they occur in various regional traditions, can best be understood on a continuum of similarities and distinctions.*

Certain Dr. Watts performance styles begin with deliberate and formal rhythms, then push the tempo and intensity as far toward moments of spirit possession as the occasion will allow. Others, in their slow and deliberate movement, behave like a winding spring that draws disparate forces together in a creative tension that sets the stage for the percussive, movement-centered, and possession-directed release that will likely follow at some point, perhaps far enough removed in the ritual sequence to seem unrelated.

Chapter 6

"Go Preach My Gospel, Saith the Lord"

Words as Movers and Shakers
in African American Music

Go preach my gospel, saith the Lord
Bid the whole earth my grace receive
He shall be saved that trusts my word
And be condemned that not believe.

ISAAC WATTS, *1707*

As sermons unfold the scriptures in black worship, hymns and songs freight spoken symbols with the burden of human thoughts and feelings. These words are the very marrow out of which the bones of black song live, move around, and have their being. No less germane to this way with words are the wordless (and thus so-called inarticulate) cries, calls, hollers, and moans that animate the palette of vocal colors that is particular to the tradition. Whether worded or wordless, songs and singing emerge from heightened speech utterances.

In practice, the stimulus for raising a particular song in a worship service can arise from a sermon or testimony, or it can emerge from some other impulse. Songs that follow from the impetus of words assume a kind of speech rhythm that is not so much natural (or conversational) as stylized to fit the sense of metrical rhythm and periodicity. Such stylized speech rhythms generate the momentum that produces strictly measured speech rhythms. But where no such explicit rhythms are found, the moaning impetus flies more freely upon the wings of the sound; these wordless sounds and vocal gestures implicate what can, in their richest forms, become a variegated surplus of meanings. Of course, the most rhythmically and verbally articulate songs are not altogether separate and distinct from hollers, cries, and moans with only a word here or there, and vice versa. Certain songs and certain style traditions draw from both wells.

Chapter 5 described four analytical categories of rhythmic movement which, though grounded in vocal gestures and spoken words, can be described and appreciated in "purely musical" terms. This chapter attends more closely to the musical implications of words themselves as shapers of pitch, rhythm, and timbre. This speech-inflected style of vocal performance occurs, of course, in

forms that are more chantlike, such as intoned prayers, sermons, and testimonies, as well as within the frames provided by musical forms. At various
turns, songs and hymns either offer sharp distinctions between the wordless
cries of the penitent and the Standard English of Watts-style evangelical hymns
(as well as the rhymes and rhythms of black English), or they mingle them
together.[1] As an essential correlate to the black English used in congregational
songs (along with the Bible itself), Dr. Watts hymns became the chief musical
point of cross-influence between the African American oral tradition and the
written tradition of Standard English. Yet as a formal tradition of sacred, non-
canonic writings, the hymns stand apart from the black English (or African
American Vernacular English [AAVE]) that Rickford and Rickford—after
Claude Brown—have called Spoken Soul (2000). The latter has, of course,
developed from the interaction between British and American colonial dialects
and those from African and creole sources. Being a mediating form between
black and white traditions, and between performed speech and songs proper,
Dr. Watts hymns played a role in fomenting the plethora of African American
vocal styles prior to their twentieth-century emergence as the world medium of
popular culture. Chapter 2 made the point that the distinctiveness of Dr. Watts
hymns is greatly due to their footing in the English literary tradition. And like
the King James Version of the Bible, they have become a primary source for the
phrases and phrase patterns that are common to black worship. Regarding the
biblical influence, Henry Mitchell has quipped that "the flow and phraseology
of the King James Version will never die in America while Black Christianity
stays Black" (1970: 173). As this chapter illustrates, the linguistic-musical influence of Dr. Watts hymns upon African Americans is most obvious in the discursive pattern by which believers have committed hymn texts to memory and
have drawn upon them freely for the rhetoric of sacred songs and sayings.
Developing this theme, I further argue that such linguistic/musical interactions can be traced throughout the lineage of African American musical forms,
from the spirituals (what W. E. B. Du Bois called "sorrow songs") through blues
and jazz to the contemporary hip-hop scene, rap in particular.

    In the divisive controversy over the origins of the spirituals, the presence
of Standard English in hymns and, to a lesser extent, in spirituals has been
summoned as a politicized claim in support of white origins. Likewise, the
notion of African or Creole language sources for the vocabulary, grammar,
or pronunciation of the spirituals has been proffered in support of black
origins.[2] I wish to pursue neither course, but to explain how African Americans
have used both the Standard English of Watts-style hymns and the Spoken
Soul of the spirituals as complementary facets of an American worship context that is African-derived.

    In regard to the hymns, words and moanlike vocal sounds may be used
separately from or in combination with the alternating call-and-response
between words chanted solo and the same lines sung by the congregation.

After the completion of the hymn verse(s), the group may continue to softly moan the hymn tune as the "pray-er" begins to pray. Likewise, individual or group moans may function as ambient and improvised responses to the prayer. Concerning the use of words of hymns without the tunes, prayers often begin with an exact quotation of a hymn verse or couplet, which serves to frame the prayer event as a solemn, sacred, and personal utterance directed by the individual to God on behalf of the group. In a practical rhetorical sense, one may also see these solitary quotations as a formulaic moment, a purposeful stall for time, during which the prayer leader gathers his or her thoughts and attention and directs them toward the feeling and rhetoric of the prayer moment. For example, Walter Simmons, a praise-house elder among the Gullah people of Daufuskie Island (South Carolina), prefaced his eloquent and moving prayer with two verses he had memorized from the hymn "The Day Is Past and Gone."

> De day is past an gone.
> An de evenin shall appear
> Oh, may we all remember well
> When de night of death draw nigh.
>
> We-we'll lay our garment by
> And upon our bed to res,
> An soon, death will corrode us all
> An what we have possessed. (Quoted in Rickford and Rickford 2000: 42)

Rickford and Rickford comment about Simmons's preface and prayer: "His grammar, with the exception of a few zero copulas and unmarked pasts, is relatively standard" (44). I would also offer that this gesture of beginning with a statement rendered in the King's English—other than the King James Bible—establishes a rhetorical tone of formality that casts its influence upon the ornate word choice, balanced sentence structure, and, parallelisms that follow in the prayer. The tone, structures, and form of this prayer are similar both to those Walter Pitts observed in Afro-Baptist churches in Central Texas (1993), and to the prayer transcribed by Andrew Polk Watson that is quoted at length in chapter 1. In moods that are less meditative and more celebratory, hymn texts are also frequently quoted during the climax of black Baptist or Pentecostal sermons. In this way did the performance of "Amazing Grace" heard in *Dr. Watts* no. 7 emerge from the peroration of a sermon by the Rev. B.W. Wilson; he first quoted the verses of the hymn, then asked the hymn choir (of Boyd Hill Church, Rock Hill, South Carolina) to follow by singing as he lined them out in couplets. Whether as words alone, as wordless vocal gestures, or as an intermingling of both, the old-time hymns serve a function in black worship tradition that is distinct from yet complementary to the songs, which are sung in the language of the people.

Chapter 5 addressed the musical implications of Geneva Smitherman's theory of "songified speech"; this chapter is primarily concerned with the oral-literary framework that sustains the same phenomenon. In keeping with the musical focus of this entire study, I am concerned here not with the oral tradition as language, per se, but with its implications for vocal performance. However, a summary of the linguistic features most relevant to the composition and performance of songs will provide a basis for considering the triangular interrelationships among black song as a distinctive palette of wordless vocal sounds, the King's English of Watts hymns, and the language of Spoken Soul.

While linguists debate the relative degrees of British, African, and indigenous American influence upon Spoken Soul, they widely concur that AAVE is a distinctive language tradition with its own vocabulary, pronunciation, and grammar. Several recent sources provide lexical references for this body of words and phrases, which is in a continual state of rapid change, based upon demographics of age and social class as well as geographic region and locale (see Major 1994, Smitherman 1998, Folb 1980, and Dillard 1977). While "the distinctiveness of AAVE does not reside in the structure of its sentences," grammatical features that occur frequently in this tradition include plural *s* and *dem* ("John and *dem*" = "John and his friends"), existential *i's* ("*i's* a lot of girls" = "there are a lot of girls"), absence of third-person-singular present tense *s* ("he go" = "he goes"), absence of possessive *'s* ("that girl *house*" = "that girl's house"), invariant *be* ("*he be* talkin' all the time" = "he is constantly and continually talking"), zero copula or the absence of *is* or *are* ("people crazy!" = "people are stone crazy!"), negative forms and constructions ("I ain't" = "I am not"), and double-subject pronouns ("my mother, she told me" = "my mother told me") (Rickford and Rickford 2000: 109–28).

Black vocabulary sharply divides blacks and whites and bridges different black social classes. This distinctive identity of black vocabulary is most fully represented in its patterns of pronunciation, and, perforce, it is these sound-producing factors that have exerted the most basic and primary effect on the sound of black singing. Such features include the pronunciation of diphthongs (two-vowel sequences) as monophthongs (a single vowel) (*I* = *ah*), deletion of *l* and *r* after vowels (*he'p* = help and *yo'* = your), and the deletion of final consonants. Regrettably, although pronunciation or, more broadly speaking, phonology is the strongest linguistic marker of identity, it is the least thoroughly analyzed element of Spoken Soul. This is especially unfortunate since the phonological character of AAVE plays a major role in generating the vocal colors that have become signatures of black singing style.

The coupling between the complex social and legal significance of the black body in North American history as well as the colonial era in general (see Fanon 1967) and the obvious function of the body as a sound-producing instrument in communication and musical performance emphasizes the tendency of speech and music to function in tandem as the strongest markers of ethnic identity. Because this element of ethnic difference, which has been ever-present in the speech and song of African–Americans, is presently increasing rather than decreasing, it is crucial to understand and interpret its cultural foundations (Rickford and Rickford 2000: 221–29).

TEXTS IN CONGREGATIONAL SONGS AND DR. WATTS HYMNS

Musicologists have acknowledged the importance of speech rhythms to black music from the blues forward, but the focus of the analysis has not explained their primacy (Monson 1996, Brothers 1997). The obscurity of the hymns—despite their affinity to the spirituals that have been reinvented as a concert form—typifies the hidden significance of speech to black music. Proceeding from an English tradition that was no less oral in derivation (see chapter 2), the performance tradition of Dr. Watts hymns brought to an African oral inheritance a heightened awareness of English poetic meters and rhyming patterns, along with a racialized theology, which slaves revitalized and subverted as their own voice of liberation.

The slaves freely adapted the hymns to African patterns of music and worship along the lines of the speech-movement continuum discussed in chapter 5—portraiture sound and poetic, lyrical, and percussive rhythms. By insinuating English iambic verse forms (long, common, and short meter and their variants), the hymns promoted an ongoing process of cross-fertilization between melodies from written sources circulating between 1750 and 1850 and African approaches to music, narrative, and ritual. This African American sense of ritual time strategically integrates formulaic patterns into ways of singing that situate a range of actions—from speaking to singing to movement and dance—within the mood or frame of particular worship moments.

Written hymns and orally transmitted songs are complementary forms that have brought to black worship differing formulaic patterns that interact in the ritual context. Because they are ceremonially read from books, hymns in the opening devotions of black Baptist tradition initiate worship as a formally structured event. By contrast, orally transmitted songs stress the eminence of God by situating the particulars of utterance and action as precisely as possible within the immediate sense of a worship moment. While speech patterns are formulaic, and those of songs even more so, hymn texts are even more rigorously formulaic, as well as fixed in structure and form. Hymns and songs balance the character of black Baptist communities as outgrowths of both the antistructure[3] inherent in outdoor covert gatherings during the slave era and the formally structured and self-governing church bodies, with buildings and bylaws, that followed Emancipation. Therefore the abiding principle of the black Baptist old-time worship tradition not only welcomes but thrives upon the creative tensions that prevail between decorum and intimacy. As with all traditions, there is a sense of "this is the way we do it here." But new ideas are seldom dismissed without a hearing. Thus, in the best instances, the climate of synthesis that brought together African-derived song forms with English evangelical hymns continues.

Hymns and songs also complement each other in a more distinctly musical sense, which, unlike the differences in ritual function, apply not to the regional style as a whole but to the singing styles of individual song leaders. Whereas hymns are more often heard in portraiture sound or poetic rhythms, the regularity of a song beat is carried in lyrical and percussive rhythms. However, depending upon the gifts and disposition of the lead singer(s), any of the rhythms along the speech-movement continuum can be heard in songs or hymns.

Although hymns and songs complement each other, both genres are subject to the regional pairing between a given speech community and its vocal style. A most graphic example of such contrasts is that between song performances in Gullah communities along the South Carolina coast and those in midlands and Piedmont communities to the north and west.[4] While certain songs are shared across regions, the vocabulary, pronunciation, and grammar—along with the repertories and musical styles—differ markedly. In turn, this association between speech communities and musical styles provides an additional course for further examination of migratory patterns and other change factors. "Run, Mary, Run" and "Sign of the Judgment," two selections from Gullah communities (both heard on *Wade in the Water,* vol. 2), are both couched in symbol-rich, African-style metaphors and feature the layered sound of interlocking rhythms that produce a driving intensity. This kind of rhythmic climate implicates the movement of sacred dance as both an invitation and a potential response to the descent of the Spirit upon the worshipers. The Gullah shout-style performances deemphasize the ornate (but not necessarily *ornamental*) vocal gestures and parallel harmonies that can be heard in songs and hymns from other style areas throughout the Southeast. For example, the song "I Got a Race to Run," which is commonly heard in upland areas, puts its message more directly and less symbolically, the pronunciation pattern is far less basilectic (diverging from Standard English) than that in the Gullah performance, and the rhythmic phrasing is persistent, understated, and lyrical rather than emphatically percussive and tersely repetitive.[5] At least, at the beginning of the song the rhythmic spaces between phrases do as much as the words themselves to set a rhetorical tone, which suggests that something essential is being "said" in the song. This kind of singing—or playing, for that matter (compare the pithiness, for instance, of a Miles Davis solo on "My Funny Valentine")—draws the listener in, as it slyly yet powerfully summons and commands attention.[6]

In both traditions—low country and uplands—if the song is to be sustained for any significant length of time, its words must be freighted with something important to be said. Within the decorum of Baptist worship, a thought pressing upon a speaker may be repeated verbatim only so often. Therefore, the repetition outlined in the song's rhythmic pattern frames the idea in a socially accepted mode, wherein others will indeed help the leader say what is urgent upon the heart. In this way, while a certain song may "worry" some singer for days or even weeks, others may also come to mind more immediately in the worship moment. The opening words, whether exclaimed or half-whispered, are uttered by an individual leader somewhere between the modes of speech and song. Some leaders will introduce the song they are about to sing by saying, "I wont you to he'p me *say* a little bit o' this song." What is also significant about the dialect I have tried to represent here is that the saying of it assumes a certain rhythmic posture and lilt that is understood as a common referent for speech and, by extension, singing. Therefore, songs become a way of patenting or stylizing rhythms that are already latent in the informal language of the speech community.

As the leader repeats and varies the song's phrases, there is growing emphasis upon more distinct rhythms and pitches that can easily be replicated. This "catchiness" is not incidental but rather is essential to the ritual function of participatory worship, in which singers must rely solely upon their own bodily resources for the achievement of a full and tightly coordinated sound. These replicable patterns are the source of the many rifflike rhythms that have become idiomatic to black music. As the congregation joins with the song leader in succeeding lines, what was first stated as personal and particular experience is, by the second or third line of the song, a group affirmation that, for instance, "all of God's children got a race to run." This group entry, occurring normally in the second portion of the first line, is the point at which songs or hymns are effectively "raised," or sounded en masse by the congregation.

Text	*Syllables*	*Stress pattern*
Got a *race* to *run,* I got a *race* to *run*	11	2 + 2
All of God's children got a *race* to *run*	10	4 + 2
Got a *race* to *run,* I got a *race* to *run*	11	2 + 2
(I say) *All of God's children* got a *race* to *run*	12	4 + 2

You cain't run it for me, got a race to run, etc.
Momma cain't run it for me, got a race to run, etc.
King Jesus gonna run it with me, got a race to run, etc.
Pray for me on-a this journey, I got a race to run, etc.

This particular text is a simple yet pointed affirmation of the life journey as a pilgrimage that compels each believer as well as the whole congregation to action. This active rather than passive response to what is said in the song is critical to the performance aesthetic of black music and worship (see Maultsby 1991). The song is expected to generate the character of body movement that James Weldon Johnson describes as swing.[7] While this quality of body movement and swing is "playfully" improvisatory, it is not lighthearted. Instead, the resolute tone of the saying is comparable to that heard in such well-known spirituals as "Done Made My Vow to the Lord" and "Don't You Let Nobody Turn You 'Round."

The power of the song to move a congregation hinges upon the leader's ability to convey, through combinations of speech and movement, the song's feeling to the congregation as shared experience. Only by gathering the minds of the people into a unified rhythmic and spiritual moment—by bringing the people into one accord—can a song gain the singular force of proclamation. Thus, the songs begin slowly and without apparent rhythmic impetus. Then, with each iteration, the key phrase—the "mascom," or concentrated expression of a widely held idea or sentiment, in this case "a race to run"—gains in rhythmic impetus. In this way a pregnant thought is first stated in word, then symbolized and signified upon by the speech rhythms that bear it along in time. In this form of call-and-response the congregation reiterates and extends each new line in the pattern given out by the leader. Stemming as it does from a literal repetition of what the leader has said, the pattern represents a confluence of African call-and-response patterns with the English tradition of lining out.[8]

In performance, the ever-present "I" in "(I) got a race to run" is omitted as the understood subject in some places and, in others, stated as a point of rhetorical rhythm (see Taylor 1975). The range of verbal options for improvisation—by adding vocables or eliding syllables and words—expands in actual practice to afford the skilled leader of congregational singing a palette of rhythmic and tonal subtleties by which a congregation can be engaged in singing as a vital act of worship. Such speech rhythms are often further enlivened by the addition of portraiture sound and poetic rhythms. But of all these factors, none is more critical to the ritual outcomes than the baseline *sound* of the words themselves. Since most of the words are familiar to the congregations, the sounds as vivid aural symbols—whether slurred or sharply articulated—must convey the humanity that befits the sacred moment.

The meter of "I Got a Race to Run" includes ten to twelve syllables per line, depending upon whether the "I" is articulated. While irregular and flexible patterning makes it difficult to argue that the song is in any pure sense iambic, its accents certainly conform to this stress pattern, which is also universal in the Watts-style hymns. With or without the "I," the alliterative accents fall upon "race" and "run," and this emphatic redundancy is reinforced by

Music example 24. Transcription of "I Got a Race to Run" as sung by Rev. Waldo Robinson, Jefferson, South Carolina.

the descending third interval in which these words are always sung. (See transcription in example 24.) The greatest interruption of the iambic lilt is the musically asserted pattern of accents on each of the first five syllables in the second line (see measures 5–6). These accents being achieved through a string of syncopated notes that has become idiomatic to black music genres, the last half of the line recovers the initial pattern. The parenthetical "I say" of the fourth line is an interjection that any good song leader might place at the head of a line. Such unstressed interjections preceding stressed beats also replicate in an improvisatory structure the unaccented-to-accented pattern of iambic diction. In this way do the texts of many congregational songs betray the long shadow of English ballad meter and its variants.

While "I Got a Race to Run" is a song of moderate-to-fast tempo, the classic slow song "Sweet Home" is a more exemplary pairing of black pathos and longing with the plaint of verses drawn from popular hymns.

Text	Syllables	Accents
Sweet *home,* sweet *home*	4	2
Sweet *home,* sweet *home*	4	2
Lord, I *wonder* will I *ever* get *home*	10	4

Text	*Syllables*	*Accents*
A*maz*ing *grace,* how *sweet* the *sound*	8	4
That *saved* a *wretch* like *me*	6	3

Sweet home, sweet home
Sweet home, sweet home
Lord, I *won*der will I *ev*er get *home*

Father, I *stretch* my *hands* to *thee*	8	4
No *oth*er *help* I *know.*	6	3

Sweet home, sweet home
Sweet home, sweet home
Lord, I *won*der will I *ev*er get *home.*

The leader opens by stating the words "sweet home" and holding them as they are repeated by the congregation. Well-suited to the two-word germ of the textual idea, the two-beat pattern—coming to rest upon the second monosyllable "home" each time—graciously renders the lilt of iambic prosody. The sequence is repeated, then all join in the pensive closing line that includes ten syllables. Though not strictly iambic, the weight of emphasis is, again, unaccented ("Lord, I") to accented ("won-der"). The anapest, "will I e-ver," precedes the penultimate "get," which gains force by its placement before the long vowel "home." Therefore, when the hymn verse enters to break the repetition, the performance is heard as a rhythmic song rather than an old-time slow hymn melody. Yet the actual pace of the words is slow enough to savor the sense of each syllable like a performed moment frozen in time. Through the verse form of "Sweet Home," which lifts out the opening couplet from each of two familiar hymns rather than the full quatrain, the singers can evoke the full meaning of those hymns without having to include the remaining, equally well-known lines. In this context, the hymn couplets mark the fictive sweetness associated with "home" as earthly place or heavenly vision. Such a song is often not sung until after an especially intense worship moment or, prophetically, as an invocation of such. This kind of singing can prolong and intensify the savor of deeply felt, shared devotion that is an essential element of Christian ritual.

While the hymns most popular among black Baptists (see chapters 1, 3, and 4) emphasize the jog trot regularity of iambic feet, the stress patterns of couplets that do not derive from hymns are, like those in the songs just discussed, more freely iambic. This category would include two- and four-line "wandering verses," as Jackson calls them (1943; see his appendices 3 and 4), which are interchangeable in many different spirituals. By literal syllable count, many fit the pattern of ballad meters. A most familiar example sets forth a rhetorical contrast between the two apostles whose names and actions form alliterative pairs.

Text	Syllables	Accents
If you *cannot preach* like *Peter*	8	3
If you *cannot pray* like *Paul*	7	3
You can *tell* the *love* of *Jesus*	8	3
And *say* he *died* for *all.*	6	3

Although the syllable count of the lines resembles the form of common meter (8–6–8–6), the metrical patterns flow between iambs (-/) and anapests (—/). Similarly, a song with which this text is often paired, "There Is a Balm in Gilead," though not iambic—"there" starting as it does on a long stress that begins with an accent (somewhat equivalent to a trochee [/-] and finishing with "Gilead" on a dactyl [/—])—follows the syllable and verse pattern of ballad meter.

There is a *balm* in *Gil*ead	8	3
To *make* the *wounded whole*	6	3
There is a *balm* in *Gil*ead	8	3
To *heal* the *sin*-sick *soul.*	6	3

As an a-b-a-c rhyme form, the first line is repeated as the third line, and the second and fourth lines extend and complete the opening declaration. This use of repetition grounds the text in an oral formula that both proclaims a thought deemed worthy and facilitates memorization.

"You May Bury Me in the East," a text which Du Bois cites as one of his favorites (see the final chapter of *The Souls of Black Folk*), is still sung—with the slight verb change from "may" to "can"—in Piedmont South Carolina (see *Dr. Watts*, no. 8). It is one of only a few song forms utilized in the spirituals, and the chorus and especially the verses bear the iambic imprint. The leader begins in a speechlike singing voice that, in tandem with the group response, only defines a rhythmic tempo about halfway through the first verse. Though the phrase includes four syllables, "You can bury me" ("bury" is pronounced as one syllable) is an anapestic pattern, wherein the first two unaccented syllables are followed by a short, hard consonant on "bury" and the long appended vowel on "me." The next words, "in the east," form a balancing anapestic phrase. The repetition of this rhythmic phrasing in the following line effects a musical symmetry that intimates the spatial extremes of east and west marked off by the text. The metrical pattern also establishes a musical sequence of unaccented-to-accented beats that parallel the placement of stresses in iambic verse. The same three-syllable anapestic motif is replicated at the following line in "But I'll hear." Two regular iambs follow in "the trum-pet sound," and the anapest underscores the concluding thought "in the morning." While any number of decorations are commonly added, this first half of the chorus is a chant upon three notes: the tonic along with the fifth and sixth below it. Given its pith and brevity, the statement bears almost exact repetition. However, as the first utterance is more the leader's statement, the congregation embraces the text when it is restated and the sound of the lead voice, which is heard an octave higher the second time, rises as a soaring descant above the whole.

Based upon the way stressed and unstressed words can be ordered, elongated, or elided, each succeeding statement of the song's chorus, no matter how similar to the previous one, establishes its own linear sense of rhythmic identity. These slightly changing repetitions of the same pattern create and sustain rhythmic momentum. By contrast, the "wandering" verses, which are commonly transferred from song to song, establish relative points of fixity, focusing upon a textual idea that is more familiar but less predictable in its occurrence than the prevailing chorus. This may explain why the chorus and its variations are repeated as the tempo gradually increases from quarter note = 90 bpm to about 120. From this point of rhythmic equilibrium, verses are added, and one is less aware of the continued acceleration that reaches 140 bpm before the song's conclusion.

Text	Syllables	Accents
You can *bury me* in the *east*	7	3
You can *bury me* in the *west*	7	3
But I'll *hear* the *trumpet sound* in the *morn*ing	7 + 4	5
You can *bury me* in the *north*	7	3
You can *bury me* in the *south*	7	3
But I'll *hear* the *trumpet sound* in the *morn*ing	7 + 4	5
Gonna *sound* so *loud* till it *wake* up the *dead*	11	4
But I'll *hear* that *trumpet sound* in the *morn*ing	7 + 4	
Sound so *loud* till it *wake* up the *dead*	9	4
But I'll *hear* the *trumpet sound* in the *morn*ing	7 + 4	
In the morning, in the morning	4 + 4	1 = 1
I'll *hear* that *trumpet sound* in the *morn*ing	7 + 4	4
On the *mountaintop*, in the *valley low*	10	4
But I'll *hear* the *trumpet sound* in the *morn*ing	7 + 4	
On the *mountaintop*, in the *valley low*	10	4
But I'll *hear* the *trumpet sound* in the *morn*ing	7 + 4	
Talk a*bout shout*ing down *here* be*low*	9	5
I'll *hear* that *trumpet sound* in the *morn*ing	6 + 4	
You *wait* until I *get* on that *other shore*	11	4
I'll *hear* that *trumpet sound* in the *morn*ing	6 + 4	
I *done* been *tempt*ed, I *done* been *tried*	9	4
But I'll *hear* the *trumpet sound* in the *morn*ing	7 + 4	
I *been* to the *Jor*dan *ri*ver and I *been* bap*tized*	13	5
But I'll *hear* the *trumpet sound* in the *morn*ing		

Text	Syllables	Accents
In the morning, in the morning	4 + 4	1 = 1
I'll *hear* that *trumpet sound* in the *morn*ing	6 + 4	
In the morning, in the morning	4 + 4	1 = 1
I'll *hear* that *trumpet sound* in the *morn*ing	6 + 4	
I'm *goin' away* [and I'm *goin'* to *stay*]	9	4
I'll *hear* that *trumpet sound* in the *morn*ing		
I *won't* be *back* till the *judg*ment *day*	9	4
I'll *hear* that *trumpet sound* in the *morn*ing		
Some coming *crip*ple, and *some* coming *lame*	10	4
But I'll *hear* that *trum*pet *sound* in the *morn*ing		
Some come-a *walk*ing in my *Je*sus *name*	10	4
I'll *hear* that *trumpet sound* in the *morn*ing		
In the morning, in the morning	4 + 4	1 + 1
I'll *hear* that *trumpet sound* in the *morn*ing	6 + 4	4
In the morning, in the morning	4 + 4	1 + 1
I'll *hear* that *trumpet sound* in the *morn*ing	6 + 4	4

Other wandering verses that might be sung with this chorus include:

Talk about *shout*ing down *here be*low	9	4
(You just) *wait* till I *get* on that *oth*er *shore*	(11) 9	4

Or:

You can *weep* like a *wil*low, *moan* like a *dove*	11	4
You *cain't* go to *heav*en 'less you *go* by *love*	11	4

A most eloquent example of the tendency in congregational singing to blend the Standard English of Watts-style hymns with the Spoken Soul of the people is the Together as One Hymn Choir selection "I Was Lost but Now I'm Found," led by Ronnie Ware (see *The Together as One Hymn Choir*).[9] Its ubiquitous tune, insistent rhythms, and wandering choruses from oral tradition mark it as, strictly speaking, a song. However, the chorus itself and several of the verses are hymn texts by the Englishmen Watts and John Newton and the Scotsman Horatius Bonar.

I was lost	(leader)
Lost but now I'm found	(chorus)
I was lost	(leader)
Lost but now I'm found	(chorus)
I was lost	(leader)
Lost but now I'm found	(chorus)
I was blind but now I see	(chorus from Newton)

The repeating chorus of the song consists of only the second couplet of Newton's "Amazing Grace," and his beloved third verse—signifying upon the legacy of slavery and racial discrimination as it acknowledges present trials—is sung as a wandering verse:

> Through many dangers, toils, and snares
> I have already come
> Was grace that brought me safe thus far
> And grace will lead me home. (Newton)

> That awful day will surely come
> The appointed hour make haste
> When I shall stand before my judge
> And pass the solemn test. (Watts)

> Goin' on down to the river
> Gonna stick my sword in the sand
> Gonna shout my troubles over
> Done made it to the promised land. (From oral tradition)

> Some say "Give me silver"
> Some say "Give me gold"
> But I say "Give me Jesus"
> To save my dying soul. (From oral tradition)

> I heard the voice of Jesus say
> Come unto to me and rest
> Lay down, thy weary one, lay down
> Thy head upon my breast. (Bonar)

The borrowed chorus signifies upon the black rhetorical penchant for paired opposites (lost-found, blind-see), and in the recorded performance its effectiveness as a song germ causes one to forget about the still more common couplet, preceding it in the hymn: "Amazing grace how sweet the sound / That saved a wretch like me." For those who are skeptical about the rampant borrowing of copyrighted material in rap music, this kind of practice may pose a possible cultural precedent, whereby what is highly esteemed from sources both in *and* outside the culture becomes utilized as "mascoms" or widely accepted word-sound templates that, at best, become engorged with meanings and, at worst, become heard and felt as cliché.

The "wilderness" epoch between Emancipation and the turn of the century, when the tradition of hymn singing was ascendant in newly organized black Baptist churches, may have produced a different yet related variation upon blended sources. Singers may have composed "pre-blues" iambic hymn couplets and verses, such as the following (*Dr. Watts*, nos. 16 and 18), which are still heard in black Baptist circles. While the structure of these and other couplets heard in black churches is identical to those Jackson collected primarily among whites (1943: appendices 3 and 4), the emotional tone differs radically. I call them "pre-blues" texts because they address earthly issues of mortality, loneliness, and suffering in religious but non-Christocentric terms.

My *mo*ther's *slee*ping *in* the *tomb*	8	4
My *fa*ther's *slee*ping *too*	6	3
Be*fore* this *time* a*no*ther *year*	8	4
I *may* be *slee*ping *too*	6	3
My *work* on *earth* will *soon* be *done*	8	4
And *then* I'm *go*ing *home*	6	3
I'm *go*ing be*yond* this *vale* of *death*	8	4
And *I* won't *cry* no *more*	6	3

The tone of these songs is as dark as the poetry is plain, almost to the point of bluntness.[10] They express from a different perspective perhaps the same sense of despair Du Bois wrote about in *The Souls of Black Folk* (to which we will return shortly). Emancipation and World War I wreaked havoc upon the aspirations of those blacks who were the most socioeconomically vulnerable. Therefore, the fissures dating from slavery between the literate house servants and the oral culture of the field workers have increased with the slow growth of an upwardly mobile black middle class since Emancipation.

And black class distinctions frequently turn upon the tensions between black and Standard English.[11] In his introduction to *God's Trombones,* James Weldon Johnson tells the story of the black slave preacher who, in his sermon introduction, misappropriated the King's English to assert to his congregation in overblown language that he was going to "unscrew the inscrutable." This kind of self-deprecating humor is also heard in a tale my mother tells of a black Methodist preacher who supposedly said to his congregation in a perfect ballad-meter couplet:

My eyes are dim I cannot see
I left my specs at home.

Hearing the 8–6 iambic lilt of the words, but misunderstanding the sense of the preacher's saying, the congregation putatively raised a hymn on the text. Displeased with the futility of the misunderstanding, again, in perfect ballad-meter verse, the preacher responded,

If you don't hush I'll get my hat
And surely I'll go home.

As the story goes, they sang that too, and the preacher got his hat and went home. Whether there is a grain of truth in the story or not, it is significant that the bearer of the tale either quoted or made lines that perfectly fit the frame of ballad meter. This kind of thigh-slapping ritual of black self-denigration has persisted as a humorous yet pathetic dark side, the underbelly of the widening gap between the working poor and the middle class. Mention of this may seem unrelated to identifying speech rhythms in lining-out hymns and other forms; but the preacher who left his spectacles at home is a caricature of the rhythmic gait—what Bernard Manning calls the "jog trot"—of English iambic prosody that became incessant not only in black and white worship during the eighteenth and nineteenth centuries but within the entire American cultural scene. This sound and feeling for rhythmic speech in the English language was internalized by readers of the work of white poets, such as Emily Dickinson, and their black counterparts, such as Phyllis Wheatley and Jupiter Hammond, alike. However, the aural gait of these patterns came into black speech communities through the hymns of Watts and Wesley, and the African pattern of molding speech inflections into black song did not pass when modernity gave rise to secular blues.

FROM HYMNS TO BLUES TO RAP

Although the blues of the early 1900s broke away from the rhetorical template of iambic rhythm, the call-and-response structures and especially the sound quality of nineteenth-century hymn singing remained a basic component of blues singing styles. W. C. Handy, who through his publishing activities became known as the Father of the Blues, commented on the dialectic formed by the preacher's lining out of a hymn and the congregation's response. He felt that the impact of this sound on an unaccustomed listener "would be chaos, but at a distance the sounds merged into a strange and moving harmony" (see the full quote in chapter 4). A wailing yet stately swell of teeming sounds is apparent in Handy's description. Though what he heard in Mississippi was almost surely different in its particulars from what can still be heard in South Carolina or Texas, his concept of convergent spiraling sounds would apply there too. This notion of an expansive sense of time as a musical space where one is at liberty to make far-ranging explorations is further developed by bluesman Son House:

> People wonder a lot about where the blues came from. Well, when I was coming up, people did more singing in the fields than they did anywhere else. Time they got to the field, they'd start singing some kind of song. Tell his ol' mule, "Giddup there!" and he'd go off behind the mule, start plowing and start a song. Sang to the mule or anybody. Didn't make any difference. We'd call them old corn songs, *old long meter songs*. They'd make it sound good, too. You could hear them half-a-mile off, they'd be singing so loud. Especially just before sundown. They sure would go a long ways. Then they called themselves, "got the blues." That's what they called the blues. *Them old meter songs*.

You'd hear them talking and one would say, "you know ol' so-and-so really can sing the blues." They didn't use any instruments. Just natural voice. They could make them rhyme, though, just like the blues do now, but it would just be *longer meter.* Holler longer before they say the word. They'd sing about their girl friend or about almost anything—mule—anything. They'd make a song out of it just to be hollering. (House 1965: 45, quoted in Evans 1982: 42–43; italics mine)

House makes a strong connection among Dr. Watts, or "meter songs" as they were also known, the field hollers composed behind plow mules, and early blues. From House's thinking one can infer three stages in the development from lining out ("meter" or "long meter," as House terms it) to the blues.[12] At first, hymns (as well as hollers, work songs, and spirituals) were memorized and sung by slaves and later by sharecroppers who sang to pass the time away. The solitary settings where these people worked must have provided a nonperformative laboratory in which to explore the potentials of unaccompanied vocal singing. They also afforded introspection apart from the community focus that attended church services. The second stage of this evolution seems to have seen the "deconstruction" of the sounds of long meter and their eventual reconstruction in forms more like what have become the free-ranging imagination expressed in the lyrics and the musical structure of the blues. This transition surfaces in House's statement that, from long meter, they went on to create rhymes that sang about most anything—not only sacred topics. A structural point of transfer may also have figured in this process, whereby the three-line structure of the moans (e.g., *Wade in the Water,* vol. 2, no. 16) became the three-line formula of blues lyrics. The a-a-a form occurs in moans as well as blues, and the movement from this to the more common a-a-b blues lyric might have occurred as a signifying variation upon the older structure.

In the final stage of transition to early blues, House and other bluesmen like Charlie Patton and Robert Johnson began to master their guitars and make them "talk" out responses and accompaniments to the breath phrases that became standardized as three text lines and twelve musical bars of the blues. While such accompaniments suggested a new kind of modal-harmonic space in which to improvise melodic lines, the generative formula of these lines encompassed the rhythmic impetus of words (see Titon 1977: 178–93). In the spirituals and in certain regional styles of hymn singing, the words themselves anchor emphatic rhythmic patterns that sustain both the momentum and the expressive sense of the song. But in early blues, the rhythmic feel of the performance is established and maintained in the guitar, and its rhythms sustain both the regular sense of body rhythm that is danceable and a sense of responsiveness to vocal lines that is more speechlike. Thus, the voice itself is liberated from the time-keeping function and empowered to narrate—in what Jon Spencer might call a secular sermon—the bluesman's troubles in a freer, more lyrical counterpoint to the hard-driving feel of the guitar accompaniment (see Spencer 1996: xiii–xvii). Given this liberation of the voice from keeping time, the regularity of iambs gave way to different and more complex stress patterns in blues lines (see Titon 1977: 178–93). By such means did blues singing reinterpret the old ways of uttering words as sounds. However, the sound of the music, the "speak-singing" did not undergo radical change. The *what* of black musical expression underwent profound change in order to become the blues, but *how* sounds could be molded to encapsulate the very nuance of what words meant lost nothing in the musical and cultural transformation.

While the speech rhythms of the spirituals were enriched by the language of Dr. Watts hymns, the blues diverged from the primacy of iambic meter. However, the speakerly impetus—the voice of Spoken Soul, the language of the people—became still more pervasive in blues and subsequent black genres such as jazz, gospel, rhythm and blues, and rap. We have seen how spiritual texts either (1) freely quote couplets from familiar hymns as verses (chapter 6); (2) utilize a common stock of verse formulas that parallel the metrical patterns of common-, short-, or long-meter hymns (chapter 4); or (3) structure words in a broad range of verse forms that use these metrical patterns as tropes (chapter 5). In these ways the spirituals structure words in cyclical streams of incantation that can transform a ritual moment from a vague assemblage into an inspired communion.

While it appears to differ radically from earlier genres, rap is but a more literal representation of the song-talk sounds that link hymns, spirituals, and blues. Rap is especially distanced from prior black forms by its urban origins, the distinctly technological basis of its production, the Black Power–revolutionary locus of its rhetoric and ideas, and the more fixed distinctions in hip-hop culture among speech, singing, and beats. In its emphasis upon the manipulation of sound through electronic means, hip-hop reflects the sharpest of African American breaks to date with the agrarian cultures of the slave epoch, which placed vocalization at the center of music making. But in its use of dense, often cryptic Spoken Soul, rap music aligns itself with Gullah and other African-derived creoles as a basilectic form, far removed from Standard English. The liquid pitch inflections, the moaning sounds common to lining out, spirituals, and the blues, are replaced in rap music by a beat that replicates the hypnotic function of "chant" as a constant sound texture or background for words that occupy the foreground. Rap narratives are delivered in stylized, hard-hitting rhythms that either correspond to or produce tension in relation to background beats. The innovations of rap are also fueled by the meshing of black oral virtuosity with Latino cultures that insinuate the new creole influence of second- and third-generation immigrants from Spanish-speaking countries.

Exposed to a diverse range of influences, from the blues through jazz and rhythm and blues to rap, black religious music in general—including, to some extent, Dr. Watts hymns—has undergone periodic cross-fertilizations. Such a synthesis occurred in the 1930s when Thomas Dorsey reworked the hymn tune *Maitland,* which is paired in hymnals with "Must Jesus Bear the Cross Alone," and introduced his own text, "Take My Hand, Precious Lord," the form of which differs significantly from the former text. This seminal transfer merged the feeling and musical language of hymns and spirituals with blues style, thus inaugurating black gospel as the urban sacred counterpart of the secular blues (see Harris 1992). The same pattern has been replicated as gospel artists like Andraé Crouch in the 1960s and, more recently, Kirk Franklin continue to transgress the style boundaries between sacred and secular.

While it may not signal a trend in cross-fertilizations between hymns and rap, a striking example of this secular-sacred transfer is the recent Bobby Jones recording of the oft-lined-out hymn "What a Friend We Have in Jesus." The recording opens with a crowd cheer, followed by a bass vamp, and a backbeat. After Jones introduces emcee Donald Lawrence, the choir begins to chant:[13]

A:	*Choir's chanted call*	*Emcee's hollered response*
	A little some(th)in' for the radio	Hanh
	A little some(th)in' for the radio	Hanh
	A little some(th)in' for the saints, yo	Ah
	A little some(th)in', some(th)in' here we go	
	Say it again, say it again.	
	A little some(th)in' for the radio	Gotta back it up
	A little some(th)in' for the radio	Gotta back it up
	A little some(th)in' for the saints, yo	Gotta back it up
	A little some(th)in', some(th)in', here we go.	

After leading the choir through these texts, Lawrence introduces the soloist by saying in rhythm: "Bobby Jones on the mike." Jones then begins to chant-sing a melody that alternates between two notes for the first couplet and, in the next couplet, soars upward over a harmonic movement of rising fourths, which balances the stasis of the preceding chant.

B:

What a friend we have in Jesus	(two-note chanting pattern)
All our sins and griefs to bear.	
What a privilege it is to carry	(melodic-harmonic movement)
Everything to God in prayer.	

After a harmonized choral repetition of B, the choir repeats the rap figure of A and a return of the hymn's second verse as the B section. From this point, the song moves to a series of vamps (the gospel equivalent of jazz riffs) that complete the performance's three-part formulaic course. While the core of gospel music, like most sacred music genres, is resiliently conservative, the rhythmic feels of rap music are fast encroaching upon the accepted bounds of "contemporary" gospel.

Although deeply rooted systems of cultural signification sustain the most conservative features of black style traditions, larger forces for change exert pressure upon what remains of black culture as an autonomous American tradition. As a body of traditions that have both signification for African Americans and value as a commodity in the global marketplace of multinational corporations, black music has accumulated, in the phrase of Thomas Brothers, "meaning in the service of power." This aspect of his analysis is founded upon Charles Keil's Marxist notion of an "appropriation-revitalization process" (see Keil 1966: 43–47). "In response to white appropriation of their music, African American musicians revitalize core values. From the revitalization comes a new style that is eventually appropriated and the process continues" (Brothers 1997: 201). Although speech-song continues to pervade black music genres, the popular culture is relentlessly compressing once-profuse regional speech traditions into smaller and smaller areas. At the same time, modern media is melding the old speech communities into ever newer and larger consumer markets for popular music—a practice that is apparent in the movement from hymns and spirituals to blues, jazz, and rap. Nevertheless, while the regional basis of rap styles is urban-centered and national in scope, the speech-music correlation continues to hold between rap-style traditions and the dialects that are specific to their cities of origin (Rickford and Rickford, 2000: 85–88).

"SORROW SONGS" AND THE AESTHETIC FALLACY

Perhaps so little attention has been given to the relationship between black speech and song because cultural and political arguments for either the respectability of Standard English or the authenticity of black English have dominated public discourse on the subject. In this context, various regional dialects have been either positively or negatively associated with black speech from the agrarian epoch of slavery. Negatives have accrued from the language of works such as *Uncle Tom's Cabin* by Harriet Beecher Stowe, and from the black images portrayed through white-face minstrelsy (Toll 1974). Positive images first emerged in the writings of abolitionist chroniclers like Frederick Douglass (1845), Thomas Wentworth Higginson (1870), and William Francis Allen (1867), and later in those of W. E. B. Du Bois (1903;

see Du Bois 1997) and black renaissance writers James Weldon Johnson (1925) and Zora Neale Hurston (1934).

However, neither viewpoint has led to a discussion of the emergence, by degrees, of song from speech in the spirituals, Dr. Watts hymns, and subsequent genres of black music. One can speak of "degrees of song" because black vocal genres span the gamut from conversational speech, recitation, chant, and song to exclamation (see List 1963). Yet in this continuum, less song does not always equal less music. Instead, vocalists and musicians have adumbrated, in the categories described in chapter 5, a stunning range of shadings that merge sounds of definite and indefinite pitch.

The lack of musical attention to the prevalence of speech rhythms in music before 1900 may follow from what Radano (1996) calls "the inscription of difference." Because they are, by nature, fluid and constantly shifting in metrical and metronomic accent, speech rhythms interpose a rhythmic tension into music that is often in conflict with the motor rhythms of body movement and dance. Especially when several such rhythms are combined either with or against a prevailing beat, creative tensions often ensue between cacophony and unity. What we may call a "mythology of difference" accrued to early writings on the spirituals, which therefore obfuscate as much as elucidate how the songs are made.

Various means of writing ethnic and musical difference into the spirituals and reading them as worth, rather than liability, were presaged in Douglass's *Narrative of the Life of Frederick Douglass, an American Slave,* and culminated half a century later in Du Bois's *The Souls of Black Folk.* Born a slave, Douglass parlayed reading and writing into obtaining his freedom, and his oratorical skills led him to become the chief spokesman for the abolitionist movement. His narrative "challenges the minstrel theme of the happy 'Sambo' and makes palpable and nearly audible the anguished resonances of slave singing" (Radano 1996: 506). Douglass's decision to become literate, made after overhearing his owner say, "If you teach that nigger how to read, there would be no keeping him," may be seen as a revolutionary recognition of personal empowerment toward political ends. However, the kind of way with words embodied in congregational songs is far more indirect and less subject to rational comprehension than was Douglass's decision. *Many early accounts of black singing therefore emphasize its difference from the accepted norms.*

Offering an apology for their musical transcriptions in *Slave Songs of the United States,* William Francis Allen and his coauthors wrote that black singing was "as impossible to place on score as the singing of birds or the tones of an Aeolian harp" (1867). During the late 1800s, a like quality of musical expression was sketched by various authors as "the songful 'heart religion' of black orality" (Radano 1996: 508). Radano also argues that such perceptions of the ineffable in black song arose from the Romanticism

of Johann Gottfried Herder, who saw in folk genius a fulfillment of the orig-
inary trope of authenticity, "a free spiritual truth emanating from the time-
less impulses of nature" (512). American philosophers such as Emerson
and Whitman followed in this thinking; and by the turn of the century Du
Bois was emboldened to call these songs "the most beautiful expression of
human experience born this side of the seas" (Du Bois 1997: 186). However, notation of the spirituals in ethnographic transcriptions and concert
arrangements reduced them to whatever could be accurately inscribed in
the Western European musical system.

By contrast, Dr. Watts hymns, which did not gain currency in written
forms, have remained an ideal site for study of the role of speech rhythms
in pre-blues genres of black music. Following Emancipation, for white audiences and for those training to become the black elite—and as a symbolic
inversion of the weak over the strong—prim-and-proper concert versions of
the spirituals were lionized as symbols of America's cultural emergence
from the European shadow. At the same time, in the rural South, black Baptist congregations continued their own songs alongside the hymns they had
learned from white Baptist missionaries. In fact, the bitter irony is that the
hymns, and the hymn books from which deacons read the lines, became
symbols of status and formality for many congregations of newly freed persons who could not read.

Du Bois captured the pathetic feeling and tone of black life during this
period in his lament from *The Souls of Black Folk,* "Of the Meaning of
Progress." The essay reflects upon his sojourn in a black rural Tennessee
community, where he had taught summer school while at Fisk University.
His makeshift classroom was the first and only learning for many of his stu-
dents, and for most the process had been arduous. The experience provided an up-close sense of the hardness of post-Emancipation life for rural
black folk. Such were the times and places that gave rise to Dr. Watts hymn
singing as an institutionalized form among black Baptists, apart from the
oversight of white missionaries. Also while teaching summer school, Du
Bois visited the churches from which he gleaned his famous trilogy of black
worship, "the preacher, the music, and the frenzy." These common folk
moaned out their hymns and sang songs in dialect, and some form of the
latter accompanied the dance or "shout" that the young scholar saw as
"frenzy." However, Du Bois saw as the highest musical expression of black
folk not these complex but rough-hewn acts of worship but the Fisk Jubilee
Singers, who sang polished arrangements of spirituals in concert halls to
critical acclaim and whose international success raised the funds to build
Jubilee Hall and saved the university from bankruptcy. Thus Du Bois linked
the unadorned songs themselves to the hardness of life in rural Tennessee
and the reinvented versions of what he dubbed "sorrow songs" to the hard-
won legacy of black progress.

This distinction between the politically voiceless masses of black folk and the college-educated "talented tenth" is graphically portrayed in the organization of *The Souls of Black Folk*. Each of its fourteen chapter epigraphs juxtaposes a text from European or American literature with the opening measures of a spiritual, or "sorrow song," printed without words. This music-only metaphor acknowledges the duality whereby African sounds, articulating English words, have forged an African American musical aesthetic. The connection symbolizes the author's formulation of "double consciousness" (his insight that, because of the effects of racism, African Americans perceive themselves from two perspectives: their own and that of the dominant white culture around them) as both an abiding tension and a point of solidarity among black folk at disparate rungs of the socioeconomic ladder. The gesture also embraces the social dynamic whereby voices of difference are silenced in favor of entities that speak Standard English. Therefore, given the popular currency of white minstrelsy as a caricature of black life, white audiences could only receive the worship songs of black people through the distancing of their reinvention as concert spirituals. So rendered, they became for Du Bois the "sorrow songs." Contradicting the prevailing negative currents, he explained: "The music of Negro religion is that plaintive melody, with its touching minor cadences, which, despite caricature and defilement, still remain the most original and beautiful expression of human life and longing yet born on American soil" (Du Bois 1997: 149).

However, the presentation of musical transcriptions without texts conceals the articulate rhythmic impetus that black hymns and songs gain from the speech-movement continuum. The omission of words is ironic yet telling because the emergence of the spirituals, through literary inscription, had already marked a beginning point for what remains a persistent duality between denigration and valorization of these songs. In the writings of Douglass, Higginson, Allen, and Du Bois, the songs became musical treasures, albeit stored in "rude and barbarous" speech. Among white intellectuals, however, the hegemony of inscription had gained ascendancy throughout the nineteenth century and, for the white masses, minstrelsy abetted the myth of black inferiority that could justify Jim Crow segregation and its enforcement through official power and vigilante violence. Thus, when *The Souls of Black Folk* was published in 1903, the dialects of the spirituals were tainted with the stigma of negative images. Paul Laurence Dunbar was struggling, in vain, to transcend his early acceptance as a dialect poet; James Weldon Johnson, in his preface to *God's Trombones,* would later comment on the expressive limitation of black dialect to the extremes of either pathos or humor.

Though Du Bois sought to oppose the myth of happy slaves, the spirituals that he called "sorrow songs," like the blues that followed, moaned out the issues of life and often transcended them through celebration. Perhaps by design, he acknowledged few distinctions between the congregational songs that he heard in the rural communities and their reinvention through concert performances. The conflicting "rudeness" and "beauty" of the unadorned songs created an aesthetic tension only relievable in the realm of symbols. For Du Bois, that symbol was Jubilee Hall on the Fisk campus, which "seemed ever made of the songs themselves, and its bricks were red with the blood and dust of toil" (Du Bois 1997: 265).

Du Bois's turn of phrase transforms the stench of death and degradation into a redemptive symbol by diverting the reader's attention to the building, paid for with funds raised by the Jubilee Singers. For Du Bois, this redemption was as much social as it was aesthetic. Though he realized the importance of the songs he heard in rural Tennessee, his concluding chapter, "Of the Sorrow Songs," exults in what the songs had become. Du Bois merges the aspirations of the black masses with the status symbols of the elite in a mode of psychosocial and historical criticism that is both transcendent and particular. However, the absence of knowing attention to the benighted dialect of the spirituals in this closing essay, along with the absence of these same texts from the epigraphs, silences the very *folk* for whom he claimed to speak.[14]

Du Bois rightly heard the African character of spirituals, but his writings do not tell us how they might have been African. Olly Wilson (1974), Portia Maultsby (1991), and others have noted the elements of musical style—call-and-response structures, cross-rhythms, timbral variance, and improvisation, for example—that mark both African and African American musicality. But we cannot discern from Du Bois or others of his era enough of the spoken language that has held these disparate forces in aesthetic balance.

Continuing developments in black vocal style—each reinterpreting the gestures of song-talk to accommodate overall linguistic and socioeconomic change—seem to confirm the aesthetic fallacy in the symbolism of Du Bois. The juxtaposition of African music with English texts in his epigraphs stood well for the Romantic sign of duality that Du Bois articulated in the notion of double consciousness. But the act of speaking, and especially a black way of speaking, has remained essential to music and ritual as performance among African Americans. A younger contemporary of Du Bois, Zora Neale Hurston, certainly understood the significance of speech and especially dialect to the essence of black preaching and singing, although she did not posit any system of relationships between language and music. However, given the contentious debate in her time over black and white origins for the spirituals, she did not, perhaps could not, acknowledge the influence of Wattsian hymnody upon the spirituals' stress and rhyming patterns. Walter Pitts notes that intoned prayers and sermons begin in tersely rhythmic formulations of Standard English that give way to increasing use of black English as the passion and intensity moves from speech to chant (1993:

132–54). Such genres move from formal and measured phrasing toward the celebratory gestures of intoned speech and, driven by percussive rhythms, often culminate in spirit possession.

In his theory of rhythm in the spirituals, James Weldon Johnson makes an appropriate connection between rhythm and the bodily movements associated with work and play. However, many of the articulate structures as well as the subtleties of African American vocal style result from the interaction of the motor rhythms associated with body movement with the less predictable rhythms of speech. The tensions or rhythmic counterpoint between motor rhythms and speech rhythms, which are present but understated in hymns and songs, were heightened with the advent of the blues. Therefore early bluesmen merged what Brothers calls "the two sign vehicles of speechlike song and the polyrhythmic paradigm, each closely associated with African-American ethnic identity" (1997: 181).

The issue of social and economic validation—a cultural politics of ethnic equality—seems more complicated now than it was when Du Bois, Johnson, and Hurston wrote. However, the politics of culture precipitate a continuing discourse, with recurrent questions, about the meaning of the signs. In every epoch, the volatile question "Is it really music?" has been successively raised—about Dr. Watts, spirituals, gospel, and rap, as well as blues and jazz. Robert Walser and Tricia Rose pursue answers to the question in reference to rap, and certainly Antonin Dvorak, Henry Krehbiel, and others answered for the spirituals in their epoch. But the continuing dual signs—Brothers' speechlike song and polyrhythmic paradigm—seem to link the sharp distinctions in performance contexts of, first, hymns and songs; later, blues and jazz, gospel, and rhythm and blues; and finally funk and rap. Brothers argues that "aurality in African-American culture fosters the speechlike inflections of the blues, while literacy fosters a different set of musical values. The association of speechlike inflections with aurality may lie behind the class-based rejection of blues" (1997: 189).

Changes in folk and popular music traditions correspond to the rapidly shifting character of black English, and both reflect the interrelations of class and race in American culture. Black English has, of course, changed at a far more rapid rate than the relatively "sacred" conventions of Standard English. Therefore, the currency of popular music culture, which is driven by change as either a matter of novelty or true innovation, has galvanized around a multinational commerce in various world music traditions that employ the dual signification of rhythms that implicate body movement in conflict with or complemented by speechlike song.

Brothers has also, perhaps unintentionally, added to the popular comparisons of jazz saxophonist Charlie Parker with Beethoven by reference to the improvisations of the former as "the apotheosis of black aurality" (1997). He persuasively argues that Parker and the ragtime composer Scott

Joplin found alternative means of enjoining black oral and white written traditions: while Joplin adapted African American rhythms and feeling to European musical forms and notation, Parker's genius was in the adaptation of European harmonic-melodic resources to the inherent aurality of African American music. In this brilliant insight, Brothers has unintentionally gestured toward something that is at once attractive and repugnant in the crossover appeal of African American music: the question "Is it music?"—a question that was certainly raised about the bebop "revolution" associated by the media with Parker and trumpeter Dizzy Gillespie.

Something at once as commonplace and complex as speech rhythms underlies the feral notion of *difference* that has attended this musical tradition. Where so utilized, speech rhythms do not stand alone but, functioning in counterpoint with the embodied rhythms of dance, generate the polyrhythmic character of African American music. While in this chapter I have sought to describe aspects of this phenomenon, adequate treatment of its profuse occurrences in the various genres of black music will require much specialized study. Nevertheless, we can see in the historical movement from genre to genre a dual insistence upon articulate plainness and, at the same time, the inherent tensions and conflicts between the rhythmic attributes of various speech genres (English and African derived) and movement. The next two chapters set these ideas into perspective by viewing them in their fully integrative social and musical contexts that are not sharply defined by either genre or category.

PART II

The Proverbial Forest

Webs of Significance in African American Music Making

> *Sing for joy; O heavens, for the Lord has done this;*
> *Shout aloud, O earth beneath.*
> *Burst into song, you mountains,*
> *You forests and all you trees,*
> *For the Lord has redeemed Jacob,*
> *He displays his glory in Israel.*
>
> ISAIAH 44:23 *(New International Version)*

Chapter 7

"I Heard the Voice of Jesus Say"

The Singing Life of the Reverend Doctor
C. J. Johnson (1913–1990)

I heard the voice of Jesus say
"Come unto me and rest;
Lay down, thy weary one, lay down
Thy head upon my breast."
I came to Jesus as I was,
Weary and worn and sad;
I found in him a resting place
And he has made me glad.

HORATIUS BONAR, *1857*

The regional network of black singing styles is a patchwork of unified diversities that have been particularized through personal experiences lived out in religious communities. These styles are unified musically by common elements that are African-derived, and socially by the economic conditions of slavery and its aftermath. The diversities arise from regional and local variations in ecology, culture, and language.[1] The various style traditions are further particularized in myth-making and self-referential expressions that encapsulate personal experience in songs, which are embraced and affirmed by entire worshiping communities. It is beyond the scope of this book to closely examine the dynamics of personal interaction within communities; that would be an ethnographic project unto itself. But the autobiographical narrative of the preacher and songwriter C. J. Johnson that closes this chapter may provide an integrated personal perspective and social framework—a case in point, as it were—for observing the complementary roles of hymns and songs in a narrative context that interweaves singing and worship with other life experiences. Rev. Johnson's life also serves as a paradigm of the black middle class that began to develop in the second generation after slavery, a time of great social and economic upheaval for African Americans, and as a metaphor for the resiliency of the old hymn-singing traditions in changing times.[2]

While African ritual and musical practices were observed on ships traversing the Middle Passage across the Atlantic and in the New World throughout the slave era, the regional traditions in America that, in some measure, still continue came to public notice in the period between Emancipation and World War I. In that time, new black Baptist congregations proliferated amid the transitions, first from slavery to freedom, then from a labor-intensive farm economy to an urban, industrial setting. In the communities this social turbulence was reflected in the pull and tug between emergent ideals of black familyhood and the reality of nontraditional family backgrounds. The immediate context for these developments was the early stratification of classes within the black community, which has been addressed in studies such as those by E. Franklin Frazier (1964), St. Clair Drake and Horace Cayton (1945), Benjamin Mays and Joseph Nicholson (1969), and C. Eric Lincoln and Lawrence Mamiya (1990). But, building upon the slave narrative tradition, black novelists such as Zora Neale Hurston, James Weldon Johnson, Richard Wright, Alice Walker, and Toni Morrison have more nearly expressed the humanistic impact of these tensions between old and new, sacred and secular, haves and have-nots within tight-knit communities where status was often based upon skin color.

A "grandchild" of slavery who was born in 1891, Hurston gives voice to the tumult of these difficult times, quipping more than once that she had "been in sorrow's kitchen and licked out all the pots." Her first novel, *Jonah's Gourd Vine* (1934), lucidly explored several aspects of the crosscurrents that roiled African American communities in the early twentieth century. Its protagonist, John Pearson (modeled after Hurston's father), leaves home to escape the violence of his family life, the privation of sharecropping for poor whites, and the contempt of his stepfather, to whom he is "dat yaller bastard." He runs away to the plantation of Alf Pearson, a well-to-do white man who is likely his biological father and who treats him like a son. John falls in love with Lucy Potts, the precocious and gifted daughter of black landowners who take a dim view of their daughter "keeping company" with a "cross-the-creek nigger." He wins Lucy's heart and hand after he discovers and refines the way with words and the "straining voice" that will eventually make him a popular preacher and the mayor of their all-black Florida town. At the core, however, he is a "natchel man" whose compulsive philandering ultimately destroys his family and his career. Though the character portraits in *Jonah's Gourd Vine* fall below those in her best works, the novel vividly depicts the conflicted nature of life for light-skinned blacks in the early twentieth century. On one hand, they were resented both for the sexual transgressions their skin color symbolized and for the social status many of them enjoyed because of their blood ties with whites; thus any apparent character weaknesses in these children of relative ease were always magnified by dark-skinned blacks who considered themselves more upstanding and respectable. On the other hand, mulattos' physical features approximated the widely held popular notions of beauty, rooted in whiteness, to which many blacks subscribed as well.

Perhaps more than any of her contemporaries, Hurston studied and wrote about the place of black families and Baptist churches in this early transition from slavery to freedom. At the height of the Jim Crow era, during which she lived and wrote, skill in judging human character and potential was coveted by persons of influence on both sides of the racial barrier. This may account for the fact that Hurston's white folk are never all bad and her black characters are no angels. Yet in the sight of her peers, this utterly human sense of blurred lines and ambiguity marked her as an enigma and a woman of contradictions. Her observations of black church music and ritual are most important for her anthropological focus upon seeing the phenomena as they were rather than reinterpreted in the terms of those outside the culture. For example, in the essay "Spirituals and Neo-Spirituals," she venerates the spirituals as a worship medium rather than a concert form. However, this and the essays "Shouting" and "The Sanctified Church" are more polemics than scholarship or literature.[3]

Nevertheless, Hurston's observations remain prescient. She begins by setting the record straight, declaring, "The real spirituals are not really just songs. They are unceasing variations around a theme" (1981: 79). She adds that they are ephemeral and continually being composed, varied, and forgotten; that the texts cover the entire spectrum of life situations and attitudes; and that they are most faithfully performed only in a worship setting and context. Her observations were obviously written against the tide of the 1920s black renaissance, which held that the spirituals, blues, and other forms should be transformed into concert music as a means of gaining cultural respect for the Negro race. The implication of Hurston's aesthetic found popular acceptance only after the emergence of the black consciousness movement in the 1960s, when Bernice Johnson Reagon formed the award-winning ensemble Sweet Honey in the Rock. In public performances and recordings of these songs and hymns, this and similar groups such as Chicago a Cappella have adapted these forms to rehearsed performances before large audiences—as the Fisk Jubilee Singers did over a century ago—but without the felt need to transform vocal style to conform to a different aesthetic.

Hurston did not speak directly to the prominence of hymn singing in black churches.[4] She acknowledges the hymns but, perhaps because they did not seem to her sufficiently rhythmic, dismisses them as "Negroized white hymns." In a discussion of the hums and chanting sounds that attend black singing and praying, she tells us, "The [hymns] are not exactly sung. They are converted into a barbaric chant that is not a chant. It is a sort of liquefying of words. These songs are always used at funerals and on any solemn occasion." But neither my own experience nor any other account known to me indicates that hymns were sung only at funerals. Nonetheless, Hurston rightly notes that the hymns, often sung at extremely slow tempos, "liquefy" or elongate words in a degree that makes them unintelligible. Perhaps this seeming inarticulateness, coupled with the texts from white authors, prompted this profoundly articulate, word-centered woman to call the hymns "barbaric." While her observations are insightful on so many other points, she apparently did not hear even the moaning sound of the hymns as consistent with the style of the spirituals, prayers, or sermons, for she notes categorically that "Negro songs are one and all based on a dance-possible rhythm" (1981: 83). Despite the prominence of such rhythms in African American music, we can see from field hollers, blues, and certain jazz moments, as well as black hymn singing, the indefensibility of such a claim. However, it must be kept in mind that Hurston wrote from the perspectives of anthropology and literature, and not with particular attention to the musical significance of certain sounds or from the depth of perspective afforded by the historical distance from which we can view these phenomena.

While Hurston and other black commentators were drawn to black preaching and the songs called spirituals as noteworthy American expressions of an African heritage, in that politicized world of contested origins for the spiritual—which had been heralded by W. E. B. Du Bois, Henry Krehbiel, and others as the sole American folk song—the fullest descriptions of black lining-out hymns were being written by white observers such as George Pullen Jackson (1943). Among the prominent black scholars and composers of the early to mid century, only John Work, in his 1949 article "Changing Patterns in Negro Folk Songs," offered a detailed description of hymns performed in this style. In fact, no one till now has spoken, both at length and from an immersion in the culture, to the meaning and place of sacred songs and hymns in a life of work and worship.

This void may be filled in some measure by the excerpts from Rev. C. J. Johnson's life story included below.[5] It is a plainspoken but often eloquent account of a life in which the singing of songs and especially hymns was quintessentially important. In differing ways, hymns and songs intensify and transcend the performance moment and, in so doing, thread together the thematic connections arising from life experiences. This interwoven relationship between sacred singing and everyday life has led to my use of "singing" as an adjectival form in the title of the narrative, which follows the short biography. What is extraordinary about Johnson's story is not only the stories he has to tell but how he tells them. As a preacher and worship leader, he honed a way of speaking that moves easily from formality to informality, from Standard English to dialect, and from utter seriousness to raucous humor. First, however, as a preface to these narrative excerpts, some attention must be given to the larger family, social, and class issues that shaped African American life in the late nineteenth and early twentieth centuries.

REVEREND DOCTOR C. J. JOHNSON
AND THE RISE OF THE BLACK MIDDLE CLASS

Because biological slave families were subject to continual disruptions, the invisible institution of the slave church supplanted the family as the basic unit of social structure. Following Emancipation, the fifty-year period between 1865 and 1915 marked the early transition from slave conscious-ness to citizenship as both a form of political empowerment (Baraka 1963) and a new affirmation of African American familyhood as the primary unit of social organization. The first two generations of blacks born into free-dom came of age during this period. Their sense of dawning liberty was, of course, attenuated by rural-to-urban migration, social disruption, economic exigency, Jim Crow segregation, and white-on-black racial violence. Within this racist climate, true freedoms were limited to the space of one's own home, and this restriction emphasized the dawning significance of sustain-able family relationships. By 1900 the quest for economic and social status had produced a kind of black middle class, which was more a status group than a class in the strict sense.[6]

Three phases have marked the rise of a black middle class: "the period of the mulatto elite, from Emancipation to 1915, the period during which the old black middle class emerged, from 1915 to 1960, and the period of dra-matic growth and diversification in the black middle class, from the 1960s to the present" (Landry 1987: 23). Early class distinctions between blacks were rooted in antebellum differences between plantation slaves, who were often dark-skinned, and free blacks, most of whom were light-skinned mulattos. "By 1850, more than one out of every three free blacks was a mulatto, compared to less than one of ten slaves" (Frazier 1957: 273–75). Whereas almost 24 percent of American whites were middle class in 1910, only 3 percent of blacks could be classified as such. Having been freed because they were the offspring of white masters and slave women, many of these mulattos were able to translate this advantage into high-status posi-tions as skilled artisans, servants of prestigious whites, or small businessmen (Landry 1987: 24). For example, many operated barber shops catering only to whites.[7] Other members of the mulatto status group, such as Booker T. Washington and C. C. Spaulding, distinguished themselves as founders of educational institutions and businesses catering to the black community.

With the rise of a new white middle class around the turn of the century, there was a decline in the strength of relationships between the mulattos and the older white elite families, on which the status of the former had been dependent. Additionally, the white nouveaux riches also distanced themselves from the black elite by moving to the suburbs and hiring servants from the influx that brought more than twelve million Europeans to the United States between 1900 and 1920. Black job prospects in general improved only after the 1924 National Origins Quota Act had slowed the flow of European migration to a virtual halt (Landry 1987: 20). This growing ethnic alienation also created a vacuum in the delivery of goods and services by white merchants to black communities. That niche was filled by an emerging black middle class of doctors, dentists, undertakers, realtors, insurance agents, newspaper editors, and other small businessmen. In this new system, status in the black community could be secured by economic achievement rather than through family background, skin color, or white approval. During this period, a black class merger took place through marriages, chiefly of females from the older, status-conscious, light-skinned elite to males among the dark-skinned blacks whose prestige came from a college education or a white-collar job rather than ties to an old family (38–40).

Born in 1913 near Atlanta, C.J. Johnson grew up in the transition between the first two phases of black middle class development. He was a practicing preacher by the age of eight and married his wife, Elizabeth Daniel, whom he calls Sister Johnson, when still in his teens. To this union were born four children: Claude Joseph Jr., Jo Ann, Martha, and Robert Joseph.[8] The elder Rev. Johnson was dark-skinned, and Mrs. Johnson is brown-skinned. Skin color was a significant feature of one's place and status during Rev. Johnson's formative years, and it comes up repeatedly in his narrative. However, the conventional preference for light skin is often reversed. Dark-skinned blacks are singled out as role models, while those with light skin receive only passing acknowledgment. Rev. Johnson told his story in the 1980s, after the rise of the black consciousness movement; on the other hand, it is likely that, long before the 1960s, Young Claude (as he was called) and other blacks of deeper hue had learned to esteem themselves for who they were. The Johnsons' story, and those of similar black families, exemplifies the new sense of racial pride instilled by the black renaissance of the 1920s, which celebrated the new, if limited, economic advances realized by dark-skinned blacks during the period, and placed that pride in its social and economic context. Furthermore, during the early decades of the twentieth century, ministers, even more than teachers, constituted the bulk of the black middle class, especially in the South (Landry 1987: 41, 53). Hence, the Old World Asian-African sense of Christian ministry as a divine calling was increasingly juxtaposed with the privileges and responsibilities of middle-class status in a Western capitalist economy.

Black family relationships were nontraditional, in that children were often raised by grandparents, relatives, or adoptive parents in place of absent or deceased fathers, mothers, or both. Upon the death of his mother and in the absence of his father, Johnson's two grandmothers argued over who would take him and his two sisters, and his paternal grandmother, known as Aint Sarah, won out. Because she had the skill of midwifery and was moving to Atlanta, she could provide them with the greatest access to education and life opportunities. Young Claude's father, Will Johnson, was a noted teacher and leader of shape-note songs. This folk system of musical literacy, which had been widely popular among whites a century earlier, gained ascendance among blacks around the turn of the twentieth century.[9] Although Claude's earliest remembered performance was a shape-note song, his singing was more profoundly shaped by the older tradition of hymns and songs learned from his grandmother. Thus, in his story, where the father stands for failure and weakness, the grandmother signifies dogged persistence and strength, and his mother utters the prophetic word on her deathbed that Young Claude will be a preacher. In realizing the patterns of virtue learned from the grandmother, Claude becomes the "man of the house," a licensed minister, and pastor of a country church, all by the age of twelve. Yet he is not without strong male role models. These include his grandfather Deacon J. J. Johnson, the Revs. Money Lowe and J. M. Gates, and his beloved father-in-law, the Rev. Major Daniel. As a young man, Rev. Johnson blended the moral virtues he had imbued with the dogged strength of assertion that is required to hold one's own in the face of opposition. But the sum of Johnson's work—the singing life for which he is remembered—is the vibrantly positive force he exerted upon those around him. Though not without weaknesses, he apparently shunned the stereotypical preacher's sin of hunger for money, women, and power.

The most telling musical revelation in the narrative concerns the ways the songs provide a channel through which the weak, at length, find a mythical course toward victory over the strong. In Johnson's story we are reminded that the violence and perils of Jim Crow segregation often required shrewd and resourceful forms of retaliation, which could be either physical and direct, verbal and psychological, or humorous and oblique. The narrative reminds us that black sacred songs arise from conflict, not only on the epic scale of the quest for abolition or the Civil Rights movement but as a continuing means by which the spirits of men and women speak against less heralded and more personal threats to self, family, and community. In such moments of struggle and apparent defeat, the songs speak of hope reaching toward its fulfillment. The ballad sheets of Johnson's first song, "I Want to Go Where Jesus Is," that his grandmother sold for ten cents each became not only a means of popularizing the song but a symbol of economic redemption from the humiliation that provoked the songwriter.[10] Five themes recur in Johnson's narrative:

1. Stories of his family's African origins and slave past, gleaned from his grandmothers, evoke a picture of survival against all odds, and stand as

mythical markers for Johnson's perception of his own life pilgrimage as a movement through time against adversity. This quality of pride and assertiveness in holding one's own identifies him with strong role models, both male and female.

2. The narrative teems with an affectionate remembrance of the elders who have been rendered due honor in return for the surplus of attention they showed to Young Claude. This was true of his regard for the Revs. Lowe and Daniel, and especially for "Aint Sarah," whom he calls "Grandmaw," with a kind of swallowed resonance on the last syllable.[11] Being not only a woman but, at least in the memory of her grandson, fully in charge of life's unpredictability and meanness, she paradoxically commands a certain respect that refutes the patronizing moniker "Aint Sarah."[12]

3. Johnson's veneration of blackness as an aesthetic and social asset harmonizes with his own sense of self-esteem and unabashed desire for attention. Blackness and even "coal-blackness" are lifted up in his stories of Grandmaw Reid, the Rev. Money Lowe, and his father-in-law, the Rev. Major Daniel.

4. Johnson utilized education and economic uplift as a means of attaining social status and professional validation. He and many other black ministers have come to manhood with a sense of divine calling and a gift for preaching. Even when woefully unprepared for the rigors of higher education, they have sought by every possible means to obtain the social benefits of degrees and titles. Though his early marriage, full-time work, and ministry precluded the advantage of a baccalaureate program, Johnson completed in-service programs of study for ministers. In this sense, he might be seen as the mirror image of the Rev. M.L. King Sr., who, despite his hard-won academic laurels, participated in the folk preaching tradition throughout his life.[13]

5. For Rev. Johnson, writing and singing songs became a primary means of personal integration that, in the larger curve of his life achievements, carried economic, social, and psychological implications. The process was economic because, later in life, singing and songwriting became the most visible factor in his attainment of some prosperity and popularity as a revivalist and recording artist. It was social because family members were intertwined in the song-making process from his childhood to his old age. And it was psychological because, through sublimation of the song-making process, the harshness of life was transformed into redemptive experience.

As direct, even charismatic utterances of the human spirit, Johnson's songs are therefore "spirituals" in the most primal sense. Though performed in community, the best performances are driven by the impetus and unction of a song leader in whom the song has become embodied as

living reality. Whether extending downward from the sphere of divine revelation or arising upward from mundane experience, this immanent sense
of God's presence with us erases the paradoxical fine line between the particular and universal dimensions of human experience.

NARRATIVE EXCERPTS FROM THE SINGING LIFE OF THE REVEREND DOCTOR C. J. JOHNSON

My name is Claude Joseph Johnson, and I was born on May 16, 1913, in Douglasville, Georgia, which is twenty-six miles west of Atlanta. My people brought
me to Atlanta shortly after the start of World War I, when I was three years
old, and I've been here ever since. My mother is buried in Douglasville, and
I still go there to visit the old home place.

My maternal grandparents came to Douglasville, purchased 250 acres
of land five miles outside of town, and settled a farm after the time of the
Emancipation Proclamation. They had left their home around the Ogeechee
River near Savannah, bound for Alabama. But except for that general direc-
tion, my folks didn't know for certain where they were going when they left
Savannah; they just left.

Grandmother said white folks was kind of rough in Savannah after freedom. One of the reasons why the whites especially disliked our family, the
Reids—my mother was a Reid—was because they were hooked up with
some wealthy white people who owned land, and they had big farms, fine
mules, cows, and things like that. The [other] white folks didn't like it.

This same grandmother told us she came over on a boat to Cuba from
Africa. Then they moved them from Cuba to up by Savannah. There she
cooked as a slave until the Emancipation Proclamation. They stayed close
around the Ogeechee River. That's where all these little funny-talking
people that you call Geechees came from.

They married in Cuba. Her husband had been an ox driver in the sugar
cane fields. They would stack that cane on a two-wheel cart. This grandfather was very light, and my grandmother was real dark. She was coal black,
but he was real light. I saw his picture and he looked like a half-white man.
He was a builder. She said he built this little city up here called Winston,
Georgia. And, many years later, when I preached in revival up there, they
recognized me.

A Made-Up Thing

Both my grandmothers told me stories about life during slavery. The one
[grandmother] that I remember so well on my father's side was twelve years
old and in training to be a cook when Emancipation came. My mama's
mother was a grown woman birthing children in slavery, and she would sit

us down before a big ol' fireplace—about fifteen or twenty grandchildren—
and tell us all about slavery.

The slaves were sold right from under one another. Many of these songs
originated there. They knew about the Lord. So when a mother would be
sold or pass away and a child was in another part, they would get a song
together for the memory of that parent. The Bible does not give the backgrounds for but a few mothers. Mostly it always discusses the men. They very
seldom stress anything about the mothers in there. But when they brought
them into this land, they knew they loved their mothers. So they would get
in the cotton field and put it together. That is the way a lot of songs like this
one came about.

> I'm gonna leave you in the hand of my Lord
> I'm gonna leave you in the hand of my Lord
> Well, the mother told her child just before she died,
> I'm gonna leave you in the hand of my Lord.

> Well, my mother died and left me a long, long time ago
> I promised her that I would meet her on the Kingdom's happy shore
> Well, the day my mother died was the day I began to cry
> I'm gonna leave you in the hand of my Lord.

When the black man was first brought to America, he had that deep trom-
bone sound in his voice already. They would go to the white church and
hear about the Lord. They served a spirit in Africa. They didn't know the
real God that we know. But they served a spirit. They would see God in a
rock. They would make these songs that way. As they grew up and saw their
children sold out from under them and all of these tragedies happen right
before their eyes, they grew in the knowledge of God as they grew in the
knowledge of natural life. They would put these things together.

Composers would put these songs together. And the same thing is happening now. My wife and I have sat down together here and in our previous
homes and put songs together out of the Bible and mixed them in with
some things of our lives. I have twenty-seven songs that I have written and
recorded on the Savoy record label.

They allowed the slaves to go to church on Sunday. Where there were
Christian owners, they'd build a balcony in the church and let them go up
there. They would hear all about heaven. These songs that you hear about—

> I got shoes, you got shoes,
> All o' God's children got shoes,
> When I get to heaven, gonna put on my shoes,
> And gonna walk all over God's heaven—

that came from looking at the white man's shoes when they were barefooted.
The whites could wear shoes because they owned them. The slaves felt like,

"When I get to heaven I'm gonna have some shoes." So it's a made-up thing by what they saw, and what they saw happen in that time. This is the same reason why these songs still live, and they're going to live on as long as this world stands. These songs are going to live on, and they're going to live without the written note. It's going to live on in the heart, and they're gonna breathe it out of the heart through their voices. It's gonna be heard.

In slavery the blacks went to the white church, where they had hymnals. They would just sing straight along. But since the slaves could not read, they would have to sit and listen—and their place was in the balcony. Since they couldn't read or write, they had to memorize these hymns, and this is where it came from. They would go back to the cotton fields or whatever work they did and hum until they could pick up the tune. Once they got the tune, they could remember the words. So when black churches were organized, they remembered those hymns, and they would line them out. The minister possibly had more education than the others; he would line out the hymn, and they could remember the words and sing what he said.

I remember Grandmaw used to sing this song ["Free at Last"]. She was singing it from the day of freedom. We don't have the history of the man that started to singing it, but just along that time when the Negroes were freed, the song came out. She used to sing that with a clap and stomping of the feet and verses in it. Grandmaw and those people were singing about the war—free from being slaves. But then they pulled it over into the religion.

Most people in Atlanta when I was a boy would sing "Free at Last" with the idea of being free from sin—they were converted. If someone was saved, the Devil had loosed 'em and they were free. That's what they applied it to. Then when King came along with the March on Washington and that speech, I started singing the song again, but it wasn't recorded until after his death.

Aint Sarah

We stayed in Douglasville till Momma died. We moved to Atlanta because there came a conflict between my momma's momma and my daddy's momma about who was gonna get the children. Grandmaw Reid, Mother's mother, said she was more able to take care of the children because she had a farm, and they could learn how to work out there. That's all she knew was just farm work. But my grandmother, Aint Sarah, was raised more in the city, where she could work. She won because she, being a midwife, could bring us with her to Atlanta, where she had a sister-in-law. She brought us here to her sister-in-law, Aunt Molly, that was down in Pittsburgh section, and from that, Grandmaw got a great big house, rented some of the rooms out, and kept us all together. She wasn't just some old woman who knew how to deliver babies. She had studied under the same doctor in Douglasville that caught me when I was born, and she worked with the kinda high-up folk there in Douglasville. She knew she could make some money midwifing, washing and ironing, and meeting different white people. They love her; just to be around her was love.[14] I knew her as Grandmaw, but everybody, even my wife, called her Aint Sarah. This grandmother on my father's side, Sarah Johnson, reared me from three years old.

She was a singer. Oh my Lord, that lady could sing! She would walk the floor in a little prance, and I think I do that sometime. . . . Yeah, she'd just prance when she would sing. I've seen her turn around when she'd get to the back end of the church and then prance on back to the front singing. And she'd stir a church. Mm-muh! She'd holler out every now and then, "Come on, children." And I picked up a habit of saying, "Come on." I won't say, "Children," though; I'll say, "Come on."

When I was small, if preachers wanted me to preach, they didn't go to my father, because my father didn't rear me. He was kinda on the wild side, so they would come to Grandmaw and say, "Aint Sarah, can the boy preach for me a week?"

She'd say, "Well, he can preach for you two or three nights, but not a whole week. I got some cases, and I can't be away but three nights. I have to be there and see after him."

Then after the affair, if we were gon' stay over, they had to prepare a room for Grandmamma and me. By me being a little boy, you know, I didn't want to sleep in a room all by myself. 'Cause at home I had my little sisters.

My younger sister and I taught her to read, taught her the ABCs, and taught her how to write her name. See, she was born in slavery and was only a young girl at the time of Emancipation. We then enrolled her in night classes at the Crogman School, where I studied and where my own children would later attend. At that time we lived on Smith Street, and the school was about two blocks from home. We would go down there with her to school at night. Grandmaw got to the point where she could correct us. Oh yeah, she learned very fast. She went as far as the fourth grade. When she was promoted to the fourth grade, she went half that term and then she didn't go anymore because her work as a midwife was too heavy for her. She was licensed as a midwife before she could read. But she was good, they say. They kept her going, white and black.

As a little boy, the first real singing I heard was the [shape-]notes my daddy could sing so well. But after we came to Atlanta and, as I started school and began to spend more time around Grandmaw, I came to love the hymns and other songs I heard her sing. . . . She had her special way she would call me. She would say, "Claude, come and sit down, I want to talk to you." Those talks were always special. If she wanted to talk, I know it would be something that would help me. Then after she talked to me, she would pray with me, and she was a praying woman—she could really pray. Then she would hold me and let me know everything was all right. I really looked up to her as the mother I didn't have.

Grandmaw was a hymn singer who could raise any type of hymn. I just took it up from a little small boy following Grandmaw, holding on to her apron. Back in those days women wore aprons. They would be very long, and I would catch hold to her as she walked through the house singing a hymn.

I would listen to her, then I would get the little children . . . up under the house and teach them how to sing like Grandmaw. We would sing hymns. That is the way it started.

"Are You Like Your Grandfather?"

My middle name, Joseph, is taken from my paternal grandfather, who was known as Deacon J. J. Johnson. Jesse was his other given name. All the relatives came to see him when he was sick on his deathbed. . . . They all came that night, and we filled the room up. And, oh, they were singing. I, as a little boy around five, was trying to sing, too, because Grandfather liked to sing. After he got through singing, he says, "Give me the big Bible."

They gave him the Bible, and he opened it and began talking. He then started to get loud, went into a tune,[15] and yelled and cried. Being a little boy, I wanted to know what Grandpa was crying about. He worked his arms—I remember, look like I see him now, working his arms up and down and crossways and holding himself. He preached and hollered and went on for a few moments, and then just started to sweat. After this they told him they thought he had talked enough.

As they dried his face, he said, "Well, I've been running from preaching forty years. I've been singing in the church and I've been a deacon in the church, but I just had to preach tonight. I want you all to know that was my first and my last sermon. . . . I want to be alone now, I want all of you to go out. . . ."

So all of us went out of the room and left him. . . . I loved Grandpa because he showed so much attention to me. When we'd come out of the room, I eased back in the room, and crawled up on the bed. . . . I saw that he had his eyes shut. One of the things I did if I wanted to wake him up was to just catch his nose, pull his nose, and he'd knock my hand; he didn't want you to touch his nose. But this time I caught his nose, and he didn't knock my hand. After I did it about three times and he didn't knock my hand, I jumped down off the bed and ran in the other room and said, "Grandmaw, Grandmaw." They all broke in there and found that he had passed.

One of the things that made Grandpa run from the call to preach was his temper. He was a deacon in a pretty rough church, and in that office, he threw a man out of the window one day. In those days, you didn't call a man a lie. That was their fighting piece. . . . So this man called my grandfather a lie, and he told him twice to take it back, but he wouldn't do it. They say he just picked the man up and threw him through the window. And they had him up before the church, but they put him back on because he was a good man. He told them that he lost his temper and he wanted to be forgiven and to continue as a deacon. He had a temper and knew that if he was a preacher, he couldn't do the things that he did when he was a deacon. But the Lord just kept pushing him, kept pushing him. When he got down sick and had to lie there in that bed for so long, he finally preached that sermon and passed. He died a deacon, but I heard that they mentioned at the funeral that he did preach his first and last sermon. He was funeralized at Zion Hill Church, where Grandmaw Carver was a member and where Rev. Money Lowe was then pastor.

His membership was there when he died, but it was at Traveler's Rest Baptist Church that he threw the man out the window. This was near Morning Star Baptist, where I pastored so long. When I was interviewed for that pastorate, the people remembered him and asked me, "Are you like your grandfather? I know you sing like him." When I asked them what they were talking about, they told me what my grandmother had told me about Jesse threw a man through the window. "Are you like him?" I says, "I don't know; I don't think I'm like that." Because he was a large, strong, husky man. I've always been very small. But he was a good singer. I remember some of the songs that he did sing. And I think I have some of them recorded. One of them that I heard my grandfather sing was

> There's a dark cloud rising, let's go home
> There's a dark cloud rising, let's go home
> Don't you see the lightnin' flashin', don't you hear the thunder roll
> There's a dark cloud rising, let's go home.

I've heard my father and one of my aunts say that on a still night in the country, my grandfather would sit on the front porch and sing a hymn. His favorite hymn was "Go Preach My Gospel, Saith the Lord." And he would sing it all the time, I imagine, because he knew he was called to preach for the Lord. And they said he would have those singing moments there, and you could hear him five miles away. People that lived five miles from Grandmaw and Grandpa would say they could hear him just as clear singing the hymn:

> Go preach my gospel, saith the Lord
> Bid the whole earth my grace receive
> He shall be saved that trust my word
> And be condemned that not believe.[16]

Oh, that was a hymn! They don't sing it that much anymore. I think when I record again I'm gonna sing it. Oh, Lord, that used to be some hymn. I still sing it every time I ordain a preacher. Ooooh, and some of the old people there remember it. Oh, Lord, they used to get to shouting on that hymn. I remember at Zion Hill, Brother MacDaniel would sing it and at Georgia Avenue, Rev. C. H. Robinson. I was a little-boy preacher then.

Sing, Little Claude

When children would come to play with me, if Grandmaw wanted me to do somethin', I'd tell 'em, "I'll see you later, I got to go and help Grandmaw." And sometimes the boys would come and help me do the work, you know. Grandmaw never did say anything about that. But I would get back there and get to workin', and singin'. And the little boys and girls that were back there helpin' me learned my songs and sang right along with me. Everybody came around me had to sing, 'cause I wasn' go'n talk to them. If I would go to singing, they would try to sing. When they went home somebody would ask, "Where you learn that song?" They'd say, "Little Claude was down there singing, he sang that song." They'd say, "Oh, I'd like to heah 'im sing." They would sing it the best they could for the parents, but when they heard me sing it, then they liked it.

This is something I really like to talk about. Being a little boy, hanging around preachers, and listening to my grandmother—I always called her Grandmaw, I do that in the pulpit. And if you listen to my records, you will find that I use the word "Grandmaw." I know it's not good grammar, but I just say "Grandmaw." She was a hymn singer. She would raise any type of hymn. I just took it up from a little small boy following Grandmaw, holding on to her apron. Back in those days women wore aprons. They would be very long and I would catch hold to her and she would be walking through the house singing a hymn. I would listen to her, then I would get the little children out in the back yard—they didn't underpen houses in those days. You could go up under the house. I would get up under the house and teach them how to sing like Grandmaw. So we would sing hymns. This is the way it started. The little children would go home—probably the parents were wicked and all like that—and sing hymns. And a lot of the parents were brought to Christ through their children singing hymns. I would have children singing the hymn that's on my album that I love so well. The truth about it is that I was converted under that hymn: "I Heard the Voice of Jesus Say." . . .

Then this thing happened to me. Now I was singing the hymn, mind you, to and with the little children. But that morning I was converted, I heard that song. Nobody was singing it—but I heard it. And mostly when I'm at churches now in revivals, I sing that hymn. And you know, I tell 'em what happened to me that Friday morning. Then things get a little rough. Sometimes I get soggy and all of that. Because it happened. It happened sixty-three years ago. And I'm telling you, it's something. The hymn!

I have two sisters and no brothers. My oldest sister was Lillie Mae, Leona was the baby, and I was right in the middle. I had to have a lot of attention. I've always wanted attention and still do. My wife knew that before she married me. I just wanted a lot of attention. . . .

My youngest sister learned to sing shape notes just like I did. . . . We used to sing duets together at . . . churches here in Atlanta. She developed into a real strong voice. She used to sing—I think her song was "It's a Great Change Since I've Been Born." She could really sing that song, and I would do the tenor while she'd lead it. . . . People would just rap us back to the floor.[17] Then we would sing something like "Jesus Loves Me, This I Know." We started singing together 'round home. We were very close. She would be in there washing dishes and I would be drying; and we would just go to singing. The people living next door were members of Zion Hill Church, and they heard us singing. One Sunday we were there . . . and they went to the pastor . . . and ask him to call us to sing. We didn't know anything about it; they surprised us. They kept us singing; we did about four songs before they would let us off the floor. They'd just rap us right back. The neighbors would hear us sing in the kitchen because those houses back during World War I were built close together . . . I mean close together. . . . That's the way we got started. Later on my baby sister and Elizabeth, who is now my wife, would walk down the street together . . . singing softly little church songs. People would stop and look and turn around and ask them, "Would you sing that again?" That's how good they were. It was a great experience.

The first "dibu"[18] that I remember was at Mount Vernon Baptist Church. I was five years old. They stood me up on a center table. You don't see them now, but they had a table they called a center table. They stood me up on the center table, and I did "The Prodigal Son." I beat the time—4/4 time— and did the song. You know, I didn't get chance to finish the song. People got to hollering and running—coming down there to me. They had to gather around me to keep the people away from me. They had to take me off that table. I was five years old and, believe it or not, I'm now pastoring a lady who was there that day. You know, I just told you that I was born in 1913. She was a grown woman then. I'm pastoring her now.

Money Lowe

In church, I would listen directly to the preacher, and I loved the preachers. In that time, Rev. Money Lowe (his real name was Money) lived just a block away from us. I found out how to get to his house, and I would go away from home without even telling my grandmother and be around there with him. He was a great singer and a great preacher.

He was some preacher! I know a lot of preachers living now who remember him. They've never heard anybody like him. Just like you hear preachers such as Billy Graham pounding away at the word of God—he would say it in Greek and translate it in a tune.[19] Though he was well educated and could lecture if he wanted to, Money Lowe was a hard preacher, he was one of those way down home, go-get-'em preachers. He would preach in Greek and translate it in a tune. But he wouldn't read it; he would be preaching it. Oh, Lord, that got out here in Atlanta, and white and colored would come when he would do a revival. The churches in Atlanta wouldn't hardly hold the people.

You talkin' about dark, I haven't seen the picture or been in the presence of an African that was darker than he was. He was very dark with real nappy hair and red eyes. That man had a voice that would shake your very soul. He'd preach along like that thirty or thirty-five minutes, then back away from the pulpit and stretch both his hands out and make the sign of the cross; then the service was over. That's what started the people in Atlanta to raising collection before preachin', 'cause Money Lowe would run 'em out o' de church. They'd have to car' 'em somewhere, they couldn't come back in.

Money Lowe was the greatest preacher ever I heard in my life. I loved him—I loved that man. I was a little boy, but he took up time wid me. He lived on Golden Street right off Chappell. I'd ask Grandmaw to go over to his house. He would take me on his knee and sing to me and I would sing along with him. He taught me how to be a little-boy Christian. But he was never my pastor. He pastored Zion Hill in Douglasville. Then he was called here to Providence Baptist, where many of the presidents of Morehouse College have pastored.[20] That was the high-faluting church in that time. Oh, Lord, they respected him highly. He was somebody.

To my regret, he died before I preached my first sermon. He took sick with pneumonia and he was determined to baptize those people at Providence. He went in that water, and when he came out he took deathly sick and died. I was to preach my first sermon the coming week. I was excited about it, because a lotta the songs I learned, he used to carry me over them. He had such a heavy voice; if he hollered in church, look like the church would shake. He was some preacher.

Money Lowe passed when I was about seven years old. He would set me on his knee and sing to me. There were four songs I remember him singing to me like that: "One Morning Soon," "This Heart of Mine," "I Got a New Name Over in Zion," and "Job." He was sick during that time. I would go 'round there and bring him water, and do things for 'im. He would sit up on the side of the bed and sing, and I would sing right along with him. So when he passed, I had those songs already written down, and I was singin' 'em. Later, when I had my first church, I would sing them and I noticed that the people were familiar with the songs. They'd just catch right on. I know that those older ministers were singing them. But I heard 'em from Money Lowe.

J. M. Gates

Though I was never as close to him, Rev. J. M. Gates was also very inspiring to me. He would sing, and then he would preach. And that was my style. Even before I heard Rev. Gates, that was already my style. But when he came on and had it on the record, and I could sit and listen to him and then hear the members saying back to him "Amen"—and some of them would get to shouting, and then he would sing—it encouraged me. He had his first recordings along about the time I wrote "I Want to Go Where Jesus Is" in 1926. He wrote "The Little Black Train Is A-Coming." Now that was his song. He wrote that song.

> Oh, the little black train is a-coming
> Get all your business right
> Little black train is coming
> It may be here tonight.[21]

That was his song, and his congregation sang it right along with him, a cappella—no music. His church was out in a little settlement called Rockdale Park. A lot of his members had children going to E. A. Ware, the school that I went to. I had begun preaching because I was eight then. He was very popular, had a nice buggy and pretty red horse—oh, it was something—sportback buggy.

Rev. Gates was the only preacher in that area who had a brick church. The Methodists, AME, and CME all had plank churches like our church, Mt. Moriah. But Rev. Gates had a brick church—had it bricked after he started to making records with sermons and songs. He was pretty wealthy. It was bricked by the time I preached in it—beautiful church!

He came to Zion Hill Church, near where we lived, and all of the children were hollering, "Rev. Gates is down to Zion Hill. He's 'round there with the pretty horse." So we went down there and I got chance to see him. I went up to him, while all the other children just stood off lookin'.

I says, "How you, Rev. Gates?"

He says, "Hey, little fella."

So I tol' 'im, I says, "I'm a preacher."

He says, "What?"

I says, "Yes, I'm a preacher, I'm a member of Mt. Moriah."

He say, "You really a preacher?"

"Yessir, I have my license 'round home." So he put me in the buggy beside him and went on round on Smith Street—see, the streets weren't paved—you know, just dirt! Rode on round there, I told him, "Here where I live."

Grandmaw came out, lif' me out of the buggy, and he says, "Aint Sarah," that's what he called her—Grandmaw knew him!—say, "This yo' boy?"

She say, "Yeah, that's ma boy. He's a preacher."

He say, "He tol' me he was." And he ask, huh, "Can he preach?"

She say, "You ought to heah him."

He say, "Well, I'm gon' set a Sunday out to my church, and I wont him to come out there and preach. I'm gon' tell all the chillun, let all the school chillun come," and he did.

Grandmaw carried me out there on the streetcar; we transferred and went on out to Rockdale. That Sunday, there was mo' chilren out there—you know, from Ware School. I did "You Better Run," then behind that I preached the sermon subject "Loose the man and let him go." Ohhh, those people shouted! This came from the eleventh chapter of St. John, where Lazarus died and Jesus raised him from the dead. He was all bound, you know. I didn't know what a subject was back there. I just say, "My text is 'Loose the man and let him go.'" We had a song out, you know, 'bout that too. "Oh loose the man, loose the man, loose the man, and let him go." I think I'm gonna work on that if I record any more, because I haven't—well, I haven't heard the song in twenty-five or thirty years. Oh, I don't know who originated it, but I did hear it when I was a boy—"Loose the man and let him go."

So when the people got through shouting and all like that, well, Grandmaw, she got to shouting too. She just ran up and picked me up in her arms and walked all up and down the aisle, and I was still preaching—couldn't stop from preaching! We just had a glorious time that day. After that, those children accepted me as a preacher, and some of 'em are living now! They still respect me as a preacher. And it's been a long time since I was eight years old.

Reverend Daniel and His Daughter

I was on good terms with Sister Johnson's father as a fellow minister of the gospel, but coming to see his daughter was an altogether different thing. Her father heard me do a revival out from Fort Valley, Georgia and said to me, "Boy, you rough! I want you to do my revival." I told him, "Yessir." So I did his revival, then he asked me to come to his home—I think it was for Thanksgiving—for dinner. When I went to the home, I first saw Elizabeth. I saw the little girl in there; she had her hair fixed like an Indian; her father was part Indian. She had the plaits hanging down on the side of her head and she was just moving around doing dinner. I asked him, "Is that your daughter?" He said, "Yes." And I kept looking at her, so I told her hello. She said, "Hey," and kept waiting on the table. So I went home and told my sister about the little girl. I told her, "That's the cutest little thing I ever saw." I say, "You know her?" She says, "No, I've never seen her."

My father-in-law, Rev. Daniel—he was something else. You know, he had one of those big sixteen-cylinder Cadillacs—didn't many white people have those things. He had churches and he was a kind-a businessman 'round hotels. He was over the colored help, they worked under him. He was some-body. You should've seen how his house was furnished off. You could go to Druid Hills, Peachtree, anywhere—you didn't see any better furnished house than Rev. Daniel's.[22] He didn't throw his money away.

He weighed about 250 pounds or more, but do you know when he dressed up—he had curly hair and he'd put that hair to one side and drop it down over there, and he was dark and had smooth dark skin—you were lookin' at somebody. Man, he could sing and preach! I used to love to see him turn around and point his hand up to the ceiling and holler, then go back to singing, then the congregation would come on right behind him. We used to have a time. I loved him so hard, it took me about four or five years to get over his death.

I took sick one year not long after we got married, and I wasn't able to go to my churches. I had to send some preachers to my churches, then I could-n't go to the little bookkeeping job I had here in Atlanta. Things just went bad. Rent got behind—all that stuff. You know what he did? He came to my house and, everything that needed to be fixed, he paid and he took all that responsibility.

The Singing Family

The 1930s and 1940s were difficult years for us. The Great Depression held us down to where we could just get by on what I was bringing in. Right in the middle of this, I had married in 1933, and we started our family two years later after she finished high school. Those days before and right after President Roosevelt was elected were hard. I married right in that time. I've seen my wife take one dollar and feed a family of four: that was myself, her, and two children. One dollar! . . . while I was scuffling and trying to go to school.

Sister Johnson has been right by my side. She has worked in every church I've pastored. I have pastored fourteen churches, and I've built two. She has helped me in my schooling, and she held everything together when I was trying to go to school in the hard times. This is the thing that kept me going.

For some years there I didn't really have time to think about writing songs as I had when I was a little-boy preacher. Also, by this time I was pas-toring at Morning Star Baptist, where I would remain for twenty-five years. However, there were some times, some things I remembered and wrote down from that period that I later worked into songs. But I wasn't even thinking about writing songs or recording during Roosevelt's season.

All of the original songs that I've recorded are listed under my own name. But all the members of my family, my children, their families, and especially my wife have been involved in the writing of some of the songs. At least four of the twenty-seven songs that I've recorded as originals were writ-ten by my wife, Sister Johnson.

My children, my daughters, my grandsons, granddaughters, my son-in-law would all come over to our house on a holiday or some Sunday. It took all us to get "Daniel Read the Handwriting on the Wall." That was the hardest one we had. I wrote it one way, and it didn't come out, it wouldn't hit. One daughter finally said, "Daddy, leave off the handwriting." We left the handwriting off and said, "Read the writing on the wall." We kept on and finally got it.

A lot of the songs on the records were done this way. When the family got together we would sing the song and tape it and listen at it. And whatever needed to come out we would take that out. Once we got it right, all the family knew. Once we go to church, they'd start singing it, and the congregation would pick it up from those who already knew it.

Sometimes we would try several different tunes in these workshops and they wouldn't work. But we'd keep trying. Then it will hit. And when it hits, then it satisfies us, and then we have a feeling that it's satisfying the Lord.

These family sessions were workshops for the recording. If anybody else wanted to be here, all well and good. But the family would be willing to do it. And once we got it right, we just carried on.

I have the ballad sheet in there for "Daniel Read the Writing on the Wall." I would always type out the verses and all for songs we worked out. We would also make a practice tape of these workshop sessions.

Eagle Rocking on "My Home"

One of the songs I have recorded, which my grandmother used to sing, goes like this:

My home, my home
My home is just on the other side of Jordan
My home, my home
Never turn back no mo'.

Now, when you sing that, you go'n' stir up the congregation. It's soft, but when you know anything, you burning. Aint Sarah, my grandma, used to sing that song, and she use to have this rock like we have. She'd go up de aisle doing this eagle rock. Now that's when folks shouted. She'd start singing in the front of the church and she'd end up in the back. Then—still singing—she'd come down that aisle just like she went up that aisle.

They still shout that way down in Macon at a church where I preach a revival each year. That's the way they shout down there. You ain't got to hold nobody when they get the eagle rock. That is the prettiest thing you ever seen. Those mothers in white dresses out there doing the eagle rock. When I'd see Grandmaw do it, I could do it too! I still do it sometimes while I'm singing.

Folks got out there just—just rocking, all rockin' the same way. And the pastor was up there singing my song and rockin' wid 'em. This young man, Rev. Glover, has a large church. And when they came up here and did a revival for us, they got out there doing the eagle rock.

Eagle rock—that's what the old folks called it. You didn't have to hold nobody. Sometimes you wouldn't see 'em say a thing. They'd drop they shoulders down and go down and come up. Wooohhh, man! It's something to see.

"You Better Run"

I heard Grandmaw sing all the verses that you hear in there, and I heard Money Lowe sing "You Better Run," but he didn't sing it like that. So I took the verses that I heard Money Lowe sing. He didn't have those verses in there. He would sing

> You better run, children, you better run
> You better run, children, you better run
> God's comin', you better run
> God's comin', you better run.

I took that and worked it around, got it together. Where he said, "You better run," I put three times "better run, better run, better run." So when I got it together, I started singing it as a teenaged boy before I married.

I had started studying about the slaves in books Grandmaw had on that, because she was a slave. This was the grandmother that reared me. I started to singing the song and Grandmaw got it and then she started to singing it. The first time I did it in church as a boy, they started singing like I did it. So I added some verses from the Bible—one 'bout Samson, another 'bout Nicodemus and all of that. In other words, it's a sermon in song. I still have the books I studied out of back then. When I first started studying about the Underground Railroad, I thought it was really a railroad, . . . a train carrying people. Then I found out it was white people slipping people away. Because if a runaway slave was caught, he was whipped or killed—and sometimes they would die trying to get away. Then I got to thinking about how the slaves in the field would hear the dogs, the bloodhounds howling. The slave was trying to get to the point where they could get to the Underground Railroad. I say, "I believe I'll put this in the song—that is the city of refuge." I had preached and studied in the Old Testament that if a man committed a crime and could get to the city of refuge, he would be saved—whatever that city was.

"I Want to Go Where Jesus Is"

Until now, no one knows but my family how this song ["I Want to Go Where Jesus Is"] came about. Here in Atlanta, I would ride the streetcar to work as a little boy trying to help Grandmaw keep food on the table. I would get out of school at noon, then work from one until seven at a grocery, cleaning up the store, and delivering groceries to people on the bicycle. I made three dollars a week like that, gave it to Grandmaw, and it helped to feed us. So this time I caught the streetcar going to the West End—we were living over there on the west side—and sat down on the back seat. A white gentleman came back there and stood over me and said, "Get up, boy, and let me sit down." I say, "Mister, the law says that we can sit in the back and y'all sit in the front and I'm on the back seat." Then he slapped me down on the floor. I got up—being a child—and bit him. I got his finger in my mouth and when he drew back to hit me again, I tightened up—and I have real sharp teeth. When they got me off'n that man and I stopped biting him, then they put me off and let him stay on, and that hurt me. The conductor put me— a little boy—off the streetcar.

As I went down the street crying—I had a long ways to walk to get to the job—I thought, "O Lord, what I'm gonna do? I don' wanna live here anymore; I can't work and help Grandmaw." Once I got to work and started cleaning up back there, I said, "I know what I can do, I can go where Jesus is." Then the thought came to me, "You'll have to die to get there." And I didn't wanna die. So I got a piece of tablet paper and wrote down, "I want to go where Jesus is." And that's where the song came from.

I had seen grown white men stomp a [black] boy. Five or six of 'em just beat him down to where he wasn't even able to get up. I was there on the streetcar with ten or twelve or more whites and no blacks. But they didn't turn a hand. They didn't even stand up or move until those ladies said, "Get that boy up off-a that man." I had him down between the benches, and I was bitin' 'im all in the face and head and everywhere else. When they pulled me up, this man was in such pain that he couldn't do anything to me—I had bit him unmercifully.

So the Lord blessed us to come through a whole lot of things. And it all came from that streetcar. Now by me being black, all of those white men—it was ten or twelve of 'em on there—were supposed to have helped that man, but they didn't. When the man told me to get up and let him sit down, saying, "I'm a white man," and slapped me—I don't think they approved of it.

Now, I didn't give that to anybody, the way the song came about. I was a boy in 1926 when I wrote it. It took me three weeks to get it all down on paper. "No more trouble where Jesus is," that's one of the verses; "I got business where Jesus is," and on and on.

That song became the favorite of the country, everywhere in Georgia, South Carolina, Alabama, Tennessee—everywhere I would go and do a revival, I would sing that song. Then after I left they would sing it. My grandmother had some ballad sheets made of it and sold enough of those ballads at ten cent to buy me a suit with short pants (didn't 'low boys to wear long trousers then) and bought one of them little middie blouses with the big white collar. She also bought me a whole lotta little shoes and things out of "I Want to Go Where Jesus Is." Look how long it had been out—see, I didn't record it until 1964. People have been on their dying bed and said, "Send get C. J. Johnson and let him sing 'I Want to Go Where Jesus Is,' because that's where I'm going."

When I started to record for Savoy, Fred Mendelsohn says, "Dr. Johnson, give me the historicity of 'I Want to Go Where Jesus Is.'" I said, "I was a boy, I loved the Lord, and my goal was heaven. I thought, 'I want to go where Jesus is,' because he's the sweetest thing I know." He said, "Well, how did you create it? How did you get it in your mind, being a boy?" I said, "I was a pastor. In 1926 I was pastoring a church. I had a church of my own. They voted on me to be the pastor when I was in grade school, not high school. I want to go where Jesus is. I love Jesus and I know he loves me. Now that's my testimony."

Chapter 8

"Come Ye That Love the Lord"

The Lining Out–Ring Shout Continuum
and the Five-Key Sequence

Come ye that love the Lord
And let your joys be known;
Join in a song of sweet accord
And thus surround the throne.

ISAAC WATTS, *1707*

The practice of Dr. Watts hymn singing among black Baptists in the nineteenth century both revitalized an existing ritual context for music performance and popularized among the black masses the forms and rhythms of English verse. Paradoxically, this cross-fertilization also solidified a peculiarly African American orientation toward ritual speech as an evocation of the Spirit that culminates in the celebratory postures of movement and dance. Heightened speech as a means of conveying the surplus of divine experience has been inseparable from the history of Judeo-Christianity and religion in general (Turner 1988). However, African Americans have demonstrated an especially strong predilection toward speechlike song and its complement, songlike speech, as a deceptively simple means of evoking the divine presence. In African American worship, speech animates gesture (viewed as primal expressions that include movement), and, reflexively, gesture (and especially dance as stylized gesture) elaborates upon and informs speech. Speech is the shaping essence of what we experience as sound, and the gestures/movements that follow upon the sounds are visible and emotive expressions that embody the character of the heightened speech from which they emanate as well as the transcendence toward which true worship yearns.

Two essays on black music by Olly Wilson underscore the interrelatedness of sound and movement not only in worship but in the whole of African-derived cultures. These works substantiate my view that sound and movement converge as dialectical categories upon which strata of expressive elements recombine to generate identifiable styles. In "The Heterogeneous Sound Ideal in African-American Music," Wilson proposes an "approach to music making in which a kaleidoscopic range of dramatically contrasting qualities of sound is sought after in both vocal and instrumental music." He notes that black music can be heterogeneous in at least two ways: vertically, "in the . . . 'sound' texture of musical ensembles," and horizontally, "in the common usage of a wide range of timbres within a single line (1992: 328–29). While Wilson here emphasizes a *sound* ideal that is peculiar to black music, in an earlier essay, "The Association of Movement and Music as a Manifestation of a Black Conceptual Approach to Music-Making," he underscores the importance of *movement* to the making of black music (see also Blacking 1973: 27; Nketia 1974: 206–7). He observes that sub-Saharan African societies view music and movement "as interrelated components of the same process" and cites transfers of this African sense of movement as intrinsic to music in African American religious music, work songs, and the brass band tradition (1985: 10, 13–20).

Thinking about sounds in relation to movement anchors the sounds within their varied ritual contexts, and for Dr. Watts hymns, that context is the black church. The sociologist of religion C. Eric Lincoln argues, "The black church became African Americans' chief index of identification, because in every critical sense it was the one satisfactory projection of themselves that found least resistance from the significant others upon which its viability would ultimately depend" (1996: 109). It is significant that Lincoln's analysis does not turn upon any notion of blacks as somehow inherently religious. For while the nexus between music and religion in black culture is undeniable, the role and function of ritual in black experience have been modeled by the social forces at play in the larger culture. Therefore, the hidden significance of Dr. Watts, as a church-bound genre of black music, is most appreciable for how its perspectives can inform our view of subsequent forms and styles both sacred and secular.

No source has been more foundational to my view of black Baptist worship than Walter Pitts's study *Old Ship of Zion: The Afro-Baptist Ritual in the African Diaspora* (1993). As we have seen, Pitts has identified two ritual "frames" in black Baptist worship: the opening devotion, which may include lining-out hymns, prayers, and other cherished forms which have, over time, been formalized; and the service, including solo and choral performances, announcements, prayer and scripture readings, all directed toward the sermon as the symbolic place of divine-human interaction and the focal point of celebration. The first frame is plaintive and deferential, the second celebratory and exultant. Through the droning, hypnotic effect of lining-out hymns, songs, and prayers, the opening frame creates an experiential separation between the worshipers and their often troubled experience outside the church. The closing frame points toward celebration and, utilizing the form of the sermon as a springboard, often culminates in sacred dance or other ritualized demonstrations of spirit possession.

The most general implication of Pitts's model is the connection between the uniqueness of black Baptist worship and ritual forms throughout the African Diaspora, particularly the crossing-over rites of passage found in various forms in many cultures. Pitts appropriates Victor Turner's structure/antistructure metaphor of passage from one state to another to describe a process that begins in the ritual's first frame, with relative emphasis upon structure, transforms that emphasis through deformation, and, during the second frame, creates an antistructure coherent with yet distinct from the old formalized structure of the first frame (Pitts 1993: 155–74).[1] In Pitts's work, Thomas Dorsey's song "Old Ship of Zion" becomes a metaphor for the transportation of "the worshipper along a continuum of spiritual uplifting from the moment Devotions begin until the closing benedictory prayer" (155). Without contradicting the oft-cited coincidence that lining out represents between European and African usages of antiphonal structure, this viewpoint also sees lining out as the primary North American instance of the arcane, disembodied, and distant utterances that characterize the first frame of African-derived rituals.

My project in this chapter is to articulate in more discrete yet general as well as conceptual terms what Pitts has called "a continuum of spiritual uplifting" (1993: 155). While there is nuanced difference between our findings, resorting to Pitts's concept of worship frames has confirmed and complemented my observations. However, his model of binary ritual frames—devotions followed by service—while describing the role and function of hymns in the Central Texas churches where Pitts conducted fieldwork, does not apply equally to all regional traditions of black Baptist worship, nor to black ritual performance in general. Although the complementary and predetermined *forms* of devotions and service are plainly evident in many locations, the ritual *structures*—the smaller and more generative units of musical activity—appear to be more interchangeable and less predictable, and produce more varied and particular ritual outcomes. Devotional hymn singing or praying often balances celebratory preaching and singing, but the progression is seldom as linear as the fixed binary form Pitts has offered would suggest. The actual structuring elements of the worship ritual—what gets done when and how to fill in what are otherwise mere forms—are far more cyclical, open-ended, and unpredictable. For example, whereas certain worship services begin with a powerful evocation of the Spirit and move with that sense of authority throughout, others turn back and forth upon themselves in "layers," as if returning again and again to the same kind of place in the search for a sure and inspired point of contact with the divine Spirit. Therefore, without rejecting the anthropological notion of binary ritual frames (which is extremely relevant to the cultural and musical basis of black music), the general cases and specific musical examples set forth below seek to tease out the notion's inherent potential for nuance and flexibility.

The prominent and memorable first impression left by an old-time Baptist devotion is one of the sounds themselves. From such an opening song or hymn, subtly modulated sounds rise as a most seductive stimulus (or "call") to worship throughout the course of the first-frame events. As the ministers and choir enter and the order of worship shifts to the second frame, song, sermon, and shout affirm a more body-centered response. This is the release of the apparently uncontrolled but inwardly regulated forces that W. E. B. Du Bois characterized as "the music, the preaching, and the frenzy" (see Baker 1984: 151–57). Put another way, we could say that as sound is the primary dynamic in the first frame, so is movement (and with it, rhythm) in the second. This characterization mirrors the dialectical opposition between sound and movement in all of black music. Especially in lining out and other first-frame genres, it is the *sound* of the singing that first moves participants to awe as a primary condition for active worship. Then, without losing urgency or subtlety, the sounds insinuate and then gradually move through increasingly percussive and complex rhythmic permutations. Although Wendell Whalum (1973) argues persuasively that slaves "blackened" the hymns, it is no less true that the hymns brought to bear upon African American ritual the rhythm and rhyme of English poetry. Verses and couplets from hymns by Watts are either quoted verbatim or utilized as models for the language of songs, prayers, and exhortations as well as sermons, and the incessant iambic lilt of these couplets may even have influenced the pattern of offbeat syncopation that dominates African American rhythm. Lining out, therefore, is of critical importance not only in itself but as one of two sound portraits or primary images—the other being the ring shout—through which black music has surfaced as a vitally American creative force.

As a primary by-product of this development, the freely measured pulse of portraiture sound and poetic rhythms countervails the strictly measured speech rhythms, which often establish the rhythmic-melodic outline of hymns and spirituals. On one hand, portraiture sound makes use of subtly varying vocal inflections to implicate rhythm without embracing it. By setting into sharp relief paired contrasts such as rise/fall, loud/soft, pitched/indeterminate, accented/ghosted, these vocal gestures both sharpen the timbral force and magnify the signification of key words or phrases. On the other hand, poetic rhythms signify upon the expressive functions more commonly associated with melody and timbre on at least two levels: structurally, by segmenting a song or sermon into an improvisatory and irregular sequence of lines punctuated by natural phrase endings, "amen"-like interjections, or aspirate breath accents; and functionally, by creating rhythmic tension between two or more entities involved in a given performance. Portraiture sound and poetic rhythms are not pervasive textures but culminating gestures either foreshadowing or achieving closure of a certain metaphorically framed event. Such creative moments, or "keys," are functional points of departure or arrival—changes emerging spontaneously during devotions or service—as opposed to the formally designated "frames" of the Afro-Baptist order of worship. Such keys can turn or alter the meaning of entire worship frames by connecting an existing text with particular individual or group needs.

Such vivid "sound pictures" have flowed from both the English-Reformation tendency toward plainspokenness and the New World transfers of African tonal-linguistic patterns away from their original lexical meanings and toward expressive English meanings ensconced between speaking and singing (see chapter 3). This nuanced sense of sound as both communication and performance encourages a level of virtuosity in prayers and songs. This, like all expression, can descend into mere self-indulgence; however, the highest attribute of such stylized sound is its potential for establishing a dialectical balance with movement in the drama of black ritual and music. This is why preaching, as the most freely expansive yet formal integration of oracular sound and movement, is so critical to both the social cohesion and personal renewal that are affirmed in black Baptist worship.

The rhetorical strategy of what Henry Louis Gates (1988) terms Signifyin(g), which in a musical context refers to "commenting on other musical figures, on themselves, on performances of other music, on other performances of the same piece, and on completely new works of music" (Floyd 1995: 95), therefore functions in black worship within an implicit *syntax of ritual behaviors* that governs what is sung or spoken, for how long, in what manner, and to what end.[2] The tradition has continually refined and disseminated these comments and, out of that process, a corresponding vocabulary of musical gestures has evolved as new forms have been developed within or adapted to the ritual context. My concept of a continuum between lining out and the ring shout represents a first step toward explicating these implicit semantic domains. As such, it considers the dynamic process through which African American music is composed and performed in various genres to suit the formulaic terms of common, well-defined ritual structures.

THE LINING OUT–RING SHOUT CONTINUUM

The lining out–ring shout continuum I am proposing unfolds as a layered series of dialectical oppositions between the expressive polarities of sound and movement in black music,[3] and it provides a means for examining how such interactions bring about creative moments in performances. The polarities of lining out and the ring shout—one slow and sonorous, the other faster and movement-based—were identified in chapter 1 as complementary ritual expressions. Going beyond that observation, I see each of these genres standing as a primary symbol of the respective English and African traditions that are palpable in black worship rituals.

Whereas the ring shout was discouraged by both eighteenth-century English missionaries and nineteenth-century black religious leaders, lining out was clearly encouraged in the eighteenth and nineteenth centuries, especially the latter. In effect, lining out became a point of cultural mediation, a means of adapting European means to African ends in a way that the ring shout did not. Because of their pervasive impact as countervailing European and African influences upon black oral culture, I have coupled these forms as complementary signs for expressive polarities in a continuum which stands for all the musical genres and styles developed by African Americans in North America.[4]

The concept of a polarity between lining out and the ring shout follows from the complementary character of a dualistic range of musical genres, forms, and structures in Baptist and other black worship traditions. Metaphorically, the forms themselves signify more general spheres of emphasis in black music, wherein lining out represents a range of expressions lending themselves to verbal, melodic, and timbral lyricism, and the ring shout represents a corresponding degree of rhythmic complexity and intensity. The range of sacred expressions signified by lining out includes intoned moans, prayers, slow-tempo spirituals, gospel performances of slow-tempo spirituals or Dr. Watts hymns, and charismatic worship songs. All these modes tease out nuances of expression that lie between speaking and singing. The ring-shout polarity, in addition to the ring shout itself, ranges from jubilee spirituals, Holiness-Pentecostal church songs, charismatic praise songs, and moderate and up-tempo gospel solos or choral selections to intoned preaching, shouting, and the repetitive drone of shout music.[5]

Through lining out's adaptations to the syntax of black worship over three centuries by slaves and their progeny, an intriguing aesthetic balance has evolved wherein the principle of tension poignantly expressed in old-time hymns is balanced by the corresponding sense of release that enlivens the African-derived ring-shout tradition. Both forms utilize various degrees of call-and-response structures, cries, calls, and hollers, hand clapping, and foot patting. However, where the ring shout centers upon emphatic body movement (moving toward spirit possession) and includes percussiveness, cross-rhythms, faster tempos, monophonic singing, and constant repetition, the chantlike essence of lining out is meditation upon the Word, or Logos, characterized by slower tempos, sublimated rhythms, organumlike harmonies or heterophonic singing, bent-note inflections, poignant lyricism, and an array of ornamentations.

My vision of the lining out–ring shout continuum is indebted in part to Samuel Floyd's concept of Call-Response. By subsuming all the individual features of African American music making under this single term, Floyd implicates call-and-response (of which Call-Response is a trope) as the key structuring element in black music. Call-and-response achieves this status in black ritual and music by its *inclusive* nature, its potential to involve everyone present in the performance. While I affirm the functional primacy of call-and-response, my project places more emphasis upon its role as one of four structuring elements in forging the sound of black music: *call-and-response* stems from *heterogeneous sound* and the resultant *harmonies,* and tends toward *interpolation* and *ornamentation.* Vocal sound as comprising these elements is balanced, in turn, by body movement as a precondition for tempo acceleration, offbeat and cross-rhythms, and ritualized demonstrations of spirit possession. Thus do the dual categories of sound and movement, which are signified by the lining-out and ring-shout polarities, play distinct yet interrelated roles. The lining-out polarity, with its emphasis upon formalized, even vertical relationships between typically male celebrants and majority female congregations, signifies structure. The ring-shout polarity, through its literal and figurative movement away from fixed structure toward spirit possession as a key expression of the personal and social transformation toward which worship is aimed, focuses and ritually defines the many functional implications of body movement. Therefore, the continuum seeks to facilitate critical study of the balance of factors governing the most general range of contextual meanings that apply to black music.

Black Baptist ritual consists of fluid yet observable structures that efficiently convey the what, how, and when of group and individual identity as nurtured in worshiping communities. Psychological, social, and ritual functions establish a raison d'etre for musical structures; in turn, structures facilitate function. As an example of how the lining-out polarity of the continuum might unfold: A text chanted by a leader prompts a member to raise a hymn tune. The coupling between the two actions effects a call to worship. The ensuing congregational response signals the extent to which the initial call has been formalized. This vertically structured beginning paradoxically encourages its own deformation through random calls and responses as the hymn performance proceeds. The indirection of these random calls and responses can also thicken the texture of heterophonic singing as more persons venture to sing their own songs within the larger song. Sensing such a ripening moment, the gifted leader may perform anticipations or embellishments that encourage more congregational involvement, or he or she may offer an altogether different song which can more adequately contain the growing rhythmic and melodic exuberance. When such an opening gesture fails, the first worship frame can become an empty exercise, as members talk aloud or make other busy preparations for the "real" service that is to follow. But at its best, this kind of formalized beginning can establish a convention of ritualized openness that affirms both structure and spontaneity.

TABLE 7   The Lining Out–Ring Shout Continuum

A. Areas of Style Opposition between Polarities

1. Lining Out (Portraiture Sound)	2. Ring Shout (Poetic Rhythm)
a. Meditation-chant	a. Constant repetition
b. Moaning inflections	b. Body movement
c. Heterophonic singing	c. Monophonic singing
d. Powerful harmonies	d. Percussiveness
e. Slower tempos	e. Faster tempos
f. Sublimated rhythms	f. Polyrhythms
g. Lyricism and ornamentation	g. Spirit possession

B. Dialectical Relationship of Style Elements

1. Lining Out (Sound)	2. Ring Shout (Movement)

a. Heterogeneous vocal colors (portraiture):
  i. Bent notes, cries, calls, hollers
  ii. Whoops, hums, moans, grunts, etc.
	a. Body movement:
	  i. Hand clapping, foot patting
	  ii. Swaying, shuffling

b. Modal heterophony or harmony:
  i. Parlando
  ii. Modal intervals and chords
	b. Accelerating tempo:
	  i. Punctuations, offbeat phrasing
	  ii. Metronomic tempo

c. Call-and-response:
  i. Interlocking, repetitive
  ii. Noninterlocking, rhythmically voiced
	c. Offbeat rhythms or cross-rhythms (poetic):
	  i. Prevalent rhythmic pattern
	  ii. Game rivalry, conflicting rhythms

d. Interpolation and ornamentation:
  i. Elisions, parallel and broken thirds, interjections
  ii. Individuality, signifying revisions
	d. Spirit possession:
	  i. Metronomic pulse
	  ii. Divine or other consciousness

Similarly, in the ring-shout polarity, the functional nature of body movement can insinuate a sense of momentum toward heightened involvement in worship. This sense of physicality most often leads to some degree of tempo acceleration. In turn, the rhythmic basis for movement grows gradually or suddenly more active, often accompanied by offbeat or cross-rhythmic clapping patterns. This hastening sense of structured yet fluid movement can initiate demonstrations of spirit possession. While the possible variations upon these statements of structure (at once determined by their function and facilitating it) are endless, the model represented in table 7 should serve as a guide to interpreting such ritual and musical tendencies in actual performances. However, if it is to facilitate penetrating answers to musical and ritual questions, the method must be applied not mechanically but advisedly.

As a prolegomenon to the continuum, section A of table 7 describes contrasting features of the two polarities. To treat such distinctions between the ring shout and lining out as mutually exclusive absolutes, however, will ill-account for the variety of regional styles and variations in performance practice that enrich congregational singing and all of black music. Instead, they should be read as frequently heard functional and structural distinctions that energize the continuum with a springlike, reflexive tension. Active critical study begins with section B, which organizes the style elements under four headings (a–d) as those most traceable to lining out, as a formal means of commencing the first ritual frame, and to the ring shout, as a summation of the second ritual frame.

The elements listed under lining out in section B follow each other in a logical progression of action and consequence, each gesture hinging in some measure upon a well-defined sense of the preceding element. For example, a leader's call can elicit a group response of heterogeneous vocal colors (a)—the sounds of bent notes, cries, calls, hollers, whoops, hums, moans, grunts—and from these, heterophonies, or incidental harmonies (b), often follow. The sounds can create a repeating call-and-response pattern, stimulate noninterlocking flurries of improvised call-and-response, or do both at once (c). These improvisations can then be ornamented as signifying revisions to previously stated ideas (d). In such patterns of give and take, the leader ignites the group, the group gives back what it has received, and the whole is enlivened by spoken interjections or flights of lyrical melisma and liquid moaning gestures that "fill up" the sound. The elements listed under the ring-shout polarity follow from each other similarly. Body movement (a) is a practical precondition for accelerating tempo (b). The acceleration almost always invites rhythmic play between a prevalent rhythm and others in momentary conflict with it (c). This kind of purposeful repetition can support the range of factors culminating in sacred dance as the ultimate sign of spirit possession (d). Therefore, a variable range of elements from both polarities coalesce in manifestations of devotion, celebration, or conflations of both.

From this perspective, the two polarities can remain distinct and separate ritual modes, or they can develop interactively, such that one or the other is more emphatic at various points in the performance. When the two are combined in some degree, a single song or hymn performance can move—ever so gradually or quite suddenly—from the slow poignancy and disassociated formality of lining out to the percussive and accelerating rhythms of the ring shout. Thus the interaction between polarities is seldom linear and direct but alternates dialectically between the two within a gravitational field that steadily moves the worship ritual away from the opening frame and toward the closing one. Interrelations between the two polarities also include a rich diversity of potential correspondence between, for example, the measured parlandos, or sequenced displacements, that can follow from subtly changing vocal cries, and the cross-rhythms that can "heat up" a musical performance or hasten movement toward the ring-shout polarity. As the lining-out form is lyrically expressive with or without measured rhythms, and the ring-shout gesture is rhythmically calculated and precise, there are occasions in performance when the sound portrait effected by a lyric gesture is ingeniously conflated with the game rivalry and competition that produces complexly poetic rhythms. Such creative moments reveal striking commonalities between the piquant vocal expression of congregational song leaders like C. J. Johnson and Bernice Johnson Reagon, on one hand, and "talking" saxophonists like Charlie Parker, Charles McPherson, and Jackie McLean, on the other. Such coincidences typify cross-fertilization between genres, wherein instruments approximate the diction of speakerly singing or mellifluous speaking, and voices, in turn, rhythmically place interjections and interpolations in time so as to meet both expressive-structural (or timbral) and functional (or rhythmic) requirements.[6]

THE FIVE-KEY SEQUENCE

Figure 2 illustrates another model for the study of singing in black Baptist worship that operates in conjunction with the lining out–ring shout continuum. It presents a sequence of five performance "keys"—arrays of related activities directed toward a common purpose—that, taken together, describe the process of black ritual performance.[7] This guide, perhaps the more critical of the two models, proposes a developmental yet fluid sequence through which performances proceed, in which the various keys may become creative moments or musical "happenings." Whether actively physical or passively inward, such performances undergo five progressive stages of involvement: (1) inspiration; (2) rapport building; (3) momentum; (4) quickening; and (5) ecstasy-freedom. Each successive key encompasses an array of possible options that, along with the four other keys, can affect the ritual event as well as the holistic outcomes of the worship occasion. Although an effective performance generally depends on the successful application of at least the first two elements, any one of these keys can be deemphasized or elided entirely as a public component of the performance, depending upon the dialectics of the congregation's psychomotor and spiritual readiness. However, the contextual sense of a successful performance requires that a song leader consciously or unconsciously work through these keys *in sequence*. Because the "sequence" is seldom strictly linear but moves cyclically through the collective psyche of the congregation,

Frame Two

5. Ecstasy-freedom	Speech/song-to-gesture/movement: Testifying, hollering, embracing the self, lifting holy hands, walking the floor, jumping or running, holy dance as human responses to apprehension of divine calling
4. Quickening	Dawning awareness: Consensus, majority participation, shared purpose, revelation of numinous presence

Transition

3. Momentum	Song to song: Slow-fast, gradual-sudden, lyrical-metronomic, simple-complex, rising participation

Frame One

2. Rapport building	Transition: • Point of connection, appropriate timed (ex tempore), rising pitch/intensity, in and of the moment
1. Inspiration	Gesture/speech-to-song: Prepared, functional, understated, apparent, demonstrative

Figure 2. The five-key sequence. An elaboration of the binary frames in African American worship identified by Walter Pitts.

the various keys can operate both overtly and in more hidden ways in individual or group experiences.[8]

Because of their assigned worship functions, the forms and genres that most often occur during the first frame of worship, such as hymns, prayers, moans, and non-shout-based congregational songs, often complete themselves without entering into the keys of quickening or ecstasy-freedom. Where a single performance does not complete the sequence of keys, those omitted keys are most often deferred to a subsequent song or hymn, to the second frame, or even to a subsequent service. However, these incomplete performances may be no less important than the more celebratory ring shout or sermonic forms. Too often the latter have been lifted out of context and lionized, perhaps because they appear more authentic, exotic, or demonstrative to the beholder than the earlier events. But the critical first-frame expressions serve to freight the later events with the meanings of shared burdens or joys that can reemerge in catharsis or exultation. It is in this sense that a lining-out hymn, though performed customarily as the preparation before the sermon, can, if repeated later in the service, become a discursive means of self-reexamination that doubles back upon the soul-searching formality with which the service began. Such a moment becomes a chance to lay bare the week's burden of "blues" and worldly cares before the more irreversible ascent to the points of climax in the second worship frame. With these points in mind, a succinct description of each key should clarify the role of the performance model in explicating the implicit musical and ritual gestures.

The key of *inspiration* can bring to a performance a sparkling sense of newborn urgency, the kind of crisis-oriented vigor that drives the conception and gestation of a musical idea. As a performance begins, this sense of catalytic inspiration fuels the transition from speech to song—launching speech upon the wings of sound, as it were, transforming mere words through carefully chosen and rhythmic pitch colors into peculiarly expressive musical ideas. Inspiration can be preplanned or of-the-moment; it can also be understated, apparent, or demonstrative. But a song devoid of inspiration is doomed to failure before it even begins.

Even songs already brimming over with inspiration must be restrained long enough to secure the *rapport-building* level, the two-way trust between leader and congregation that moves the latter from passivity to sustained involvement. (The master song leader will also know when to yield on occasion to congregational reticence and call it quits.) The principle of building rapport can be taught, but the intuitive sense of exactly what to do, and when and how, approximates in oral tradition the task of an orchestra conductor, whose genius realizes the score by first negotiating an ensemble's weaknesses so as to maximize its strengths. Until rapport is achieved, no song can begin to bud or blossom. But when such factors as timing and tempo, pitch and volume, combine to breathe new life into old words, the whole exceeds the sum of its parts.

As the *momentum* key embarks, speech gives way completely to singing (speech-song yields to pure song-song), movement takes on prominence, and there is the sense of a musical body in motion whose implicit end is not yet fully determined. Depending on the particular regional style in question, this sense of momentum can occur either suddenly or gradually, but in most styles the momentum key will achieve creative moments through rises in intensity that are fed by or lead to poetic rhythms and sound portraitures.

Most often signaled by a tempo acceleration, the array of gestures imbedded in the *quickening* key reinforce the sense of movement achieved as the momentum built during the previous stage of the performance. By this time, those still on the fringes of the worship event (perhaps owing to fatigue, disinclination, or other distractions) are energized to join in by the inexorably growing musical consensus. Such a quickening, freed from the deceptively static qualities of earlier keys, can renew or transform the view of one's situation, promoting a sense of divine or personal revelation.

The *ecstasy-freedom* key is the culmination of black vernacular worship and becomes a desirable (but not inevitable) end for many performances. Here, song gives way to speech, vocables, movement, or some combination of these as functional concerns exceed the limitations of sound itself. While many events never achieve this stage, this does not mark them as incomplete. Such hymns, songs, prayers, or moans may remain within the first three or four keys throughout the performance and still serve to advance the overall progress of the worship ritual. In fact, many congregations only experience ecstasy-freedom—the sense of ultimate liberty in the worship ritual—once or twice during the course of several years. Nevertheless, such mountaintop experiences are critical to the corporate life of black Baptist congregations.

Once a performance has manifested inspiration and rapport, it has met the minimum requirement for effectiveness. The inspiration is an outward demonstration that conveys to the other participants that the hymn raiser or song leader really does have something urgent and significant to say through the words he or she is singing. The "call" of these opening verses beckons an earnest, nonformulaic "response," which signifies that the message of the song has struck home in the hearts of the auditors. The rapport stemming from that inspired call and deeply felt response connects the leader and the group in an interdependent cycle of communication.

By way of a spoken interlude, the song leader or another person might offer a testimony or brief exhortation, which more sharply defines the sense of inspiration that provoked the song. By contrast, a retreat from a song's opening lines may signal a new song or a complete change in direction. Wherever a powerful basis of inspiration is coupled with rapport, the succeeding stages—momentum and quickening—may be compressed or telescoped and difficult to observe. Singers describe the ability to know where one is in the service and to intuit what comes next as a talent from God, freely given. This is the mythical character of African American ritual, which has too often been sensationalized in sacred and secular contexts by blurring the lines between the stereotypes of "natural" musicianship and the reality of acquired skills that always enhance the gift. The communal sense of the music acknowledges the power of individuals to make a difference in the ritual, but the means to power often lie hidden within the dynamic interaction between various individuals and the group. This is one of the reasons why so much lore—some true, some not—follows the preachers, singers, and jazz musicians who hold the reins of this social and ritual power.

THE CONTINUUM AND FIVE-KEY SEQUENCE EXEMPLIFIED
IN A CONGREGATIONAL SONG

As an example of applying the lining out–ring shout continuum (and the five-key sequence) to a specific sacred performance, this chapter closes with an account of a performance of the song "I'm Going On to See My Lord." In this extraordinary performance, all five keys were struck, moving from inspiration and rapport-building through momentum and quickening and finally achieving complete ecstasy-freedom. I found the intensity of the rendition, which I witnessed firsthand, singularly moving as both worship and performance, and its impact remains vivid in memory. It is a paragon of the structural and timbral subtleties, the moods and interactive dynamics, as well as the broad formal outlines that are distinctive in African American sacred (and secular) performances.[9]

The occasion was the monthly meeting of the Washington-Baltimore chapter of the United Southern Prayer Band, held on November 15, 1997. The body was an aggregation of African Americans from various churches in the Carolinas and the Washington-Baltimore area, many of whom had migrated north from a common region of Piedmont South Carolina, near Rock Hill and Chester. The fifty-nine-year-old organization's local chapters meet monthly for an extended period of devotional singing, praying, and testifying on a Saturday evening at 9 and continue until about 1 A.M. The monthly meetings are, in effect, extended devotionals without the preaching service, which follows on Sunday.

Grounded in speaking more than singing, the deceptively simple texts of congregational songs turn upon a hook, or engaging sound idea, that is both musical and rhetorical. The effectiveness of congregational singing is measured not by the abstract quality of vocal sounds or "pure music," but by the effect of spoken/chanted words upon listeners and participants. Because the effect of the singing hinges upon an idiomatic flow of words as shapers of sound nuances, a song leader must persuasively impress the sense of the text upon the hearts and minds of the congregation in the opening lines.

Leading lines that are answered by the same group response throughout is the form typical of the low country and Sea Island shout spirituals with cross-rhythmic (as opposed to offbeat) clapping that have been particular to coastal Gullah traditions. By contrast, Piedmont chant-based and inflected song styles more often quote hymn verses or hymnlike verse forms—"wandering verses"—which have been transmitted for generations through oral tradition. This Prayer Band meeting brought together in one setting both the hymnody and the oral traditions, including the lining-out hymns themselves, songs with hymn texts as verses, and the orally transmitted stock of verses that are interchangeable between songs, yielding a sum much greater than either of the parts.

Until about 11 P.M., the meeting had proceeded at an even intensity, without large peaks or valleys. Change was signaled when a man I will call Brother Unknown came into the meeting.[10] He sat quietly, singing along on several songs and at first showing little sign of assertiveness or physical involvement in the event. But the moment of inspiration came when, in the course of the song "It's a Good Time in Zion, I Believe," Brother Unknown apparently became "full" and ready to venture the leading of "I'm Going On to See My Lord." Having arrived late, he had no way of knowing that the song had been sung earlier in the evening. Beginning in a somewhat detached yet expressive parlando, a foot-patting rhythm quickly suggested an underlying pulse, although the rhythmic outlines remained far from evident. This early paradox between rhythmic discursion and incision was uncanny, and the very manner of his early delivery portended what was to come (see example 25).

Everything about Brother Unknown's singing and presence was, in one way, odd and out of joint—he wore a medium gray suit whereas all the other leaders wore subdued blacks and blues—but his sense of rapport with the group seemed immediate, and his gestures, though ungainly, were utterly on the mark. At one point, he even covered his face with his hands—as if to signify upon selflessness!—for what seemed like an eternity (perhaps five seconds) between verses, but because clapping and patting in a powerful swing rhythm were already pushing the tempo, the song could well afford the luxury. Brother Unknown sang and carried himself in such a way that the air became charged with an "anything can happen" kind of expectancy. His gestures and bearing made a distinction between the leader as a soloistic presence who also facilitated by driving the rhythm and intensity of the singing through his focused unpredictability and the chorus who followed his structured yet flexible variations. His distinctive timbre guided without dominating the singing, and the solid rhythmic pulse created momentum and direction; but the recurring hints of reticence between verses also withheld momentarily the fulfillment we were, by that time, insisting upon. In the hindsight of transcription (see example 25), I can see that although he was in most cases only delaying the rhythmic flow by inserting an occasional 2/4 measure into the prevailing 4/4 rhythm, this signifying strategy was extremely effective.

After five riveting choruses of the song's a-b-c-b form, a quickening took place soon after Brother Unknown playfully said to the group, "You know, 'I'm 'on' git out ch'all's way." He must have been testing us to see if we liked what was happening as much as he did, and if so, the sisters did not disappoint him; the chorus of injunctions included, "You ain't in de way," "Help yo'self," "Brother, work on it," and "Sing it some mo'!" Mother Williams, in her nineties but feisty and spirited, stood up, shook her finger at him, and put the matter most forcefully: "No you ain't, let's get on with it." This

Music example 25. Transcription of "I'm Going On to See My Lord."

spoken chorus created a commotion, underscoring the dawning sense of expressive liberty. By now everyone was standing up, and perhaps this was the spur Brother Unknown had expected. In this movement to ecstasy-freedom, he sang two more choruses, then gave way to another leader, who in turn was relieved by another, extending the song to more than nine minutes to make it one of the lengthiest of the evening.[11] Though length is one indication of a song's fundamental viability in most congregational styles, it does not of itself always indicate intensity; more often, it conveys an implied consensus that the song in progress *needs* to be sung. Such had also been the case with the previous song, "It's a Good Time in Zion," sung in the chantlike Piedmont style, in which songs develop momentum slowly and require more chorus repetitions to arrive at peak intensity. Brother Unknown sang "I'm Going On to See My Lord" in the more volatile inflections of the sandhills style, which are graphic and immediate in their use of poetic rhythms and portraiture sound, but seldom sustain their energies toward the high points of quickening or ecstasy-freedom, which are more common in the Piedmont tradition.

Knowing that he had the floor, Brother Unknown moved ahead with a performance that was as much visual as aural. The mix of smiles, frowns, face-hiding, bravado, walking the floor, and hand gestures heightened the implied connections between lived experience and performance. It is in this sense that the best performers cause us to forget the fact of their persons as distinct from their engagement in both the dynamics of group activity and the metacommunications that ritually comment upon deeply felt personal experience.

The performance's foundation was a rooted yet flexible portraiture sound, manifested as a strong but ever-pliant sense of pulse. For although it was performed in a manner that constantly exploited the tensions between speech and motor rhythms, a powerful, coherent pulse was never in doubt. A gifted song leader must anchor his or her singing in the common ground of a pulse, even while the words of the choruses float upon the free and natural quality of speech rhythms. Here, the portraiture quality featured actual speech sounds and irregular, freely measured speech rhythms as much as moaning, liquid pitch sounds.

Examining the performance of "I'm Going On to See My Lord" in greater detail, we can see the interaction of rhythmic momentum with events occurring out of rhythm and more generally see the warp and woof of interactive elements unfolding in the ritual process. As Brother Unknown begins, his voice soars over the ambient sounds of group members talking here and there. His first statements draw quiet but affirmative responses from individuals. First, an "hmmm" sound in a male voice, as if a man in the group is savoring the goodness of the opening phrase he has heard. A sister then interjects her answer—a well-defined "yes"—in the same phrase. In the next phrase, a muted treble laugh is heard, a sound that chuckles with rather than at the song leader. A line or so later, a more obviously male voice sustains a laughing sound, which implies that the song-thought is resonating with his mood. Then another male voice tells Brother Unknown to "roll it" (which is to say, go on with it), then there is another laughing sound. These sounds, all occurring within the span of the first chorus, set the stage for the ritualized mayhem that will soon signal the group's vigorous approval of the song and its leader.

Ambient sounds are as absent from the second chorus as they were present in the first, as pure singing takes over. This contrast suggests that those who were either listening to or actively commenting upon Brother Unknown's narrative in the first chorus have either affirmed their trust in his leadership or, for whatever reasons, decided that he indeed has a song to sing and it is time to help him sing it. There are some emphatic hand claps here and there, but the rhythmic pulse is still being felt more than heard.

The idiosyncratic way in which Brother Unknown's first chorus makes the meaning of the text deeply felt—for example, the speechlike appeal to the Lord that begins the song, "Fix me, Jesus, fix me right"—also identifies the song as his in particular, despite the fact that it had been sung earlier that evening. His uncanny sense of timing and strong vocal presence identifies the song with his person as a singular and embodied point of origin. One example of the leader's—and increasingly the group's—purposeful idiosyncrasy occurs at measure 27, where the upper line sings "in-to the light" rather than "in the light." This simple variation enriches and energizes the rhythmic counterpoint.

As the second chorus ends, one of the brothers tells the leader to "Work it," and another can be heard laughing as if to say, "We've really got something here." When heard as counterpoint to the call-and-response structure of the song, these ambient calls and responses create a third layer of rhythmic and timbral counterpoint, which serves to ground the experience more securely in the life experience of the participants as a community. The scattered sounds are also not unrelated to the gathering verbal interjections that twice interrupt the performance, but this metacommunication about and around the worship process may be seen as a seething pot of energy that ebbs and flows—not counter to the singing but in concert with it. I could not know, based upon a chance visit to this event, all the ramifications of why Brother Unknown's song garnered such an affirmative response. But I inferred that the respondents expected him to lead this particular song sooner or later in the meeting, and now that the time had come, they were not at all disappointed. Such approvals of the performance are often expressed implicitly in the round-about, indirect nature of the talking.

By the beginning of the third chorus, the felt rhythmic sense has become fully articulated in an audible beat, and the leader's opening line is uttered so as to draw attention to the beat by syncopating certain words in the line "Done been tempted and I done been tried." The volume of the song is now rising, and the discernable rhythm is an offbeat clapping pattern. The train, as it were, of a certain quality and intensity of movement is now rolling down the track.

Another focal point of the song becomes the "Oh!" exclamation that begins the second half of the chorus form. The exclamation is sounded in a major interval between the tonic of the key (in the melody carried by men's voices) and the third above (from the women). This being the most prominent tertian harmony in the song, its soaring heights suggest a kind of arch-form melody, gradually rising to that point and falling from there to the final cadence. Such harmonies, sprinkled here and there through a texture that is dominated by heterophony and organumlike open sounds, may be read within the fabric of a hymn or spiritual as part of a process of "getting on one accord" that is musical, spiritual, and social.

In the chorus "You weep like a willow, you moan like a dove," the leader and others push or seek to move the rhythm faster at points, and the tactus has become solid enough to absorb the gradual acceleration without losing its stability. In the latter half of the chorus, male voices further encourage the leader with asides like "Yeah" and "Work it." At the next chorus, "Come on, brother, take a walk with me," the hand-clapping rhythm grows yet more stable, the asides become both spoken and sung, and every conceivable rhythmic space is being filled by a group or individual sound.

The fifth chorus, as it returns to "You fix me Jesus, you fix me right," continues this sense of fullness, which is consistent with the tendency outlined in Olly Wilson's essay "The Heterogeneous Sound Ideal in African-American Music." Having tested the waters of inspiration and rapport and found both in abundance, Brother Unknown is emboldened to continue for two more choruses. From that point on, two other leaders move the text along for five more choruses, there is another break in the song for rejoicing, signifying, and testifying, followed by a two-chorus reprise. The first of these two final choruses begins with a short, staccato accent on the words "I stepped," which creates a dramatic sense of physical motion. The climax of the performance is heard in Brother Unknown's timbrally brilliant and rhythmically consistent holler at measure 112. This hauntingly onomatopoetic sound rings as a birdlike exclamation.

The leader began the song by deftly asserting through sung-spoken word and rendered gestures that the words of the song carry real meaning for him. The group's attention was captured by the end of the first chorus, and given this growing rapport with the leader's vision of the song, they sought to make it theirs as well. An offbeat hand-clapping pattern firmly established the tempo in the third chorus, and by the fourth and fifth, an apparent momentum was quickly moving toward increased participation and a greater degree of rhythmic and melodic flexibility by individuals as well as the aggregate. Brother Unknown's ritualized demurral—"I'm 'on' git out ch'all's way"—only added fuel to the fire of the group's readiness, and by the sixth and seventh choruses, a quickening was apparent in the steadily accelerating tempo and growing body movement. When two other brothers took up the lead and continued the song for another five choruses, the movement into ecstasy-freedom was complete. Another break in the singing gave way to a vociferous second round of affirmations and rejoicing, after which two more choruses brought the song to a close.

The great strength of this performance of "I'm Going On to See My Lord" was the fullness of joy and communion signified by the exclamations and affirmations freely interjected between verses. These exchanges quickened and produced a certain ecstatic liberty, which was more apparent in the mood of the ritual than in the purely musical sense of how the performance held together. The musical intensity lagged when, after seven choruses led by Brother Unknown, the singing lost both the solid ground of a strong pulse and a playfully unpredictable tension upon that pulse. Two subsequent leaders took the reins of the song, but the rhythmic footing became less sure and their rhythmic inventions less vividly expressive. However, musical limitations notwithstanding, the ritual impact of this song performance—including the secondary leads—was the riveting peak of the entire service.[12]

The gap in the circle of continuity between leaders may have also been due to the regional style differences represented in these singers, many of whom had migrated north from neighboring but different regions of the Carolinas. These two related and proximate yet distinct regional styles— one broadly centered in expressive movement, the other focused primarily upon shouting and spirit possession per se—mediate between the Anglo-American ideal of minimal physical expression and the possession-centered African American ring-shout tradition. Against the background of regional traditions discussed in chapter 2, the singing in this Prayer Band meeting was balanced between two neighboring up-country style traditions. Perhaps the offbeat shout (of the Central Piedmont) and inflective moaning styles (of the sandhills) have become what they are over a prolonged course of continuing change and adaptation. In still more general terms, the lining out and ring shout polarities—the former found to the east of the Catawba River and the latter to the west—have balanced each other in the formation of these style traditions.

Chapter 9

"God Moves in a Mysterious Way"

*The Lining Out–Ring Shout Continuum
beyond Church Walls*

> *God moves in a mysterious way*
> *His wonders to perform*
> *He plants his footsteps in the sea*
> *And rides upon the storm.*
> WILLIAM COWPER, *1779*

While the primary focus of this book is black Baptist ritual, its general significance extends to nonchurch forms and contexts that developed in the
generations immediately following the ascendancy of Dr. Watts among black
Baptists. The black music forms that emerged in the twentieth century—
blues, gospel, rhythm and blues, and jazz—all drew upon the common body
of ritual and musical elements that developed along with nineteenth-century
congregational singing. Though reinterpreted in the terms of their secular
settings, Signifyin(g) parallels and allusions to black worship permeate secular genres as well as the concert music of many composers, white as well as
black. From blues exclamations of "Oh Lordy" to the call-and-response-
laden riffs of the big-band era to the irregularly phrased sermonic solos of
the bebop era, tokens of sacred ritual proliferate throughout the corpus of
black music. Nonetheless, the jazz context—as performance rather than
ritual—together with the greatly enhanced technical facility and expressive
range of professional performers, has elevated the music from its religious
(or social) function to a new role as the sum and focal point of the event.

Exemplary performances provide illustrations of the range and significance of interrelationships between these style traditions, as well as
instances of secular applications of the lining out–ring shout continuum
and the five-key sequence. This chapter discusses such interrelationships in
terms of several classic blues performances, all of which can be heard on
The Blues: A Smithsonian Collection of Classic Blues Singers.[1] Then it goes on to
describe and critique three seminal jazz tracks as embodiments of the ritual
form and styles included in the lining out–ring shout continuum: Billie
Holiday's signature song, "Strange Fruit"; Charlie Parker's modern jazz

improvisation on the blues, "Parker's Mood"; and the landmark collective improvisation led by Ornette Coleman, "Free Jazz."[2]

THE LINING OUT–RING SHOUT TRADITION IN THE BLUES AND BEYOND

In congregational singing, blues, and jazz alike, melodies are often composed or reworked through improvisation based upon the speech rhythms of either Standard English or regional dialects. This concept of melody emphasizes the inherent reflexivity that associates the expressive range of words with their rhythmic fluency. The *way* something is said is as important as *what* is said. Therefore, in the development of black vocal styles from Dr. Watts to blues to jazz, rhythmic placement, more than pitch organization (but not to the neglect of it), has become the primary ordering principle from which melodies and harmonies derive their shape and meaning. This sense of rhythmic placement does not generate itself but accrues from the patterns of rise and fall, vocal color, accent, and timing that are associated with speech. Without undermining the importance of timbre and pitch in these traditions, this suggests a hierarchy of ordering elements derived from speech and implicating movement. Within the development of black speech patterns from the slave era until now, epochal shifts in the semantics and sociology of language have prefigured or followed musical developments. Chapters 3 and 4 pondered the range of ways that performances of hymns and songs have occupied the spaces between speech and song, and this attribute is no less present in the early blues, which Son House linked to hymn singing (see chapter 6).

Many early blues singers manipulated words to create the grooves that have become most identified with the blues. They used repetitive guitar rhythms to accompany speechlike vocal rhythms that, although not shaped by the verse patterns of Dr. Watts hymns, reflect patterns in the lining out–ring shout continuum. The lesson of these musical narratives, for then and for all time, is that the range of personal styles which can be brought to telling one's story is inexhaustible, always adapting and changing with the situation and function of language at a particular time. The myriad blues vocal styles can be placed within the terms of the lining out–ring shout continuum. Blind Lemon Jefferson's deliveries, for example, are deeply grounded in the lining-out polarity, making fluid yet focused use of expressive freedom to exploit timbral extremes and nuances. In "That Black Snake Moan" and "Match Box Blues," phrases are freely sped up or slowed down as the rhetorical flow and dramatic impact of his statements dictates. Wailing swoops up to long notes complement rhythmically punctuated verbal statements that advance the narrative. The structural relation between long-note wails and quicker, rushing rhythms is a microcosm of the larger dramatic effect produced by alternations between operatic recitatives and arias.

The opposite, ring-shout polarity prevails in Papa Charlie Jackson's narration of "Shake That Thing" over his banjo accompaniment. The twelve-bar introductory groove is a series of three-against-two syncopations occurring over backbeats that underscore beats two and four in 4/4 meter. The mix of backbeats and syncopation suggests the rhythmic feel of the New Orleans second-lining street band tradition. The three-note descending figure is outlined in the opening four measures in a quarter-note syncopation, then it is transposed at the fifth measure to fit the subdominant chord change and quickened to an eighth-note rhythm. The four eighth notes followed by a quarter note in measure six declare a "solid" ending to what has been a "liquid" or floating rhythm.[3] The D-sharp to E alternations that begin the succeeding measure "float" the melody once again. Although two syncopations break the scalar melody in measures 9–12, the straight rhythms of this turn-around phrase balance the syncopated riffing in measures 1–9, and prepare for the more even and danceable reiterations of the succeeding vocal line.

The vocal utilizes the descending scalar figure (which has been hammered out in the introduction) to narrate the foregrounded humor and sexual implications, which are vocalized in strict rhythm. The incessant three-note descending figure creates a playful frenzy that uses the spirit possession of the ring shout as a trope to insinuate more earthy ecstasies. In this context, Jackson must tease words to fit rhythms. This extroverted approach contrasts with the subtle rhythmic liberties of Blind Lemon Jefferson, whose rhythms remain subject to the natural flow of his words. Hence Jackson is centered in the ring-shout polarity and Jefferson in lining out. Both singers slur beginning and ending consonants so as to produce an uninterrupted flow of either foregrounded or backgrounded rhythms, the former building intensity through repetition, the latter achieving similar ends through pitch bends and color changes within the blues modality.

The sense of each of these styles is also conveyed in the two Ma Rainey selections in the Smithsonian collection: the wails, moans, and liquid feel of the lining-out polarity evident in "Countin' the Blues," and the use of rhythm to develop a groove in "Shave 'Em Dry." This notion of *groove* became the generating force in the development of rhythm and blues, and it is wonderfully felt in Big Mama Thornton's belting 1952 performance of "Hound Dog," the tune that Elvis Presley covered for white audiences three years later.

These, along with other jazz and blues performances, underscore the widening range of contexts and settings for black music making which became manifest between the two world wars. The conflation of the lining-out and ring-shout polarities, synthesized into blues and jazz traditions, occurred on a wide scale in sacred as well as secular black traditions. During this era of continuing South-North migration, small urban churches were formed of family and friends coming from common rural locations and singing in similar styles. But larger black congregations, which were receiving new members from many different origins, undoubtedly faced the necessity of coming up with new, hybrid styles in which large-group singing could be rhythmically and musically guided by piano (and later, Hammond organ) accompaniment.[4]

As fixed-pitch instruments hastened the demise of congregational singing traditions, gospel flourished, but only after Thomas Dorsey and others had synthesized the concept of gospel as a sacred form expressing the emotional depth of the blues (Harris 1992). Early gospel in the Chicago tradition, like the blues itself, embraced both the powerful interaction of the quartets in the Southern tradition and the solo performers who plugged the new gospel songs in the North. The musical interactions between quartets or choirs and soloists reinterpreted call-and-response structures, such that the conventional leader-group sequence was varied as accompanying instruments often "answered" soloists and soloists sang trailing exclamations underscoring group declamations.

Outside the churches, jazz was supplanting the blues as the social music of choice by the late 1920s, and, by the early 1930s, Thomas Dorsey's concept of gospel blues would stir controversy and point to new directions in black church music. By the late 1930s, jazz drummers were once again taking an increasingly well-defined and central role in fostering and nurturing the creativity of improvisers. With jazz drummers Kenny Clarke and Max Roach at the center of 1940s bebop, the role of the drums in not only playing "time" but gauging and stimulating the dramatic flow of the performance—in effect, framing it as a performed *ritual*—became an accomplished fact. Though modern jazz rhythm sections are rarely foregrounded (indeed, as we shall see, jazz has increasingly spotlighted the "front line" soloist), they have recontextualized the essential interactions that circumscribe congregational singing. Guiding and facilitating the formulation of groove or swing in the performance, jazz drummers thus mirror the role and function of congregational song leaders.

Of primary importance in the harmonic developments that marked the bebop era was the piano; however, the style was defined above all by the front-line man who could make his horn "talk." Once again, what is significant here is the extent to which black music is rooted in the potentials of speech for evoking action as a manifestation of its innate character. Marked by back-and-forth movement between "down-homeness" and urbanity, such musical narratives conflate the regularity and movement of the ring-shout polarity with the soulfulness and rhythmic freedom of lining out. From time immemorial, singers of congregational songs and hymns had been utilizing poetic rhythm and portraiture sound in a much less precise and demanding rhythmic context. The genius of Charlie Parker, Ornette

THE PROVERBIAL FOREST

Coleman, and other masters of bebop and free-form jazz improvisation captured a comparable speechlike fluency on musical instruments instead of
human voices. This was the artistic essence of the transformation of expressly
social communities—whether sacred or secular—into a concert tradition
that was increasingly formalized and specialized by the technical demands
of its highly competitive orientation.

BILLIE HOLIDAY'S "STRANGE FRUIT"

If the verse forms that the hymns bequeathed to the spirituals were dispensed with entirely by the blues, then the question arises as to what—
other than moaning inflections—blues singers retained from the older
forms. One answer lies in the chantlike minimalist concept of vocal melody,
which balances the rhythmic inventiveness and textual innuendo in the
work of blues singers as well as jazz vocalists like Louis Armstrong and, most
notably, Billie Holiday. In both regular choruses and scat singing, Armstrong
simplified melodies and then infused what remained with the emphatic
momentum of swing rhythms (compare his scat singing in "Hotter Than
That" with the opening melody; see *Smithsonian Collection of Classic Jazz*,
vol. 1). This melodic minimalism follows from the "flattening out" of
melodic contours discussed in chapters 2 and 5, and it builds upon the
impetus of recitative chant that is so fundamental to both Dr. Watts hymn
singing and black preaching.

The power and directness of Billie Holiday's singing reflected, without
imitating, that of her stylistic "mentor," Bessie Smith. Both of these most
original approaches to vocalization were premised upon relentless media-
tions between the continuum's two poles; in their best performances, both
women maintained swinging rhythms (ring-shout polarity) and a natural
sense of speakerly timbral inflections (lining-out polarity). Typical of
Bessie's gift for flowing seamlessly between the two is "Jailhouse Blues" and
"Mama's Got the Blues," in both of which she approaches a range of held
notes with pitch inflections that implicate black speech rhythms. Billie Holiday became legendary for her ability to create semantic implications that
transformed banal tunes such as "Tea for Two," "What a Little Moonlight
Can Do," or "Me, Myself, and I" into interesting musical expeditions. This
"less is more" principle of chantlike rhythmic grooves was also inherited
from early bluesmen like Robert Johnson, Papa Charlie Jackson, and others
who appropriated melodic-rhythmic motives to vocalize not just logical
statements but allusions, insinuations, and storytelling metaphors that
weave together musical, social, and personal meanings.

Along with the plainspoken emotional directness that Holiday shared
with Smith, the stylized rhythmic patterns of swing, while understated,
are very present in Holiday's eloquent delivery of "Strange Fruit." The

inimitable sense of drama that galvanizes this performance is grounded in the concept of swing, which Holiday, along with Armstrong, Lester Young, Count Basie, and others, helped to develop and refine. While the song does not actively "swing" like a medium or up-tempo jazz performance, there is a knowing placement of the syllables in time that is stylized by the rhetorical vocabulary of dotted and triplet rhythms that comprise the lexicon of swing.

While her performances of jazz and pop standards like "I Can't Give You Anything but Love," "Them There Eyes," and "Gimme a Pigfoot"—especially in the early years of her career—play upon the ring-shout end of the continuum, Billie Holiday is best remembered for her way with slower tunes and compositions that suited her deep sense of drama and poetic expression. Her renditions of tunes like "I Love You, Porgy," "Good Morning, Heartache," "God Bless the Child," and "Don't Explain" thus exploit the possibilities of the lining-out polarity. It is this end of the continuum that is so brilliantly explored in the Lewis Allen song "Strange Fruit"—written as a protest of the lynchings that enforced Jim Crow justice—which became her vocal signature. The 1945 recording of this selection reveals both the discipline and power of Holiday's melodic concision and the swing roots of her rhythmic concept (see *The Jazz Singers*, vol. 3).[5] As in other performances, her approach is to understate and insinuate ideas and, in so doing, to imbue the thoughts with a life of their own. Here, the airily understated force of her demeanor balances the weight of virtually every line in the song text. This indirection maximizes the song's biting irony and must have mediated between the dual sensibilities represented by the integrated audiences to which she sang it.

The complexities begin with the text itself. The lyrics unfold in a series of short, irregular phrases, each line consisting of two phrases held in an antecedent-consequent relationship—a relationship that is mirrored throughout in Holiday's phrasing. The first stanza is:

Southern trees bear strange fruit	(3 syllables + 3 syllables)
Blood on the leaves and blood at the roots	(4 + 5)
Black bodies swinging in the Southern breeze	(5 + 5)
Strange fruit hanging from the poplar trees	(4 + 5)

Such poetic "sound bites" are similarly apparent in Thomas Dorsey's signature gospel song, "Take My Hand, Precious Lord." In this case, the phrases are used as rhythmic hooks that build and maintain the momentum of the song once a tempo is established:

Precious Lord, take my hand	(3 + 3)
Lead me on, let me stand	(3 + 3)
I am tired, I am weak, I am worn	(3 + 3 + 3)

This way of delivering short phrases followed by silences, then gradually lengthening them to become more lyrical statements is also common in black preaching and praying.[6] Because the gesture does not depend for its effect upon the particulars of speech—whether Standard English or dialect—as much as upon rapport and momentum, it is as often found among seminarians as among ministers without formal training.

Whereas melodic contours have been compressed or flattened out by many black vocal bards (known and unknown), the "Strange Fruit" narrative is already heavy with recitativelike note repetitions telling the poem's story. Therefore, in Holiday's performance, she uses the melody line's upper and lower neighbors and chord tones beyond the fifth to tickle and tease out expressive and harmonic nuances.

This most unromantic ballad is sung in a freely measured style that, despite constant rubato, never loses its tautness. This steadiness is largely due to the supreme rhythmic control exercised by Holiday. The pianist, Milt Raskin, awaits her every move, and though never in a hurry, she does not waste time. Moving more here or holding back there, a steady, expressive continuity links the stand-alone quality of the lyrical subphrases noted above. There are many repeated notes, and most of the movement is in seconds, chiefly downward. These purposeful yet gentle undulations create a flow of understated movement wherein each word is "placed" and framed with a certain tone quality and inflection, so as to play a strategic role in moving us to the unexpected but poignant ending, when the singer suddenly drops down to touch a low F before swooping up an octave to the bent-note conclusion. Without establishing a strictly measured pulse, the rhythmic movement is organized around long-short and short-long sequences of eighth and sixteenth notes in quadruple time, with contrasting triplet rhythms for textual emphasis or at phrase beginnings. This alternation between triple and duple patterns intimates rather than explicates swing and establishes a rhythmic informality that is almost conversational.

While cliché references to moaning or blue-note intonation are noticeably absent, Holiday's grace notes, slides, and undulations implicate the blues tradition. This phrasing pattern is set in the first eight measures, where stepwise scalar movements or undulations away from and back to the same note dominate in her delivery of the first, second, and fourth lines of the poem. The plane of this melodic contour is broken in the third line by the drama of ascending minor thirds which foretell the arrival of the diminished chords that end the phrase.

Reaching down to F below middle C and up a minor tenth to the A-flat above, the melody line is "through-composed" by Holiday (no doubt from her many previous performances between 1939 and 1945). It begins in her low-medium "talking" register and sustains its melodic flatness through a gradual ascent to the dramatic climax of the final measures, where the surprise ending encompasses an octave leap from her lowest note. This F avoids the obvious sound of the tonic B-flat. Inasmuch as the low F is used only six times—chiefly as a pedal tone to achieve dramatic effect—the melodic movement is concentrated in the minor seventh between the tonic B-flat and the seventh above, A-flat. The melodic references to the F that dominate the final moments of the song create a fitting relief from the ponderous tonic B-flat that Holiday emphasizes at the start of the song. These tonal references to the low F as a pedal tone or kind of vocal launching pad are fitly consummated by the octave leap from it that ends the piece. This, coupled with the undulation to the lower neighboring tone in the final phrase, establishes a melodic coherence that balances the freshness of improvisation with the stratagems of forethought. In this sense, the movement of the piano (from the seventh of the B-flat minor chord down to the sixth on the final note) responds to Holiday's closing insinuation of the lower neighboring tone, and to the dissonant and brutal irony of the song's mood.

Absent from this performance (and from most Holiday interpretations) are the asides and exclamations commonly interjected as jive talk in blues and jazz and as affirmation in spirituals, hymns, and gospel. This reticence suggests the attitude and spirit of "coolness," which both linked her artistic and personal sensibilities with those of tenor saxophonist Lester Young and established a precedent for the creative reticence that would mark the cool jazz of the early 1950s. In the absence of the interjections which underscore the communal dimension of other black music forms, Billie, Lester, and their cool-jazz disciples embraced the concept of swing rhythm as a musical code of commonality, which replaced the more outward expressions of community in earlier styles as a metalinguistic and musical code of behavior and speech.

"PARKER'S MOOD"

Part of my project in *Lining Out the Word* is to explain certain paradoxical continuities in the stylistic development of African American music. Among these is the coincidence of rhythmic patterns—especially poetic rhythms and portraiture sound—in sacred songs and modern jazz. This kind of linkage can be heard between, say, Rev. C. J. Johnson's treatment of the hymn "I Heard the Voice of Jesus Say" (*Dr. Watts*, no. 10) and the bebop classic "Parker's Mood" (*Smithsonian Collection of Classic Jazz*, vol. 3). The glib response to my claim might be that this coincidence is neither indirect nor paradoxical. But anyone who has listened extensively to congregational songs and hymns, to blues and rhythm and blues, and to jazz singing realizes that the riffs and licks I call poetic rhythms were not apparent in the lexicon of jazz improvisation until *after* the bebop foment. Although jazz singing since the coming of Louis Armstrong has teemed with the liquid sounds of moaning (resituated and desacralized as "blue" notes) and with the rhythmic freedom that accrues from the commingling of speech inflections with a regular pulse, it was only with 1940s jazz that a new rhythmic synthesis was achieved between these poles of abandon and regularity—or artistic freedom and the discipline from which it stems. Although such musical gestures had long been implicated in the instrumental improvisations of seminal figures like Louis Armstrong and Lester Young, hastened by changes in the larger society as well as the quality of community among musicians, such flights of rhythmic virtuosity became commonplace in jazz only during and after the 1940s bebop era. Just as congregations sing sacred songs for their own edification, so did bebop musicians—as well as certain vocalists like Billie Holiday and Sarah Vaughan—utilize jam sessions and other performances as occasions for explicitly musical interaction and competition.[7] Hence continuities that lie at the heart of black music making were implicit but less than apparent in the commercial and dance-oriented context of jazz performance before the 1940s.

It would have been a logical continuity for such gestures to have surfaced in the early jazz styles, which were heavy-laden with blues. Instead, it required the virtuosity that became the standard for jazz performers during the bebop era to seamlessly and fluently incorporate the vocal gestures of black hymn singing. Such a once- or twice-removed reinterpretation of a particular element is certainly not an uncommon cycle of artistic renewal—leaping forward by jumping backward, as it were. This perspective upon Dr. Watts as a particular vocal genre that has had a prismatic, multivalent influence upon other genres has prompted me to reflect upon the basic elements and organizing principles of black music.

Thomas Brothers (1997) clearly articulates the role of harmony in bridging the transition between "autonomous" black music genres, like the spirituals and field hollers, and "crossover" forms like blues, rhythm and blues, and jazz. The interesting paradox about the jazz of the 1940s is that as harmonies became more complex and sophisticated, in the functional Western sense, they also became more subtly and flexibly adapted to the tonal inflections of the blues. What is more, this new subtlety was as much rhythmic as it was melodic and harmonic. The essence of this new way of approaching rhythm pushed the boundaries in both directions and, in so doing, paradoxically blurred the lines in between. On the lining-out end of the continuum, during the 1940s, the aesthetic of the blues—which has never sought to apologize for a good gut-wrenching moan—became not less emphatic but somehow more abstract, or at least more expressive over a wider range, without a loss of immediacy. At the ring-shout polarity, the blinding speed of up-tempo bebop tunes stylized the moods of (social) partying and (religious) celebration as well as (hard) work that had formed the rhythmic basis of swing. Tunes or improvisations in slower tempos, which frequently called upon double-time passages and irregular rhythms, drew upon both expressive poles in the formation of a musical language that could encompass the worldwide range of commercial and art music subsumed in the jazz rubric. This is the kind of watershed in music history that caused so many musicians to feel that Charlie Parker had extended the language of music in the direction toward which they had been striving. Such terms of merger between old and new are illustrated nowhere better than in Bird's 1948 blues improvisation "Parker's Mood" (*Smithsonian Collection of Classic Jazz*, vol. 3).[8]

The fanfarelike opening of "Parker's Mood" is a blues cry upon the G-minor triad that parallels the B-flat major tonality of the piece. While the figure features the minor parallel of the major triad that becomes a primary theme in Parker's celebrated improvisation, the triplet rhythms that will also unify and add interest to the solo are not heard until the first chorus. Pianist John Lewis's response to Parker's opening call extends his melodic line and, along with the brush work of Max Roach on drums, lays down a quadruple rhythmic pad, which insinuates triplet rhythms. The slow, shuffling triplet evokes the rhythm and blues of 1940s jump bands, like that of saxophonist Louis Jordan, that were playing tunes in a slow 4/4 meter, compounded by a triplet figure on every beat. Of course, earlier styles of blues, gospel, and jazz had also used triplets alongside and against duple rhythms as a means of heightening rhythmic tension. However, this shuffle beat is at the heart of the major-triad figure that opens Parker's solo proper, and it presages the faster sixteenth-note triplets that will recur throughout.

The beginning of the tune establishes a sense of regularity via the first and clearest of many references to shuffle rhythm throughout the piece. Two parallel phrases create a four-measure period, which is left open by a half cadence on the tonic (major-minor) seventh chord, anticipating the standard blues change of harmony to the subdominant in measure 5. Until now, grace-note blues inflections have colored the members of the major-minor seventh chord in a way that applies what we have discussed as portraiture sound. But in measures 5 and 6, Parker inserts a compelling jazz adaptation of poetic rhythm featuring the repetition of a motive or lick that, without doing violence to the flow, pulls greatly upon the regularity of the rhythmic feel. His triplet figure, which features the thirteenth of the chord (or the sixth, if you choose) and its upper neighbor, the seventh, sounds first on beats two and four; then, in the next measure, it is displaced a half beat ahead to the upbeats of one and three. The phrase ends by restating the rhythmic pattern of four sixteenth notes followed by the triplet that marked the opening phrase. In measure 8 he "runs the changes" by outlining the scales corresponding to the ii-V, bop-style chord substitution inserted by pianist Lewis. Measures 9–11 bring a return to the triplet figure, this time moving it downward in a sequence of six repetitions that dance across the beats without the tension of syncopation that marked the earlier triplets.

The next chorus is introduced by a one-measure fanfarelike motive that alludes to the statuesque isolation of the figure that opened the piece. This is followed in measures 14 and 15 by a different kind of poetic rhythm, one that implicates portraiture sound. The evocation is achieved by its fluid treatment of rhythm and melody, but save a single grace note on the last beat of measure 14, its speechlike character is achieved by a knowing sequence of triplets, followed by quintuplets and sextuplets, all of which lend a cascading push to the rhythm and create the illusion of playing out of time yet firmly within the meter. By contrast, the phrase in measures 16 through 18 begins in the urbane reserve of chordal improvisation, only to be extended through repetition that winds its way back to the rhythmic poetry of blues licks as it draws near to its terminus on the first note of measure 19. While colored by blues inflection, the interest is sustained in the closing phrase of the chorus by a Bach-like series of chromatic tones that converge, first upon a B-flat, then upon a D that begins the final measure of this chorus.

After a solo piano chorus by Lewis, Bird's third chorus begins with a "preaching blues" triplet figure, which ends on a deftly placed, shoutlike fall away from the thirteenth of the E-flat chord in the second measure. The phrase and this emphatic closing note mark the expressive climax of the whole performance. As before, a contrasting phrase follows in chromatic tones, which create melodic gravity toward the G in measure 3 and the F that begins measure 5. As he did at the parallel point in the previous choruses, Bird calls upon the syncopation of rhythmic poetry to create tension and excitement in measures 5 and 6, which is resolved by the downward-tending phrases and logical voice leading of measures 7 and 8. Perhaps the longest whole-cloth repetition among many repetitions of shorter licks, the last phrase repeats the quick rise and downward fall heard at the same point in his first two choruses, and closes with a scalar passage that fills in the outline of altered chord tones first heard in the penultimate measure of the first chorus.

What kind(s) of musical discourse are we hearing in "Parker's Mood"? The work opens and closes with a mythic fanfare—in hindsight, a moment parallel in significance to the point when a preacher pontifically takes his text before preaching the sermon. Each of the three choruses begins with a gesture, an audible representation of what Agawu describes as "the physical manifestation of a more fundamental communicative urge" (1995: 27). Each of these is a kind of holler, a riffing yet slow and deliberate pattern, which becomes the linchpin for what happens in the remainder of each blues chorus. The first of these is a classic antecedent-consequent phrase (a-b-a-b'), and the remaining two pose a similarly striking melorhythmic idea, from which the rest of the chorus unfolds. The middle of each chorus (approximately bars 4–8 of the blues form) proceeds from a rhetorical stutter to establish a stylized gesture, a kind of sonic dance in which the seeming stutter is redeemed and elaborated into a fuller melorhythmic statement that imposes the tension of syncopated two-against-three (vertical) or two-followed-by-three (horizontal) rhythms. His closing gesture in all three choruses is a pattern of converging melodic lines, one sequence of pitches descending and the other ascending to the target note of the phrase. So, within a conservative economy of ideas, the range of expression is stunningly coherent. As in congregational singing, the effect of the musical moment is always contingent upon and particular to the quality of interaction that is occurring within the ensemble. For example, while the stutter-dance syncopation is heard in all three choruses, the sense of rhythm is far less syncopated and more stylized in the second chorus. Here, Parker quickly responds to the lightness, almost frivolity, implicated by the swinging flow of Lewis's piano and the double-time swing that Roach teases from the snare drum with his brushes. This stylized sound becomes a strut, as it were, which calls to mind the pugnacious adolescence of what Louis Armstrong did so many years before on the tune "Strutting with Some Barbecue" (see *Smithsonian Collection of Classic Jazz*, vol. 1). In that piece, one hears what is essentially one quality of expression—call it jubilation, celebration, or what you will. But in the Parker solo, the range of expression is constantly, adroitly shifting from one melorhythmic mood to another and is therefore much less predictable. A special dimension of the musical language that Bird helped to transform in modernity was his ability to "speak" with a certain lucidity yet quickly turn that simple eloquence in myriad expressive directions without losing coherence. In the degree to which each could be subverted to his purposes, he mastered the musical equivalents of both Spoken Soul and Standard English, and plied them seamlessly between the poles of the lining out–ring shout continuum.

ORNETTE COLEMAN'S "FREE JAZZ"

The place of the piano in the mediation between the blues and jazz has been a two-edged sword: on one hand, the sophisticated adaptations of the blues sound formulated by artists like Duke Ellington, Theolonius Monk, Bud Powell, and Horace Silver were foundational to improvisational flights like those of Charlie Parker and John Coltrane, which extended jazz tonality to its limits; on the other hand, Ornette Coleman and other performers of extended-tonality jazz have argued that the piano imposes a harmonic preoccupation that hinders the sense of musical freedom inherent in music of African American heritage. Building upon the styles of foundational figures such as Louis Armstrong and Lester Young, bebop, cool jazz, and hard bop consolidated the centrality of individual soloists who improvised over the harmonic "changes" or chord progressions. Notwithstanding the crucial but less visible interactions within rhythm sections and between rhythm players and soloists, modern jazz placed soloists, rather than band-leaders, in the foreground. This development, coupled with advances in jazz harmony, produced a creative tension between individuals and groups that could only be fulfilled in the new jazz that was attaining self-conscious-ness as an art form. In reaction to the harmonic and technical intensity of bebop, some critics and patrons of jazz facilitated a revival of New Orleans jazz during the late 1940s and 1950s. In turn, the impact of collective improvisation—the hallmark of the New Orleans tradition—found new res-onance within the terms of the jazz avant-garde of the 1960s. Perhaps the general tendency of artistic style evolutions to reach back in order to leap forward prompted the avant-garde musicians to reevaluate the role of the soloists in relation to the group. This collective improvisation was a jazz realization of music making's principal function in African American set-tings, that of affirming a sense of community and belonging.

The alto saxophonist and composer Ornette Coleman organized the col-lective improvisation "Free Jazz," which was released by Atlantic Records (ATL1361) in 1961 as a thirty-eight-minute album of the same name. It has become a lasting sign of the changes that were afoot in jazz and a testament to a special assemblage of great musicians. The recording has achieved long-term visibility through an excerpt from Coleman's solo, which is included in the *Smithsonian Collection of Classic Jazz*. However, the larger out-lines of the performance, especially as a *ritual* form, are only discernable in the full performance. The ensemble character of the "Free Jazz" recording is defined both by the conspicuous absence of the piano and by the pres-ence of two bassists, Scott LaFaro and Charlie Haden, and two drummers, Billy Higgins and Ed Blackwell.[9] The horns feature the blues tonal sound of trumpeter Freddie Hubbard and tonally shifting yet rhythmically stylized improvisations by Coleman on alto saxophone and Don Cherry on trum-pet, with the borders in between straddled by bass clarinetist Eric Dolphy.

The recording session's stereo mix emphasizes the eight-man lineup as a double quartet rather than an octet, although there is considerable spillover of the sound between channels and interaction across the two groups. Cole-man, Cherry, LaFaro, and Higgins are heard on the left channel; Dolphy, Hubbard, Haden, and Blackwell on the right. The recording session was a carefully planned event. Coleman seems to have chosen the musicians with a knowing hand, aware of their complementary skills and orientations. An ensemble interlude was loosely scored, or at least planned so as to effect consistent transitions between solos by each of the performers. The resul-tant LP record, which featured the Jackson Pollock painting *White Light* on the cover, preserved the second of two studio takes.

In his liner notes for the LP, Ornette Coleman describes several of the nine interludes that frame the collective improvisation as "harmonic unisons," in which "each horn has its own note to play but they are so spaced that the result will not sound like harmony but like unison." Like Dr. Watts hymn singing, these vocally conceived lines, clustered together, can be heard as a singular mass of porous "blocks" which form an imposing "wall" of sound. Although Dr. Watts harmonies are more sharply defined by organumlike movement in parallel fifths, the less-predictable harmonic unisons of "Free Jazz" share with hymn singing the illusion of vast and uncharted spaciousness.

Nine ensemble passages frame "Free Jazz" into a sequence of eight solos, each followed by collective improvisation. The opening "harmonic unison" is balanced by a similar closing gesture; between them, seven interludes precede solos by each member of the ensemble. During the horn solos, in particular, instruments "hold court" (or "have church") by way of call-and-answer dialogues from soloist to group and among the musicians.

Following a frenetic five-second crescendo of cascading rhythm vamps and horn lines, the opening harmonic unison consists of seven prolonged three-note cluster chords that, without the complete loss of tension, grow progressively thinner and less complex as they ascend in pitch and intensity. Lasting about fifteen seconds, these slow-moving chords manage to hang together as a progression without calling attention to themselves as harmony per se. Perhaps this is the magical paradox of the phrase "harmonic unison." Under the chords, the drummers establish a frenetic sense of double-time rhythm which adds a rhythmic dimension to the intensity of the dissonant yet coherent harmonies.[10]

The opening solos, by Eric Dolphy, then Freddie Hubbard, each following a harmonic unison interlude, establish a certain sense of the soloist's role in relation to the ensemble of improvisers. Absent the pervasive chordal harmonies of jazz, the sound space is framed by the ride-cymbal rhythms and walking-blues bass lines underneath, which lend a stylized sense of jazz normalcy to this pianoless instrumentation. While the bass lines all point toward a tonal goal, each is provisional and constantly shifting. Predictably, the horn solos and improvised responses from the other three horns all emerge as foregrounded figures, movements, and images. First we hear Dolphy alone, then the collective of other wind instruments answer his calls and sustain dialogues with him and among themselves. About five minutes into Dolphy's solo, a sense of melodic focus and emotional intensity emerges. Then Freddie Hubbard's trumpet solo continues and hastens the slow-developing sense of inspiration and rapport. Later, as the process unfolds, it is Coleman's solo that generates the momentum, which quickens collective energies and propels the whole into high celebration.[11]

If the whole work can be heard as a sermon, we come to the (perhaps premature) climax in Coleman's solo. It is a tonal conception—bluesy, funky, and highly melodic—yet as it avoids predictably functional tonality, the melodic-harmonic focus never gets stale. He also produces a very pure and vital alto saxophone sound, one utterly unconstrained by conventional technical limitations. While his work here evokes Charlie Parker, Sonny Stitt, Charles McPherson, Phil Woods, and other great stylists, it is irreducible and free of received mannerisms.[12] In response to the fluid and forceful stream of ideas, his fellows engage Coleman in a series of riffs, licks, and hits, each more intense than the last. Table 8 charts the progression of themes and ensemble responses during Coleman's solo.

Singling out Coleman's solo is not a negative critique of the others but an observation about where it stands in relation to the musical events that come before and after. Dolphy's and Hubbard's solos, which precede it, and Don Cherry's, which follows it, are improvised in harmonic-melodic styles, which avoid any apparent sense of key or tonal center. However, Coleman's outing is striking for its seemingly inexhaustible sense of tonal movement from place to place, with strong melodic coherence and few redundancies.[13] It is a veritable kaleidoscope of themes, key centers, and textures; as a balance to the unpredictable yet refreshing shifts of tonality, his melodic statements are anchored by heavily formulaic, shall we say "bluesy," rhythms. It may seem peculiar to speak of blues rhythms, as such, because inflections—blue notes and scales—have become the musical sign of "blues." But blues music, as such, may be heard as a range of stylized rhythms—licks, riffs, and hits—performed either as an integrated continuum or as elements which have been abstracted (emphasized) or sublimated (deemphasized) to fit the expressive needs of a given compositional context. In the avant-garde jazz context, these rhythms are less predictable than the freely measured and strictly measured rhythms of hymn singing. However, they are no less identifiable as style elements.

With help from the other horns and the rhythm section, Coleman sustains a ten-minute run of creativity that forms the momentum-filled and quickening core of "Free Jazz." Coleman has structured a form and style of improvisation in which he is most fluent, and the players respond well to his tuneful and vividly phrased rhythms. Staying in each modal orientation just long enough to establish a groove or sense of connection with the ensemble, the soloist is constantly shifting the tonal-harmonic orientation of his tuneful blues riffing. He also proves adept at instigating a surplus of melorhythmic activity, hearing and exploiting the sound of the whole yet moving on from that point to sustain his own train of thought and to initiate a new direction.

The very force and clarity of Coleman's ideas seem to compel a remarkable degree of focus and consensus from the other horns. A Blackwell drum roll builds under a wailing high note, and a series of rapid but judicious interactions unfold between soloist and collective. After the drum roll, the

TABLE 8   Improvised Themes and Ensemble Responses during Solo by Ornette Coleman

Minutes elapsed	0	1	2	3	4	5	6	7	8	9	10
Solo	I (rhythm)[a]		II (set-up)	III (lick)	IV (snakes)	V (boogie-jingle)	VI (calypso)			VII (jamming)	
Ensemble		A (drums roll-lick) B (finish)	C (long-short) D (lick)	E (funk)		F (jangle)	G (calypso)		H (noisy)	I (jamming)	

[a]Parenthetical terms are the names I have assigned to each of Coleman's thematic ideas to connote their moods.

other horns begin their first of several licks, this one repeated verbatim in unison more than a dozen times. Immediately after, the other horns complete and extend a phrase begun by Coleman, which gives him time to breathe and then head off in a different direction. By the two-minute mark in Coleman's solo, the collective has come to a most imaginative two-part textured accompaniment to the solo, featuring a cycle of long notes in one instrument balanced by a bevy of syncopated single-note exclamations in the other.

Thus far, the solo has featured a fluent stream of rhythmic, bebop-esque eighth-note phrases, all building in rhythmic momentum. With this rhythmic feel firmly established, Coleman initiates a more rapidly shifting series of thematic ideas. During the last two minutes of the solo, both soloist and ensemble reach a peak of sustained improvisatory celebration that evokes the sense of ecstasy-freedom described in chapter 8. Not only because of Coleman's inspired virtuosity but through the sustained and sensitive interaction between the musicians, this entire section masterfully exemplifies the qualities of ritual performance and prolonged, gradually swelling sense of community embraced in the lining out–ring shout continuum.

Following a unison melodic passage—what Coleman calls a "transposed unison" of what was heard at the opening of his own solo—trumpeter Don Cherry's solo opens side two. Though less prolix and complicated, his work is a deftly rhythmic continuation of the subtle interactions between a soloist and the collective. As in Coleman's solo, it seems that as the performance develops, the chorus of collective improvisers is increasingly attuned and responsive to the whims and fancies as well as the driving impetus of the soloist himself. Cherry's solo is unique in that the horns perform a harmonic unison underneath him; a drummer—Blackwell, I believe—sends him off again upon a new direction; and the two-part form of his solo closes with an effectively conversational flurry of lines from the horns. After the next interlude, the bassists, Haden and later LaFaro, quickly retreat to a much more calm and quiet melodic and spatial groove, but one that does not shrink from the established rhythmic vitality of the cymbal work by Blackwell and Higgins.

The bass solos are about half the length of the horn solos that preceded them, and the even shorter drum solos that follow feel incredibly rushed. One has to wonder if the recording engineer signaled to them that time was running out. First from Blackwell, then Higgins, we get only a glimpse of what each has to say in relation to what has gone on before. This is where, for me, the performance falls short. What could have been a powerfully ecstatic and free expression of rhythm and timbre, perhaps eliciting interaction from the horns as well, does not occur. Instead, we get two painfully brief cameos, reminiscent of the kinds of short eight- or sixteen-bar solos drummers played in swing-era band arrangements. Of course, the drummers

TABLE 9   Order and Length of Events in the Recorded
Performance of "Free Jazz"

Event	Approximate Length in Clock Time
Opening harmonic unison	00:22
Dolphy solo (bass clarinet)	04:57
Harmonic unison	00:24
Hubbard solo (trumpet)	04:15
Transposed unison	00:20
Coleman solo (alto saxophone)	09:40
Transposed unison	00:14
Cherry solo (trumpet)	05:42
Harmonic unison	00:09
Haden solo (bass)	04:27
Harmonic unison	00:09
LaFaro (bass)	03:50
Harmonic unison	00:14
Blackwell (drums)	01:18
Harmonic unison	00:09
Higgins (drums)	01:07
Total elapsed time	37:28

may have simply exhausted what they had to say, or expended their available energies, before these closing statements. Taking an even more positive attitude, one might hear the closing drum solos as preludes to the harmonic unison that closes the piece—preludes that balance the improvisatory cascade of horn lines that led into the opening harmonic unison.

Building upon the foregoing description, we can hear "Free Jazz" with particular attention to its progress along the five-key sequence. While Coleman's playing is inspired in itself, the matter of selecting, assembling, and organizing this collective improvisation was no mean feat. In this sense, we can say that *inspiration* is the ability to intelligibly communicate one's musical vision, urgency, or moment to others. This is the sense of participation that Portia Maultsby (1991) places at the core of the African-derived musical aesthetic that stresses the relationship between performance and lived experience within the circle of community. Even with professional musicians, *rapport* is neither a given nor, once it is established, a constant. Whether "Free Jazz" grew out of previous musical encounters, whether it was a rational, communication-based conversation, or whether it just "happened," these musicians came into the performance with solid rapport and maintained it throughout. Following upon an established sense of inspiration and rapport, the *momentum-producing* phase of the thirty-eight-minute jam occurs as Coleman is soloing at about the midway point of the piece. The collection of riffs and licks that emerges repeatedly out of the mix owes to the funky feel of piquant rhythms and melodies heard at the interstice between Blackwell's drum parries and Coleman's horn statements.

It is neither the improvisations nor the structural concepts but the form of the work as a whole that flounders toward the end. The overall conception of the piece proves either unrealized or unrealizable. I rather believe it is the former case: though difficult, it is possible for an improvisation of substantial length and complexity to be successfully performed. In all venues, such miracles of formal cohesiveness do occur with some frequency, but not with great predictability. Where the elements of black ritual that define the five-key sequence concur, a certain church service, sermon, or jazz performance may excel. Attempts at making the ritual more predictable tend to constrain the capacity of the performance to respond to the particularities that define each time and place. As the pressure to produce more predictable forms has multiplied with the onset of technology and the growth of the recording industry, there has been a decline in the inward vitality of the religious traditions sustained by the five-key sequence. In this sense, it is not only the market-driven pressure from *without* to conform that compromises the culture of an underprivileged ethnic minority, but also (to put it in Marxist terms) a range of needs *within* the proletarian ranks to conform to the modes of production that stem from the sources of power.

My notion of aesthetic "success," then, is the achievement of the five stages of ritual development—inspiration, rapport, momentum, quickening, and ecstasy-freedom. Rituals that are not primarily musical can succeed by simply achieving various extramusical functions within, say, the first three stages of inspiration, rapport, and momentum without going further. In many ritual settings, the advanced stages of quickening and ecstasy-freedom occur only on rare occasions. However, specifically musical contexts—even those that are generally speaking "professional," whether aesthetic or commercial—assume a higher level of technical competence and a creative ability to make extraordinary things happen (with some predictability) in the performance context. (For composers, who are by definition not improvisers, the challenge is to create something that is not only compelling, powerful, true, or beautiful, but replicable and less unpredictable.)

For such reasons, a number of outstanding musicians with jazz backgrounds have come to see the formal resources of jazz, gospel, and other popular genres—a chorus or main idea followed by an improvisation—as far too formally simplistic to spur reliable aesthetic outcomes beyond those rare and perspicacious ritual moments when things "magically" come together. On the other hand, for ritual specialists and performers in all media, there is always that realm of the inexplicable, when things spontaneously happen during performances as if by their own accord.

Congregational singing emanated from spaces defined by their particularity, wherein music was performed by communities for their own enjoyment and edification. The effectiveness of such performances has never turned upon an extravagant range of technical resources but has relied upon maximum utilization of a limited range of low-tech assets. However, such specialized, specifically functional contexts for music making cannot venture beyond a range of moods and ideas that are at once accessible, acceptable, and effective.

In slaveocracy, black musicians' performance of secular social music for blacks and, especially, for whites defined their state of privileged subservience. Later, black minstrelsy created social spaces in which performances of black music could satisfy white audiences' appetite for diversion and ideas of essentialism. For the black performers who donned blackface, this mastery of the (racial) mask facilitated modes of Signifyin(g) through which performers could send dual messages to black and white audiences. Inasmuch as interracial religious events had proven problematic even in the fervent context of the early-nineteenth-century camp meetings that characterized the Second Great Awakening, this point of mutual acceptability was critical. The blues and, in a more radical way, jazz effected larger musical and social designs for escaping the affronts and stigmas of slavery without renouncing the refinements of black vocalization and gesture descended from both visible and invisible settings for music making—that is, the "visible" professional performances for whites and "invisible" slave worship communities. The underlying sense of rhythmic groove or swing overlaid with more liquid poetic rhythms, the ambient heterophony resulting from such rhythmic textures, the positive tensions between expressive timbres and propulsive speech rhythms, all led to an enhanced capacity for sending numerous messages at the same time. These propensities—coupled with the mastery of brass and woodwind instruments (which became more available to blacks following the Industrial Revolution) and the social upheavals set in motion by Emancipation and the urban migrations—fostered new modes of black musical discourse, situated in the terms of modernity, which challenged the subjugation of slavery and Jim Crow segregation. In the jazz age, the nightspots of Harlem became the racial promised land of soaring hopes and aspirations, and the enabling musical force of instruments functioning as voices produced, from these beginnings, the sense of virtuosity first personified in the trumpet and vocal improvisations of Louis Armstrong. Singers like Billie Holiday and Ella Fitzgerald reasserted the role of the voice in virtuoso improvisation, and bebop instrumentalists and composers fully adapted instrumental forces to the dual terms of the lining out–ring shout continuum.

Emerging within the vocal textures of the continuum, African American music's distinctive character has developed from the tension between freely measured and strictly measured rhythms. Important as the concept of swing was to the evolution of jazz styles in the 1900s, that rhythmic moment was allied with gestures and speech patterns that, especially in the past thirty years, have undergone rapid change. Thus the sounds of spirituals, blues, gospel, rhythm and blues, and jazz have begun to take on a historical quality—a sense that while these traditions will live on, the time of their currency is past, and the dawn of a new cultural moment is here. This changing epoch brings African American musical culture to a new place of "youthful maturity," where the sounds of the agrarian Old South—the discernable connections to slave culture—continue alongside the teeming diversity of the New South and of the urban North and West. In this chaotic changing of the guard, the palace soldiers of modern jazz hold the battlements uncertainly against a horde of young turks who march to the rhythms of rap, speak in the language and moment of this generation, and see dimly, if at all, the ancient shoulders on which they stand.

Conclusion

Regional traditions of hymn singing continue in the hallowed places of black worship, under the cloak of autonomy and outside the domain of what some observers—and many of the participants—consider to be "music." I consider this book a first step in what should be an ongoing study of lining out and the congregational singing tradition. I have begun with a genre study instead of a specific ethnographic instance because without such a study, the gaps between the conceptual frames provided by existing studies of black sacred music, my own comparisons of regional styles of lining out, and the issue of interrelations between lining out and other black music genres seem too wide. I hope that further studies will move from this general case of attention to a single genre across regions and through time to localized field research, with the potentials for delimitation and elegance of design that it affords.

An outstanding example of such an ethnographic study, and relevant to *Lining Out the Word*, is Kofi Agawu's *African Rhythm: A Northern Ewe Perspective* (1995). Although it came to my attention after this writing was substantively complete, my conclusions about speech and rhythm concur with his findings. He articulates in detail a concept of rhythm in African (and, I submit, by extension African American) music that builds upon other scholars' descriptions of the coexistence of "free and strict rhythms" in various African music traditions (73–74, 80–82). The crux of this model is a network of apparent interrelations among gesture (as the "primordial communicative urge"), the spoken word, vocal music, instrumental music, and dance as stylized gesture (28, 181). A similar study of the generative musical power of speech and its bearing upon rhythmic styles would, I believe, reveal a closely related yet distinct semantic and expressive ordering of elements.

The "trees" of African American music have provoked certain questions—about hymns, speech-song, free and strict rhythmic styles, and ritual contexts where these forces interact—and the cultural "forest" (Clifford Geertz's "webs of significance") points to answers lying within African Americans, their music, and their rituals. While examining some of the musical trees in some detail, I have only glanced at the forest of African American culture, which can yield a greater range of musical understanding than I've drawn upon here. Five kinds of "trees" have occupied my attention in this study: (1) the ever-changing field of unified diversities that make African American music identifiable as such; (2) the processes of cultural change by which the tradition renews and adapts itself to obvious and subtle shifts in the social stratification of African Americans in relation to other groups in the United States; (3) the patterns of musical change and nonchange observable through particular attention to the role(s) of lining out in black worship; (4) the process by which North American language contact apparently modified, without fundamentally changing, African approaches to the generative relationship between speech and music; and (5) as a larger expression of the speech-music relationship, a ritual tradition that eloquently integrates music making with the whole of human reality and life experience. As a means of integrating these findings about Dr. Watts into a broad range of performance contexts, a theory—at least a hypothesis—of black music as ritual has emerged, which I call the lining out–ring shout continuum. "Either/or" questions have prolonged debates over black and white origins for the spirituals and jazz, and have failed to provide ethnic but nonracialized models for critiquing black performances. Though founded upon a present-tense, empirical base of recent fieldwork, as well as archival studies, my claim of a historical process that emphasized linguistic and musical interrelationships has led to a theoretical reconstruction of the early development of black lining out. This hypothesis both conceptualizes some nonchanging patterns of musical expression that were codified during the slave era and affords a new perspective for criticism of other music genres built upon the same aesthetic principles. By illustrating a diverse family of related yet distinct regional performance styles, *Lining Out the Word* also challenges the essentialist fallacy of identifying any one style as the singular model of black authenticity.[1]

In the course of this book, I have observed that black music performance is consistently integrative, interactive, movement-centered, and transformative. This awareness rests upon four premises: (1) Most black music genres rely upon an immediate connection between the sounds and a sense of moment—the sense that something important or influential is being "said" in the music—and this signification most often derives from the interstice between speech and song, as well as from that between the musical act and other dimensions of life. (2) As the signification is often based in links between the phenomenological experience of music making and other

aspects of life, whether spiritual or mundane, so do performances potentially include not only anyone who has something of moment to "say" but,
potentially at least, everyone present. (3) The concept of movement, which
contains various qualities of rhythmic expression (many of which are not
metronomic) is as central to African American music as it is to its African
prototypes. (4) To call a music functional says nothing about *how* it functions, and to what end. Whether they tear the church up or help everybody
let the good times roll, Dr. Watts hymns, congregational songs, blues, and
many other forms are intended to produce degrees and types of altered
consciousness. As noted in the introduction, Kwame Anthony Appiah has
observed about the nature of identities that they are multiple and complex
responses to change which oppose other identities; that they flourish
despite their "roots in myths and lies"; and that their construction is not
guided by rational forces (1992: 178). The question of identity is important
to the hymns and their genesis in the speech act because speech (or, in linguistic terms, phonology) is the strongest linguistic marker of identity in
any given culture (see Rickford and Rickford 2000: 221–29); moreover,
because the lining-out form integrates speech and singing, it has more
often marked continuities than changes.

In the larger context, social changes have spurred musical changes, and,
of these, urban migration was the most constant element of social change
that propelled musical innovations between the Emancipation Proclamation of 1863 and the Civil Rights Act of 1964. This process of change
involved both "letting go" of and "holding on" to traditions that emerged in
the rural byways of the former slave states.[2] There has been a rush to study
blues, gospel, and rhythm and blues, perhaps because these forms say more
about what it meant to *let go* of Southern rural cultural traditions. Continuing study of the ring shout, hymns, spirituals, and secular forms that developed earlier should expand our understanding of what it meant to *retain*
deeply held ways of making music.

This dialectic between social change and musical nonchange can be
observed in black communities from Emancipation until now. Although
inspirational and deeply meditative when well performed, Dr. Watts ceased
in certain places simply for lack of a strong singer who could command
authority in the style. Where such weaknesses were apparent in the elders,
youth sought their own ways of participating in the worship. In many places,
this meant adding a piano or guitar or other instrument. Nonetheless, these
changes were not radical innovations that would transform the received
earthy and rural sound template; instead, several generations of youth
replaced the old-time congregational singing with a hybrid that remained
an essentially Southern blend of diction, vocal timbres, and, grammar.

In the late 1970s, as the move to the cities became a matter of accomplished fact, rap sprang up as what sounded almost like a foreign language.

Yet it was not at all foreign; rather, the city-speak that had been heard for years was now producing its own sound template, one distinct and removed from the country feel of slurred articulations and pitches that mark congregational singing, blues, gospel, rhythm and blues, and, to a lesser extent, jazz. While changes in the vocal sounds of blackness may be obvious, rap as a changed way of speaking signals a more profound shift in the racial and cultural identity of a people. Whether for rich or poor, black or white, city values carry their own code of ethics. For example, almost no one would deny that the reserve, defensiveness, and slickness of urban culture is different from, even alien to, the down-home feeling of community that marks rural culture. If not utterly divergent ways of being, they are profoundly different lifestyles, each demanding its own code by which sound symbols are imbedded with meaning. With the onset of rap, the sounds of rural blackness—the slurs, whines, and moans which marked sacred and secular music from the slave quarters to rhythm and blues—became submerged in the landscape, or absent altogether. In their place arose the bumpin', thumpin', sharply articulated percussiveness of "cityfied" Spoken Soul. Rap's emergence stands as confirmation that the field-to-factory mass migration, which lasted for nearly a century between Emancipation and the Civil Rights Act, was now an accomplished fact.

The Dr. Watts tradition is rooted in what Appiah calls "myths and lies." The form sprang into the lap of black mother wit, out of the mouths of those who espoused that slaves should be obedient to their masters. To the black middle class that was utterly concerned with literacy, economic agency, and social status, this antipathetic way of receiving culture represented a stigma, if not a backwards glance, with which few forward-thinking African Americans would wish to associate. The masses, however, transformed the trashy off-scouring into rare treasure.

The greater social challenge for Dr. Watts is that, unlike the spirituals, which have been reinvented, the hymns are an inheritance from archaic old-line Calvinism, which stubbornly rejects all moves to transform its boundaries so as to admit any whiff of secularism. Within the limits of old-line authority from which it stems, black Baptists (and some Methodists as well) have infused the form with the very soul of what is musical about African American culture. It is a bedrock element in what is so utterly black, culturally speaking, that few middle class or well-educated blacks care to contemplate it for long. It is irrelevant to some of their deepest and most up-to-date (dare we say white) hopes and aspirations.

Conforming to Appiah's last point, the construction of the Dr. Watts hymn-singing sound—not as a tradition but as a continuing symbol of identity for certain African American worshiping communities—does indeed defy logic and reason. We can better understand why this may be so by attention to the "opposing identities" from Appiah's first point; for the dialectic of opposition—the heat of battle, as it were—compels courses of action which are contingent and unpredictable.

Black Christianity in general has established an identity that opposes, even as it stands with, white Christianity. As a ritual agent of both alignment with and autonomy from the larger society, Dr. Watts has played a quiet yet persistent role in the deep cultural ambivalence (the daunting "doubleness" that Du Bois pondered) of African Americans. There are certain blacks whose lifestyles and religious traditions are far removed from the cradles of Dr. Watts hymn singing; yet they are interested in and apparently moved by the tradition as a musical sign of blackness. By contrast, certain blacks who grow up in the bedrock of the tradition are entirely unaffected by the music and are disassociated from its sound. My concern, however, is not with variations in personal taste but with the creative sustenance of the practice as an element of cultural more than personal identity, as well as its relevance to the larger community. Moreover, the construction of a thing so subtle as identity can never be a completed project but remains an ongoing process.

There is a general logic that explains the continuance of Dr. Watts in certain churches and not in others. As an oral practice among those denied access to literacy, it afforded a socially dignified and culturally adaptable means of conducting worship in styles and forms that embedded European Protestant practices into African ritual forms. Yet the practice has not ceased with the onset of literacy; that reason alone cannot explain the here-and-there map of locations that continue the tradition, and the preponderance of exceptions calls into question the logic of the general explanation. Yet the fact that Dr. Watts is more widespread among blacks than whites is a paradox only explicable by the continuing relevance of oral culture to African Americans. Even among blacks, whether the growing middle class or the masses, the form is still practiced by a minority within the minority, who continue the tradition with unflagging vitality. Such locations are important sites for further study because the construction of the practice, especially as a sign of identity, is a continuous activity. In this dynamic sense, wherever the process is vital, there are cycles of construction, deconstruction, and reconstruction by which song leaders, hymn choirs, and congregations navigate the peaks and valleys that come with the passage of time. This is because, except in large, complex, and highly specialized ministries, worshiping communities are focused not solely upon musical matters but also upon the day-to-day experiences of the life passage. Such small and moderate-sized church bodies afford ideal sites for investigating the integrative process by which speech, song, and music embody and express the sense of community that is foundational to African American worship.

In the lining-out hymns African Americans received and developed a worship form that has acquired cultural agency in communities, for good or evil, for gain or loss, for building up or for tearing down. Unlike the cultural and social symbolism allied with the spirituals, which have become less autonomous, hymn singing proved less adaptable to championing social and cultural goals that have advanced the fortunes of African Americans in the larger order of American society. Therefore, as a form more fixed and less moldable, it has often been perceived as a regressive if not expendable cultural expression, of which race men and race women have often been ashamed before the bastions of the larger society. For in order to sing the hymns as they should be sung, the speaker-singers must perforce evoke the musical equivalent of the Spoken Soul, which has long been heard among those who are the least well-educated and socially mobile. In the formation of identities, then, black intellectuals are often alienated from the sound imprint of what lacks currency among their white counterparts, and the urban black masses reside in a culture increasingly removed from the rural sites and moments that infused the Dr. Watts sound with symbolic meaning.

The heritage of Dr. Watts does not cease when a church like Gum Springs Baptist, where I first heard the hymns as a boy, no longer raises hymns in the old-time way, for the life of the tradition can be no less vital in transformation. Musical change is not only fashioned from continuity, but marked by apparent disjunction as well. Our potential for insight lies in the interrelationship between these ways of seeing. Sketching the course of history, the dots representing isolated genres and styles must be more securely connected by the force of reflection. The connections should reveal both the musical elements, which are shared across genres, and the structural patterns that linked most forms of black music to a larger culture from about 1800, the peak period of slave importation, to 1970, when the sounds of the agrarian South were beginning to wane in African American music. Then perhaps the whole can appear in the merging lights of affinity and distance that can lead to a fuller appreciation of African American music and ritual.

I no longer bemoan the passing of specific regional traditions of congregational singing. However, I do believe it is easier to arrive at a conceptual basis for black music in the United States while a quorum of living archaic traditions continues than to face the task of recovering forms from the remnants of what was. This is the challenge defiantly confronted by Stuckey (1987) and others who have been and still are interpreting the ring shout. Though widespread in the nineteenth century, it is known to continue in but a few coastal communities of South Carolina and Georgia. The ring shout is an ideal site for study of how Africans adapted ritual traditions of music and dance in North American settings. The present study suggests that lining out afforded a complementary occasion for enslaved Africans to assimilate and adapt the language and moods of Dissenting Protestant ritual to the needs of worshiping slave communities.

The hypothesis that African Americans adapted linguistic and musical patterns from African cultures to oral traditions forged in North America points to the need for systematic study of the poorly documented range of African American regional styles, their relation to corresponding speech communities, and possible linkages between Spoken Soul and the concept of tonality in African languages. Those who concur with at least the direction of these analogies—that through linguistic-musical contact, a new system of speech signs was subverted to the terms of residual but nonsemantic structures—may prefer a different course of explanation; but it is beyond question that slaves and their progeny developed a diverse yet coherent system of lining-out styles, a synchronic range that has mirrored in space the unrelenting diachronic movement in American music from the colonial era to the modern day and beyond.

APPENDIX A

Selection of Transcribed
and Discussed Performances

The performances included here comprise the recording *Dr. Watts Hymn Singing among African Americans,* compiled by William T. Dargan and available at the Center for Black Music Research, Columbia College, Chicago.

KEY TO COLLECTORS

AEJ	Alan and Elizabeth Lomax and Lewis Jones
AL	Alan Lomax
AP	A. A. Pinkston
DA	Drew Armstrong
EE	Elise Eppes
FM	Fred Mendelssohn
GCC	Guy and Candie Carawan
JAL	John A. Lomax
JF	John Faulk
JRL	John A. and Ruby T. Lomax
JT	Jeff Todd Titon
JW	John Work
LWJ	Lawrence Jones and Willis Laurence James
RS	Robert Sonkin
WTD	William T. Dargan

State: South Carolina
Selection number: 1
Title: "What a Friend We Have in Jesus"
Performer(s): Mr. Mackey, Mrs. Bligen, and others, Watchnight Service
Location/date/collector: John's Island, SC/January 1964/GCC
NCFC (North Carolina Folklore Collection) no. 3538

No. 406, *Baptist Hymnal*
Composer: Joseph Scriven, 1855

What a friend we have in Jesus
All our sins and griefs to bear
What a privilege to carry
Everything to God in prayer
O what peace we often forfeit
O what needless pain we bear
All because we do not carry
Everything to God in prayer.

I love Jesus, I love Jesus
I love Jesus, I love Jesus
I love Jesus, yes, I do
I love Jesus, I love Jesus
I love Jesus, I love Jesus
I love Jesus, yes, I do

I love him because he bled for me
I love him because he bled for me
I love him because he bled for me, yes, I do
I love Jesus, I love Jesus
I love Jesus, I love Jesus
I love Jesus, yes, I do

Feed me, Jesus, feed me, Jesus
Feed me, Jesus, feed me, Jesus
Feed me till I want no more
Feed me, Jesus, feed me, Jesus
Feed me, Jesus, feed me, Jesus
Feed me till I want no more

(Lordy, with the)

Bread of heaven, bread of heaven
Bread of heaven, bread of heaven
Feed me till I want no more
Feed me, Jesus, feed me, Jesus
Feed me, Jesus, feed me, Jesus
Feed me till I want no more

State: South Carolina
Selection number: 2
Title: "Come Ye That Love the Lord"
Performer(s): Jerusalem Baptist Association, Oak Grove Baptist Church
Location/date/collector: Salters, SC/November 7, 1994/WTD
No. 350, *Baptist Hymnal*
Composer: Isaac Watts, 1707

Come, ye that love the Lord
And let your joys be known
Join in a song of sweet accord
And thus surround the throne

Let those refuse to sing
Who never knew our God
But children of the heavenly King
May speak their joys abroad.

The hill of Zion yields
A thousand sacred sweets,
Before we reach the heavenly fields
Or walk the golden streets.

Then let our songs abound,
And every tear be dry;
We're marching through Immanuel's ground,
To fairer worlds on high.
[Moaning chorus]

State: South Carolina
Selection number: 3
Title: "Go Preach My Gospel, Saith the Lord"
Performer(s): Kingston Lake Baptist Association, Flag Patch Baptist
      Church
Location/date/collector: Loris, SC/October 14, 1994/WTD
No. 559, *Baptist Hymnal*
Composer: Isaac Watts, 1707

Go preach my gospel, saith the Lord;
Bid the whole earth my grace receive;
He shall be saved that trusts his word,
And be condemned who'll not believe.

"I'll make your great commission known;
And ye shall prove me gospel true
By all the works that I have done
By all the wonders ye shall do."

"Teach all the nations my commands;
I'm with you till the world shall end;
All power is trusted in my hands
I can destroy, and I defend."

He spake, and light shone round his head;
On a bright cloud to heaven he rode:
They to the farthest nations spread
The grace of their ascended God.
[Moaning chorus]

State: South Carolina
Selection number: 4
Title: "Father, I Stretch My Hands to Thee"
Performer(s): Rev. L. L. Lewis, Cedar Creek Baptist Church
Location/date/collector: Wadesboro, NC/August 3, 1981/WTD
AFS number: 26,865
No. 293, *Baptist Hymnal*
Composer: Charles Wesley, 1741

[Pastor Rev. Lewis: (We ask someone) for the tune, common meter, while we sing.
We ask everybody in the building, Let's sing to the glory of God.
It may be our last time
We may not get back tomorrow night
But let's do what we can now.]

Father, I stretch my hands to thee
No other help I know
If thou withdraw thyself from me,
Ah, whither shall I go?

What did thine only Son endure
Before I drew my breath!
What pain, what labor, to secure
My soul from endless death

[Rev. Lewis continued:
Sometimes when I feel so guilty
I feel like I done wrong
And it (be)gin to press on us
I bow on my knees sometimes
I bow myself alone
And I look up and say,]

Author of faith, to thee I lift
My weary longing eyes
O may I now receive thy gift
My soul without it dies
[Incomplete]

State: South Carolina
Selection number: 5
Title: "A Charge to Keep I Have"
Performer(s): Deacon Mack Bittle, St. Paul Singing Union, Gum Springs
    Baptist Church
Location/date/collector: Mt. Croghan, SC/August 30, 1981/WTD
No. 454, *Baptist Hymnal*
Composer: Charles Wesley, 1741?

A charge to keep I have
A God to glorify
Who gave his Son my soul to save,
And fit it for the sky.

To serve the present age
My calling to fulfill
Oh, may it all my powers engage
To do my Master's will.
[Moaning chorus, incomplete]

State: South Carolina
Selection number: 6
Title: "Father, I Stretch My Hands to Thee"
Performer(s): Gethsemane Baptist Church
Location/date/collector: Kershaw, SC/July 20, 1981/WTD
AFS number 26,857

See text for number 4, above.

State: South Carolina
Selection number: 7
Title: "Amazing Grace"
Performer(s): Deacon J.H. Watson, Boyd Hill Baptist Church Hymn Choir
Location/date/collector: Rock Hill, SC/February 1992/WTD
No. 492, *Baptist Hymnal*
No. 3, *Primitive Hymns*
Composer: John Newton, 1779

Amazing grace, how sweet the sound,
That saved a wretch like me!
I once was lost but now I'm found:
Was blind, but now I see.

'Twas grace that taught my heart to fear,
And grace my fears relieved;
How precious did that grace appear,
The hour I first believed!

Through many dangers, toils, and snares,
I have already come;
'Tis grace has brought me safe thus far,
And grace will lead me home.

[Repeated final couplet]
'Tis grace has brought me safe thus far,
And grace will lead me home.
[Incomplete]

State: South Carolina
Selection number: 8
Title: "You May Bury Me in the East"
Performer(s): Community Hymn Choir
Location/date/collector: Rock Hill, SC/May 3, 1996/WTD
Anonymous text of traditional song (note slight verb change from "may" to
    "can" in this performance)

You can bury me in the east
You can bury me in the west
But I'll hear the trumpet sound in the morning
You can bury me in the north
You can bury me in the south
But I'll hear the trumpet sound in the morning

[Repeat of first chorus]

Gonna sound so loud
Till it wake up the dead
But I'll hear that trumpet sound in the morning
Sound so loud
Till it wake up the dead
But I'll hear the trumpet sound in the morning

In the morning, in the morning
I'll hear that trumpet sound in the morning

On the mountaintop
In the valley low
But I'll hear the trumpet sound in the morning
On the mountaintop
In the valley low
But I'll hear the trumpet sound in the morning

Talk about shouting down here below
I'll hear that trumpet sound in the morning
You wait until I get on that other shore
I'll hear that trumpet sound in the morning

I done been tempted, I done been tried
But I'll hear the trumpet sound in the morning
I been to the Jordan river and I been baptized
But I'll hear the trumpet sound in the morning

In the morning, in the morning
I'll hear that trumpet sound in the morning
In the morning, in the morning
I'll hear that trumpet sound in the morning

I'm going away [and I'm going to stay]
I'll hear that trumpet sound in the morning

I won't back till the judgment day
I'll hear that trumpet sound in the morning

Some folks come cripple, some folks come lame
But I'll hear that trumpet sound in the morning
Some folks come walking in Jesus' name
I'll hear that trumpet sound in the morning

In the morning, in the morning
I'll hear that trumpet sound in the morning
In the morning, in the morning
I'll hear that trumpet sound in the morning

State: South Carolina
Selection number: 9
Title: "Jesus Invites His Saints"
Performer(s): Phinizy Chorus, Aiken County
Location/date/collector: New Ellenton, SC/September 3, 1994/WTD
No. 451, *Baptist Hymnal*
No. 244, *Primitive Hymns*
Composer: Isaac Watts, 1707

Jesus invites his saints
To meet around his board;
Here pardoned rebels sit, and hold
Communion with their Lord.

This holy bread and wine
Maintain our fainting breath
By union with our living Lord,
And interest in his death.

[Comment of approbation by leader, Brother Joseph Wilborne, after
    rehearsal performance:
. . . I'm sorry, I'm ready for my bread and wine (followed by group laughter)
. . . Now that's it;
Now if you don't hear it like that, that's not it
. . . Not in this area.]

State: Georgia
Selection number: 10
Title: "I Heard the Voice of Jesus Say"
Performer(s): Rev. Dr. C. J. Johnson
Location/date/collector: Brooklyn, NY/NA/FM
AFS number: Savoy 14126
No. 487, *Baptist Hymnal*
Composer: Horatius Bonar, 1846

I heard the voice of Jesus say,
"Come unto me and rest:
Lay down, thy weary one, lay down
Thy head upon my breast."

[Rev. Johnson: You know, this verse is the one that I love so well:
I came to Jesus—
I wonder are y'all holding me
I, I, I came, I came to Jesus
I didn't wait till I got a new pair o' shoes
I came to Jesus
I didn't wait for my little sisters and brothers
Every now and then my burden get heavy, my trials give misery (?)
And I like to get away and say,]

I came to Jesus as I was,
Weary and worn and sad,
I found in him a resting-place,
And he has made me glad

State: Florida
Selection number: 11
Title: "A Charge to Keep I Have"
Performer(s): Rev. Cross
Location/date/collector: Florida/NA/AP
AFS number: 19,128
No. 454, *Baptist Hymnal*
Composer: Charles Wesley, 1741?

See text for number 5, above.

State: Mississippi
Selection number: 12
Title: "A Charge to Keep I Have"
Performer(s): Rev. Ribbins and Congregation, Pastor, First Baptist Church,
    Jackson, TN
Location/date/collector: Mississippi/NA/AEJ
AFS number: 4757 B2
No. 454, *Baptist Hymnal*
Composer: Charles Wesley, 1741?

[Exhortation of the host pastor or deacon: "I want to ask you to join in and sing two verses of a hymn. You know, we just can't get away from those good ol' hymns. They will stir you when nothing else will. You can get (up) some morning feeling bad and feeling tired and feeling worn out. And just go to humming one of those ol' hymns that you used to hear Mother hum and walk around the floor and hum them until the Spirit of God would come and get in her soul and cause a great shout. Let us sing this hymn. . . ."]

See text for number 5, above.

This hymn has the unison sound of melismatic style, with only slight heterophony, that is similar to the Memphis and Chicago (Shinault) performances (see *Negro Church Music*, Alan Lomax, ed., Atlantic 1351). The melody is the same as that sung in nos. 5, 11, and 14. (Rev. Ribbins, the guest speaker, is from Jackson, Tennessee, and he apparently is not the one who lines out and leads the hymn singing.)

State: Louisiana
Selection number: 13
Title: "Amazing Grace"
Performer(s): Huddie Ledbetter
Location/date/collector: Shreveport, LA/August 1940/AL
AFS number: 4470 B5

Amazing grace, how sweet it sounds
That saved a wretch like me
I once was lost but now I'm found
Was blind but now I see

As I went down in the valley to pray
And m'soul got happy an' I stayed all day
I once was lost but now I'm found
Was blind but now I see

[As clapping rhythm continues, shouted words are unintelligible.]

Must I be carried to the skies
On flower beds of ease
And must I fight to win the prize
And sail through bloody seas

State: Texas
Selection number: 14
Title: "Must Jesus Bear the Cross Alone"
Performer(s): St. Stevens Baptist Church
Location/date/collector: Austin, TX/August 1941/JF
AFS number: 5444 A1
No. 449, *Baptist Hymnal*
Composer: George Nelson Allen, 1852?

Must Jesus bear the cross alone
And all the world go free

No: there's a cross for everyone
And there's a cross for me.

How happy are the saints above,
Who once went sorrowing here!
But now they taste unmingled love
And joy without a tear.

State: Texas
Selection number: 15
Title: "I'm Not Too Mean to Serve the Lord"
Performer(s): St. Stevens Baptist Church
Location/date/collector: Austin, TX/August 1941/JF
AFS number: 5444 B2
Source: Unknown
Text of traditional wandering verses

I'm not too mean to serve the Lord
He done so much for me
My mother's sleeping in the tomb
My father's sleeping too

Before this time another year
I may be sleeping too.

State: Michigan
Selection number: 16
Title: "Before This Time Another Year"
Performer(s): C.L. Franklin and congregation
Location/date/collector: Detroit, MI/NA/JT
AFS number: 22,500
Source: Unknown
Text of traditional wandering verses

Before this time another year
I may be dead and gone
I'll let you know before I go
What will become of me

State: Kentucky, North Carolina, Virginia (performed at a meeting of the
      regional association of churches from all three states)
Selection number: 17
Title: "What a Friend We Have in Jesus"
Performer(s): Shiloh Primitive Baptist Church, *Love and Praise,* vol. 1
Location/date/collector: Elkin, NC/1997/DA

See text for number 1, above.

State: Kentucky, North Carolina, Virginia (performed at a meeting of the
    regional association of churches from all three states)
Selection number: 18
Title: "My Work on Earth Will Soon Be Done"
Performer(s): Shiloh Primitive Baptist Church, *Love and Praise,* vol. 1
Location/date/collector: Elkin, NC/1997/DA
Source: Unknown
Text of traditional wandering verses

My work on earth will soon be done
And then I'm going home
I'm going beyond this vale of death
And I won't cry no more.

State: Texas
Selection number: 19
Title: "A City Called Heaven"
Performer(s): Barton Creek Baptist Church
Location/date/collector: Austin, TX/1941/JF
AFS number: 5488

Sometimes I am tossed and driven
Sometimes I [don' know] where to roam
I heard o' that city called heaven
I started to make it my home

While I'm in this wide world of sorrow
No charity, no comfort have I
No hopes in this world for tomorrow
[Unintelligible line]

Sometimes I am tossed and driven
Sometimes I['ve] nowhere to roam
I heard o' that city called heaven
I started to make it my home

My mother done reached that glory
My father's still walking in sin
My sisters and brothers won't own me.
Because I am trying to get in

Sometimes I am tossed and driven
Sometimes I['ve] nowhere to roam
I heard o' that city called heaven
I started to make it my home

[Intoned testimony:]
I just wonder why they saying
Ain't you sometimes tossed in this wide world
I, I couldn't sleep at night
There are times when I lay on my pillow right there
But I decided in my mind
That I heard of that city called heaven
And I'm surely gonna make it my home
Mmmm, yes, I'm gon' make it my home
Somebody over there that I just might see
Because [if you] looking for me in this world
[Unintelligible] when I fall
When I'm tossed to and fro
Sometimes when it's dark and gloomy
They're watching me over there
Over yonder, over yonder
Won't be no more sorrows
Won't be no more dark clouds [going to clear]
God's [unintelligible] shine eternally in the kingdom over there
So glad, so glad.
I'm like Job, my destiny's on high
My name is written 'fore the Lamb's book of life
Come out and snatch the branch from eternal burning
Burdens in my life gonna stop [unintelligible] one day
[Unintelligible]

State: Texas
Selection number: 20
Title: "A Few More Years Shall Roll"
Performer(s): Barton Creek Baptist Church
Location/date/collector: Austin, TX/1941/JF
AFS number: 5488
No. 631, *Baptist Hymnal*
Composer: Horatius Bonar, 1857

A few more years shall roll
A few more seasons come
And we shall be with those that rest
Asleep within the tomb

A few more struggles here,
A few more partings o'er
A few more toils, a few more tears,
And we shall weep no more.

State: Michigan
Selection number: 21
Title: "Remember Me"
Performer(s): New Bethel Baptist Congregation
Location/date/collector: Detroit, MI/NA/JT

> See text for number 7, above.
> [Incomplete]
>
> Remember me
> Remember me
> O Lord, remember me
>
> Father, I stretch my hands to thee
> No other help I know
>
> Remember me
> Remember me
> O Lord
> Remember me
> [Incomplete]

CATEGORIZATION OF EXAMPLES ACCORDING TO RHYTHMIC STYLE

The following distinctions in rhythmic style result not in distinct singing *styles* but in alternate and complementary means of *structuring* a performance into a whole. Despite the practical inseparability of performance and composition in this context, the rhythmic distinctions are more compositional than stylistic. Styles go further to identify the singing as similar to or different from particular ethnic, social, musical, and linguistic sources. (All numbers refer to *Dr. Watts*. Not all examples listed above are included here.)

Timeline (Speech or Percussive Rhythms)

1. What a Friend We Have in Jesus
2. Come Ye That Love the Lord
6. Father, I Stretch My Hands to Thee
7. Amazing Grace
8. You May Bury Me in the East
9. Jesus Invites His Saints
13. Amazing Grace
17. What a Friend We Have in Jesus
19. A City Called Heaven

Poetic

10. I Heard the Voice of Jesus Say
13. Amazing Grace
16. Before This Time Another Year
20. A Few More Years Shall Roll

Portraiture

3. Go Preach My Gospel, Saith the Lord
4. Father, I Stretch My Hands to Thee
5. A Charge to Keep I Have
11. A Charge to Keep I Have
14. Must Jesus Bear the Cross Alone
15. I'm Not Too Mean to Serve the Lord
21. Remember Me

APPENDIX B

Partial Annotated List of Recorded Lining-Out Performances Held in the Archive of Folk Culture, Library of Congress

AFS 75 B1: Lining-out hymn. Sung by congregation of a Negro Baptist church, Alexandria, Virginia. Recorded by John A. Lomax, September 1933. Duration ca. 2'02".

AFS 75 B2: In That Land. Sung by congregation of Negro Baptist church, Alexandria, Virginia. Recorded by John A. [and Alan] Lomax, September 1933.

AFS 75 B3: Sermon. Spoken by minister of Negro Baptist church. Alexandria, Virginia. Recorded by John A. Lomax, September 1933. Fragment.

AFS 75 B4: Hymn. Sung by congregation of Negro Baptist church, Alexandria, Virginia. Recorded by John A. Lomax, September 1933.

AFS 103 A1 and A2: Remember Me. Sung by congregation of Baptist church, Alma Plantation, Baton Rouge, Louisiana. Recorded by John A. and Alan Lomax, July 1934.

AFS 103 A1 and A2: Jesus Died a Sinner's Friend. Same location as preceding. (Listening deferred due to technical problem—side A blank including AFS 101A–106B.)

AFS 1304 A2, B1, and B2: Lining-out hymns and Remember Me. Sung by Negroes from Wadmalaw Island, Charleston, South Carolina. Recorded by John A. and Ruby T. Lomax, July 1937. In the play *Plantation Echoes* by Rosa Warren Wilson. (Words unintelligible on recording.) Duration 6'55".

AFS 1315 A1 and A2: Mournin' Song. Sung by Dock Reed and Vera Hall, Livingston, Alabama. Recorded by John A. Lomax, July 1937. (Call-and-response phrase is shortened.) Duration 2'47".

AFS 2684 A1: Amazing Grace. Sung by Jesse and group of Negroes, Livingston, Alabama. Recorded by John A. and Ruby T. Lomax, May 1939. (LWO 4872, reel 172B mid.) Duration 2'48".

257

AFS 2686 A1 and A2: Jesus the Man I Long to Know and When I Can Read My Title Clear. Sung by Vera Hall and Dock Reed, Livingston, Alabama. Recorded by John A. and Ruby T. Lomax, May 1939. Duration 5'50".

AFS 2721 A4: Communion hymn [Go Preach My Gospel]. Sung by Phil Butler, Brady Walker, Thomas Trimmer, William Gant, and Mary Lee, Clemson, South Carolina. Recorded by John A. and Ruby T. Lomax, June 1939. Duration 1'40".

AFS 3005 A1 and A2: Amazing Grace. Sung by Mrs. Mary Shipp, Byhalia, Mississippi. Recorded by Herbert Halpert, May 1939. Duration 4'41".

AFS 3005 B1: I Love the Lord, He Heard My Cry [sic]. Sung by Mrs. Mary Shipp, Byhalia, Mississippi. Recorded by Herbert Halpert, May 1939. (Excellent fragment.) Duration 2'20".

AFS 3014 B1: Somebody Knockin' at Yo' Door. Sung by Negro men and women, Cockrum, Mississippi. Recorded by Herbert Halpert, May 1939.

AFS 3067 A1: I Know I Am a Child of God. Sung by four women and two men, Edwards, Mississippi. Recorded by Herbert Halpert, May 2, 1939. (Taping continues through next selection.)

AFS 3067 A2: I Wish I Had a Mother Here. Sung by four women and two men, Edwards, Mississippi. Recorded by Herbert Halpert, May 2, 1939. (Excellent fragment.) Duration 3'50" for this and the preceding performance.

AFS 3977 B3: Father, I Stretch My Hands to Thee (following prayer and Amazing Grace). Sung by Winnie Terry, Merryville, Louisiana. Recorded by John A. and Ruby T. Lomax, October 1940. Duration ca. 4'00".

AFS 4020 A2: When I Can Read My Title Clear. Sung by Dock Reed and Vera Hall, Livingston, Alabama. Recorded by John A. and Ruby T. Lomax, October 1940.

AFS 4020 A3: On Jordan's Stormy Banks [I Stand]. Sung by Dock Reed and Vera Hall, Livingston, Alabama. Recorded by John A. and Ruby T. Lomax, October 1940.

AFS 4022 B1: Hark, from the Tomb a Doleful Sound. Sung by Betty Moore and Liza Witt, Livingston, Alabama. Recorded by John A. and Ruby T. Lomax, October 1940. (Excellent fragment.) Duration 1'53".

AFS 4040 A and B: On Jordan's Stormy Banks [I Stand]. Sung by congregation in funeral service for Sally Ann Thomas at Brown Chapel Baptist Church, Livingston, Alabama. Recorded by John A. and Ruby T. Lomax, October 1940. (Includes moaning; very good.) Duration 2'50".

AFS 4470 B3, 4, and 5: Amazing Grace. [Lined out] and sung by Huddie Ledbetter. Recorded by Alan Lomax, August 1940, at the Library of Congress (continues through B6).

AFS 4470 B6: Down in the Valley to Pray. Sung by Huddie Ledbetter. Recorded August 1940. Duration ca. 5'00".

AFS 4757 B2: Long meter hymn [A Charge to Keep I Have]. Sung by Rev. Ribbins and congregation, Mississippi. Recorded by Alan and Elizabeth Lomax and Lewis Jones, 1942. (Excellent performance.) Duration ca. 6'00".

AFS 4761 A1: I'm Going Home on the Morning Train. Sung by Rev. Ribbins and congregation, Mississippi. Recorded by Alan and Elizabeth Lomax and Lewis Jones, 1942. Duration 2'30".

AFS 4761 A2: Long meter hymn [I Love the Lord, He Heard My Cries]. Led by the deacon with congregation, Mississippi. Recorded by Alan and Elizabeth Lomax, 1942. Duration ca. 2'20".

AFS 4761 A3 and A4: Long meter hymn. [My Soul Be on Thy Guard]. Announcement by deacon. Led by deacon and congregation, Mississippi. Recorded by Alan and Elizabeth Lomax with Lewis Jones, 1942. Duration ca. 8'00".

AFS 4761 B: Soon I'll Be at Home. Sung by Negro quartet, Mississippi. Recorded by Alan and Elizabeth Lomax with Lewis Jones, 1942. Duration ca. 2'15".

AFS 5064 B and 5064 A: A "moan" by Deacon Collins Pettway, Gee's Bend, Alabama. Recorded by Robert Sonkin, July 1941. Duration 4'25".

NOTES

INTRODUCTION

1. Lining out is "a method of performing a psalm or hymn, in which the clerk or leader gives out either the words or the melody, or both, one line at a time, to be followed by the congregation. The practice began in the early 17th century in British parish churches as an aid for the illiterate. It had disappeared in England by 1800 but is still used in churches in the rural south-eastern USA" (*The New Grove Dictionary of Music and Musicians,* edited by Stanley Sadie, 20 vols. [London: Macmillan, 1980], 11: 7).

2. Because of the extreme slowness of their performance, George Pullen Jackson (1943) felt that Dr. Watts hymns were without rhythm. I, too, once thought of hymn singing as arhythmic; but this perspective changed as I began to participate regularly in hymn singing, to transcribe and analyze the performances, and especially to hear and experience multiple regional traditions. I discovered that while Dr. Watts rhythms are not strictly metrical in a musical sense, rhythmic gestures embedded in a range of formulaic melodic patterns operate expressively within relative but not metronomic rhythmic structures. African-derived rhythmic styles can be heard in Dr. Watts performances over a continuum that ranges from hymns that sublimate rhythm in favor of more freely expressive melodic-timbral gestures to hymns that develop rhythmic and semantic ideas through incessant repetition and variation.

3. See "Pony Blues" in the recorded anthology *The Blues: A Smithsonian Collection of Classic Blues Singers,* vol. 2.

4. The tradition of congregational singing, from which the popular genre of "spirituals" emerged, consists of orally transmitted songs and hymns lined out from word-only hymn books. The chantlike devotional singing is accompanied only by hand clapping, foot patting, or idiophones that generate percussive sounds, such as rattles or sticks tapped on the floor. Beginning in the outdoor secluded spaces where slaves worshiped, the modern-day essence of the sound is a play of voices, clapping hands, and patting feet resonating within wooden spaces framed

by walls, ceilings, and church pews. For a visual sense of these simple wooden buildings that dot the countryside of former slave states, see Rankin 1993.

5. See Stuckey 1987 and Floyd 1995.

6. Some of the most resistant mysteries about music in African American worship have been rendered intelligible by Pitts's skill at balancing a clear conception of key problems and issues with empathetic ethnography and archival resourceful-ness. His work has blind spots and weaknesses, but some of my criticisms are pos-sible only because of the plateau Pitts has established by setting the whole cultural context of black worship and music into sharper relief. I never knew him, but his curiosity about black worship was apparently fired by a social-scientific perspective rooted in anthropology and linguistics, and his ethnographic research, as an outsider to the Afro-Baptist tradition, was facilitated by his service as a pianist in the churches where he conducted field work. By contrast, my spe-cific and general involvement in lining-out hymn singing was indelibly shaped by long-term relations with the elders who sang them, and I am an ethnomusicolo-gist concerned with how archaic worship forms—lining out and the ring shout in particular—might inform a larger understanding of black music. Just as he sought to achieve linguistic and cultural particularity, in this book I attempt to see the most general significance of lining out to African American music.

   On call-and-response structure in lining out, see Gilbert Chase 1987: 55–71, 213–31; Charles Hamm 1983: 24–46, 111–39, 261–78; Wiley Hitchcock 1988: 103–5; Wilfrid Mellers 1965: 264–65; and Eileen Southern 1983: 30–31, 76–77, 167, 207, 446–47.

7. Jackson's description of the mazelike, thronging sound of the hymns, in which it is difficult to distinguish the parts from the whole, confirms his impression of them as "exotic and weird." The singing, he wrote, "seems perfectly simple and easy for the singers. But the listening white person is utterly confused, cannot make musical head or tail out of what he hears. . . . He cannot even check the trend by the words he has heard lined out; for the singing surges on with so many graces and strings of graces . . . that all words, syllables even, lose their identity and evade recognition. It becomes vaguely evident simply that each complicated tone surge or tone constellation accompanies a single syllable of text" (1943: 248–49).

8. John Blacking's (1995: 154) observation concerns music in general, but I find it especially applicable to Dr. Watts hymn singing. He continues, "This is why truly musical changes are not common and why they reveal the essence of music in a society."

9. This is the meaning suggested by the Horatius Bonar hymn "I Heard the Voice of Jesus Say."

10. African musical intonations are commonly derived from speech intonations. The study of linguistic intonation is a branch of phonology concerned with the effect of rhythm, stress, and pitch upon speech communication.

11. Although, in chapter 8, I refer to the lining out–ring shout continuum as the basis for a "theory" of black music, it must be apparent to any critical reader that this work is speculative and general, and must be followed with a more spe-cialized and carefully restricted study of language and speech within a particu-lar community.

12. Weinreich (1953) defines "interference phenomena" as instances of deviation from the norms of either language that occur in the speech of bilinguals as a result of language contact, and "language loyalty" as "a principle . . . in the name of which people will rally themselves and their fellow speakers consciously and explicitly to resist changes in either the functions of their language (as a result of the language shift) or in the structure or vocabulary (as a consequence of interference)" (1, 99).

13. These include the essentially African form of work songs, the African-derived ring shout, mid-1700s lining-out hymn singing, the late-1700s African American sermon, early 1800s spirituals, 1890s dialect poetry, the rise of blues and related forms since the 1920s, reinterpretation of the spirituals in the Civil Rights movement of the 1950s and 1960s, and the aesthetic of the late-1960s black arts movement.

14. This is a major theme in LeRoi Jones's *Blues People* (1963), which, despite gaps and weaknesses, remains a pertinent explanation of the significance of black music to the American experience. Perhaps such a book could not have been written until after Herskovits argued for New World Africanisms in *The Myth of the Negro Past* (1941). In the 1970s, following upon Jones's criticism and led by Eileen Southern's example, black music attracted a cadre of scholars, who are still laying foundations.

15. Of course, this has had as much to do with the economic and political hegemony of the United States following the world wars as with the cultural meaning of African American music.

16. This idea is adapted from Pitts 1993: 124–25.

17. The concept of performativity denotes an emphasis upon "the emergence of verbal art in the social interaction between performers and audiences" (Baumann and Briggs 1990: 59–60).

18. While sacred and secular in other cultures, including eighteenth-century Europe, also bear such similarities, in black experience they are defined more by context and setting than by gesture and signification. Just as the blues and lining out share elements, so do certain black secular dance traditions compare closely with the sacred ring shout and holy dance traditions.

19. I have adapted this convention from the organization of that canon of black culture, W.E.B. Du Bois's *The Souls of Black Folk*, which I have also sought to criticize fairly (see chapter 6).

20. In more than twenty years of attending Christian worship services throughout the United States in the course of my work, I have never heard either of these hymns sung in a predominantly white body. By contrast, perhaps because of the relevance of their message to the toils and snares that have been built into black experience, these texts are frequently quoted from and sung in black Baptist and Methodist worship.

CHAPTER 1. "BLEST BE THE TIE THAT BINDS": PART I

1. Although Pitts (1993) observed that shouting was discouraged during devotions within a particular association of Central Texas Missionary Baptist churches, no such rigid distinction can apply to the general case.

2. These points are adapted from my own field observations and from the nine attributes of black Christian worship and religious experience set forth by Nathan Jones (1982).

3. A sermon by Jonathan Edwards, "A Divine and Supernatural Light," seeks to explicate this religious perspective. An excerpt can be found in George and Barbara Perkins, *The American Tradition in Literature (Shorter Edition in One Volume)*, 8th ed. (New York: McGraw Hill, 1994), 93–98.

4. Early in the twentieth century, Pentecostals broke with the old-time Baptist devotional frame and began the worship ritual with a "praise and testimony" service. In addition to piano and electronic organ, such services were often accompanied by instruments not found in Baptist churches, such as guitar, bass, drums, and washboard, as well as multiple tambourines. After an opening scripture and prayer, many of the personal testimonies were prefaced with an inspirational song. The songs were highly rhythmic, and at peak points of expression the alternation between speech and song would give way to episodes of the holy dance known as shouting, performed by individual members. Such intensity was often followed by a more intimate and reflective worship moment, out of which certain Church of God in Christ congregations developed the "yes, yes, yes" chant, after which their official hymnal is named. This chant might be considered a black Pentecostal analogy to Baptist moaning, an effort to express at either emotional extreme—joy or sadness—that which is unspeakable.

With the mid-century rise of the more ethnically diverse Charismatic and full-gospel churches, their "praise and worship" services became more structured by the guidance of appointed song leaders and less contingent upon the participation of individual members. Whereas Pentecostal praise and testimony services encourage all members to bear witness to God's goodness in song, words, or both, Charismatic praise and worship services proceed under the direction of pulpit-centered praise teams who lead a preselected sequence of songs. While the sequence of songs and their tempos can vary with the emotion and spirituality of the moment, medium and up-tempo praise songs typically begin the ritual, and the twenty- to thirty-minute service culminates in slower, more intimate songs of worship. There is a ritual and semantic parallel between this concluding worship in Charismatic congregations, the Pentecostal chant, and Baptist moaning. While no tradition is rigidly fixed as to when such a key moment may occur, Pentecostal and Charismatic worship often culminate in an awe-inspiring quietude, while the first-frame placement of Baptist moaning more often opens into the celebration and release of shouting. Despite the prevalence of the binary devotions-service form in black Baptist worship, the felt need to follow a period of intense celebration with more inward and personal acknowledgment of the divine presence can also result in ritual forms that are more ternary than binary.

As the socioeconomic profile and status of Pentecostal and Charismatic groups has risen, and with the passing of the older folk who can sing the hymns and songs, praise and worship services have become common in numerous Baptist churches, whose welcome is often extended to the same pool of working- and middle-class blacks. These influences can be reflected in a number of ways, including the use of instrumental accompaniment (once the key of a song has been established by a song leader), the inclusion of women in leadership roles formerly occupied by men, the particulars of whether leaders stand or sit and how many are utilized, and the mixing of song repertories from the old-time Baptist, Pentecostal, and Charismatic traditions.

5. See thoughtful discussions of the concept in Hinson 2000: 89–91, 93, 98–99, 102, 320–21.

6. The term "lining out" connotes a deceptively disembodied neutrality and objectivity. The more specific designation "meter hymns" seems dry and noncommittal. The verb "deaconing" suggests the formal and male-dominated tradition wherein hymns are read or chanted from the front by an authority figure. I have come to rest upon the title reference "Dr. Watts" because of the particularity it connotes, both as used by members of speech communities where lining out is performed and as a reference to the form's English origins. I am especially grateful to Terry Miller for mentioning that while he has heard blacks speak of "Dr. Watts," he has not heard the same usage among whites. This impression has been reinforced in conversations and correspondence with other colleagues, such as Ronald Pen and Warren Steele, who have studied white traditions of lining out among Old Regular and Primitive Baptists. See the entry for "lining out" in *The New Grove Dictionary of Music and Musicians*, cited in note 1 for the introduction, and liner notes by Reagon and Brevard for *Wade in the Water*, vol. 2. Wyatt Tee Walker, pastor of New York City's Canaan Baptist Church, devotes a chapter to meter hymns in *"Somebody's Calling My Name": Black Music and Social Change*, 1979.

7. See William Tallmadge (1984), "Folk Organum: A Study of Origins." Although he examines the European roots of such parallel fourth and parallel fifth harmonies, one is prompted by the diversity of black lining-out styles to allow for African sources as well. (See Nketia 1974: 147–67 on melody and polyphony in African vocal music.)

8. For example, "Amazing Grace" and "I Heard the Voice of Jesus Say" are common meter hymns with eight syllables per lines one and three, and six syllables per lines two and four. "A Charge to Keep I Have" is in short meter, and "Go Preach My Gospel, Saith the Lord" is in long meter. See Lovelace 1963 for a detailed explanation of poetic meters commonly employed in hymns.

The definition of hymn meters has been a recurring point of disagreement between researchers and members of various African American speech communities. For example, in his 1940 interview with Alan Lomax, Huddie Ledbetter defined common meter as that which was most popular among Baptist churches in his Louisiana childhood memory, long meter as more melodically active and sustained than common meter, and short meter as a shoutlike hymn singing style, common in Methodist revival meetings. Such emic definitions—of the *sound* (as opposed to the given form)—of the singing by those who participate vary with regions, styles, and individual sources.

9. Despite glaring fallacies (see refutations in Epstein 1983), George Pullen Jackson's 1943 study, *White and Negro Spirituals*, contains prescient thinking and observations about lining out in black Primitive Baptist settings. Eschewing racial bias as an explanation for difference, Brett Sutton (1982) and Joyce Cauthen (1999) have clarified and focused such ethnic, musical, and cultural comparisons in more recent studies of hymn singing among black and white Primitive Baptists.

10. See Collins 1992.

11. This selection can be heard on *Wade in the Water,* vol. 2.

12. When a black Missionary Baptist congregation becomes full-gospel Baptist or entirely nondenominational there is a shift in the worship tradition away from lining out and the spirituals and toward praise and worship songs that follow upon the contemporary gospel sound of Andraé Crouch, the Hawkinses, Bill and Gloria Gaither, and others. Where churches maintain an active lining-out and spiritual-singing tradition, they are likely to practice doctrinal tenets consistent with the General Baptist brand of the Arminian faith. While naming the churches and the pastors would compromise the confidentiality of my sources, this viewpoint can be substantiated by reference to a conversation I had on May 14, 1997 with two pastors in South Carolina, one ("John") whose church continues a rich lining-out tradition and one ("Peter") who recently resigned from a Baptist pastorate and, soon after, founded a nondenominational body in the same city. Within the terms of their friendship, John acknowledges the rightness of what Peter has done, because although Peter's congregation was moving in the direction of full-gospel faith, it was apparently divided as a body, with a small majority holding to traditional Baptist doctrine. However, despite their friendship, John is likely to continue to lead the large congregation he pastors, despite their readiness *not* to move in some of the more doctrinally progressive directions. Whereas John's congregation lines out hymns every Sunday, Peter's church almost never lines a hymn. Herein is the implicit connection between musical form and what people believe.

13. Lining out is not antiphonal in the style tradition of the Italian Renaissance, wherein the two groups of singers or instrumentalists were spatially separate and sang or played a verbatim musical echo of the other. The antiphony of lining out is in the verbatim repetition of the leader's *words* by the singing congregation.

14. The Gullah people are the descendants of slaves from the same or similar African tribes who were concentrated on the Sea Islands of South Carolina. Due to their high concentration in the area, they were able to maintain many of the cultural traditions from their native Africa. After the Civil War, many plantation owners either fled their plantations or sold the land to the Gullah people, who continue to live on and farm the land to this day. The Gullah language peculiar to this group is roughly an English-based creole language heavily influenced by several West African languages. For more on the Gullah language and Sea Island culture, see Nancy Rhyne, *Chronicles of the South Carolina Sea Islands* (Winston-Salem, N.C.: John F. Blair, 1998).

15. In this sense, one might argue that the ring shout signifies "deformation of mastery," in Houston Baker's terms, while lining out conveys the corresponding "mastery of the mask." As interrelated and dynamic polarities in American racial politics, these rhetorical modes—one dancing and rejoicing, the other moaning and crying—have moved back and forth across the landscapes of both geography and history. See Baker 1987: 20, 21, 25, 31–32. For a reading of the musical impact of these ideas, see Floyd 1995: 87–99.

16. Floyd 1995. Floyd builds upon the assumption that "African survivals exist not merely in the sense that African-American music has the same characteristics as

NOTES TO PAGES 35–44   267

its African counterparts, but also that the musical *tendencies,* the mythological beliefs and assumptions, and the interpretive strategies of African Americans are the same as those that underlie the music of the African homeland, that these tendencies and beliefs continue to exist as African cultural memory, and that they continue to inform the continuity and elaboration of African-American music" (5).

17. Throughout this book, arranged or notated versions of black religious songs in the nineteenth-century unaccompanied tradition are called spirituals. I also call them spirituals when I am addressing general developments in black music, without reference to a particular location or situation. However, where the reference is to a particular setting or context, they are called congregational songs, or simply songs. This distinction, an acknowledgment of what they are called by the people who sing them, derives from several conversations I had in the 1980s with Bernice Johnson Reagon.

18. The most comprehensive study of the spiritual has been that by John Lovell Jr., *Black Song: The Forge and Flame—The Story of How the Afro-American Spiritual Was Hammered Out* (New York: Macmillan Company, 1972). Providing limited coverage of the ring shout, he ascribes no significance to lining out as a major factor in the development of the spirituals. Reasoning from the basis that the peculiar quality of the spirituals developed in spite of rather than due to the lining-out tradition, literary and theological studies of the form inevitably read lining out in opposition to the ring shout and other more apparently African traditions. But in black lining out's *musically* distinctive way of saying and singing, it appears that black congregations were doing much more than mimicking their white counterparts. The hymns seeded a "low-ground of sorrow, weeping, and wailing" from which the singers cried out for deliverance and found faith for their own struggle within the bounds of what white missionaries offered as approved religious expression during the antebellum period. Thus the sound itself of their plaints, such as "I Love the Lord, He Heard My Cries," rang with a witness of truth against injustice that could not long be denied. On many occasions, ring shouts had to be deferred until after the approved forms of service, but the hymns could be wailed out under the watchful eye and directly within earshot of the oppressor. Shrouded until the nineteenth century by the secrecy of brush arbor meetings, which were secret religious meetings in any number of temporary structures—though most commonly under tree cover—in which words were disallowed, the *sound* itself signified an already palpable human search for divine deliverance.

19. Less particularly but more broadly, Harris defines "moaning" as "a set of performance practices, usually embellishments, that were applied to any of the genres of religious song that blacks then sang" (1992: 22).

20. Here, as throughout, I am building inferences from a nonsystematic range of locations and types of churches that I have visited. However, there is a need for more systematic and full-scale study of regionalism in black congregational singing traditions.

21. See Washington 1986. These heading phrases are used with some frequency throughout a chapter of his book.

CHAPTER 2. "BLEST BE THE TIE THAT BINDS": PART II

1. While the most detailed treatment of hymn singing among Missionary Baptists has been that by Walter Pitts in his book *Old Ship of Zion: The Afro-Baptist Ritual in the African Diaspora* (1993), he attends solely to the structure of worship and linguistic patterns he observed in Central Texas and to their correlates in Africa and the Diaspora, and does not consider the diversity of regional styles checkered throughout the former slave states. A broader range of style traditions among Missionary Baptists is well-represented on the compact disc *Wade in the Water,* volume 2. It includes an excellent and rare example of the traditional prayer with moans and five different regional singing traditions, situated in the Eastern Seaboard states from Maryland to Georgia. Also featured is a re-creation of historic lining-out performances like those that took place in "Mother Bethel" in Philadelphia, the home of the African Methodist Episcopal Church, whose founder and first bishop, Richard Allen, also compiled and published its first hymnal in 1801.

   While *Wade in the Water* is a comprehensive treatment of songs and hymns from several black regional traditions, the other two collections referred to in this book are focused upon hymn singing in particular. *Benjamin Lloyd's Hymn Book* is a comparative study of ethnic and regional traditions among the Primitive Baptists, and the *Dr. Watts* collection inventories black hymn-singing styles throughout the Southeast.

2. Shape-note singing is a practice associated with

   > a body of rural American sacred music published in any of several musical notations in which a note head of a certain shape is assigned to each of the solmization syllables *fa, sol, la, mi* (in the four-syllable "fasola" system) or *do, re, mi, fa, sol, la, si* or *ti*. Most shape notations (also sometimes called "buckwheat," "character" or "patent" notations) employ key signatures, deploy the notes on a five-line staff and use the rhythm signs of conventional notation. They are intended to help singers with little musical expertise to sing at sight without having to recognize pitches on the staff or understand the key system. (*The New Grove Dictionary of Music and Musicians,* edited by Stanley Sadie, 20 vols. [London: Macmillan, 1980], 17: 313–19)

3. The *Original Sacred Harp* is a shape-note hymnal first published by Benjamin Franklin White in 1844. Its most recent revision was published in 1991.

4. Although *Dr. Watts* no. 11, "A Charge to Keep I Have," is performed solo here by Rev. Cross, in an informant interview, the interviewer, Alfred Pinkston, notes that in worship the melody is heard with "a second part which is usually pitched a perfect fifth lower," creating a strict organum effect (1975: 96).

5. See the discography for recorded performances of hymns by Aretha Franklin, Mahalia Jackson, Rev. J.M. Gates, Whitney Houston, and Rev. Carlton Pearson. Although additional fieldwork might disprove this speculation, it appears that in the unaccompanied regional styles these tune-based melodies are less frequently performed than the more ornate melodies which bear the style features of oral transmission.

6. My sense of this performance has been helped greatly by Ruth Crawford Seeger's transcription and the accompanying discussion in Jackson (1943: 250). The transcription itself appears on an unnumbered insert at the end of that book.

7. The Gullah language and Sea Island ring shout traditions are older than the Piedmont Carolinas' syncopated shout tradition, in which there is no ring formation. While radical economic and cultural change have reduced the number of Sea Island locations to the point where one can find shouters in only a sparse handful of locations along the Eastern Seaboard, the more gradual and mediated Piedmont change, in which hymns and shape-note singing likely played greater roles, has been apparently less disruptive to the old-time tradition. Thus, while there seems to be no active correspondence between the disparate groups who still perform the ring shout, an active network of churches and choirs in the Piedmont continues the anniversaries, revivals, and other cyclical occasions that perpetuate the tradition.

8. This map of hymn singing in the Southeast and elsewhere in the United States is based primarily upon an inventory of recorded hymn performances archived at the American Folklife Center of the Library of Congress. The map of singing styles in South Carolina is contiguous from region to region based on Project Senior Culture, which surveyed congregational singing throughout the state (Dargan 1995). However, no such detailed coverage of the entire southeastern United States is currently available. Despite this disparity in the amount of available data, it is possible to hazard a description of these regional styles and an account of how the styles developed as regional traditions.

9. These already appear in arranged spirituals, jazz band arrangements, and transcribed jazz solos. The ways in which certain African American composers and arrangers have notated their ideas so as to establish a sense of idiomatic rapport with their performers' capacities for interpreting the music they write or arrange could form the topic of an interesting study. Rightly applied, such an ideal of consistency should facilitate style analysis and illustrate inherent connections between lining out and related genres.

CHAPTER 3. "OUR GOD, OUR HELP IN AGES PAST"

1. King also notes that "gospelling poetry represents a practical application of ideas that were current in *Paraclesis* and in Protestant biblical commentaries by Bullinger, Jud, and Calvin" (1982: 210–20).

2. The terms "Puritan," "Nonconformist," and "Dissenter" are related, but in their day they conveyed differing if overlapping perspectives for the parties they designated. The spirit of Puritanism was a "combination of piety and realism, of humility and self-assertion, of deference and rebellion" (M. Watts 1978: 16), rooted in the conviction that the Church of England had not gone far enough in its break with Roman Catholicism. As used in the early seventeenth century, "Nonconformity" "referred to beneficed members of the established church whose Puritan convictions led them to omit some parts of the liturgy and to refuse to conform to some of the ceremonies laid down in the Book of Common Prayer and the canons of the church." During the Restoration period, the meaning of Nonconformity grew to encompass everything from the moderation of

Presbyterians, who differed with the established church primarily on questions of polity, to the radicalism of Quakers, who renounced all semblance of outward ritual and stressed the primacy of inward experiential religion. Under the guidance of Oliver Cromwell, Nonconformists sought during the 1650s to establish a presbyterian polity in the Church of England and to replace the monarchy with a republican form of government. In the politicoreligious intrigues of the 1660s, "conforming" Episcopalians began referring to Nonconformists as Dissenters, and by the early eighteenth century "it was the universal term for all the non-episcopal congregations of England" (Keeble 1987: 7, 41). For nearly thirty years, between the 1662 Act of Uniformity and the 1689 Act of Toleration, Nonconformist/Dissenters endured legal harassment and imprisonment, and were sometimes killed. In this period, the rejected parties created a compelling literary vision of themselves as a people called out by God who were enduring persecution for the strength of their inward convictions. Forged out of such introspection, the immediate and personal voice of Watts hymns, along with the grandeur of their praise and celebration, would afford them a new resonance with larger and still more disparate North American audiences in the eighteenth century.

3. Psalmody consists of biblical psalms rendered in metrical English translations, which are more or less literal, e.g., "Our God, Our Help in Ages Past" is a translation of Psalm 90. Hymns are also metrical songs of praise to God, but they are not restricted to the literal content of scripture and may include freer renderings of the psalms, metrical settings of scriptures other than the biblical psalms, or metrical verses adhering to scriptural doctrines but not traceable to a specific source, e.g., "Joy to the World"; Watts's paraphrase of Psalm 98, "Must Jesus Bear the Cross Alone," by Charles Wesley; and "Amazing Grace," by John Newton. Although Watts wrote "hymns"—which, though freer in form than those of his predecessors, remained faithful to the spirit if not the letter of Hebrew and Greek texts—he set a precedent for freely interpreting the scriptures that those who followed, such as Wesley and Newton, extended still further.

4. Although phrases included here suggest an indirect pattern of repetition, which may or may not have been conscious, certain phrases of the two versions of Psalm 90—the enduring one in common meter and the other in long meter—are more apparently similar, suggesting that there may have been a conscious reworking of not only words and phrases but also the ideas they convey. An example of the latter, more conscious reworking of ideas can be seen in the following long-meter (L.M.) and common-meter versions of the same verse of Psalm 107, v. 6:

O may the sons of men record   L.M.
The wondrous goodness of the Lord!
And let their thankful off'rings prove
How they adore their Maker's love.

O that the sons of men would praise   C.M.
The goodness of the Lord!
And those that see thy wondrous ways,
Thy wondrous love record.

5. This popular Watts hymn is included in neither the *Psalms of David Imitated* nor *Hymns and Spiritual Songs* but is appended to the sermon by Watts, "Holy Fortitude or Remedies Against Fear," included in the third volume of his *Sermons*, which were collected and published by John Clark and Richard Hett between 1721 and 1724.

6. Paralleling these images of the English as the "chosen people" are infrequent statements that are seen today, in retrospect, as anti-Semitic, such as this verse in short meter (S.M.):

See what a living stone
The builders did refuse;
Yet God hath built his church thereon,
In spite of envious Jews. (Ps. 118)

CHAPTER 4. "FATHER, I STRETCH MY HANDS TO THEE"

1. If Dr. Watts hymns were the genotype, the genetic constitution, then the songs and spirituals are the phenotype, "the visible properties of an organism that are produced by the interaction of the genotype and the environment" (*Merriam-Webster's Collegiate Dictionary*, 10th ed.). While I do not intend to make an association between physical genetics and a certain way of making music, the metaphor of submerged genotype and revealed phenotype certainly describes the current relationship between Dr. Watts hymns and congregational songs in African American worship. The "environment" that Dr. Watts hymns interacted with as they spread from region to region was the distinctive character of each speech community and the patterns of movement associated with local worship practices. Because Dr. Watts has permeated singing traditions more in certain locations than in others, the apparent extent of this hymn-to-song—or conversely, song-to-hymn—style influence varies from region to region. Although the songs and hymns have interacted reflexively with each other, I have characterized the hymns as "genotype" because they have remained far more submerged and less visible than the songs or spirituals.

2. Brothers identifies four stylistic codes that are important to the sound of African American music: harmony, the concept of a "piece" of music, speechlike song, and polyrhythmic textures.

3. See the citations for sources on call-and-response structure in lining out in the introduction, n. 6.

4. For the former style, see *Musiques de l'ancien royaume Kuba*, Disques Ocora OCR 61, Republique du Zaire (see side B, no. 7, "Dirges," Women from Pombo Bulombo, recorded April 12, 1970, at Pombo Bulombo, Ngeende tribe). *Dr. Watts* no. 13, "A Charge to Keep I Have," and no. 15, "Must Jesus Bear the Cross Alone," are examples of the latter style.

5. A variety of dirge singing styles—free and strict rhythm as well as a merger of both—can be heard on nos. 16, 18, and 19 of the compact disc accompanying Agawu's 1995 book, *African Rhythm: A Northern Ewe Perspective*.

6. The common ritual structure Walter Pitts identifies includes two frames: a secret first frame that utilizes the singing or chanting of esoteric texts to induce

somnolence or loss of self-consciousness, and a public second frame that seeks possession trance by pairing body movement with repetitive singing and drumming. As the first frame contains European-derived practices and the second African-derived ones, the tone and mood of worship move from the languidness of slow chanting to percussive rhythms and possession trance (1993: 91–92). After Fernandez (1973), Pitts defines a frame as "a bound [performance] event that assumes affective value through the vehicle of metaphoric expression" (31–33). Pitts also found that initiation rituals in Africa and the Diaspora share a two-frame structure. Following the rite of passage, the novice is to possess two personalities: the old socially conditioned self (the outward mask) and the (ritually liberated) self that emerges through the conditioned reflex of possession trance (Verger 1957: 72–73).

Although I concur with the *formal* concept of dual and complementary frames that Pitts has identified in both African and African American worship, the *structure* of black Baptist worship is more fluid and variable than what Pitts describes. Forms describe the larger order of worship, but structures of a ritual evolve and unfold through the peaks, plains, and valleys of expression that occur in performance. The primary events of black worship are preaching, singing, shouting, conversion, prayer, and testimony, as described by James Cone (1978). What actually occurs in the progress of each event as performed becomes its *ritual* structure. Therefore, devotionals are a *form* consisting of hymns, prayers, and songs as *structured* events, each guiding the whole toward certain ritual outcomes. Just how these events proceed hinges upon a range of still smaller components—questions, answers, phrases, interjections, speaking, chanting, singing, and the whole gamut of musical gestures Samuel Floyd subsumes under what he terms Call-Response (1995: 96), a broader conceptual category than the structural entity call-and-response.

These are the building blocks, the musical and dramatic means of ordering time and sound in black Baptist ritual. Each event—and the gestures that guide it in one direction or another—is important to the worship tradition because, while the binary *formal* relationship between devotions and preaching service is fixed, smaller binary *structures* may be freely replicated or inverted, turned this way and that, during the course of any ritual event. In this sense, while the ritual *form* is predetermined, each discrete event is *structured*—in an emergent sense—toward certain acts of worship (and away from others) only in the course of performance. Before the sermon, for example, a hymn choir may retreat to the decorous reflection of a Dr. Watts hymn (first frame) to set a worship tone that entreats the preaching of the gospel. Then the sermon may culminate in celebration or shouting (second frame). In certain regional styles, the course of a single song or hymn performance may offer a microcosm of both the first and second frames as it moves from slow but emphatic speech rhythms, through accelerating tempos, to the intensity of a percussive shouting rhythm. This first frame–second frame order, by far the most common, may also be modified so that a kind of "holy hush" (or quieter worshipful singing that offers thanks to God for the release and rejoicing expressed in the shout) *follows* rather than precedes a shouting episode.

7. Framing his study as a macroanalysis of why and how Africans in the Diaspora adapted European forms for lining out, praying, and preaching to African ritual

functions, Pitts's field research and analysis inventoried eight black vernacular English variables isolated in the speech of central Texas preachers as indices of ritual change from standard to black vernacular English. Quantitatively analyzing worshipers' speech in conversations, prayers, and sermons for the frequency of these variables, he found that Standard English was most dominant in the speech conventions of black prayer language, that conversational speech represented a middle ground, and that the emotional climax of sermons was laden with black vernacular speech (1993: 132–45). Although Pitts gives extensive attention to hymns and songs, his linguistic analysis is limited to sermons and prayers.

8. The relative prominence in American slave society of cultural influences from each of these African regions is difficult to estimate. Although the role of individual leaders and musicians is pivotal in processes of musical change, the factors of non-change that are under consideration were reinforced by more broadly shared social patterns. However, in the experience of slaves who had been transported by land and sea to a frighteningly permanent new home, the "non-change," as either retention or reinterpretation, became perforce a form of change. While the roles of individual leaders and musicians were pivotal in such transformations, those singular adjustments were also contingent upon the social resonance that could issue from groups sharing similar backgrounds and experiences.

9. Letter of March 2, 1756, quoted in Pilcher 1971: 112. See also Epstein 1977 and Southern 1983.

10. Perhaps we cannot know the extent to which these reports were accurate or whether they were written with the intent of generating aid from church officials and supporters.

11. This description carries my own memory back to my early years when, having already been drawn to more conventional popular music of the 1950s, I heard lining out and wondered how it could sound so different from anything else I'd ever heard.

12. The impact of this kind of singing can hardly be captured through typical field recording techniques. It would require a microphone for every person, or at least for each principal singer within the congregation.

13. "Hush arbor" and "brush arbor" are similar names for the same space: "brush" references the covering of tree limbs that structured the space, and "hush" suggests the secretive and subversive status of slave worship, apart from the supervision of masters or overseers.

14. The fourth edition of this hymn book shows a 1906 copyright. Obviously reprinted without modifications, as of this writing the fourth edition is available from the National Baptist Publishing Board.

15. This information was obtained by the author in a May 1999 telephone conversation with Dr. T. B. Boyd III of the National Baptist Publishing Board and in follow-up correspondence with Ms. Mary Green, administrative assistant to Dr. Boyd.

16. Other twentieth-century accounts of Dr. Watts performances include those by Joyce Cauthen (1999) from Alabama, Geneva Smitherman (1977) and Ben Bailey (1978) from Mississippi, John Wesley Work III (1949) from Tennessee, and Brett Sutton (1982) from Virginia. In addition, dissertations on the topic cover the genre in other regions, including Florida (Pinkston 1975), South

Carolina (Duncan 1979), North Carolina (Crowder 1978), and Kentucky (Smith 1987).

17. Though born into the tradition, I also had difficulty deciphering the gloriously atmospheric sound presence surrounding me in those worship services. And the sounds that Jackson heard in Alabama were likely even more heterophonic than the organum harmonies heard in my region of South Carolina. His bafflement may have been compounded by differences in regional styles among the areas of Alabama, Florida, and Tennessee where he worked.

CHAPTER 5. "I LOVE THE LORD, HE HEARD MY CRIES"

1. Although "drum languages" continue in certain African locations, Agawu and others writing throughout the twentieth century noted the sharp decline in the number of drummers who actually knew the correspondence between certain rhythmic phrases and what they represent in meaning.

2. Although Smitherman is right that one approach to lining out is "long, slow, and drawn-out," as indicated in chapter 1, other regional styles begin slowly only to gradually or suddenly accelerate.

3. This diverges from the observation by John Work III that the rhythm of Dr. Watts hymns is "spun-out melismatically with no rhythm derived out of measure and beat, only punctuated by the wordphrase of the leader" (quoted in Southern 1983: 284). He describes his impression as one of song riding unbounded upon the wings of speech. However, understated though it may have been, the Primitive Baptist singing he heard—likely similar to no. 20 from *Benjamin Lloyd's Hymn Book*, "Father, I Stretch My Hands to Thee"—must have been framed by a definite pulse. Work does not deny that there was a beat, only that what he heard derived not from measure or beat but from the speech impetus. He describes a single tradition; however, in the multiplex of regional styles, neither the rhythms of natural speech nor the force of a definite beat has overpowered the abiding creative tension between the two that runs like a thread through the entire corpus of Dr. Watts.

4. Vocables are nonsense syllables that add to the rhythmic momentum of a phrase. For example, the phrase "fix me Jesus" becomes "fix-a me Jesus" in a verse couplet often added to spirituals. See Whalum 1971: 390–91 for a description of this leading line and repetition form and its variants.

5. Although others offer hearty affirmations like "Sing your song" and "go 'head," it seems that only the leader and his daughter know the hymn, which is being sung at an annual gathering of Primitive Baptist churches in Western North Carolina.

6. Also as metacommunication, but apart from the melismatic intensity of poetic rhythms, speech rhythms may be either spoken or sung as short interpolations between the phrases of a song, such as the lead-in "I want you to . . . ," which a singer might logically insert after "Precious Lord, take my hand" and before "lead me on and let me stand" in Thomas Dorsey's classic gospel song "Take My Hand, Precious Lord."

7. See List 1963 for a chart that gradates the modes of speaking between speech and song.

8. While the melodic sources have not been identified, *Benjamin Lloyd* no. 9, "O May I Worthy Prove," and *Dr. Watts* no. 9, "Jesus Invites His Saints," also sound like tune book melodies. However, neither of these hymns has been rhythmically transformed by either the speechlike character of free rhythms or the metronomic insistence of percussive rhythms.

9. Performed by the Shiloh Primitive Baptist Association (including churches from North Carolina, Virginia, and Kentucky), the percussive rhythms present on *Benjamin Lloyd* no. 8 may be part of a larger regional style holding currency among Primitive and Missionary Baptists in the Piedmont Carolinas. Although a clapping pattern does not accompany "Dark and Thorny," its rhythmic character approximates the accelerating tempos and intensity one can hear further south in the Charlotte–Rock Hill region of the Carolinas. *Dr. Watts* nos. 7 and 8 (the hymn "Amazing Grace" and the song "You May Bury Me in the East"), as well as *Wade in the Water*, vol. 2, no. 8 ("I Heard the Voice of Jesus Say"), all also exemplify this style. (Although the latter is performed by the Baltimore chapter of the United Southern Prayer Band, many of its members migrated there from this Piedmont region of South Carolina.)

10. The alliterative relation between portraiture sound and poetic rhythms is a coincident reminder that because of their common North American origin in what Collins describes as the moaning-prayer event, the two are interrelated elements of Afro-Baptist worship. Given the high level of integration between these two style features, I have categorized performances based upon which of them is most apparent in the approach of the lead singer(s).

11. Anglo-American congregations came to decry the "old way" for the confusion of sounds evoked in its arhythmic, slow, and lugubrious style. The "regular way" was not only faster; it was promulgated through published tune books and designed to facilitate a new musical literacy in choirs and congregations.

12. See, e.g., "Pony Blues" on *The Blues: A Smithsonian Collection of Classic Blues Singers,* vol. 1.

13. Ironically, contemporary claims that rap is not "music" bear a striking resemblance to nineteenth-century descriptions of spirituals that benighted that form for its supposed "barbarism" (Walser 1995).

14. "Papa's Got a Brand New Bag," parts 1, 2, and 3, and "The Funky Drummer" can be heard on *James Brown: Star Time,* discs 1 and 3.

15. Cooke's especially stylized way of applying poetic rhythms as a kind of ululation in triplet rhythms can be heard on "Touch the Hem of His Garment" and "I'll Come Running Back to You." See *The Two Sides of Sam Cooke.* Aretha Franklin's use of the same is apparent in "Drown in My Own Tears" on *Aretha Franklin: I Never Loved a Man the Way I Love You.*

16. Rev. Johnson can be heard in *Dr. Watts* no. 10, and Rev. Franklin's congregation can be heard in *Dr. Watts* nos. 16 and 21.

17. Two sides of a single coin, portraiture sound and poetic rhythm are really complementary expressions of the heterogeneous sound ideal posited by Olly Wilson (1992), who cites prevalent tendencies in black music, including (a) rhythmic and implied metrical contrast, (b) percussiveness, (c) call-and-response structures, (d) high density of musical events within a short time frame, and (e) the incorporation of body movement with music making. With

the possible exception of body movement (which is subdued but not lacking), these tendencies identified by Wilson play key roles in both portraiture sound and poetic rhythm.

CHAPTER 6. "GO PREACH MY GOSPEL, SAITH THE LORD"

1. Although I have consulted linguistic sources that coincide with the claims made in this chapter about the structure and signification of African American song-talk, my focus is not so much upon the linguistic character of words, but upon what those words as performed speech utterance do to drive or generate the composition and performance of Dr. Watts hymns and congregational songs.

2. Along with the origins controversy concerning the spirituals, two schools of thought have prevailed about the origins of black English, one arguing that it is derived from white American and English dialects and the other arguing that its sources are in the pronunciation and grammar of African languages (see Rickford and Rickford 2000: 91–128). Pursuing neither course, this discussion considers the cross-fertilization of styles that has occurred between hymns and songs as respective English and African ways of patterning words into songs.

3. "Antistructure" is based on Victor Turner's concept of the unity of *communitas*, or coming together in the ritual process, as opposed to the more rigid or outward structures by which social unity is maintained.

4. Because I believe that the Gullah-style songs, though dispersed over a smaller area, have received more attention in print and on record, and because hymn singing is more foundational to the character of uplands styles, the bulk of this chapter's analysis centers on the latter.

5. The discussion that follows is based on my recollections of several performances as well as a 1996 telephone interview with Rev. Waldo Robinson, pastor and moderator of the St. Paul Baptist Association, which has member churches through Chesterfield County, South Carolina, and a well-known host of a Sunday-evening gospel music radio program in that region.

6. An example of this kind of beginning might be *Dr. Watts* no. 8, "You May Bury Me in the East," which begins in a slow, indefinite rhythm and gains in emphasis and tempo throughout.

7. Wendell Whalum summarizes Johnson's description of swing as "that subtle and elusive thing that results from the swaying of head and body. The 'swing' is spontaneous. It is a form of the rhythmic aspect of rendering the music but is separated, by Johnson, from the rhythm created and guided by the patting of the feet and hands" (1971: 391). This description is prescient especially if we can envision in it the studied yet unconscious movements a human body makes that can appear to be "dancing without dancing." Such gyrations of the head, torso, or buttocks often accompany nonmusical activities such as sitting, working, playing, or walking. They can and frequently do also accompany social or creative dance, but the improvisatory, almost absent-minded freedom of this rhythmic movement develops fluidly from the perception of a dynamic sequence of interactive moments in time.

8. Since the congregation is repeating or completing what the leader has initiated, this exchange is really a verbal cueing process rather than a clear case of

antiphony—i.e., calls that provoke a corresponding response rather than an exact repetition—between leader and congregation.

9. Ware also leads *Dr. Watts* no. 9, "You May Bury Me in the East."

10. If these hymn texts are pre-blues utterances, then the song by Thomas Dorsey, "I Don't Know Why," may be heard in the same way. Although its form is the sixteen-bar gospel blues, and the hymn "God Moves in a Mysterious Way" is inserted as one of the verses, the song chorus never mentions God or Jesus:

I don't know why
I have to cry sometime
No I don't know why
I have to sigh sometime
It would be perfect day
But so much trouble in my way
I don't know why
But I'll find out by and by

The Lord, he moves in a mysterious way
His wonders to perform
He plants his footsteps on the sea
And he rides in every storm.

(As sung by Bessie Griffin on Thomas Dorsey, *Precious Lord: Recordings of the Great Gospel Songs of Thomas A. Dorsey.*)

11. The social tension between speakers of AAVE and Standard English in the late nineteenth and early twentieth centuries was apparent both in the church and in the world of literature. A poem by Daniel Webster Davis, "De Linin' ub de Hymns," portrays a dispute between proponents of lining-out hymns and those who are for reading them from hymnals (*Weh Down Souf and Other Poems* [Cleveland: Helman-Taylor, 1897], 54–56). Although the entire poem concerns the conflict between those who read and those do not, the following lines address hymn singing in particular:

De young folks say 'tain't stylish to lin' um out no mo';
Dat dey's got edikashun, an' dey wants us all to know
Dey likes to hab dar singin'-books a holin' fore dar eyes,
An' sing de hymns straight along "to manshuns in de skies."

In a brief article on the 2000 production of Scott Joplin's *Treemonisha* staged by the Opera Theatre of St. Louis, Edward Berlin quotes from program notes by Gerald Early, which, despite some historical errors, offer a prescient justification for the use of AAVE in the production. Early notes that "in most black literature of [the early twentieth century] the rule was simple: educated black characters did not speak in dialect; uneducated ones did." By retaining the use of dialect in the St. Louis production, Berlin concludes, "the Opera Theatre . . . presents a *Treemonisha* that has both theatrical spirit and artistic integrity" (*Center for Black Music Research Digest* 13, no. 2 [fall 2000]: 18–19).

12. Although "long meter" in standard usage designates a four-line iambic quatrain with eight syllables in each line, the term has been generalized in many black

communities to designate an especially slow and ornate style of lining out. This sense of rhythmic and melodic freedom is likely what House is talking about here.

13. In rap terminology, the emcee, or master of ceremonies, is the rapper or lead voice. This usage is traceable to the late-1970s origins of rap in the Bronx, New York, where emcees were so designated because their role was to deliver a constant stream of jive talk on the microphone, while disc jockeys manipulated turntables and mixers to enhance the rhythmic sound of funk recordings from the 1960s and 1970s. These focal activities provided music for dancing in the parks by African American and Hispanic youth who were either too young or too afraid to attend clubs in ghettoes beset with ethnic and gang violence (see Keyes 1996).

14. For a detailed discussion of the song texts omitted from the epigraphs in *The Souls of Black Folk* as well as an interpretive reading of Du Bois, Hurston, and others on the spirituals, see Sundquist 1993: 457–539.

CHAPTER 7. "I HEARD THE VOICE OF JESUS SAY"

1. For a discussion of the methodological issues engaged by crosscultural analogies and crossregional comparisons, see Gerhard Kubik 1998.

2. In the early 1980s, upon learning of my interest in black hymn singing, the gospel music writer and collector Doug Seroff mentioned C. J. Johnson to me as someone who had recorded hymns and who was still singing and preaching. From our initial meeting in 1982 until his death in 1990, Rev. Johnson and I worked continually to bring hymns to younger audiences and to record his life story for posterity.

3. Hurston's essay "Spirituals and Neo-Spirituals" is prescient for its insights into the dynamics of black worship. Likewise, the collection of essays published in *The Sanctified Church* is rich in insights into black church culture. However, because of her difficult experiences growing up in the midst of a very deeply wounded home and church community, which suffered for her father's sexual indiscretions, her memories of the black Baptist church seem to have been laden with heavy psychological baggage that even her ethnographic skills found difficult to throw off. While her subjectivity did not hinder the mechanics of her prodigious fieldwork, it seems to have bifurcated her perspective of the black church. On one hand, she celebrated the vitality of the worship tradition as a literary source; on the other, she felt that participation in the black church tradition was a sign of weakness and only good "for those who need it." For example, see her essay "Religion," in *Dust Tracks on a Road* (1942).

4. Nor did her contemporary James Weldon Johnson. For his perspectives, see chapter 10 of his novel *The Autobiography of an Ex-Coloured Man* (1912), in which the protagonist journeys to the South to conduct fieldwork in the course of writing a great musical work that he feels will redeem the cultural legacy of the Negro. (He later scraps this plan and decides to forego his artistic aspirations altogether, passes for white in pursuit of status, and "sells his birthright for a mess of pottage.") See also Johnson's nonfiction treatment of the spirituals in his introduction to *The Books of American Negro Spirituals* (1969); also Whalum's essay on the theoretical significance of Johnson's claims in this introduction (1971).

5. From my interview with Rev. Johnson at his Atlanta home. The recent publication of Deacon William Reardon's story (see Reagon 2001) makes available another important resource for understanding the congregational singing tradition in its social context.

6. Bart Landry explains that while "status groups emerge out of the *subjective evaluation* of community members, classes are based on *objective positions* within the economic system" (1987: 25). "The meaning of class revolves around the ownership and use of capital"; it is a fundamental distinction, not between "haves and have-nots," but between "those who hire and those who are hired" (ibid.).

7. By convention, the middle class has included professionals (such as doctors, lawyers, teachers, and ministers), nonowning managers, sales workers, clerical workers, and small businessmen (Landry 1987: 5). In 1910, only 3 percent of blacks were professionals, 8 percent constituted a skilled working class of artisans and foremen, 39 percent belonged to an unskilled working class, and 50 percent worked on farms (1987: 21).

8. As of this writing, Johnson's wife and all his children still live in Atlanta. The daughters, who are nearing retirement as factory laborers, have lived with their mother since the elder Johnson's death in 1990. The oldest son is a building contractor, and the younger son pastors Victory Baptist Church, a large congregation in the southeast quadrant of the city.

9. In *Jonah's Gourd Vine*, John Pearson gets close to Lucy Potts by joining the choir and learning to sing the shape notes at the Baptist church where many of the "uppity" black people worship (Hurston [1934] 1990: 49–57).

10. Hurston calls attention to this practice of selling ballad sheets, noting the changing role but continuing presence of the spirituals in early-twentieth-century black worship: "The makers of the songs of the present go about from town to town and from church to church, singing their songs. Some are printed and called ballads, and offered for sale after the services at ten and fifteen cents each" (1981: 79).

11. In the documentary film *Wild Women Don't Have the Blues,* the pianist Danny Barker uses this same speech inflection on the word "Maw" to venerate Ma Rainey, giving the same the sense of ownership and affection in the gesture of pronunciation. Of course, Sarah Johnson was by no means the same as Gertrude Rainey. One was a praying woman, the other a blues woman. Yet, each in her own setting commanded the ultimate respect. This sense of black womanhood might be seen as profoundly assertive yet utterly feminine and even respectable to Victorian sensibilities.

12. As early as the Reconstruction era, blacks frowned upon being called "Aunt" or "Uncle" So-and-So by whites; educated blacks, especially, have studiously avoided or discouraged this practice.

13. Note that many black ministers, as an additional mark of status and a means of standing at a discreet distance from the flocks they pastor, have also identified themselves by initials instead of a first or middle name, e.g., C. J. Johnson, C. L. Franklin, M. L. King.

14. Subverting the stereotypical image of the male or female Negro who indiscriminately panders to whites, Johnson casts his grandmother in the role of one who is gifted, skilled, and genuinely charming. Hence, whites as well as blacks are

drawn to the sense of personal magnetism she exudes. Whether Sarah Johnson was or was not this way is not the issue. The quality of her grandson's remembrance and his gift for characterization are at play in the storytelling process.

15. In other words, he began preaching in an intoned, chanting style.

16. Holding wide currency among black Baptists who continue the hymn tradition, this Isaac Watts hymn is no. 128 in *Hymns and Spiritual Songs*, vol. 1. See Watts 1707.

17. That is, they called them back with great applause.

18. A performance of special significance, possibly a corruption of "debut."

19. A reference to intoned or chanted preaching.

20. There is no record that Rev. Lowe ever pastored the Providence Baptist Church in Atlanta, which is historically allied with Morehouse College.

21. See discography for *Rev. J. M. Gates: Complete Recorded Works in Chronological Order.*

22. See Landry's discussion of how blacks kept to themselves socially during this period of overt racial discrimination and furnished their homes as lavishly as possible (1987: 79).

CHAPTER 8. "COME YE THAT LOVE THE LORD"

1. See Turner 1969. Turner's model for the study of ritual has also been adapted by Houston Baker to describe the literary-historical evolution toward the point of creative fruition or ripeness that he calls "Black (W)holeness." See Baker 1984: 180–84.

2. See Floyd 1995 and Gates 1988. Floyd's point in *The Power of Black Music* is that not only can the meanings derived from vernacular contexts inform criticism of jazz and black concert music, but the very grammars of the latter often build upon the former. In this light, Wilson's heterogeneous sound ideal becomes a key identifying element in the *sound* of black music. Building upon Wilson and Pitts as well, my project works from Floyd's Call-Response construct— especially for its value as a thick description of black music vernacular's structural components—to elaborate a system for critical study of vernacular performances with or without reference to other styles. I agree with Floyd and Gates that the act of musical Signifyin(g) is central to the black vernacular, and I applaud the range of elements and procedures situated in what Floyd terms Call-Response, to which we will return.

3. This is not to be confused with the binary opposition of the structuralist school of anthropology advanced by Levi-Strauss and Chomsky and critiqued in ethnomusicological terms by Feld (1974). Here, *dialectical* describes a relationship between sound and movement in black music that is wholly neither one nor the other but is ever intersecting, merging, diverging, and always requiring both elements in relative balance with each other to compose the whole.

4. The coupling of lining out and the ring shout can also be seen as an early seed of the black modernist synthesis commented upon by Houston Baker— "mastery of the mask" and "deformation of mastery," respectively (1987: 20–21, 25, 31–32). For a reading of the musical impact of these concepts, see Floyd 1995: 87–99.

5. In the following discussion, the term pair "moaning"/"shouting" is sometimes substituted for "lining out"/"ring shout." In general, however, I prefer the latter terms since they underscore the relationship between the ritual-musical process and its historical context.

   The ring-shout polarity would also include nonmusical or indeterminate ecstatic behaviors such as running, screaming, laughing, or being "slain in the spirit," which is to lie down in a prone position and perhaps experience trance-like states of altered consciousness. The inclusion of these elements derives from the importance of the concept of heterogeneous sound to both African and African American music. Because these motions or postures implicate either sound or silence, and because they color the tone and meaning of certain worship moments, they bear directly upon the musical as well as ritual outcomes of a worship event.

6. Though not unrelated to it, these vocal practices long predate modern scat singing as a consciously stylized Signifyin(g) revision of instrumental sounds. I see the relationship between scat and the freely measured rhythms in songs and hymns as once-removed and indirect. These vocal gestures were surely evident in the repertoire of gifted song leaders long before similar concepts of the balance between rhythmic constancy and freedom crystallized in the melodic, harmonic, and timbral flights of Charlie Parker's saxophone.

7. See Baumann 1977 and Goffman 1974. While Baumann uses the terms "frame" and "key" synonymously, I make a distinction between the formal frame of worship and the unplanned changes of key within it.

8. The sequential nature of this five-part process may appear untenable if one takes the stereotypical view of ecstatic worship as orgies of emotional abandon. Such abandon undoubtedly occurs in both black and white circles, but it is not particularly relevant to the critical category of music. The present examination is limited to those forms of ecstatic worship that are explicitly musical. Close examination confirms that ecstatic worship, relying as it does on a wide range of orally transmitted, formulaic words and actions, must be carefully observed if one is to apprehend the signals that move the music and worship from one key to the next.

9. Though the performance was extraordinary as a ritual experience, the recording equipment available to me on that chance visit could not fairly capture the complex web of sounds. Therefore no recording of the performance is available publicly. This I deeply regret, as this performance remains one of the most graphic examples of the principles described here that I've ever witnessed.

10. I have chosen this pseudonym because, to my great regret, I did not learn the man's name at the time and, as a visitor and a stranger, was subsequently unable to retrace the path and identify him.

11. This suggests an indirect parallel between congregational singing and jazz contexts, wherein the role of the song leader—as analogous to that of the drummer, who sets the tempo and monitors intensity and group interaction in general—can and does frequently shift, like that of the jazz soloist, during extended performances from one person to another.

    In the hymn choir tradition around Rock Hill and Chester, South Carolina, from where many Prayer Band members originate, such lead changes occur frequently. In this tradition, it is a mark of discretion or maturity in a song leader to sustain a song only long enough to achieve rapport and garner momentum. If the performance has moved his or her fellow worshipers, someone will continue the song or encourage the leader to do so. As in the gospel quartet tradition, lead changes also afford resting intervals for leaders, who spend their vocal resources quickly in the rising volume, pace, and intensity.

12. Conversely, it would have been possible for the performance to excel musically but fail to achieve the minimum levels of rapport and momentum required in such a worship service.

CHAPTER 9. "GOD MOVES IN A MYSTERIOUS WAY"

1. *The Blues: A Smithsonian Collection of Classic Blues Singers* contains many more classic examples, including Charley Patton's "Pony Blues," Robert Johnson's "Believe I'll Dust My Broom," Henry Thomas's "Bull Doze Blues," Sonny Boy Williamson's "Good Morning, Little School Girl," Blind Boy Fuller's "Step It Up and Go," and Bobby Blue Bland's "Farther up the Road." See also Blind Willie Johnson's "If I Had My Way I'd Tear the Building Down" on *The Complete Blind Willie Johnson* (Columbia/Legacy C2K 052835, 1993).

2. Due to copyright restrictions, the complete lyrics to "Strange Fruit," along with transcriptions of all three tunes, could not be included in this book.

3. The professional jazz musicians who were the informants for Monson's ethnographic study (1996) spoke of "liquid" rhythms as freer, or going against the prevailing pulse, "solid" rhythms as those that create and sustain the groove so central to various African American vernaculars.

4. Data concerning the state of congregational singing in large urban churches during the urban migrations are anecdotal and sketchy, but Baptist pastors and area moderators, such as Dr. C. J. Johnson and Dr. Waldo Robinson, have indicated to me the challenges stemming from efforts of groups from differing regions to sing together. Such events seem an ironic rehearsal of both the African dilemmas of tribal difference and the early social challenges that arose from the intentional confounding of African languages and cultures by North American white slave traders and owners.

5. Holiday first recorded the song in 1939 and reprised it numerous times in succeeding years.

6. See Eric Sundquist's comparison of the lyricism of oral tradition (illustrated in Zora Neale Hurston's transcription of a folk sermon) and a similar passage in a sermon poem written by James Weldon Johnson (Sundquist 1992: 49–91).

7. For an account of the growth of jam sessions before and during the bebop era, see DeVeaux 1997.

8. In Carl Woideck 1996, this studio recording is listed as version 5 of "Parker's Mood," and versions 2 and 4 are also referenced. All three were issued on *The Complete Savoy Studio Sessions*, Savoy ZDS 5500, 2000.

9. Ed Blackwell plays the role of foil here to the more straight-ahead drumming of Billy Higgins. Though also deeply grounded in the pulse-keeping function, Blackwell is perfectly suited to such a task, playing with, stirring up, and responsive to what is going on around him in the ensemble. I have always thought of

him as the prototype of the jazz drummer as the "mother" who takes care of all her "children" (the other voices in the ensemble), seeing to it that each individual, seeking his or her own direction, finds one that harmonizes with the direction of the whole. His rare gift was this ability to shift, play, work, push, pull, and, above all, negotiate the uncharted territory of a jazz performance. I therefore attribute the genius of the "hambone rhythms" (see n. 11) that come into play during Coleman's masterful solo as much to Blackwell's inspiration and instigation as to the chorus of horns that foreground those rhythmic figures.

10. Especially in the opening and closing statements, the harmonies are freely atonal, in that each pitch in the twelve-note chromatic scale is strategically employed, not to avoid the implication of harmonic gravity or pull altogether but to achieve that musical effect without the use of the traditional harmonic language of tonality or modality.

11. Martin Williams calls some of these high-energy moments "hambone rhythms." If one is listening with a bias toward a rigorous economy of ideas stated and developed in relation to time as the formal framework, then, according to Williams's claim, that these rhythms are arguably overdone. But forming, as they do, the celebratory pinnacle of the performance, the rhythms proceed from and retreat into an entire musical statement that, without the relief from cerebration afforded by the celebration of the hambone jive, might prove tedious and academic.

12. In this sense, Coleman is to the great alto stylists before him as Brahms is to Bach. The ideals are the same, but the later figure has attained a privileged place of technical facility and aesthetic refinement that is premised upon the prior genius.

13. The jazz style and context insist upon repetition as a key element in the way a theme is handled or developed. However, Coleman's fantasylike solo moves from one theme or idea to the next, and once he has left a certain idea he does not overtly return to it. I do not know if this solo has been transcribed, but if not, it really should be, so that we can see the mix of plain and simple melodies and imaginative, nonformulaic harmonies that keeps Coleman's groove so focused and intense yet free from stylized forms and patterns.

CONCLUSION

1. Paul Gilroy (1991) and others have persuasively countered that position, and their arguments might be further strengthened by fuller knowledge of Dr. Watts and other early black genres.

2. A graphic illustration of the contrast I am suggesting between "letting go" and "holding on" with reference to the old culture can be seen in hymn-singing episodes from two films. In *The Preacher's Wife* (the less successful remake of the classic film *The Bishop's Wife*), Whitney Houston plays the prototypical minister's spouse of the black church tradition who, at the proverbial ritual moment when he needs her most, leads the choir in a stirring rendition of the Watts hymn "I Love the Lord, He Heard My Cries." However, this occurs in a strictly urban scenario, complete with a Richard Smallwood melody that both charms the soul in

its simplicity and demonstrates conversance with the romantic stratagems of Western concert music. By contrast, the Wesley hymn "A Charge to Keep I Have" signals the denouement in *Murder in Mississippi,* a documentary film on the Civil Rights movement. The hauntingly spacious sound of "A Charge to Keep I Have," sung unaccompanied (to a tune within the family of melodies that are apparently traceable to the shape-note tune *Idumea*), implicates the worship culture associated with a black church edifice, which is then burned by members of the Ku Klux Klan.

BIBLIOGRAPHY

Agawu, Kofi. 1995. *African Rhythm: A Northern Ewe Perspective.* Cambridge and New York: Cambridge University Press.

Aghahowa, Brenda Eatmon. 1996. *Praising in Black and White: Unity and Diversity in Christian Worship.* Cleveland, Ohio: United Church Press.

Alexander, Bobby C. 1991. *Victor Turner Revisited: Ritual as Social Change.* Atlanta: Scholars Press.

Allen, William Francis, Lucy McKim Garrison, and Charles Pickard Ware. [1867, 1929] 1951. *Slave Songs of the United States.* New York: Peter Smith.

Appiah, Kwame Anthony. 1992. *In My Father's House: Africa in the Philosophy of Culture.* New York and Oxford: Oxford University Press.

Asante, Molefi Kete. 1990. African Elements in African-American English. In *Africanisms in American Culture,* edited by Joseph Holloway. Bloomington: Indiana University Press.

Bailey, Ben E. 1978. The Lined Hymn Tradition in Black Mississippi Churches. *Black Perspective in Music* 6 (1): 3–17.

Bailey, Guy, and Erik Thomas. 1998. Some Aspects of African-American Vernacular English Phonology. In *African-American English: Structure, History, and Use,* edited by Salikoko S. Mufwene et al. London and New York: Routledge.

Baker, Houston A., Jr. 1972. *Long Black Song: Essays in Black American Literature and Culture.* Charlottesville: University Press of Virginia.

———. 1984. *Blues Ideology, and Afro-American Literature: A Vernacular Theory.* Chicago and London: University of Chicago Press.

———. 1987. *Modernism and the Harlem Renaissance.* Chicago and London: University of Chicago Press.

———. 1988. *Afro-American Poetics: Revisions of Harlem and the Black Aesthetic.* Madison: University of Wisconsin Press.

Ball, Charles. 1837. *Slavery in the United States: A Narrative of the Life and Adventures of Charles Ball, a Black Man. . . .* New York: J. S. Taylor.

Baptist Hymnal for Use in the Church and Home. [1883, 1920] 1991. Valley Forge, Penn.: Judson Press.

Baraka, Imamu Amiri [LeRoi Jones]. 1963. *Blues People: The Negro Experience in White America and the Music That Developed from It.* New York: William Morrow and Company.

Barthes, Roland. 1972. The Structuralist Activity. In *Critical Essays,* translated by Richard Howard. Evanston: Northwestern University Press.

Bascom, William R. 1969. *The Yoruba of Southwestern Nigeria.* New York: Holt, Rinehart and Winston.

Baumann, Richard. 1977. *Verbal Art as Performance.* Prospect Heights, Ill.: Waveland Press.

———. 1992. *Folklore, Cultural Performances, and Popular Entertainments: A Communications-Centered Handbook.* New York and Oxford: Oxford University Press.

Baumann, Richard, and Charles Briggs. 1990. Poetics and Performance as Critical Perspectives on Language and Social Life. *Annual Review of Anthropology* 19: 59–88.

Baumann, Richard, and A. Paredes, eds. 1972. *Toward New Perspectives in Folklore.* Austin: University of Texas Press.

Bebey, Francis. 1975. *African Music: A People's Art.* Translated by Josephine Bennett. New York: Lawrence Hill.

Bell, Catherine. 1992. *Ritual Theory, Ritual Practice.* New York and Oxford: Oxford University Press.

Bellah, Robert, et al. 1985. *Habits of the Heart: Individualism and Commitment in American Life.* Berkeley: University of California Press.

Benson, Louis F. 1915. *The English Hymn: Its Development and Use in Worship.* New York: George H. Doran.

———. 1927. *Hymnody of the Christian Church: The Lectures on "The L. P. Stone Foundation,"* Princeton Theological Seminary, 1926. New York: George H. Doran.

Berry, Jack. 1970. Language Systems and Literature. In *The African Experience,* edited by John Paden and Edward Soja. Evanston, Ill.: Northwestern University Press.

Berry, Jason. 1988. African Cultural Memory in New Orleans Music. *Black Music Research Journal* 8 (1): 3–12.

Billington, Ray Allen. 1973. *Frederick Jackson Turner: Historian, Scholar, Teacher.* New York: Oxford University Press.

Bishop, Selma L. 1962. *Isaac Watts: Hymns and Spiritual Songs 1707–1748.* London: Faith Press.

———, ed. 1974. *Isaac Watts's Hymns and Spiritual Songs: A Publishing History and a Bibliography.* Ann Arbor: Pierian Press.

Blacking, John. 1973. *How Musical Is Man?* Seattle: University of Washington Press.

———. 1995. *Music, Culture, and Experience: Selected Papers of John Blacking,* edited by Reginald Byron. Chicago and London: University of Chicago Press.

Blum, Stephen, Philip V. Bohlman, and Daniel M. Neuman. 1991. *Ethnomusicology and Modern Music History.* Urbana and Chicago: University of Illinois Press.

Bontemps, Arna. 1958. Rock, Church, Rock! In *The Book of Negro Folklore,* edited by Langston Hughes and Arna Bontemps. New York: Dodd, Mead.

Bremer, Fredrika. 1924. *America of the Fifties: Letters of Fredrika Bremer.* New York: American-Scandinavian Foundation.

Brothers, Thomas. 1997. Ideology and Aurality in the Vernacular Traditions of African American Music. *Black Music Research Journal* 17 (2): 169–209.

Bruce, Dickson. 1974. *And They All Sang Halleluia: Plain-Folk Camp-Meeting Religion, 1800–1845*. Knoxville: Tennessee University Press.

Cauthen, Joyce. 1999. *Benjamin Lloyd's Hymn Book: A Primitive Baptist Song Tradition*. Montgomery: Alabama Folklife Association.

Chase, Gilbert. [1966] 1987. *America's Music: From the Pilgrims to the Present*. 3rd ed. Urbana: University of Illinois Press.

Chesnut, Mary Boykin. 1949. *A Diary from Dixie*. Edited by Ben Ames Williams. Boston: Houghton Mifflin.

Coke, Thomas. 1793. *Extracts of the Journal of the Rev. Dr. Coke's Five Visits to America*. London: G. Paramore.

Collier, James Lincoln. 1978. *The Making of Jazz: A Comprehensive History*. London: Macmillan Publishers Limited.

———. 1993. *Jazz: The American Theme Song*. New York: Oxford University Press.

Collins, Willie. 1992. An Ethnography of the Moan-and-Prayer Event in Two African American Baptist Churches in Southeast Alabama. In *African Musicology: Current Trends: A Festschrift Presented to J. H. Kwabena Nketia*, vol. 2, edited by Jacqueline Cogdell DjeDje. Los Angeles: African Studies Center, University of California.

Collinson, Patrick. 1988. *The Birthpangs of Protestant England: Religious and Cultural Change in the Sixteenth and Seventeenth Centuries*. New York: St. Martins.

Cone, James. 1972. *The Spirituals and the Blues*. New York: Seabury Press.

———. 1978. Sanctification, Liberation, and Black Worship. *Theology Today* (July) 139–52.

Coolen, Michael Theodore. 1982. The Fodet: A Senegambian Origin for the Blues? *Black Perspective in Music* 10 (1): 69–84.

Cornevin, Robert. 1966. *Histoire du Congo, Léopoldville-Kinshassa: des origines préhistoriques à la République Démocratique du Congo*. Paris: Berger-Levrault.

Costen, Melva Wilson. 1993. *African American Christian Worship*. Nashville: Abingdon Press.

Courlander, Harold. [1963] 1992. *Negro Folk Music U.S.A.* New York: Dover.

———. 1976. *Afro-American Folklore*. New York: Crown Publishers.

Crawford, Richard A. 1968. *Andrew Law, American Psalmodist*. Evanston, Ill.: Northwestern University Press.

———. 1993. *Our American Musical Landscape*. Berkeley: University of California Press.

Creel, Margaret W. 1988. *"A Peculiar People": Slave Religion and Community-Culture among the Gullahs*. New York: New York University Press.

Cressy, David. 1980. *Literacy and the Social Order: Reading and Writing in Tudor and Stuart England*. London: Cambridge University Press.

Crosby, Tho[mas]. 1738–40. *The History of the English Baptists from the Reformation to the Beginning of the Reign of King George I*. 4 vols. in 2. London: by the author. Reprint, Lafayette, Tenn.: Church History, Research and Archives, 1978.

Crowder, William S. 1978. A Study of Lined Hymnsinging in Selected Black Churches of North and South Carolina. Ed.D. diss., University of North Carolina at Greensboro.

Curtin, Phillip. 1969. *The Atlantic Slave Trade: A Census*. Madison: University of Wisconsin Press.

Dalby, David. 1972. The African Element in Black American English. In *Rappin' and Stylin' Out*, edited by Thomas Kochman. Urbana: University of Illinois Press.

Dargan, William. 1995. Congregational Singing in South Carolina. *Black Music Research Journal* 15 (1): 29–73.

Davies, Horton. 1961. *Worship and Theology in England.* Vol. 3, *From Watts to Wesley to Maurice, 1690–1850.* Princeton: Princeton University Press.

———. 1975. *Worship and Theology in England,* Vol. 2, *From Andrewes to Baxter and Fox, 1603–1690.* Princeton: Princeton University Press.

Davis, Arthur P. 1943. *Isaac Watts: His Life and Works.* London: Independent Press.

Dennett, John Richard. 1965. *The South As It Is: 1865–1866.* Edited with an introduction by Henry M. Christman. New York: Viking Press.

DeVeaux, Scott. 1995. *Jazz in America: Who's Listening.* National Endowment for the Arts, Research Division Report #31. Carson, Calif.: Seven Locks Press.

———. 1997. *The Birth of Bebop: A Social and Musical History.* Berkeley: University of California Press.

Dillard, J. L. 1972. *Black English: Its History and Usage in the United States.* New York: Random House.

———. 1977. *Lexicon of Black English.* New York: Seabury Press.

Dilthey, Wilhelm. 1961. *Meaning in History: W. Dilthey's Thoughts on History and Society.* London: George Allen and Unwin.

DjeDje, Jacqueline Cogdell. 1978. *American Black Spiritual and Gospel Songs from Southeast Georgia: A Comparative Study.* Los Angeles: Center for Afro-American Studies, University of California.

———, ed. [1989] 1992. *African Musicology: Current Trends. A Festschrift Presented to J. H. Kwabena Nketia.* 2 vols. Los Angeles: African Studies Center, University of California.

———. 1998a. West Africa: An Introduction. In *Africa,* vol. 1 of *Garland Encyclopedia of World Music,* edited by M. Ruth Stone. New York: Garland Publishing.

———. 1998b. African American Music to 1900. In *Cambridge History of American Music,* edited by David Nichols. Cambridge: Cambridge University Press.

Drake, St. Clair, and Horace R. Cayton. 1945. *Black Metropolis: A Study of Negro Life in a Northern City.* New York: Harcourt, Brace.

Du Bois, W. E. B. [1903] 1997. *The Souls of Black Folk.* Edited with an introduction by David Blight and Robert Gooding-Williams. Boston and New York: Bedford Books.

———. 1971. Of the Faith of the Fathers. In *The Black Church in America,* edited by Hart Nelson, Raytha Yokley, and Ann Nelsen. New York: Basic Books.

Duncan, Curtis. 1979. A Historical Survey of the Development of the Black Baptist Church in the United States and a Study of Performance Practices Associated with Dr. Watts Hymn Singing: A Source Book for Teachers. Ed.D. diss., Washington University.

Dyen, Doris Jane. 1977. The Role of Shape-Note Singing in the Musical Culture of Black Communities in Southeast Alabama. Ph.D. diss. University of Illinois at Urbana-Champaign.

Dyson, Michael Eric. 1993. *Reflecting Black: African-American Cultural Criticism.* Minneapolis and London: University of Minnesota Press.

Eames, Wilberforce. 1905. Introduction to *The Bay Psalm Book, Being a Facsimile reprint of the First Edition, Printed by Stephen Daye at Cambridge, in New England in 1640.* New York: Dodd, Mead and Company.

Earl, Riggins. 1993. *Dark Symbols, Obscure Signs: God, Self, and Community in the Slave Mind.* Maryknoll, N.Y.: Orbis Books.

Eighmy, John Lee. 1969. The Baptists and Slavery: An Examination of the Origins and Benefits of Segregation. In *Blacks in the United States,* edited by Glenn D. Norval and Charles M. Bonjean. San Francisco: Chandler Publishing. First published in *Social Science Quarterly* 49 (December 1968): 66–73.

Epstein, Dena. 1973. African Music in British and French America. *The Musical Quarterly* (59): 61–91.

———. 1977. *Sinful Tunes and Spirituals: Black Folk Music to the Civil War.* Urbana: University of Illinois Press.

———. 1983. A White Origin for the Black Spiritual? An Invalid Theory and How It Grew. *American Music* 1 (2): 53–59.

Escott, Harry. 1962. *Isaac Watts: Hymnographer.* London: Independent Press.

Evans, David. 1982. *Big Road Blues: Tradition and Creativity in the Folk Blues.* Berkeley: University of California Press.

Fanon, Frantz. [1952] 1967. *Black Skin, White Masks.* New York: Grove Press.

Faulk, John H. 1983. *Fear on Trial.* Austin: University of Texas Press.

Feld, Steven. 1974. Linguistic Models in Ethnomusicology. *Ethnomusicology* 18 (2): 197–217.

Fernandez, James. 1973. Analysis of Ritual: Metaphoric Correspondences as the Elementary Forms. *Science* 182: 1366–67.

———. 1974. The Mission of Metaphor in Expressive Culture. *Current Anthropology* 15: 119–45.

Finnegan, Ruth. 1976. What Is Oral Literature Anyway? Comments in the Light of Some African and Other Comparative Material. In *Oral Literature and the Formula,* edited by Benjamin A. Stolz and Richard S. Shannon III. Ann Arbor: University of Michigan Center for the Coordination of Ancient and Modern Studies.

Fisher, Miles Mark. 1933. *A Short History of the Baptist Denomination.* Nashville: Sunday School Publishing Board.

———. 1963. *Negro Slave Songs in the United States.* Ithaca, N.Y.: Cornell University Press.

Floyd, Samuel A. 1991. Ring Shout! Black Music, Black Literary Theory, and Black Historical Studies. *Black Music Research Journal* 11 (2): 267–89.

———. 1995. *The Power of Black Music: Interpreting Its History from Africa to the United States.* New York: Oxford University Press.

Folb, Edith. 1980. *Runnin' Down Some Lines: The Language and Culture of Black Teenagers.* Cambridge: Harvard University Press.

Foote, Henry Wilder. 1940. *Three Centuries of American Hymnody.* Cambridge: Harvard University Press.

Foster, Richard J. [1978] 1998. *Celebration of Discipline: The Path to Spiritual Growth.* San Francisco: HarperSanFrancisco.

Frazier, E. Franklin. 1957. *The Negro in the United States.* Rev. ed. New York: Macmillan.

———. [1964] 1974. *The Negro Church in America.* New York: Schocken Books.

Frey, Sylvia R. 1993. Shaking the Dry Bones: The Dialectic of Conversion. In *Black and White Cultural Interaction in the Antebellum South,* edited by Ted Ownby. Jackson: University Press of Mississippi.

Gaillard, Samuel Gourdin. 1956. Recollections of Samel Gourdin Gaillard. *South Carolina Historical Magazine* 57: 119–33.

Gates, Henry Louis, Jr. 1987. *Figures in Black: Words, Signs, and the "Racial" Self.* New York and Oxford: Oxford University Press.

———. 1988. *The Signifying Monkey: A Theory of Afro-American Literary Criticism.* New York: Oxford University Press.

———. 1992. *Loose Canons.* New York and London: Oxford University Press.

Gaunt, Kyra Danielle. 1997. The Games Black Girls Play: Music, Body, and "Soul." Ph.D. diss., University of Michigan.

Gennari, John Remo. 1993. The Politics of Culture and Identity in American Jazz Criticism. Ph.D. diss., University of Pennsylvania.

Genovese, Eugene. 1974. *Roll, Jordan, Roll: The World the Slaves Made.* New York: Pantheon Books.

Gilroy, Paul. 1991. Sounds Authentic: Black Music, Ethnicity, and the Challenge of a Changing Same. *Black Music Research Journal* 11 (2): 111–36.

Godrich, J., and R.M.W. Dixon. [1969] 1997. *Blues and Gospel Records, 1890–1943.* New York: Oxford University Press.

Hall, Robert H. 1984. "Do Lord Remember Me": Religion and Cultural Change among Blacks in Florida, 1565–1906. Ph.D. diss., Florida State University.

———. 1993. Commentary in Response to "Shaking the Dry Bones." In *Black and White Cultural Interaction in the Antebellum South,* edited by Ted Ownby. Jackson: University Press of Mississippi.

Hamm, Charles. 1983. *Music in the New World.* New York: W.W. Norton.

Handbook to the Baptist Hymnal. 1992. Nashville: Convention Press.

Handy, W.C., and Abbe Niles. [1926] 1990. *Blues: An Anthology.* New York: Da Capo.

Haraszti, Zoltan. 1956. *The Enigma of the Bay Psalm Book.* Chicago: University of Chicago Press.

Harding, Vincent. 1981. *There Is a River: The Black Struggle for Freedom in America.* New York: Harcourt Brace Jovanovich.

Harris, Michael W. 1992. *The Rise of Gospel Blues: The Music of Thomas Andrew Dorsey in the Urban Church.* New York and Oxford: Oxford University Press.

Herskovits, Melville. 1941. *The Myth of the Negro Past.* New York: Harper and Brothers.

Herzog, George. 1964. Drum-Signaling in a West African Tribe. In *Language in Culture and Society: A Reader in Linguistics and Anthropology,* edited by Dell Hymes. New York: Harper and Row.

Higginson, Thomas Wentworth. [1870] 1960. *Army Life in a Black Regiment.* East Lansing: Michigan State University Press.

Hillerbrand, Hans J., ed. 1996. *Oxford Encyclopedia of the Reformation.* New York: Oxford University Press.

Hilton, Bruce. 1969. *The Delta Ministry.* New York: Macmillan.

Hinson, Glenn. 2000. *Fire in My Bones: Transcendence and the Holy Spirit in African American Gospel.* Philadelphia: University of Pennsylvania.

Hitchcock, H. Wiley. [1969, 1974] 1988. *Music in the United States: A Historical Introduction.* 3rd ed. Englewood Cliffs, N.J.: Prentice Hall.

Hitchcock, H. Wiley, and Stanley Sadie. 1986. *The New Grove Dictionary of American Music.* 4 vols. London: Macmillan; New York: Grove's Dictionaries of Music.

Holland, Bernard. 1997. Jazz Musicians with Nothing Better to Do? *New York Times,* Sunday, July 27, H25.

Holloway, Joseph, ed. 1990. *Africanisms in American Culture.* Bloomington: Indiana University Press.

Hood, George. 1846. *A History of Music in New England.* Boston.

House, Son. 1965. I Can Make My Own Songs. *Sing Out!* 15:3 (July): 38–47.

Hurston, Zora Neale. [1934] 1970. Characteristics of Negro Expression, Conversions and Visions, Shouting, Spirituals and Neo-Spirituals, and The Sermon. In *Negro: An Anthology,* edited by Nancy Cunard, abridged edition by Hugh Ford. New York: Frederick Unger.

———. [1934] 1990. *Jonah's Gourd Vine.* New York: HarperCollins.

———. [1942] 1995. *Dust Tracks on a Road: An Autobiography.* New York: Harper-Collins.

———. 1981. *The Sanctified Church.* Berkeley: Turtle Island.

Jackson, George Pullen. 1937. *Spiritual Folk Songs of Early America: Two Hundred and Fifty Tunes and Texts with an Introduction and Notes.* New York: J. J. Augustin.

———. 1943. *White and Negro Spirituals: Their Life Span and Kinship.* New York: Da Capo Press. Reprint, New York: J. J. Augustin, 1944; New York: Da Capo, 1975.

———. 1952. *Another Sheaf of White Spirituals.* Gainesville: University of Florida Press.

Jackson, Joyce M. 1981. The Black American Folk Preacher and the Chanted Sermon: Parallels with a West African Tradition. In *A Tribute to Alan Merriam,* book 2 of *Discourse in Ethnomusicology,* edited by Caroline Card et al. Bloomington, Indiana: Ethnomusicology Publishing Group.

James, Willis Laurence. 1955. The Romance of the Negro Folk Cry. *Phylon* 16 (1): 15–30.

———. 1970. Liner notes for *Afro-American Music: A Demonstration Recording.* Folkways 2692. New York: Aasch.

———. 1995. *Stars in de Elements: A Study of Negro Folk Music.* Edited by Jon Michael Spencer with an introduction by Rebecca T. Cureau. Durham, N.C.: Duke University Press.

Jenkins, Everett, Jr. 1996. *Pan-African Chronology: A Comprehensive Reference to the Black Quest for Freedom in Africa, the Americas, Europe and Asia, 1400–1865.* Jefferson, N.C.; London: McFarland and Company.

Johnson, Claude Joseph. 1990. The Singing Life of the Reverend Doctor Claude Joseph Johnson: A Narrative Portrait. As told to William and Janice Dargan. Unpublished manuscript.

Johnson, Daniel M., and Rex R. Campbell. 1981. *Black Migration in America: A Social Demographic History.* Durham, N.C.: Duke University Press.

Johnson, James Weldon. [1927] 1989. *The Autobiography of an Ex-Coloured Man.* With a new introduction by Henry Louis Gates, Jr. New York: Vintage Books.

———. [1927, 1969, 1976] 1990. *God's Trombones: Seven Negro Sermons in Verse.* New York: Penguin Books.

Johnson, James Weldon, and J. Rosamond Johnson. [1925, 1926] 1969. *The Books of American Negro Spirituals.* New York: Da Capo Press.

Jones, Charles Colcock. 1842. *Religious Instruction of the Negroes in the United States.* Savannah: T. Purse.

Jones, Frederic C. 2000. A Comment on Rev. Paul Moseley's Sermon—I'm Looking for a City—From a Linguistic Perspective. Paper read at the Twenty-Sixth

Annual Society for American Music Meeting, Charleston, South Carolina, March 1–5.

Jones, George Fenwick, ed. 1985. *Detailed Reports on the Salzburger Emigrants Who Settled in America. . . . Edited by Samuel Urlsperger.* Vol. 8: *1741.* Athens: University of Georgia Press.

Jones, LeRoi. See: Imamu Amiri Baraka.

Jones, Nathan. 1882. *Sharing the Old, Old Story.* Winona, Minn.: St. Mary's Press.

Jones, Ralph H. 1982. *Charles Albert Tindley: Prince of Preachers.* Nashville: Abingdon Press.

Jones-Jackson, Patricia. 1987. *When Roots Die: Endangered Traditions on the Sea Islands.* Athens: University of Georgia Press.

———. 1994. Let the Church Say "Amen": The Language of Religious Rituals in Coastal South Carolina. In *The Crucible of Carolina: Essays in the Development of Gullah Language and Culture,* edited by Michael Montgomery. Athens: University of Georgia Press.

Jordan, Winthrop D. [1968] 1969. *White over Black: American Attitudes toward the Negro, 1550–1812.* Baltimore, Md.: Penguin Books.

Joyner, Charles. 1971. *Folk Song in South Carolina.* Columbia: University of South Carolina Press.

———. 1975. A Model for the Analysis of Folklore Performance in Historical Context. *Journal of American Folklore* 88: 254–65.

———. 1984. *Down by the Riverside: A South Carolina Community.* Urbana: University of Illinois Press.

———. 1993. A Single Culture: Cultural Interaction in the Old South. In *Black and White Cultural Interaction in the Antebellum South,* edited by Ted Ownby. Jackson: University Press of Mississippi.

Keeble, N.H. 1987. *The Literary Culture of Nonconformity in Later Seventeenth-Century England.* Athens: University of Georgia Press.

Keil, Charles. 1966. *Urban Blues.* Chicago: University of Chicago Press.

———. 1985. People's Music Comparatively—Style and Stereotype, Class and Hegemony. *Dialectical Anthropology* 10: 1 and 2 (July): 119–130.

Keil, Charles, and Steven Feld. 1994. *Music Grooves.* Chicago: University of Chicago Press.

Keyes, Cheryl. 1996. At the Crossroads: Rap Music and Its African Nexus. *Ethnomusicology* 10: 2 (spring/summer): 223–248.

Kimberlin, Cynthia Tse. 1989. Ornaments and the Classification as a Determinant of Technical Ability and Style. In *African Musicology: Current Trends: A Festschrift Presented to J.H. Kwabena Nketia,* vol. 1, edited by Jacqueline Cogdell DjeDje. Los Angeles: African Studies Center, University of California.

King, John. 1982. *English Reformation Literature: The Tudor Origins of the Protestant Tradition.* Princeton, N.J.: Princeton University Press.

Krehbiel, Henry. [1914] 1962. *Afro-American Folksongs: A Study in Racial and National Music.* New York: F. Ungar.

Kubik, Gerhard. 1989. Alo—Yoruba Chatefables: An Integrated Approach towards West African Music and Oral Literature. In *African Musicology: Current Trends: A Festschrift Presented to J.H. Kwabena Nketia,* vol. 1, edited by Jacqueline Cogdell DjeDje. Los Angeles: African Studies Center, University of California.

————. 1998. Analogies and Differences in African-American Cultures across the Hemisphere: Interpretive Models and Research Strategies. *Black Music Research Journal* 18 (1 and 2): 203–27.

Labov, William. 1998. Coexistent Systems in African-American Vernacular English. In *African-American English: Structure, History, and Use,* edited by Salikoko S. Mufwene et al. London and New York: Routledge.

Landry, Bart. 1987. *The New Black Middle Class.* Berkeley: University of California Press.

Latrobe, Benjamin Henry. 1980. *The Journals of Benjamin Henry Latrobe, 1799–1820: From Philadelphia to New Orleans.* 3 vols. Edited by Edward C. Carter, II, John C. Van Horne, and Lee W. Formwalt. New Haven: Published for the Maryland Historical Society by Yale University Press.

Lawrence, Beverly Hall. 1996. *Reviving the Spirit: A Generation of African Americans Goes Home to Church.* New York: Grove Press.

Lee, Jesse. 1810. *A Short History of the Methodists in the United States of America: Beginning in 1766 and Continuing till 1809.* Baltimore: Magill and Cline.

Levine, Lawrence. 1978. *Black Culture and Black Consciousness: Afro-American Folk Thought from Slavery to Freedom.* New York: Oxford University Press.

Levy, Eugene. 1973. *James Weldon Johnson: Black Leader Black Voice.* Chicago and London: University of Chicago Press.

Lewalski, Barbara. 1979. *Protestant Politics and the Seventeenth-Century Religious Lyric.* Princeton: Princeton University Press.

Limon, J. E., and M. J. Young. 1986. Frontiers, Settlements, and Developments in Folklore Studies. *Annual Review of Anthropology* 15: 437–60.

Lincoln, C. Eric. 1974. *The Black Church since Frazier.* New York: Schocken Books.

————. 1984. *Race, Religion, and the Continuing American Dilemma.* New York: Hill and Wang.

————. 1996. *Coming through the Fire: Surviving Race and Place in America.* Durham and London: Duke University Press.

Lincoln, C. Eric, and Lawrence H. Mamiya. 1990. *The Black Church in the African American Experience.* Durham and London: Duke University Press.

Lischer, Richard. 1995. *The Preacher King: Martin Luther King, Jr. and the Word That Moved America.* New York and Oxford: Oxford University Press.

List, George. 1963. The Boundaries of Speech and Song. *Ethnomusicology* 7:1 (January): 1–16.

Locke, Alain. [1925] 1968. *The New Negro: An Interpretation.* New York: Arno Press.

Locke, David. 1990. *Drum Damba: Talking Drum Lessons.* Crown Point, Ind.: White Cliffs Media.

Lord, Albert B. 1960. *The Singer of Tales.* Cambridge: Harvard University Press.

Lovelace, Austin C. 1963. *The Anatomy of Hymnody.* New York and Nashville: Abingdon Press.

Lovell, John, Jr. 1972. *Black Song: The Forge and the Flame.* New York: Macmillan Company.

Lowens, Irving. 1955. The Bay Psalm Book in 17th-Century New England. In *Journal of the American Musicological Society* 8 (1): 22–29.

Major, Clarence. 1994. *Juba to Jive: A Dictionary of African-American Slang.* New York: Viking/Penguin Books.

Mallard, Robert Q. 1892. *Plantation Life before Emancipation*. Richmond, Va.: Whitet & Shepperson.

Malmstrom, Jean, and Annabel Ashley. 1963. *Dialects—USA*. Champaign, Ill.: National Council of Teachers of English.

Malone, Bill C. 1993. Blacks and Whites and the Music of the Old South. In *Black and White Cultural Interaction in the Antebellum South*, edited by Ted Ownby. Jackson: University Press of Mississippi.

Manning, Bernard L. 1942. *The Hymns of Wesley and Watts: Five Informal Papers*. London: Epworth Press.

Marks, Morton. 1974. Uncovering Ritual Structures in Afro-American Music. In *Religious Movements in Contemporary America*, edited by Irving Zaretsky and Mark Leone. Princeton: Princeton University Press.

———. 1982. You Can't Sing Unless You're Saved. In *African Religious Groups and Beliefs*, edited by Simon Ottenberg. Meerut, India: Archana.

Marsh, J. B. T. 1903. *The Story of the Jubilee Singers: Including Their Songs*. London: Hodder and Stoughton.

Martin, Stefan, and Walt Wolfram. 1998. The Sentence in African-American Vernacular English. In *African-American English: Structure, History, and Use*, edited by Salikoko S. Mufwene et al. London and New York: Routledge.

Maultsby, Portia. 1985. West African Influences and Retentions in U.S. Black Music: A Sociocultural Study. In *More than Dancing: Essays on Afro-American Music and Musicians*, edited by Irene V. Jackson. Westport, Conn.: Greenwood Press.

———. 1990. Africanisms in African-American Music. In *Africanisms in American Culture*, edited by Joseph Holloway. Bloomington: Indiana University Press.

Mays, Benjamin E., and Joseph Nicholson. 1969. *The Negro Church*. New York: Russell and Russell.

McBrier, Vivian Flagg. 1977. *R. Nathaniel Dett: His Life and Works (1992–1943)*. Washington, D.C.: Associated Publishers.

McKim, James Miller. [1867] 1969. Negro Songs. In *The Social Implications of Early Negro Music in the United States*, edited by Bernard Katz. New York: Arno Press.

McLoughlin, William G. 1978. *Revivals, Awakenings, and Reform: An Essay on Religion and Social Change in America 1607–1977*. Chicago and London: University of Chicago Press.

McNeil, W. K. 1993. *The Blues: A Smithsonian Collection of Classic Blues Singers*. Sony Music Special Projects RD 101–2 A4 23981. Washington: Smithsonian Institution Press. Booklet accompanying the recording.

McRae, Barry. 1988. *Ornette Coleman*. London: Apollo Press Limited.

Meacham, James. 1912, 1914. A Journal and Travel of James Meacham, 1789–1797. *Annual Publication of Historical Papers of the Historical Society of Trinity College* (Hartford, Conn.), 9: 66–95; 10:87–101.

Mellers, Wilfrid. 1965. *Music in a New Found Land: Themes and Developments in the History of American Music*. New York: Knopf.

Meyer, Leonard. 1956. *Emotion and Meaning in Music*. Chicago: University of Chicago Press.

Michaels, Walter Benn. 1995. Race into Culture: A Critical Genealogy of Cultural Identity. In *Identities*, edited by Kwame Anthony Appiah and Henry Louis Gates, Jr. Chicago and London: University of Chicago Press.

Miller, Keith D. 1992. *Voice of Deliverance: The Language of Martin Luther King, Jr. and Its Sources*. New York: Free Press.

Miller, Terry. 1984. Oral Tradition Psalmody Surviving in England and Scotland. *The Hymn* 35: 15–22.

Mitchell, Henry. 1970. *Black Preaching*. Philadelphia and New York: J.B. Lippincott.

Monson, Ingrid. 1996. *Saying Something: Jazz Improvisation and Interaction*. Chicago: University of Chicago Press.

Morgan, Edmund S. 1975. *American Slavery, American Freedom: The Ordeal of Colonial Virginia*. New York: W.W. Norton.

Myrdal, Gunnar. 1944. *An American Dilemma*. New York: Harper and Row.

National Baptist Hymn Book (Worded Edition). 1906. 4th ed. Nashville: National Baptist Publishing Board.

Nettl, Bruno. 1995. *Heartland Excursions: Ethnomusicological Reflections on Schools of Music*. Urbana and Chicago: University of Illinois Press.

Nketia, J.H. Kwabena. 1955. *Funeral Dirges of the Akan People*. Exeter, U.K.: Achimota.

———. 1963. *Drumming in Akan Communities of Ghana*. Edinburgh: Thomas Nelson and Sons.

———. 1971. Surrogate Languages of Africa. In *Linguistics in Sub-Saharan Africa*, edited by Jack Berry et al. *Current Trends in Linguistics* 7, edited by A. Sebeok. The Hague: Mouton.

———. 1972. The Musical Languages of Africa. Summary of report presented at the meeting "Musical Traditions in Africa," organized by UNESCO in Yaounde, Cameroon, February 23–27, 1970. Published in *African Music*. Paris: La Revue Musicale.

———. 1974. *The Music of Africa*. New York: W.W. Norton.

Oliver, Paul. 1970. *Savannah Syncopators: African Retentions in the Blues*. New York: Stein and Day.

———. 1984. *Songsters and Saints: Vocal Traditions on Race Records*. Cambridge: Cambridge University Press.

Oliver, Paul, Max Harrison, and William Bolcom. 1986. *The New Grove Gospel, Blues, and Jazz*. New York and London: W.W. Norton.

O'Meally, Robert. 1991. *Lady Day: The Many Faces of Billie Holiday*. New York: Arcade Publishing/Little, Brown and Company.

Ong, Walter. 1982, 1989. *Orality and Literacy: The Technologizing of the Word*. London and New York: Routledge.

Owens, Leslie Howard. 1993. Commentary in Response to Article by Bill Malone and Others. In *Black and White Cultural Interaction in the Antebellum South*, edited by Ted Ownby. Jackson: University Press of Mississippi.

Owens, Thomas J. 1995. *Bebop: The Music and Its Players*. New York and Oxford: Oxford University Press.

Parrish, Peter, J. 1989. *Slavery: History and Historians*. New York: Harper and Row.

Parsons, Charles Grandison. 1855. *Inside View of Slavery: or a Tour among the Planters*. Boston: J.P. Jewett.

Patterson, Beverly Bush. 1995. *The Sound of the Dove: Singing in Appalachian Primitive Baptist Churches*. Urbana and Chicago: University of Illinois Press.

Patterson, Daniel W. 1982. Word, Song, and Motion: Instruments of Celebration among Protestant Radicals in Early Nineteenth-Century America. In *Celebrations:*

Studies in Festivity and Ritual, edited by Victor Turner. Washington, D.C.: Smithsonian Institution.

Payne, Daniel Alexander. 1968. *Recollections of Seventy Years.* New York: Arno Press.

Payne, Wardell J., ed. 1991. *Directory of African American Religious Bodies: A Compendium by the Howard University School of Divinity.* Washington, D.C.: Howard University Press.

Perlman, Alan M., and Daniel Greenblatt. 1981. Some Observations on Jazz Improvisation and Language Structure. In *The Sign in Music Literature,* edited by Wendy Steiner. Austin: University of Texas Press.

Pilcher, George William. 1971. *Samuel Davies: Apostle of Dissent in Colonial Virginia.* Knoxville: University of Tennessee Press.

Pinkston, Alfred Adolphus. 1975. Lined Hymns, Spirituals, and the Associated Lifestyle of Rural Black People in the United States. Ph.D. diss., University of Miami.

Pitts, Ann. 1978. A Prosodic Analysis of a Chanted Formulaic Sermon. *Rackham Literary Studies* 9: 89–96.

Pitts, Walter F. 1988. Keep the Fire Burnin': Language and Ritual in the Afro-Baptist Church. *Journal of the American Academy of Religion* 56: 77–97.

———. 1993. *Old Ship of Zion: The Afro-Baptist Ritual in the African Diaspora.* New York: Oxford University Press.

Plant, Deborah G. 1995. *Every Tub Must Sit on Its Own Bottom: The Philosophy and Politics of Zora Neale Hurston.* Urbana and Chicago: University of Illinois Press.

Porter, Lewis. 1985. John Coltrane's *A Love Supreme:* Jazz Improvisation as Composition. *Journal of the American Musicological Society* 38: 593–621.

Potter, Russell A. 1995. *Spectacular Vernaculars: Hip-Hop and the Politics of Postmodernism.* Albany: State University of New York Press.

Powell, Richard. 1997. *Black Art and Culture in the Twentieth Century.* London: Thames and Hudson.

The Psalms, Hymns, and Spiritual Songs of the Old and New Testament: Faithfully translated into English Metre: For the Use, Edification, and Comfort of the Saints in Publick and Private, especially in New England. 1744. 26th ed. Boston: J. Draper for J. Blanchard.

Raboteau, Albert J. 1978. S*lave Religion: The "Invisible" Institution in the Antebellum South.* New York: Oxford University Press.

Radano, Ronald. 1996. Denoting Difference: The Writing of the Slave Spirituals. *Critical Inquiry* 22:3 (spring): 506–544.

Raichelson, R.M. 1975. Black Religious Folksong: A Study of Generic and Social Change. Ph.D. diss., University of Pennsylvania.

Randolph, Peter. 1855. *Sketches of Slave Life.* Boston: James H. Earle.

Rankin, Tom. 1993. *Sacred Space: Photographs from the Mississippi Delta.* Jackson: University Press of Mississippi.

Rawick, George, ed. 1972. *The American Slave: A Composite Autobiography.* Westport, Conn.: Greenwood Press.

Reagon, Bernice Johnson. 1989. Sing till the Power: The Survival of the Congregational Singing Tradition. Paper presented at the conference Contemporary Black American Congregational Song and Worship Traditions, sponsored by the National Museum of American History and the Program in African American Culture, Smithsonian Institution, Washington, D.C., February 2–4.

———. 1993. *We Who Believe in Freedom: Sweet Honey in the Rock—Still on the Journey.* New York: Anchor Books/Doubleday.

Reagon, Bernice Johnson, and Lisa Pertillar Brevard. 1994. Liner notes for *Wade in the Water.* Vol. 2, *African American Congregational Singing: Nineteenth-Century Roots.* Produced in collaboration with National Public Radio. Smithsonian Folkways SF 40073.

———. 2001. *If You Don't Go, Don't Hinder Me: The African American Sacred Song Tradition.* Lincoln and London: University of Nebraska Press.

Reed, Andrew, and Matheson, James. 1835. *A Narrative of the Visit to the American Churches by the Deputation from the Congregational Union of England and Wales.* 2 vols. London: Jackson and Walford.

Rhyne, Nancy. 1998. *Chronicles of the South Carolina Sea Islands.* Winston-Salem, N.C.: John F. Blair.

Richey, Russell E. 1985. From Quarterly to Camp Meeting: A Reconsideration of Early American Methodism. *Methodist History* 23: 199–213.

Rickford, John Russell, and Russell John Rickford. 2000. *Spoken Soul: The Story of Black English.* New York and Chichester: John Wiley and Sons.

Ricks, George Robinson. 1977. *Some Aspects of the Religious Music of the United States Negro: An Ethnomusicological Study with Special Emphasis on the Gospel Tradition.* New York: Arno Press.

Roberts, John Storm. [1972] 1998. *Black Music of Two Worlds.* New York: Schirmer.

Robinson, William H., Jr. 1969. *Early Black American Poets: Selections with Biographical and Critical Instructions.* Dubuque, Iowa: William C. Brown.

Rogal, Samuel. 1991. *A General Introduction to Hymnody and Congregational Song.* Metuchen, N.J., and London: Scarecrow Press.

Rosenbaum, Art. 1998. *Shout Because You're Free: The African American Ring Shout Tradition in Coastal Georgia.* Athens and London: University of Georgia Press.

Rosenberg, B.A. [1970] 1988. *The Art of the American Folk Preacher.* Urbana: University of Illinois Press.

Rouget, Gilbert. 1966. African Traditional Non-Prose Forms: Reciting, Declaiming, Singing and Strophic Structure. In *Proceedings of a Conference on African Language and Literature,* edited by Jack Berry, Robert Plant Armstrong, and John Povey. Evanston, Ill.: Northwestern University Press.

Routley, Erik. 1952. *Hymns and Human Life.* London: J. Murray.

Saintsbury, George. 1919. *Historical Manual of English Prosody.* London: Macmillan.

Scholes, Percy A. 1934. *The Puritans and Music in England and New England: A Contribution to the Cultural History of Two Nations.* London: Oxford University Press.

Sernett, M.C. 1972. Black Religion and American Evangelism. Ph.D. diss., University of Delaware.

———. 1985. *Afro-American Religious History: A Documentary Witness.* Durham: Duke University Press.

Shapiro, Nat, and Nat Hentoff. 1955. *Hear Me Talkin' to Ya: The Story of Jazz as Told by the Men Who Made It.* New York: Dover Publications.

Smith, Arthur L. 1970. Socio-Historical Perspectives in Black Oratory. *Quarterly Journal of Speech* (October): 264–69.

Smith, Carl Henry. 1987. The Lined Hymn Tradition in Selected Black Churches of Eastern Kentucky. Ph.D. diss., University of Pittsburgh.

Smith, Edward D. 1988. *Climbing Jacob's Ladder: The Rise of Black Churches in Eastern American Cities, 1740–1877*. Washington: Smithsonian Institution Press.

Smitherman, Geneva. 1977. *Talkin and Testifyin: The Language of Black America*. Boston: Houghton Mifflin.

———. 1994. *Black Talk: Words and Phrases from the Hood to the Amen Corner*. Boston: Houghton Mifflin.

———. 1998. Word from the Hood: The Lexicon of African-American Vernacular English. In *African-American English: Structure, History, and Use*, edited by Salikoko S. Mufwene et al. London and New York: Routledge.

Sobel, Mechal. 1979. *Trabelin' On: The Slave Journey to an Afro-Baptist Faith*. Westport, Conn.: Greenwood Press.

———. 1987. *The World They Made Together: Black and White Values in Eighteenth-Century Virginia*. Princeton: Princeton University Press.

Sosnoski, James J. 1995. *Modern Skeletons in Postmodern Closets: A Cultural Studies Alternative*. Charlottesville and London: University of Virginia Press.

Southern, Eileen. [1971] 1983. *Readings in Black American Music*. New York: W. W. Norton.

———. [1971, 1983] 1997. *The Music of Black Americans*. New York: W. W. Norton.

———. [1972]. An Origin for the Negro Spiritual. *Black Scholar* 3 (10): 8–13.

———. [1977]. Musical Practices in Black Churches of Philadelphia and New York, ca. 1800–1844. *Journal of the American Musicological Society* 30: 296–312.

Spencer, Jon Michael. 1987. *Sacred Symphony: The Chanted Sermon of the Black Preacher*. Westport, Conn.: Greenwood Press.

———. 1990. *Protest and Praise: Sacred Music of Black Religion*. Minneapolis: Fortress Press.

———. 1992. *Black Hymnody: A Hymnological History of the African-American Church*. Knoxville: University of Tennessee Press.

———. 1996. *Re-Searching Black Music*. Knoxville: University of Tennessee Press.

Stearns, Marshall. [1956, 1962] 1972. *The Story of Jazz*. London and New York: Oxford University Press.

Sternhold, Thomas, and John Hopkins. 1562. *The Whole Booke of Psalms*. London: John Day.

Stokes, Martin. 1994. *Ethnicity, Identity and Music: The Musical Construction of Place*. Oxford and Providence, R.I.: Berg Publishers.

Stowe, David. 1995. *Swing Changes: Big-Band Jazz in New Deal America*. Cambridge and London: Harvard University Press.

Stuckey, Sterling. 1987. *Slave Culture: Nationalist Theory and the Foundations of Black America*. New York and London: Oxford University Press.

Sundquist, Eric J. 1992. *The Hammers of Creation: Folk Culture in Modern African-American Fiction*. Athens and London: University of Georgia Press.

———. 1993. *To Wake the Nations: Race in the Making of American Literature*. Cambridge and London: Belknap Press of Harvard University Press.

Sutton, Brett. 1982. Liner Notes to *Primitive Baptist Hymns of the Blue Ridge*. UNC 39088. Chapel Hill: University of North Carolina Press.

Tallmadge, William H. 1961. Dr. Watts and Mahalia Jackson: The Development, Decline and Survival of a Folk Style in America. *Ethnomusicology* 5 (2): 95–99.

———. 1975. Baptist Monophonic and Heterophonic Hymnody in Southern Appalachia. *Yearbook for Inter-American Musical Research* 11: 106–136.

————. 1979. The Nomenclature of Folk Hymnody. *The Hymn* 30 (October): 240–42.

————. 1981. The Black in Jackson's White Spirituals. *Black Perspective in Music* 9: 139–60.

————. 1984. Folk Organum: A Study of Origins. *American Music* 2–3 (Fall): 47–65.

Taylor, John E. 1975. Somethin' on My Mind: A Cultural and Historical Interpretation of Spiritual Texts. *Ethnomusicology* 19:3 (September): 387–99.

Temperley, Nicholas. 1979. *The Music of the English Parish Church.* Vol. 1. Cambridge: Cambridge University Press.

————. 1981. The Old Way of Singing: Its Origin and Development. *Journal of the American Musicological Society* 34: 511–44.

Thomas, Lorenzo. 1994. The Bop Aesthetic and Black Intellectual Tradition. In *The Bebop Revolution in Words and Music,* edited by Dave Oliphant. Austin: University of Texas.

Thompson, Robert Farris. 1990. Kongo Influences in African-American Artistic Culture. In *Africanisms in American Culture,* edited by Joseph Holloway. Bloomington: Indiana University Press.

Tirro, Frank. [1977] 1993. *Jazz: A History.* New York: W. W. Norton.

Titon, Jeff Todd. 1977. *Early Downhome Blues: A Musical and Cultural Analysis.* Urbana: University of Illinois Press.

Toll, Robert C. 1974. *Blacking Up: The Minstrel Show in Nineteenth-Century America.* New York: Oxford University Press.

Turner, Victor W. 1969. *The Ritual Process: Structure and Anti-Structure.* Chicago: Aldine Publishing.

Turner, William C. 1988. The Musicality of Black Preaching. *Journal of Black Sacred Music* 2: 1 (spring): 21–34.

Vass, Winifred. 1979. *The Bantu-Speaking Heritage of the United States.* Los Angeles: Center for Afro-American Studies, University of California.

Vaughn-Cooke, Faye. 1972. *The Black Preaching Style: Historical Development and Characteristics.* Language and Linguistics Working Papers 5, edited by William K. Riley and David M. Smith. Washington, D.C.: Georgetown University Press.

Verger, Pierre. 1957. *Notes sur le Culte des Orisa et Vodun à Bahia.* Dakar: IFAN.

Walker, Sheila S. 1972. *Ceremonial Spirit Possession in Africa and Afro-America.* Leiden: E. J. Brill.

Walker, Wyatt Tee. 1979. *"Somebody's Calling My Name": Black Sacred Music and Social Change.* Valley Forge, Penn.: Judson Press.

Walser, Robert. 1995. Rhythm, Rhyme, and Rhetoric in the Music of Public Enemy. *Ethnomusicology* 39: 2 (spring/summer): 193–217.

Washington, James Melvin. 1986. *Frustrated Fellowship: The Baptist Quest for Social Power.* Macon, Ga.: Mercer University Press.

————, ed. 1994. *Conversations with God: Two Centuries of Prayers by African Americans.* New York: HarperCollins.

Washington, Joseph, Jr. 1972. *Black Sects and Cults: The Power Axis in an Ethnic Ethic.* New York: Doubleday Anchor Press.

Waterman, Christopher Alan. 1990. *Juju: A Social History and Ethnography of an African Popular Music.* Chicago and London: University of Chicago Press.

Watson, Andrew Polk. 1932, Primitive Religion among Negroes in Tennessee. M.A. thesis, Fisk University.

Watt, Tessa. 1991. *Cheap Print and Popular Piety (1550–1640)*. Cambridge and New York: Cambridge University Press.

Watts, Isaac. 1707. *Hymns and Spiritual Songs in Three Books with an Essay Towards the Improvement of Christian Psalmody by the Use of Evangelical Hymns in Worship, as well as the Psalms of David*. 3 vols. London: Printed by J.H. for M. Laurence.

———. 1719. *The Psalms of David, Imitated in the Language of the New Testament and Applied to the Christian State and Worship*. London: J. Clark.

———. 1997. *The Psalms and Hymns of Isaac Watts*. Morgan, Penn.: Soli Deo Gloria Publications.

Watts, Michael. 1978. *The Dissenters: From the Reformation to the French Revolution*. Oxford: Clarendon Press.

Weinreich, Uriel. 1953. *Languages in Contact: Findings and Problems*. New York: Linguistic Circle of New York.

Wesley, John. 1837. *The Journal of the Reverend John Wesley, A.M. First Complete and Standard American Edition from the Latest London Edition*. 2 vols. New York: T. Mason and G. Lane.

West, Cornel. 1988. *Prophetic Fragments*. Grand Rapids, Mich.: William B. Eerdmans; Trenton, N.J.: Africa World Press.

Westcott, William. 1993. African-American. In *Ethnomusicology: Historical and Regional Studies*, edited by Helen Myers. New York and London: W.W. Norton.

Whalum, Weldell. 1971. James Weldon Johnson's Theories and Performance Practices of Afro-American Folksong. *Phylon* 32: 4 (winter): 383–95.

———. 1973. Black Hymnody. *Review and Expositor* 70: 3 (summer): 341–55.

White, Benjamin Franklin. [1844] 1971. *Original Sacred Harp*. Denson Revision. Cullman, Ala.: Sacred Harp Publishing.

White, James F. 1982. *Introduction to Christian Worship*. Nashville: Abingdon Press.

Wicks, Sammie Ann. 1998. Point of View: The Monocultural Perspective of Music Education. *The Chronicle of Higher Education,* January 9: A72.

Wiley, Electra C., and Robert L. Wiley. 1984. The Plaintive Sound: The Rhetoric of Despair in Black Churches in Arkansas. *Journal of Communication Studies* 2:5–10.

Williams, George W. 1968. *History of the Negro Race in America 1619–1880*. New York: Arno Press and the New York Times.

Williams, Martin. 1970. *The Jazz Tradition*. New York: Oxford University Press.

Wilson, Olly. 1974. The Significance of the Relationship between Afro-American Music and West African Music. *Black Perspective in Music* 2: 1 (spring): 3–21.

———. 1983. Black Music as an Art Form. *Black Music Research Journal* 3: 1–22.

———. 1985. The Association of Movement and Music as a Manifestation of a Black Conceptual Approach to Music-Making. In *More than Dancing: Essays on Afro-American Music and Musicians,* edited by Irene V. Jackson. Westport, Conn.: Greenwood Press.

———. 1992. The Heterogeneous Sound Ideal in African-American Music. In *New Perspectives on Music: Essays in Honor of Eileen Southern,* edited by Josephine Wright with Samuel Floyd Jr. Warren, Mich.: Harmonie Park Press.

Wimberly, Edward P., and Anne Streaty Wimberly. 1986. *Liberation and Human Wholeness: The Conversion Experiences of Black People in Slavery and Freedom.* Nashville: Abingdon Press.

Woideck, Carl. 1996. *Charlie Parker: His Music and Life.* Ann Arbor: University of Michigan Press.

Work, John W., II. [1915] 1969. *Folk Song of the American Negro.* New York: Negro Universities Press.

Work, John W., III. 1949. Changing Patterns in Negro Folk Songs. *Journal of American Folklore* 62: 136–44.

Wright, Ellen, and Michel Fabre. [1971, 1978] 1997. *Richard Wright Reader.* New York: Da Capo Press.

Wright, Richard L. 1976. Language Standards and Communicative Style in the Black Church. Ph.D. diss., University of Texas at Austin.

DISCOGRAPHY

ANTHOLOGIES

American Folk Music. Vol. 2, *Social Music.* Edited by Harry Smith. Folkways FA 2952. Recorded originally in 1927. Includes two black lining-out hymns (listed under the names of the sermons they followed on the original recordings) led by Rev. J.M. Gates.

Benjamin Lloyd's Hymn Book: A Primitive Baptist Song Tradition. Montgomery: Alabama Folklife Association. 1999. This is the CD accompanying the book with the same title by Joyce Cauthen, listed in the bibliography. Referred to throughout this book as *Benjamin Lloyd.*

The Blues: A Smithsonian Collection of Classic Blues Singers, vols. 1–4. Sony Music Special Projects RD 101-2 A4 23981. 1993. This CD collection includes a booklet with the same title, authored by W.K. McNeil, listed in the bibliography.

Dr. Watts Hymn Singing among African Americans. Compiled by William T. Dargan. Unpublished recording available at the Center for Black Music Research, Columbia College Chicago. Referred to throughout this book as *Dr. Watts.*

Elder Songsters 1 and *Elder Songsters 2.* Vols. 6 and 7 of *Music from the South.* Folkways FP 2655, FP 2656. Recorded originally in 1954, released in 1956. Includes several black lining-out hymns recorded in Alabama and Louisiana.

Ghana: Ancient Ceremonies, Songs, and Dance Music. Recorded by Stephen Jay. Elektra Nonesuch CD 9 72082 2. 1991. First released 1979.

The Jazz Singers 1919–1994. 5 vols. Smithsonian Institution, A-28977, A-28978, A-28979, A-28980, A-28981. 1998.

Musiques de l'ancien royaume Kuba. Disques Ocora OCR 61. Republique du Zaire. First released 1972. See side B, no. 7, "Dirges," by women from Pombo Bulombo, recorded April 12, 1970, at Pombo Bulombo, Ngeende tribe.

Negro Blues and Hollers, AFS L59, 12-inch LP. 1962. Includes Son House performance of "Camp Hollers."

Negro Church Music. Edited by Alan Lomax. Atlantic 1351. 1960. One lining-out hymn by Rev. R.C. Crenshaw and congregation, Memphis, Tennessee.

Primitive Baptist Hymns of the Blue Ridge. Recorded by Brett Sutton. UNC 39088. 1982. Chapel Hill, North Carolina: University of North Carolina Press. Includes liner notes by Brett Sutton, listed in the bibliography.

Roots of Blues. Edited by Alan Lomax. New World NW 252. 1977. Includes lining-out hymn and prayer by Rev. R. C. Crenshaw and congregation, Memphis, Tennessee.

Roots of Rap: Classic Recordings from the 1920s and 1930s. Yazoo 2018. 1996.

Singing Preachers and Their Congregations (Negro Religious Music), vol. 3. Blues Classics 19, Ping 1005. 1968. Reissues of old commercial recordings. Includes two lining-out hymns recorded in Chicago in 1956, led by Deacon L. Shinault.

The Smithsonian Collection of Classic Jazz. 5 vols. Smithsonian Institution, A-21730, A-21731, A-23732, A-23733, A-23734. 1987.

Sorrow Come Pass Me Around: A Survey of Rural Black Religious Music. Edited by David Evans. Advent 2805. 1975. Includes a solo version of a lining-out hymn.

The Together as One Hymn Choir: A Collection of African-American Spirituals and Metered Hymns. Vol. 2. Crusader Broadcasting Ministry, TA1VOL2. 1999.

Wade in the Water. Vol. 2, *African American Congregational Singing: Nineteenth-Century Roots.* Conceived and compiled by Bernice Johnson Reagon and Lisa Pertillar Brevard. Recorded in 1989 and 1992; produced in collaboration with National Public Radio; Smithsonian Folkways SF 40073. 1994. Referred to throughout this book as *Wade in the Water,* vol. 2.

INDIVIDUAL RECORDINGS

Brown, James. *James Brown: Star Time.* 4 discs. Polydor 849 109-2, 849 110-2, 849 111-2, 849 112-2. 1991.

Burnett, Rev. J. C. *Amazing Grace.* Decca 7494. 1938.

Campbell, Rev. E. D. *Come Let us Eat Together.* Victor 35824. 1927.

Coleman, Ornette. *Free Jazz: A Collective Improvisation by the Ornette Coleman Double Quartet.* Atlantic 1364. 1960. Liner notes by Martin Williams.

Cooke, Sam. *The Two Sides of Sam Cooke.* Specialty SPCD 2119-2. 1970.

Dorsey, Thomas A. *Precious Lord: Recordings of the Great Gospel Songs of Thomas A. Dorsey.* Columbia/Legacy CK 57164. [1973] 1994.

Edmonds, Rev. P. E. *There's a Hole in the Wall.* Paramount 12876. 1929.

Franklin, Aretha. *Aretha Franklin: I Never Loved a Man the Way I Love You.* Atlantic 8139. 1967.

———. *Aretha Franklin: Amazing Grace with James Cleveland and the Southern California Community Choir.* Atlantic 2906. [1972] 1987.

———. *Aretha Gospel.* Chess CHD 91521. 1991.

Gates, Rev. J. M. *Rev. J. M. Gates: Complete Recorded Works in Chronological Order.* Volumes 1–9. Document Records DOCD 5414, 5432, 5433, 5442, 5449, 5457, 5469, 5483, 5484. 1995–96.

Houston, Whitney. *The Preacher's Wife.* Arista 18951. 1996.

Jackson, Mahalia. *Gospels, Spirituals, and Hymns.* Columbia/Legacy: C2K 47083, C2K 47084, C2K 47085. 1991.

Johnson, C. J. *Dr. C. J. Johnson Presents the Old Time Song Service.* Vols. 1 and 2. Savoy MG 14126. 1965. Black congregational singing from Georgia; one lined-out hymn on each disc.

Pearson, Rev. Carlton. *Live at Azusa.* Vol. 2: *Precious Memories.* Warner Brothers 46354. 1997.

INDEX

"I'm Gonna Leave You in the Hand of My
    Lord," 178
"I'm Not Too Mean to Serve the Lord," *81*,
    252
induction, 24
industrialization, 104
inspiration (performance "key"), 202, 204,
    207, 212, 227, 231
interference phenomena, 12, 263nn12–13
interpolation, 199
intonation, linguistic, 262n10
"It's a Good Time in Zion, I Believe," 207,
    210
"It's a Great Change Since I've Been Born,"
    184
"I Want to Go Where Jesus Is" (Johnson),
    175, 187, 190–92
"I Was Lost but Now I'm Found," 152–53

Jackson, Ed, xi–xii
Jackson, George Pullen: on cultural trans-
    fers, 51; on hymns in slave culture, 8,
    101–2; lining out described by, 116, 172,
    262n2, 265n9; on portraiture sound,
    127; "pre-blues" iambic couplets and,
    153–54; Primitive Baptist hymn singing
    and, 28; on wandering verses, 149
Jackson, Jesse, 124
Jackson, Lillie Mae, xii
Jackson, Mahalia, 14, 127
Jackson, Papa Charlie, 216, 218
James, Willis Laurence, 16
jazz: asides/exclamations in, 221; bebop,
    221–25; blues and, 217, 220; commer-
    cialization of, 159; congregational
    singing and, 214, 281–82n11; five-key
    sequence and, 205; free-form improvisa-
    tion in, 218, 221–25; harmony in, 222,
    226; linguistic/musical interaction in,
    141; lining out–ring shout continuum in,
    214–15, 217–34; notational conventions
    in, 269n9; percussive rhythms in,
    128–29; poetic rhythms in, 137, 219–20;
    rhythm in, 172, 216, 282n3; soloists fore-
    fronted in, 225–26; speech-movement
    continuum in, 217–18; speech rhythms
    in, 157, 222; speech-song and, 120, 122,
    220–21; swing, 217–21
Jefferson, Blind Lemon, 215, 216
Jefferson (SC), *148*
"Jesus Invites His Saints" (Watts), *71*, 249
"Jesus Loves Me, This I Know," 184

jive talk, 221
"Job," 185
Johnson, Blind Willie, 60
Johnson, C. J.: birth of, 174, 177; elders and,
    176; ensemble support of, 60; family of,
    174–75, 177, 184, 188–89; influences
    on, 60; lining out–ring shout continuum
    and, 202; marriage of, 188; poetic
    rhythms of, 128, 137; recorded perfor-
    mances of, 29, 33, 60; role models of,
    175–76, 179–88; sacred/secular interre-
    lationship and, 221; signature hymn of,
    29, 128; significance of, 169, 172–73;
    singing life of, 183–84, 188–89; skin
    color and, 174, 176, 185; on slavery,
    177–79; songs of, 175, 176–77, 187,
    189–92; storytelling ability of,
    279–80n14
Johnson, Elizabeth Daniel ("Sister
    Johnson"), 174, 184, 187–88
Johnson, James Weldon: black class stratifi-
    cation and, 170; black speech and,
    159–60, 162; on black/Standard English
    tensions, 154; hymn singing overlooked
    by, 171, 278n4; poetic rhythm and, 128;
    on rhythm in spirituals, 164; on swing,
    147, 276n7
Johnson, J. J., 175, 181–83
Johnson, Robert, 156, 218
Johnson, Sarah ("Aint Sarah"), 180–81, 183,
    189, 190, 191, 279n11, 279–80n14
Johnson, Will, 175
Jonah's Gourd Vine (Hurston), 170, 279n9
Jones, Bobby, 158–59
Jones, Charles Colcock, 4, 111, 112
Jones, LeRoi, 173, 263n14
Jones, Nathan, 264n2
Joplin, Scott, 164–65, 277n11
Jordan, Louis, 223
"Joy to the World" (Watts), 96
jubilee spirituals, xiii, 198

Keach, Benjamin, 94
Keeble, N. H., 95, 98, 106
Keil, Charles, 159
Kentucky, Dr. Watts hymns in, 32
Keyes, Cheryl, 38
"keys," performance. *See* performance "keys"
King, John, 269n1
King, Martin Luther, Jr., 44, 124, 179
King, Martin Luther, Sr., 176
King James Bible, 9–10, 33, 141

oral traditions: Afro-European influence on,
198; Dr. Watts hymns and, 25, 101–2, 105,
141, 239; literacy and, 114; moaning styles
and, 51–52; musical influence of, 5–6; in
slave culture, 107; written hymns and, 144
organum, 50–51, 58, 59–60, 265n7
Original Sacred Harp, 51, 268n3
ornamentation, 199
ostinato, 133
"Our God, Our Help in Ages Past" (Watts),
96, 270n3

Pageland Religious Folksong Documentation project, 4
"Papa's Got a Brand New Bag" (Brown),
136–37
Paradise Lost (Milton), 93
Parker, Charlie, 228, 281n6; black
oral/white written traditions enjoined in,
164–65; lining out–ring shout continuum and, 202, 217–18; "Parker's Mood,"
14, 214–15, 221, 223–25; poetic rhythms
of, 127, 137
Particular Baptists, 94
Patrick, John, 94
Patton, Charlie, 2, 104–5, 156
Paul, Saint, 100–1
Pen, Ronald, 265n6
Pentecostalism, 109, 198, 264–65n4
percussive rhythms, 119, 130–32, 255, 275n9
performance "keys," 202–5; in blues, 214;
ecstatic worship and, 281n8; example of,
206–13; "frames" vs., 281n7; in jazz,
227–32
performativity, 263n17
Phinizy Chorus, 53
piano, 217, 225
pidgins, 103, 107
Piedmont Carolina: African musical influences in, 133; Dr. Watts hymns in, xi–xiii;
hymn choir tradition in, 281–82n11;
moaning styles in, 50, 102; percussive
rhythms in, 275n9; prayer bands from,
206; regional style traditions in, 54–55, 58,
145, 150, 206, 210; research projects in, 4;
shout styles in, 40–41, 42, 213, 269n7
Pilgrim's Progress (Bunyan), 93
Pinkston, A. A., 273n16
Pisgah, 53–54
pitch, words as shapers of, 140
Pitts, Walter, 8, 11, 46, 135, 142; on Afro-
Baptist church, 31; on binary mood

frames in black Baptist worship, 43, 107,
194–95, *203,* 271–72n6; on black vocal
style, 163–64; linguistic analysis of, 17,
272–73n7; regional singing styles uncon-
sidered by, 268n1; scholarly significance
of, 262n6; on slave conversions, 110
plainspokenness, 105–6, 197, 218
poetic rhythms: African influences on, 133,
134–35; in black Baptist worship,
196–97; in Dr. Watts performances,
127–28, 138–39, 256; portraiture sound
as complement of, 275n10, 275–76n17;
sacred/secular occurrences of, 137,
219–20, 221, 223–25, 275n15; semantic
content conveyed by, 138–39; in speech-
movement continuum, 125, 127–28
Pope, Alexander, 93
popular culture, 3, 18, 91, 159
portraiture sound: African influences on,
133–34; in black Baptist worship,
196–97; in Dr. Watts performances, 139,
256; poetic rhythm as complement of,
275n10, 275–76n17; sacred/secular
occurrences of, 137, 221; semantic content conveyed by, 139; in speech-movement
continuum, 125–27
poverty, xiii
Powell, Bud, 225
Powell, Richard, 103
The Power of Black Music (Floyd), 16, 280n2
prayer: in black Baptist worship, 25; in
Dr. Watts performances, 37; intoned,
163–64; linguistic/musical interaction
in, 142; lining out polarity and, 198;
musical influence of, 220; portraiture
sound in, 125
prayer bands, 58, 206–13
The Preacher's Wife (film; 1996), 283–84n2
preaching: in black Baptist worship, 24–25;
five-key sequence and, 205; intoned, 25,
163–64; C. J. Johnson and, 181–82,
184–88; musical influence of, 220; portraiture sound in, 125; ring shout polarity and, 198
Presbyterianism, 94
Presley, Elvis, 216
Primitive Baptists: black vs. white lining-out
practices of, 38, 265n9; Dr. Watts hymns
and, 25, 27–28, 32; Dr. Watts hymns
recordings of, *83, 84–85,* 268n1, 274n3;
hymn repertory of, 27; lining out by,
116; portraiture sound of, 127; recorded

Romanticism, 98, 115, 160–61
Roosevelt, Franklin D., 188
Rose, Tricia, 164
"Run, Mary, Run," 145

Samuel, William, 91
The Sanctified Church (Hurston), 278n3
Savoy (gospel label), 60, 178, 192
scat singing, 136, 218, 281n6
Sea Islands (SC/GA): African influences
   in, 133–34; cross-rhythmic clapping
   styles in, 206; cross-rhythmic shout style
   in, 40–41, 58–59; Gullah people in,
   266n14; lining out in, 112–13, 114;
   percussive rhythms in, 130; shout spirituals in, 206; shout styles in, 53, 60,
   133, 145–46, 269n7
segregation, 2, 162, 171, 173, 175, 191, 219,
   280n22
semantics, tonal, 123–24
sermons: "Free Jazz" (Coleman) as, 227–28;
   intoned, 163–64; linguistic influence on,
   263n13, 273n7; as stimuli for song-
   raising, 140
Sermons (Watts), 271n5
Seroff, Doug, 278n2
"Set Down, Servant," 31
"Shake That Thing" (Jackson), 216
shape-note hymnody, 51, 59, 127, 180,
   268n2
sharecropping, 156
"Shave 'Em Dry" (Rainey), 216
sheet music, 3
short-meter hymn singing, 265n8
shout music, 198
shouts/shouting: African/English influences
   on, 105; African influences on, 122, 133;
   in congregational singing tradition,
   35–36, 39–42, 102; cross-rhythmic,
   40–42, 53, 60; definition of, 25; lining
   out–ring shout continuum and, 198,
   281n5; percussive rhythms and, 130;
   regional variations in, 52–54, 58, 190,
   206, 213; response to, 41; as sound gesture, 122. *See also* lining out–ring shout
   continuum; ring shout
signification, 123, 139, 159, 236–37
Signifyin(g), 197, 214, 280n2, 281n6
"Sign of the Judgment," 145
Silver, Horace, 225
Simmons, Walter, 142
Sinclair, Hardin, xii

Sinclair, Rene, xi–xii
singing, definition of, 25
slave culture: African cultural expressions
   in, 103–4, 106–8, 135, 273n8; Bantu
   language influence in, 106–7; Baptist
   missions and, 7, 59, 102, 109, 111–12;
   cultural change in, 103–4; hymn singing
   in, 7–8, 101–2, 111–13, 156; illiteracy
   enforced in, 104, 110; C. J. Johnson on,
   177–79; lining out and, 7, 34–35, 104,
   108–9, 112–13; rap as break from, 157;
   regional style traditions and, 56, 58–59,
   170; ring-shout tradition and, 40–41,
   113; ritual in, 8, 112; social hierarchies
   in, 107; Standard English performativity
   and, 9–10; tonal semantics in, 124;
   Watts's influence on, 100–2; worship in,
   6, 111–13, 116–18
slave drums, 103
slave rebellions, 103
Slave Songs in the United States (Allen; Ware;
   Garrison), 112, 123, 160
Sloane, Hans, 103
Smith, Arthur L., 123
Smith, Bessie, 129, 218
Smith, Carl Henry, 27, 274n16
Smitherman, Geneva, 273n16; on AAVE,
   143; on lining-out tempo, 274n2; on
   shout-style hymn singing, 41; speech-
   song parallels and, 16, 121; on tonal
   semantics, 123–24, 125
Smithsonian Collection of Classic Jazz (recording), 226
Smithsonian Institution Workshop on Black
   Congregational Singing (1989), 4
Sobel, Mechal, 103
social class, xiii; black gospel music and, 2–3;
   black vs. Standard English and, 154–55;
   civil rights movement and, 44; devotional
   lining out and, 31–32; Emancipation
   and, 154, 170, 173–74; meaning of,
   279n6. *See also* black middle class
"Somebody's Calling My Name" (Walker), 34
song leaders: continuity between, 212–13;
   five-key sequence and, 205; impact of
   lack of, 237; lining out–ring shout continuum and, 199, 202; ritual and, 210;
   role of, in black Baptist worship, 147,
   199, 207–13, 281–82n11; vocal gestures
   of, 281n6. *See also* Johnson, C. J.
The Souls of Black Folk (Du Bois), 160,
   161–63

Text:	10/12 Baskerville
Display:	Baskerville
Compositor:	International Typesetting & Composition
Printer and Binder:	Thomson-Shore, Inc.